H‌ S

TOM CLARK writes daily editorials on economics, politics and society for the *Guardian*. He runs the newspaper's opinion polling, and hosts a weekly podcast. He previously advised the last Labour government, after five years at the Institute for Fiscal Studies where he published peer-reviewed papers on poverty, inequality and social security. He has co-authored a book on ethnic diversity, *The Age of Obama* (2010).

ANTHONY HEATH is professor of sociology, University of Manchester, and emeritus professor at the University of Oxford. In 2013 he was awarded a CBE in the Queen's Birthday Honours List. His most recent book is *The Political Integration of Ethnic Minorities in Britain* (2013).

HARD TIMES
INEQUALITY, RECESSION, AFTERMATH

TOM CLARK
WITH ANTHONY HEATH

YALE UNIVERSITY PRESS
NEW HAVEN AND LONDON

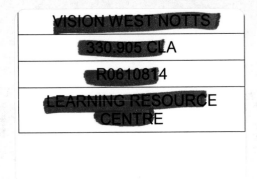
For information about this and other Yale University Press publications, please contact:
U.S. Office: sales.press@yale.edu   www.yalebooks.com
Europe Office: sales@yaleup.co.uk   www.yalebooks.co.uk

Set in Sabon by IDSUK (DataConnection) Ltd
Printed in Great Britain by Hobbs the Printer Ltd, Totton, Hampshire

Library of Congress Cataloging-in-Publication Data

Clark, Tom, 1976–
   Hard times : the divisive toll of the economic slump / Tom Clark, with Anthony Heath.
      pages cm
   Includes bibliographical references and index.
   ISBN 978-0-300-20377-6 (alk. paper)
   1. United States—Economic conditions—2009– 2. United States—Social conditions.   3. Great Britain—Economic conditions—1997– 4. Great Britain—Social conditions.   5. Recessions—Social aspects.   6. Global Financial Crisis, 2008–2009—Social aspects. I. Heath, A. F. (Anthony Francis) II. Title.
   HC106.84.C53 2014
   330.973—dc23

                                                                    2014002243

A catalogue record for this book is available from the British Library.

ISBN 978-0-300-21274-7 (pbk)

10 9 8 7 6 5 4 3 2 1

For my mother

T.C.

Contents

Foreword to the paperback edition: 'Recovery' 2015

John McArthur knows a good deal about recession in post-industrial Britain, and he has recently been learning something about the nature of the current jobs recovery too.[1]

A 59-year-old electronics specialist with a rich CV, he previously worked factory floors, trained and retrained, moved into product development, and even started his own company. But like many others in his part of Lanarkshire, in the central lowlands of Scotland, he has also endured extended spells without work. During the depths of the Great Recession, he put himself forward, through a government-backed scheme, to work for LAMH Recycle Ltd in Motherwell, a social enterprise that reconditions computers and other materials. 'It was minimum-wage work, but I was more than happy to do it', he tells me in gentle, intelligent tones. 'I had experience to share. They'd be rekitting televisions and things that would otherwise be getting thrown out, and I'd sit at the end of line, doing the final quality check, signing things off as good to go.'

He was well prepared for the fact that this work would abruptly come to an end at some point, as it duly did in 2011 – 'I always knew the placement would stop, because it had this government backing, and these things do run out.' Nothing, however, could prepare him for what happened next.

The Future Jobs Fund, which had supported the original place-ment, was axed soon after David Cameron's arrival in Downing Street in 2010, but in fits and starts his coalition government came forward with make-work schemes of its own. And it was through one of these, 'community work placements', that John was informed in August 2014 there was once again a post for him at LAMH. The new 'offer', however, came with one significant twist: John would be going back to his old job without a wage. He was now being ordered, on pain of losing his benefits, to put in 30 hours per week while continuing to scrape by on Jobseekers' Allowance. The usual weekly rate in 2014/15 is £72.40.

For John, as for many others, the message of this recovery has been, 'Yes, you can work, but it might not be work as you used to under-stand it.' For some, what's gone is the presumption of a single work-place with a stable body of colleagues, and all the social connections that come with that. For others, such as the growing army of zero-hours workers, what's vanished is the idea of a fixed working week. And for very many others again, another traditional notion has been upended – the old expectation that pay would never actually fall, and would instead tend to creep up over time. As 2014 drew to a close, Britain's economists disagreed about whether or not earnings growth, when properly measured, had truly caught back up with inflation at long last. But all agreed that real-terms pay had been steadily sinking for six straight years. That made for the sharpest pay squeeze since the 1860s, and the most sustained decline on record.[2]

John's invitation to toil for nothing at all might thus be seen as a case of the adverse trends affecting the wider workforce being pushed to a logical extreme. But the case is emblematic, too, of something else that *Hard Times* talks about – of welfare provisions that had origi-nally been put in place to help people through an hour of need being refashioned into an instrument of punishment. To those on the sharp end, at least, it increasingly feels like strictures that purport to encourage people to pick themselves up are instead operating to keep claimants in their place.

There was, John says, 'stony silence' when he asked what he was meant to gain in experience from going back to a job he had already done. 'It was being done as punishment, and I felt like dirt. I just think it morally reprehensible that a person is expected to work for no wage, it is as simple as that.' So he wrote to his prospective wage-free employer, LAMH, explaining to them why he felt he had to decline. He received no reply; instead, he found his benefits duly 'sanctioned' for a full six months.

A miniscule pension from a previous job is now all that he has to keep body and soul together, and – as of Christmas 2014 – he describes himself as getting by with 'potato scones – special offer 8 for 6, 49p at Lidl – which does me for breakfast and lunch'. And for dinner? '16p tins of spaghetti hoops from Aldi, which I usually have every night.' The diet is 'monotonous', but he doesn't complain, observing that things must be unimaginably worse for sanctioned families raising children.

Perhaps the most poignant feature of John's story – with all the humiliation, as well as the hardship – is that it is playing out during what really ought to be the return of happier economic times. This recovery may have been the slowest to get going in a century, but by summer 2014 it was without question real, and the GDP figures confirmed that the UK economy was bigger than it had been before 2008. *Hard Times* emphasised that employment had fallen far less than many had feared during the crisis, and, as the recovery beds in, the jobs numbers are continuing to surprise on the upside. In autumn 2014, the employment rate was only a fraction of a percentage point below the pre-crash record.

But all this good news misses the point. For the central argument in the book is that the deep societal problems laid bare by the recession – problems of anxiety and isolation – were always more structural than cyclical. A rich country should be perfectly able to endure getting a bit poorer during a passing downturn. The UK did *not* run into all the dislocation that we uncover because the crisis suddenly created frailty in downtrodden communities. The role of the slump was rather to expose problems with deep roots in the long decades that came before, decades in which inequality had run out of control. The return of growth was never, on its own, going to undo all the damage – and especially not under a version of austerity that passes on so much of the bill run up by the bankers to the poor.

Hard Times draws on almost as much American as British data, highlighting how ordinary workers in the US have been denied any share in a growing economy for a generation or more – for 25 years when family finances are considered in the round, and for 40-plus years where individual male workers are singled out from their wives. The question underlying these transatlantic comparisons was whether the UK is switching to a new American-style normal, in which there is no longer any automatic connection between an expanding economic pie on the one hand, and, on the other, a growing slice for regular employees. The final verdict is still not in, but another year into the recovery, such a suggestion is increasingly hard to dismiss.

In explaining the worrying trends in pay and security, *Hard Times* points to the substitution of cheap, deunionised labour for costly capital investment. It stresses, too, the disappearance of middling clerking and technical jobs, in a labour market where all the new openings seem to lie in providing care for the elderly, and servicing the well-to-do in restaurants and hotels. All of this stands up well in the unfolding recovery, but, a year on, the connection between low pay and the assault on social security is becoming clearer.

This is true in the latest academic studies, which increasingly register the potential importance of welfare reforms in explaining stagnant pay.[3] But it is true at the level of common sense and anecdote too. Minimal welfare with maximum stigma is, after all, as Chapter 8 explains, a mix that has long been familiar in low-pay America. The more that stories like John McArthur's come to light – stories of hardship and harsh rules pressing penniless people into taking inappropriate work – the less surprised we should be if employers are holding back on pay rises for their existing staff. What John calls 'an army of conscripts from the Department for Work and Pensions' are providing a ready cut-price alternative.

In this emerging link between squeezed pay for the majority and reduced benefits for the vulnerable few, there really ought to be an opening for solidarity, progressive resistance and then progressive reform. *Hard Times*, however, points to the deep difficulties in the way of building the sort of electoral coalition that might finally turn the tide on inequality. For one thing, we report in Chapter 9 that very many of those who are in work deeply resent those who are without it, a resentment wholeheartedly encouraged by certain politicians and newspaper editors. For another, we uncovered jealousies flowing in every direction in and amongst the dispossessed, with people on one sort of benefit often disdaining those on another.

Can such divisions be overcome? It all depends on which of the two divides discussed in *Hard Times* emerges as more salient. The first big split is that between the safe (if squeezed) majority, and the large minority that is most insecure, and often dependent on benefits. The second and more politically promising split is the chasm that separates the rich, whose pay and assets have raced away from everybody else for a third of a century, from the rest. And 'the rest' here is an overwhelming majority – *Hard Times* shows that the squeeze on pay goes at least nine-tenths of the way up the scale. That includes graduates who are settling for the sort of second-best future that all the study and the student debt was meant to save them from. It includes, too, families who have always worked and often done OK, but who now, in this recovery, are raising children in rented homes, where they would once have expected to buy, and generally feeling that life is proving more of a stretch for them than it ever was for their parents. During the last year both these divisions have, in different ways, hardened in the recovering economy. So which is now looking like emerging as the defining divide?

The poor: always with us, at least in this recovery

The immediate effect of the Great Recession on family incomes was, *Hard Times* reports, *not* in fact disproportionately felt by the poor: state action, through taxes and benefits, ensured that the initial squeeze was shared far and wide. But the book also points out that both unemployment proper, and the newer, more distinctive blights on working life in this recession – underemployment and zero-hours contracts, for instance – were heavily concentrated at the bottom end. And it warned, too, that the post-crisis assault on welfare benefits could yet push more of the pain onto the most vulnerable.

A year on, these judgements seem, if anything, too nuanced. Important new work from the Institute for Fiscal Studies has unpicked the standard crude assumption that a single inflation rate affects the whole population equally, and instead examined separately the cost of living for different sorts of families.[4] During the years since the crisis, a number of things that weigh especially heavily in the budgets of poorer families, such as the cost of heating, have risen in price particularly

Being poor got more expensive: average annual effective inflation by income bracket, 2008/09–2013/14

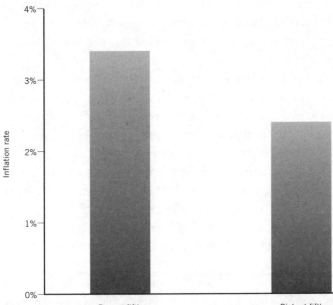

Source: Institute for Fiscal Studies.

rapidly, whereas that greatest of middle-class costs, mortgage interest payments, has fallen through the floor. Put it all together, and as the chart on the previous page shows, inflation has been running at between one-third and one-half higher for the poor than for the rich. Factor in this differential, and the apparent decline in income inequality that registered in the immediate aftermath of the crisis largely disappears.[5] As for the subsequent years of austerity, with these true costs of living factored in, the rise in absolute poverty is that bit sharper.[6]

Looking further ahead, the last year has borne out our claim that penury could intensify into the recovery. The University of Essex and the London School of Economics have just produced the first independent study to analyse the UK Coalition's tax and benefit policies, in isolation from those it inherited from the last Labour government.[7] This has confirmed that the Cameron government has taken most from the income of poorer groups, at the same time as it has advantaged most of those in the top half – including within the very top 1%. As our book argues, too, the pattern of gains and losses has more to do with political choice than economic necessity: the LSE/Essex study concludes that the mix of reductions in direct tax and cuts to welfare payments have yielded no overall gain for the Exchequer.

With unregulated rents continuing to rise, and low wages unaddressed, the underlying pressures for spending on housing benefit and tax credit top-ups for pay packets remain in place. Indeed, the latest official analysis implies that the government will fall short on the welfare savings it promised to secure as a consequence of these pressures.[8] But instead of searching for new strategies to reduce the demand for state support, the year 2014 saw the Conservative Party resolve to redouble its strategy of reducing benefit entitlements.

In his Budget, Chancellor George Osborne capped non-pension social security expenditure, stipulating that it would no longer be allowed to rise faster than price inflation. Put like that, it sounds reasonable, but over the decades what this assumes is that, however strong the economy, the sick and the workless will never be entitled to any share in rising national prosperity. With rents rising, pay stagnant and population increasing, capped expenditure seems almost certain to leave the poor getting poorer.

At the Conservative Party conference, Osborne put in another 'tough guy' turn, proposing to freeze benefits, including for low-paid workers, for two further years at the end of the prolonged squeeze already imposed. Days later, Cameron showered away all the resultant savings (and more) by promising £7 billion in income tax cuts, some aimed well up the scale. And he promised an even more imbalanced austerity than we have had so far. Where the Conservative John Major had repaired battered public finances after the 1990s recession with a rough 50:50 mix of taxes and spending cuts, the Coalition has relied on a ratio of roughly nine parts cuts to (largely social) expenditure, to only one part tax. In his next term, Cameron said, 'I am confident we will find the savings we need through spending cuts alone', implying a fiscal 'mix' of 100:0. That leaves the state's share in the economy being rolled back to 1930s proportions. Those who depend on IT should be very afraid.

On the raw finances, then, there is now less need for some of the careful caveating that marked out our hardback edition. The poor were not after all much better protected than anyone else when the storm first hit, and the government's evolving direction of travel will push ever more of the pain of adjustment their way. Looking beyond income to economic security – the thing *Hard Times* argues is so important for community and family life – there are, despite the remarkable jobs growth, stubborn problems at the bottom end of the labour market.

'Underemployment', as measured by those part-timers who would prefer to be working full-time, stood at 1.34 million in the November 2014 data release, which is, as one would expect, down on the dark days of two years before, when this group numbered 1.41 million.[9] But this is a decline of only around 5%, far smaller than a parallel fall in unemployment of nearly 30%. The band of temporary employees who would rather be full-timers is also proving hard to shrink, remaining at just under 600,000, compared with something more like 350,000 before the slump hit. As for zero-hours working, the ultimate form of commodified labour, the evidence is at least suggestive of continuing growth. Official statistics here are still in their infancy, so it is not yet possible to strip out seasonal variation, but the spring 2014 tally of workers employed in this way stands at 622,000, as against a late 2013 estimate of 583,000.[10]

Since *Hard Times* was published, the importance of yet another new form of casualisation has come into the spotlight: 'self-employment'. Between 2008 and 2014, an extraordinary two-thirds of the total growth in jobs came from an apparent freelance boom. In the first flush of the recovery, this boom concealed a withering away of employed posts in much of the country away from London. To the extent that rising self-employment reflects a new spirit of entrepreneurialism it might be welcome, but something very different appears to be happening at the bottom end. Whereas average real wages for employees have fallen by around 8% since the crisis, official figures put the cumulative decline in median self-employed earnings at 22%.[11] Civil servants, who are tasked with trying to prevent fake self-employment being used to reduce National Insurance contributions, speak privately of hotel chambermaids, shepherds and forestry staff being lopped off the payroll and then asked to come straight back as hired guns.

Much like zero-hours workers, unwilling freelancers have no certainty about what they will be paid or when. This is economic insecurity of exactly the type that will warp first into anxiety, and then into arguments within the home – and broken community connections beyond it. Chapter 6 sets out how a precipitous withering of social involvement accompanied the recession, a decline much more marked on the poorest streets. But it also concluded that there were some tentative signs of civic engagement bouncing back with the economy. Alas, the most recent data suggests that the seeming improvement has not been sustained. Between 2012/13 and 2013/14, the latest government figures show that the proportion of citizens engaged each month in formally organised volunteering or even in trading favours with neighbours has slipped back again. This new decline, which looks even sharper when other forms of civic activism are factored in, appears particularly marked in England's struggling North-East.[12]

The economy is still a long way from booming, but if it does get the chance to go at full-throttle before some new crisis emerges, then *some* of the problems that plague low-paid workers should begin to abate. With truly buoyant demand for labour, employers will find themselves competing with each other to hold on to staff, and no longer able to disregard their wishes in relation to terms and conditions. Other difficulties of struggling families (benefits and tax credits being high on the list) appear set to drag on indefinitely, however, unless something changes. To try and ensure that it doesn't, the political right, ably assisted by its media cheerleaders, will continue stoking middle-class resentment against a subsidised underclass. This tactic will only work if the great squeezed middle can be convinced that it is not 'in it together' with the poor.

Squeezed middle, narrowed futures

Pay, *Hard Times* reports, has been reduced way up into the ranks of the comfortable – nine-tenths of the way up the scale. But we argue that this, on its own, will not do all that much to disrupt middle-class security, particularly if this ultimately proves to be a passing squeeze. Nor will it do much to foster a sense of solidarity with the most vulnerable – a sentiment which the middle class always fears could land it with a tax bill.

Things could play out very differently, however, if the middle class came to feel that its own plans for the future were being threatened by the post-recessionary economy. We report in Chapter 7 on various signs that, for younger people at least, aspirations in terms of home ownership and earnings had taken a serious blow. There was, we explained, an enduring wage penalty to be paid for graduating into a recession, and over the last year new evidence has emerged on the extent to which the young, although on paper the best-qualified generation in history, are earning and owning far less than they would have expected. Home ownership rates for twenty-somethings have halved over the last 20 years, younger adults' pay has stagnated at ages where it always used to rise, and this pattern of making less progress than generations gone by extends even to university graduates.[13]

Middle-class parents might imagine that inherited property will eventually correct some of this for their offspring, but what if there is now a more fundamental block on getting on and getting ahead? Most of the evidence about social sclerosis in *Hard Times* concerns inherited disadvantage at the bottom of the heap, particularly in relation to unemployment. But perhaps the single most intriguing finding to emerge over the last year concerns adverse patterns in social mobility with far wider potential ramifications.

Piecing together data from all the main UK tracking surveys, which follow real individuals on their journey through life, the sociologist Erzsébet Bukodi and Oxford and LSE colleagues have counted the number of steps that successive generations of Britons have taken up and down the class ladder (as defined by occupational grade).[14] The charts record how many young men and women, assessed at age 27, have advanced or fallen back from the place that their own families occupied on the societal spectrum.

The results show, first, that the earliest baby boomers – born in 1946, and turning 27 at the very end of the post-war 'Golden Age', in 1973 – were very lucky indeed. With both managerial and professional positions proliferating at the top, roughly twice as many young men and women were able to move up as were condemned to move down. Subsequent cohorts, maturing in more unequal times, did not have it quite so good. But right through the 1980s and 1990s there continued to be more steps up than steps down. For those who came of age during the Great Recession, however, things are different – and, for young women at least, there has recently been marginally more downward than upward mobility.

In such data we are, perhaps, witnessing where the great casualisation of labour could take society. Yes, 27 is nowadays rather young to reach a final verdict on a cohort's prospects, and it is conceivable that the picture will brighten for the babies of the 1980s as they move into their thirties. But it is surely conceivable, too, that some of the adverse trends that Chapter 4 reports on as afflicting the low-paid are slowly

Opportunity knocked: downward social mobility is up, and upward social mobility down for successive generations of British:

(a) men

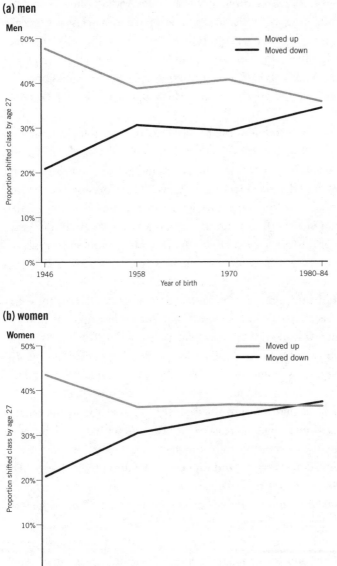

(b) women

Source: Bukodi et al. (2014).

making themselves felt farther up the range. Outside of the technology sector and a few elite professions, there is often dwindling room at the top, and dwindling security everywhere else. And of course, the prospects of climbing the ladder in the traditional middle-class way are not helped by the great concentration of wealth at the very top end. Wealthy families can easily stump up for costly Master's degrees and mortgage deposits for their own children – selective advantaging that can often have the effect of diminishing opportunities for everyone else.

It is too early to know what such disturbing sociological patterns will do to political attitudes, although the UK's 2015 general election could provide one early test. The latest updates of the British Social Attitudes data that we analyse in Chapter 9 have been mixed, but are not especially encouraging for the welfare state. The exaggerated perception of mass fraud appears to have eased somewhat, but other varieties of mistrust remain. Excessive benefits are still seen as encouraging idleness, and a seeming swing away from this view in 2012 was not sustained into 2013. Most chillingly, and in line with our argument about political fragmentation *among* recessionary victims, there has recently been a particular decline in support for unemployment benefits among working respondents who are struggling financially.[15]

But ebbs and flows in support for particular policies and institutions will always come and go. The deeper tide of ideas takes longer to turn, yet is ultimately more powerful. The closing chapter of *Hard Times* asserts that 'the lop-sided pattern of rewards in the Anglo-Saxon economies' will 'increase volatility', and with it the dangers of fresh financial crises. It calls for such arguments to 'escape the economics seminar room' and find their way into public debate. The year 2014 has seen this begin to happen. In the spring, Thomas Piketty's *Capital in the 21st Century* pipped Disney's *Frozen: Journey to the Ice Palace* to the top spot in the Amazon bestsellers book chart. The huge interest in the French economist's data-rich discourse reflected his emphasis on 'patrimonial capitalism', a system in which great and often inherited wealth will trump any amount of thrift, talent or industry from the middle and lower classes.

This is certainly not the first sign of a new interest in inequality since the crisis. Just after it broke, in 2009, Richard Wilkinson and Kate Pickett became (surely) the best-selling epidemiologists in history, with *The Spirit Level*. This sweeping, controversial and contested analysis, subtitled *Why more equal societies almost always do better*, traced the roots of social ills from crime to obesity back to the income gap. Like Piketty, whose scholarly and little-noticed earlier books feature in our endnotes, Wilkinson had written a good deal before, including in books that had set out the same basic argument with some of the same data. The income inequality numbers may not have changed all that much with the Great Recession, but the mood undeniably did.

Other of this last year's books confirm as much. David Marquand's *Mammon's Kingdom* bemoaned the warping effect of wealth worship on culture and value in Britain. Sir John Hills' *Good Times, Bad Times* revives the old argument for the welfare state as something that can help everybody, the middle classes included, through all those financial pinch points that inevitably litter the long road between cradle and grave. On top of these new books comes a previously unimaginable level of interest in inequality at the World Bank, the IMF and on the comment pages of the *Financial Times*. And, of course, all this interest comes on top of the latest scholarly papers and data that this Foreword has already reviewed.

The best of the analysts and intellectuals emphasise that we are living in interesting times, during which creative options for policy really should be opening up rather than being closed down. Of course, there are real fiscal pressures, but Chancellor Osborne continues to place the deficit ahead of every other objective, promising austerity without end. And yet at the same time the Bank of England is sat on piles of public debt – bonds which it bought with magicked-up money – and shows little sign of wishing to dump onto the market. Even as such a fetish is made of the debt, then, it is becoming possible to see how it could end up being whittled away through quantitative easing, in much the same way that inflation ate into the huge national debts of the past. Official practice is evolving faster than official policy here, a sure sign that it is time to challenge some of the conventional macro-economic wisdom.

New ideas for the labour market are likewise overdue. The unanticipated strength of the bounce-back in jobs holds out the prospect that unemployment could fall to rates not seen since the post-war golden age. Neither inflation nor 'pricing workers out of jobs' are the clear and present dangers that they once were. This invites a less inhibited discussion about regulating labour standards than we have had for a very long time.

Such heretical conversations may not yet be found within the walls of Her Majesty's Treasury. But in the academy, big questions are being asked afresh, and most especially about inequality. There was a time, not so long ago, when the issue of who got what was regarded, at best, as rather tangential to economics proper and, at worst, as a dangerous distraction. The Nobel Laureate, Robert Lucas, spoke for the mainstream when he said that 'of the tendencies that are harmful to sound economics, the most seductive, and in my opinion the most poisonous, is to focus on the question of distribution'.[16] Having started my career analysing the UK inequality numbers in the 1990s, I remember that mood in economics only too well – as does Piketty, who complains of his own discipline's prioritising of 'highly ideological speculation' over evidence and insight. Today, however, Piketty is himself a real Nobel contender.

The irony is that it was in the 1980s and 1990s, the long years when inequality was ignored, that the economic gap truly shot out of control. It took the Great Recession to wake the world up to what had happened. The hocus pocus of the money men had promised to enrich everyone, but after 2008 the public watched as the alchemy unravelled – and then raged at being handed the bill. As we put it in this book, the tide turned abruptly on the old way of doing business and, as it went out, a lot of rot that had been lurking under the surface suddenly came into full view.

After the long years of neglect, re-engaging with the question of 'who gets what' is not easy. Certainly, mainstream party politicians and establishment policy-makers are struggling to come up with answers that are equal to the mood. But the task of tackling inequality is every bit as urgent in the sort of recovery that is now taking shape as it was in the depths of the Great Recession. And if, as Keynes wrote, the ideas of 'academic scribblers' are indeed 'more powerful than is commonly understood', then, sooner or later, change is going to come.

Tom Clark
London, 2015

Authorial note

As the Acknowledgements make plain, large parts of this book are, in an important sense, the product of a whole team of researchers, whose work on 'hard times' themes was overseen by Professor Anthony Heath. Through seminars and correspondence, Tom Clark played an active part in the work of this team, and in the text thus uses the collective first person – e.g. 'we discovered', 'our findings' – in discussing the research undertaken as part of a five-year collaboration between the University of Manchester and Harvard University, known as Social Change: A Harvard–Manchester Initiative (SCHMI).

Beyond that, Tom Clark had editorial control of the text – adding opinions and observations, as well as knitting in other sources of research, as he saw fit. Where the book ranges beyond SCHMI's work, therefore, the text often reverts to the first-person singular, to make clear that the observations and opinions are Tom Clark's alone.

Introduction

The men of Marienthal were so depressed that you could see it in the very way they walked. Most trudged along at two miles an hour, and nine out of every ten crossing the few hundred yards of their village would find an excuse to stop en route, often dithering along their brief way. The slump's poison had seeped out of silent factories, and ended up somewhere under the skin. We know all of this – and much more about daily life in this one tiny Austrian town in the 1930s – because pioneering young sociologists went there to find out what happens when everyone is thrown out of work, as virtually everyone had been when Marienthal's flax mill fell victim to the credit crunch of 1929.[1]

Eighty years later, a true economic hurricane again engulfed the rich world, for the first time since the 1930s. In the UK at least, the statistics confirm that national income took a bigger cumulative hit than during the Great Depression itself. You might imagine that there would be vast social consequences, but – thanks to the burgeoning of data and computers to crunch it – there is no need to rely on the imagination, or indeed on anecdotes from one village in the Austrian hills. Drawing on the social scientific research of a distinguished transatlantic team of scholars – headed by Manchester University's Anthony Heath and Harvard's Robert D. Putnam – this book treats the contemporary Anglo-American economies as one giant Marienthal. Through one-to-one interviews with recessionary victims, as well as detailed analysis so up-to-the-minute that it has yet to reach the academic journals, it maps out the ways in which bad financial news pours off the business pages and onto the streets of our communities.

Back in Marienthal, there was, of course, material hardship: hunger was so rampant that a family whose dog had gone missing would no longer bother to report the loss. The Viennese researchers who entered the village documented a degraded diet and worn-out clothes, just as they had expected. Far more disturbing, however, was what they learnt about the impoverishment of the spirit. Despite boundless time, free library tickets and discounted newspapers, the townsfolk somehow did not get around to reading, even though they had been enthusiastic readers when they were still busy with work. The small town was once blessed with rambling clubs, sports teams and discussion groups that had passed time pleasantly and at minimal cost. Yet when the slump bequeathed all those spare hours to fill, instead of booming, many such societies folded.

The researchers asked townsfolk to keep diaries of their days. They found hours accounted for with baffling entries such as 'in the meantime midday comes around'[2] – entries documenting how the clocks tick differently after all hopes of prosperity and purpose have died.

Far away, in the United States of the same era, the Depression's great chronicler, John Steinbeck, was writing that it was 'in the souls of the people' that 'the grapes of wrath are filling'.[3] This time around, little of what has been written and broadcast about the new global slump has had anything to do with the soul. The news reports have been delivered against a backdrop of the trading-room floor's flickering screens. We read that the animal spirits of investors had fallen into depression. But perhaps it is time to inquire about spirits more generally, and to ask whether we collectively sank into a Marienthal-style social slump – the sort of slump to snuff out the happiness of the individual, the life of the community and the dreams of the next generation.

For anyone who is interested in what happens next, it is just as important to investigate the public mood that has emerged from stagnation – and the direction in which it is pushing politics and society. Hardship can set attitudes on different paths: in Marienthal, some stricken citizens would manage to rustle up a bowl of soup for an even more stricken neighbour; others, overpowered with bitterness, would trump up allegations about fellow townsfolk transgressing the unemployment benefit rules.

Are our own hard times splintering opinion into a thousand varieties of resentment – pitting victims against one another, leaving them not only despairing, but also ripe to be divided and ruled? Or could this still prove to be one of those crises from which progressive opportunities eventually emerge? In our quest for answers, we will mine a wealth of data from the US, as well as the UK, and will also hear direct from two dozen British families at the sharp end.

The *economic* parallels with the 1930s are hard to resist. The Great Recession that began in 2008 soon engulfed the whole world, just as the Depression had done.[4] And – just as in the United States of the 1930s – the recent bust was preceded by a roaring boom, powered by high-octane debt. On both occasions, too, this vast debt was distilled and disguised by financial wizardry, as the moneymen built Jenga-style towers that were doomed to come crashing down. In words that could just as well have been written about Lehman Brothers in 2008, J.K. Galbraith wrote of a long-forgotten investment bank in *The Great Crash 1929*: 'As Kreuger and Toll moved down to its ultimate value of nothing, leverage was also at work – geometric series are equally dramatic in reverse.'[5] The malady in the eurozone today resembles that in the gold standard back then. The slow-burning (and still unresolved) crisis in the vaults of the continent's banks carries echoes of the 1931 collapse of Credit-Anstalt – the financial explosion that pushed the Depression into its second phase.[6]

The *societal* parallels are, thus far, less clear. The fall-out from the last great slump was seared into British folk history by the Jarrow March and *The Road to Wigan Pier*, just as the desperate, dusty dislocation of the American West in the 1930s was immortalised in *The Grapes of Wrath*. There is hard data, as well as literature, to record how the Depression translated into a societal slump, at least in the US. Witness the precipitous depressionary drop in membership of

The social slump: US civic society membership rates dived during the Great Depression

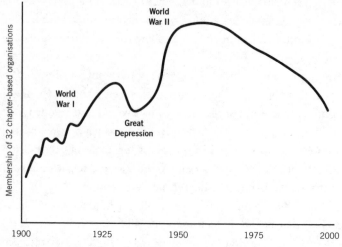

Source: Putnam, *Bowling Alone*. Scaled by a composite of membership rates.[7]

32 chapter-based civic American organisations recorded in the chart above, reproduced from Robert Putnam's book *Bowling Alone*.

These organisations are diverse – they range from the Elk fraternity through to the Scouts; from the Jewish B'nai B'rith through to the League of Women Voters. But what they had in common was a devolved structure and an expectation that their members would come out and actively participate in some way in their local community. They were the warp and weft of the organised community life for which America was traditionally known. On this hundred-year chart there are, of course, sweeping secular trends unrelated to any recession – these form the chief subject of *Bowling Alone* – but the great civic slump during the early 1930s is nonetheless stark. It captures in a picture the same story told in all those Marienthal reports of defunct social clubs and walking groups. Putnam's underlying analysis of the individual organisations confirms that 'the membership records of virtually every adult organization in this sample bears the scars' of this period.[8]

Other, more qualitative, analyses carried out during the Depression era underline the same conclusion. Mirra Komarovsky's classic study of 59 unemployed men and their families near New York documented how economic misfortune warped relations within the home, and then spilled over into the community and 'reduced the social life'. People who 'used to visit and entertain friends' suddenly did so 'hardly at all'. One former electrician put it particularly bluntly: 'You don't have any friends unless you have got the dollar.'[9] Few aspects of community life were untouched. *Bowling Alone* also documents how membership of parent–teacher associations and professional associations took a dive, which paralleled the big dip in the economy. There was even a slump in sales of playing cards, with which people had used to while away the evenings together.[10]

Meanwhile – at least until Franklin Roosevelt's energy channelled discontent into something more positive – the political mood in this splintering American community turned to rage. In Iowa, farmers blocked highways and punctured tyres with pitchforks; in Wisconsin, dairy herdsmen fought battles with deputy sheriffs; and in Nebraska, angry smallholders threatened to bring 200,000 men to Lincoln to 'tear that new State Capitol Building to pieces'.[11] The Tuskegee archive registers a tripling in the number of African Americans lynched between 1929 and 1933.[12] A 1931 *New Republic* story explicitly spelt out a link between a stricken labour market and such racial violence: 'Dust had been blown from the shotgun, the whip and the noose, and Ku Klux practices were being resumed in the certainty that dead men not only tell no tales, but create vacancies.'[13] Closer to Marienthal, the political consequences of the Depression then emerging in German-speaking Europe are so infamous that they hardly need describing.

In speaking of the 'Great Recession' we nod to those years; but we are not suffering from the same mass unemployment as then, and – in any case – should we really expect passing economic troubles to dislocate today's vastly richer societies? Developments in the worst-hit parts of the world create varied impressions.

In Greece, as a six-year slump drags on, some of the soup kitchens that initially sprang up to rescue the desperate have been wound up for want of help, and in 2013 the Orthodox Church scheduled a summer break for food handout centres on the grounds that 'the women volunteers who cook in church kitchens . . . need to have a rest'.[14] A visiting American journalist, Michael Lewis, encountered angry crowds 'wielding truncheons disguised as flagpoles', and concluded that the community was coming to behave 'as a collection of atomized particles, each of which has grown accustomed to pursuing its own interest at the expense of the common good'.[15]

If that sounds like a good working definition of outright social breakdown, it is also a contrast with what Lewis found in Ireland, seat of one of the biggest banking busts. While 'important-looking foreigners' chased investors' debts, a traditionally poor population that never quite believed in boom-time riches laboured under impossible retrenchment 'with scarcely a peep of protest'.[16] Irish resignation may be less frightening than Greek rage, but it is hardly healthy either.

Our aim in this book is to identify the distinctive social maladies that flow from economic stagnation away from the peculiarities of the eurozone crisis, in Britain and the United States. Before the storm hit, the thing that marked out these two societies was the steady opening-up of a vast economic gap. Indeed, the world's leading authorities on the distribution of income have published a book that draws on decades of evidence, with the subtitle: *A contrast between continental European and English-speaking countries*.[17] All rich societies levelled out over most of the twentieth century; the great contrast emerged after the 1970s. Britain and America – unlike France, Germany or, until recently, Japan – began recreating the economic divisions of the past.[18]

Such was the drag on low pay during the supposed boom that for poorer Britons and Americans it is pertinent to ask: When exactly did the hard times begin? But the great divide was always likely to have very particular consequences during a serious bust. For if a first sensible thought is that a depression in today's advanced society – richer by far than 1930s Marienthal – should bring nothing like the same hardship, a sensible second hunch is that a lot will depend on how the pain is shared.

The sky-scraping opulence on display in London's Shard or New York's Bank of America Tower never did trickle down to the ordinary streets below, where many damp and cramped homes remained. We will ask whether these proved more vulnerable to the ravages of 'the storm'. Indeed, a more fitting metaphor turns out to be a tornado that rips a narrow strip through a Midwestern city, destroying some blocks while leaving others eerily untouched.

So this is unashamedly a book about inequality, as well as about recession: it has to be. Drawing on extraordinarily rich data, we are able to explore not merely *what* is happening, but also *how* and sometimes even *why*. We discover that the effect of the slump has been not so much to widen the financial divide, as to deepen it, and turn it into a societal schism. David Cameron used to talk up the pursuit of 'general well-being' and a 'Big Society' as a means of smoothing the rough edges of vigorous capitalism; but we will establish that the slump has converted unequal economies into unequal communities, hammering happiness and putting strain on families across great swathes of both the UK and the US, and most particularly their poorest streets. And we will see that, on some measures at least, the overall 'social recession' was actually deeper than the economic decline.

The Great Recession puts on trial not merely the consequences of vastly dispersed incomes, but also the way of running an economy that brought these into being. In the tables of regulatory protection for workers produced by the Organisation for Economic Co-operation and Development (OECD), Anglophone countries are bunched at the bottom.[19] The fruits of boom-time growth were grabbed by the rich (to varying degrees) in New Zealand, Canada and Australia, as well as in Britain and America.[20] Churchill wrote romantically of the 'English-speaking peoples'; de Gaulle less benignly about 'the Anglo-Saxons'. Either way, by 2008, the idea of a distinctive Anglo-Saxon way of doing business no longer sounded so anachronistic. And one of our most frightening findings is that, in line with the uneven damage of the great storm, political opinion has polarised in a way that could frustrate hopes of either country changing its ways. Nonetheless, the world needs to know how societies that run along these laissez-faire lines cope in the face of hard times – and how they recover.

An intriguing early exchange that was reported between Barack Obama and his Treasury secretary betrayed possible presidential unease on this last point. 'Your legacy is going to be preventing the second Great Depression', said Tim Geithner; 'That's not enough for me', replied the president.[21] Perhaps Obama sensed that there was something beyond the absence of growth that had landed America in its mess, and that it might thus take something more than the restoration of growth to repair the damage. Perhaps he had hoped to do something more than get back to American business as usual.

But a few years on, and to the extent that variable recoveries allow it, both Britain and the US *are* heading back towards business as usual. The basic model has not been reformed. In the UK, new analysis of official data shows that the proportion of bank lending going to productive businesses is actually lower than it was before the bust.[22] Meanwhile, orthodox voices such as Sir Mervyn King, former Bank of England governor, openly worry that a recovery pumped by so-called quantitative easing – the policy of printing money to pour into financial assets – could even inflate a fresh bubble.[23] If that is right, another bust could become conceivable sooner than anyone would like to imagine. But even if the recovery is sustained, it is built on the same old foundations. Both British and American societies will live with the consequences, as the effects of the Great Recession – which might soon be forgotten in more prosperous neighbourhoods – dog poor communities into the indefinite future.

Aside from boom-time inequality, Britain is an interesting society for the wider world to watch in hard times, because it is putting something else on trial, too: namely, the doctrine of so-called 'expansionary fiscal contraction'. This is the strategy, freely pursued by the coalition government after 2010, of reducing public expenditure in advance of an established recovery. Whether consciously or not, Chancellor George Osborne has echoed retrenching predecessors from the 1930s: whole passages of Neville Chamberlain's 1932 Budget – which mixed boasts about how austerity was restoring confidence at home with grim forebodings of chill winds blowing in from the Continent – could have been delivered by Osborne.[24] Whereas Obama's priority after his inauguration was his stimulus bill, Britain's new chancellor, only in office for a matter of weeks, argued that government cut-backs could actually create growth, by clearing away an overblown state that was 'crowding out private endeavour'. 'Some have suggested', he added, 'that there is a choice between dealing with our debts and going for growth. This is a false choice . . . [U]nless we deal with our debts there will be no growth.'[25] On that basis, the cutting began . . .

Subsequently, as the US gradually entered a half-throttle economy, the UK initially sank into a second period of stagnation – to all intents and purposes a modest double-dip recession.[26] In the process, it became a favourite case study for progressive Americans in how *not* to deal with depression. Bill Clinton's former labour secretary, Robert Reich, told me that 'Americans worried about austerity increasingly use Great Britain as *the* example of why the strategy is dangerous'.[27] At the *New York Times*, Paul Krugman regularly referred to 'the economic consequences of Mr Osborne'.[28] As far away as Australia, as Kevin Rudd briefly gathered the reins of his country's premiership in summer 2013, he warned that the opposition would 'copy the British Conservatives – launch a national slash and burn, austerity drive and drive the economy into recession as happened in Britain'.[29]

More recently, Osborne claimed vindication as growth finally returned; but his glowing self-appraisal remains bitterly contested.[30] Even the British business secretary, Vince Cable, publicly worries that the recovery is being fuelled by new rises in house prices – the very form of growth that proved unsustainable in the past.[31] However the British economy develops over the next few years, the chancellor's fiscal plans rely on retrenchment for very many years to come. So protagonists on both sides of the world's great austerity argument should surely also be interested in the way that British society fares as it swallows the Coalition's bitter medicine.[32]

Despite the distinctive twist of the austerity experiment in the UK, on the two sides of the Atlantic the basic picture remains one of shared rather than separate experience. Here are two rich but unequal societies, with large financial sectors and flexible labour laws, both hitting the buffers at once. We know that the recent slump cost the British and American economies more in lost output than any downturn since the Second World War, but – until now – it has been hard to be sure how much damage has truly been done to the fabric of the two nations.

In the broad-brush picture that comes across in news reports, occasional hopes that this might be a moment for renewal have jostled with darker fears in both countries. In the US, the depressed years saw the electorate bury ancient hatreds by twice electing the first black president; meanwhile, a sanguine newspaper commentator claimed to spot a burst of 'neighboring' on American streets.[33] On the other hand, at the political and even the cultural level, the US remains deeply divided. Every slump-induced need for a tweak to federal fiscal policy sparks brinkmanship that threatens to turn polarisation into paralysis. As for Britain, it has certainly clung to its famous ability to put on a brave face for the world. In the depths of the second bout of stagnation in 2012, a stately jubilee for the Queen passed off with popular support, and then London staged a successful Olympics, the opening ceremony of which was hailed as making every diverse community feel part of the national story. Billions of viewers across the planet saw nothing to indicate that a mere 11 months earlier this nation had briefly appeared to be coming unstuck, with summer riots spreading like wildfire across English towns and inner cities the previous August.

The evidence from day-to-day life is just as confusing. Every so often you might catch a glimpse of something suggesting trouble just below the surface – a gleaming shop window, say, which on inspection turns out to be hawking loans to the desperate, with interest charged at an annual rate of 4,000%. But if you pass your days in the more comfortable parts of town, it is often hard to pin down exactly what has changed. Walking around my own patch of East London, a few hundred metres can determine whether or not you perceive society to be unravelling: walk ten minutes in one direction and you find yourself amidst organic greengrocers and purveyors of pricy wooden toys, with no trace of recession evident. But walk ten minutes in the other direction and you hit the junction of Amhurst Road and

Mare Street – the grimy asphalt intersection that achieved nationwide recognition as the flaming heart of those 2011 summer riots.

Even in London, then, where house prices and wages have not fallen to the same extent as in most of Britain or the US, one can find images to support any chosen interpretation of the slump – from the Panglossian to the panicked. So to judge which is the more instructive impression of Anglo-American communities, you need to do more than trade anecdotes: you need to delve into the data.

The shape of things to come

We start out in Chapter 1 by reviewing the big economic picture and asking whether – in our vastly more affluent world – the Great Depression comparison really stands up to scrutiny. There are solid economic reasons why we *ought* to have been able to avoid 1930s-style societal ruin, and yet – as Chapter 2 asks – just how much protection against penury do the undoubted riches built up before the bust really provide when they were grabbed by so few hands?

The book moves on to trace the path of our tornado through a depressed labour market. Overall unemployment did not return to the highs seen in the 1930s, but – as Chapter 3 asks – how much bleaker do things appear if we soar down from the aerial view afforded by statistical averages and wander through the younger, blacker and poorer streets of our communities? The misery of the jobless was undoubtedly the chief societal poison during the Depression; but in Chapter 4 we explore the low pay, casual contracts and unpredictable shifts which combined during the recent recession to bring hard times to much of the working population too – and in a manner that is dragging on into the recovery.

The next stage of our inquiry moves out of the jobs market and into the communities, the homes and the hearts where the human consequences unfolded. Chapter 5 looks at family life and individual well-being, drawing on the new science of happiness and the oldest statistical indicator of its absence – the suicide rate. Chapter 6 then steps out of the home and onto the streets, to gauge the strength of social networks. Throughout, we ask whether hard times are re-inforcing pre-existing divisions by blighting the vulnerable more.

With the American recovery well under way and the British economy finally picking up, too, we consider whether we might soon be able to forget a passing storm. After all, recent English data on volunteering has been seized on as suggesting 'a civic recovery'. But Chapter 7 peers over the horizon and asks: Just how long will it be until cash-strapped families can once again dream of getting ahead? Just how easy is it for alienated individuals and atomised communities to bounce back after recession? And, looking further ahead, will the bitter experiences of today's jobless fathers be visited on their children, too?

The last time the storm hit this hard, Roosevelt in the US (and later, Beveridge in Britain) responded with a bold agenda that did not merely clear up the immediate disaster, but also sought to ensure that no future gale could bring the same misery. Alongside the aim of creating a full-employment economy to provide decent jobs, the ambition then was to build a comprehensive welfare state that would provide shared shelter whenever the economy faltered. Although policy has followed somewhat different paths in London and Washington this time, the recent record of both – upon which Chapter 8 concentrates – could reasonably be caricatured as knocking down storm defences.

Chapter 9 asks why, and looks for signs of opinions polarising along faultlines that have been sharpened by the slump. In increasingly unequal societies, it is becoming evident that the real pain of recession is not dished out randomly, but reserved for hard-pressed 'usual suspects'. That renders the old argument about weathering the storm collectively less persuasive to well-to-do communities who feel they are not much at risk, and thereby retards hopes of a common response. Chapter 10 wraps things up and insists that – for all the difficulties of constructing shared shelters today – the ruin uncovered along the line of the tornado imposes an obligation to try.

1

Not quite 1933

*Where is all this money, all this electronic money that's gone
missing? How has it gone missing? Who is accountable for it? None
of this is happening.*
'Winston', 47, jobseeker from Stanmore (on the outskirts
of London), speaking about the slump

The storm came out of a clear blue sky. In his 2007 Budget speech,
Chancellor Gordon Brown could boast that Britain was enjoying 'the
longest period of economic stability and sustained economic growth in
our country's history', just before he moved unchallenged into No. 10
Downing Street.[1] The long expansion in the US economy had been briefly
interrupted by 9/11, but felt just as assured. Few outside the financial
sector discerned the first whispers of a credit crunch during that notably
wet English summer,[2] but then September brought something unseen
since 1866 – a run on a British bank. It was not yet obvious that the
queues of savers that formed outside branches of the smallish, provincial
Northern Rock represented a threat to the financial universe as we knew
it. But a year later – almost to the day – Lehman Brothers came crashing
down in New York, heralding the start of the most catastrophic phase of
the crisis. Within weeks, America's biggest insurer, AIG, the Washington
Mutual Bank and Britain's own financial giant, RBS, would be respectively bailed out, bust, and bought up by the taxpayer.

As the towers of high finance shook, ordinary citizens watching from the streets below were entitled to ask what on earth the panic gripping the investing classes had to do with them. What passed for explanation on the news involved a series of acronyms – MBSs, CDSs and CDOs – that all turned out to be cunning schemes to make money out of debt which had suddenly proved to be not so cunning after all. In describing his bewilderment to us, 'Winston', a lean man with an urgent, expressive voice, speaks for the many. But six years on, 'Winston' finds himself uprooted and living alone, miles from his family, and – as we shall see – with every aspect of his life, from his diet to his dwindling dealings with relations, warped by the fall-out from those far-away financial dramas.

There is no doubt that for 'Winston', as for the least-fortunate minority in Britain and America, a financial slide has ended in personal misery. But how far has economic turmoil spilled over into a *wider* social malaise? Our Introduction pointed to reports from Austria's Marienthal and records of American civic associations to suggest that such a malaise did indeed set in during the Great Depression. However, does it really *feel* as if society has come crashing down again – as though the 1920s world of Fitzgerald's Jay Gatsby has suddenly transformed into something more like the 1930s world of Steinbeck's Tom Joad? This chapter attempts a cool appraisal of the average force with which the contemporary storm has blown.

Anyone who has lent even half an ear to the news in the past five years cannot have failed to gather that this was no ordinary slump. This was the big one, or so they said – the 'once in a century' event, as Alan Greenspan put it in 2008.[3] But the financial elite is interested in financial phenomena – share-price swings and overnight interbank rates – that are only of direct concern to itself. If we're talking people instead of percentages – and talking particularly about the majority of people who do not dabble in stocks or in interest-rate swaps – then is a purely financial crisis *really* such a big deal? Is there any serious reason to think that disruptive events in the alien world of Wall Street or the City of London would leave us all living in a world turned upside down?

The *economic* case for saying that they would do so starts with the historical observation that slumps which follow financial crises are invariably more significant. The disrupted flow of capitalism's monetary life-blood means that unemployment typically rises and output typically falls by twice as much – and for twice as long.[4] Six years on from the financial drama, a sober reading of the figures on the amount of real 'stuff' that the economy is churning out confirms that, in Britain at least, the ensuing slump has proved, if anything, worse than the Depression.

The figure below compares the profile of the decline in the UK's national income since 2008 with what unfolded at the beginning of the 1930s. The great contraction in 1931–32 was scarcely any sharper – about 7% of total output lost at the trough on both occasions. This is absolute GDP: if we looked instead at GDP per head (to take account of the fact that the more recent recession occurred at a time of faster

Greater than great? The course of the post-2008 UK slump compared with the 1930s

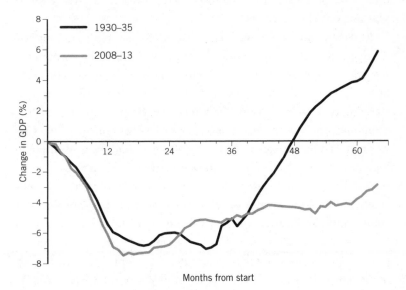

Months from start

Source: National Institute of Economic and Social Research, London.

population growth), then the downturn this time would appear relatively steeper.[5] And since the sort of social processes that we will be investigating take time, the duration of the loss is probably more important than its magnitude. On that count, the twenty-first-century slump is the more severe. In mid-2013, 64 months into the downturn, output was still 2% below where it started, whereas the full depth of the dip in the Depression was recovered within 48 months. Again, this sustained decline would be even more marked if we looked at national income per head.

For the US, the figure opposite tracks the recent slump against the two nastiest recessions since the Second World War.[6] The American slide that began with the credit crunch in 2007 is confirmed as both deeper and more enduring than any since the 1930s. The oil shock of 1973 called time on America's motoring way of life, forcing the introduction of a national speed limit and requiring President Nixon to plead with filling stations not to sell fuel on Saturdays; but the crisis of 2008 knocked half as much again off GDP. The great Reagan industrial shake-out of the 1980s felt as though it dragged on for ever, but the graph shows that after the recent recession it took GDP a whole year longer to bounce back.

Moving from facts to feelings, we can also establish without any difficulty that the public noticed – and long continued to notice – something awry. In spring 2013 (so more than three years into the technical US recovery), the pollsters YouGov found 64% of Americans claiming that their own lives had been significantly affected by 'the economic problems in your country' – an overwhelming majority. This was matched by a weighty 57% of Britons who said the same thing to the selfsame question.[7] The mood that surrounds money has a funny way of affecting things that are not obviously related to it; in a characteristic flourish, Keynes once ventured that Shakespeare's genius could only have thrived in the exuberance of an inflationary era.[8] Conversely, in the cautious mood of economic depression, one contemporary American writer has observed that people 'date less, sleep more and spend more time at home', while 'pop songs become more earnest, complex and romantic'.[9] No Briton old enough to recall

Worst since the War: the course of America's Great Recession compared with the downturns of the 1970s and 1980s

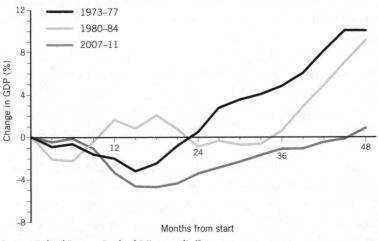

Source: Federal Reserve Bank of Minneapolis.[10]

Morrissey crooning about unfulfilled love as unemployment topped 3 million will dispute the last point, even if the recessionary connection then was not as stark as with John Rich's 'Shuttin' Detroit Down'.

Flickers of a Depressionary social psychology can also be detected in the sales of those few things to have bucked the downward trend. In 1930s America, the yen for escape rendered cigarettes and cinema tickets about the only goods to record rising sales; meanwhile, the flurry of new chocolate bars on the other side of the Atlantic led Roald Dahl to venture that interwar Britain was to confectionery what the Italian Renaissance was to art. Today, Kantar's market research reveals that Britons have, once again, developed a taste for more sugary and fattier foods.[11] And on the basis of 34,000 consumer interviews conducted during the economic trough of 2009, YouGov reported large proportions of UK shoppers switching to supermarket own brands, drinking less in the pub and cooking with leftovers (or at least claiming to do these things).[12] By January 2010, 31% said they were doing more home-baking, 19% more mending of clothes and 20% more vegetable growing; a full 77% claimed to be doing more of one or other of the money-saving activities suggested than before the downturn.

Yet a nation of thrifty bakers and vegetable growers is hardly a social catastrophe. And while a recessionary passion for sugary and fatty snacks may well be storing up health problems farther down the track, establishing that comfort consumption is back on the menu is not the same thing as proving that our communities are going to the dogs.

It may be as well to pause here and consider a much more sanguine interpretation of what has been going on. The Great Recession may be the worst American slump *since* the Depression, but that does not mean it is anything like as bad as the Depression was; the sheer scale of the slide witnessed in the US in the 1930s defies contemporary comparison. The total decline in real GDP then was something like one-quarter when measured between the calendar years 1929 and 1933;[13] it was more like one-third from precise peak to trough; and it was virtually one-half for industrial production.[14] These thumping great fractions – a half, a third, a quarter – are declines of another order from the knock of 7% or so that the UK suffered both back then and now, or the 5–6% hit to GDP that America suffered between 2007 and 2009.

The grim tales in our Introduction about social atomisation in the 1930s came from a village in Austria (a nation where industrial production dropped by nearly 40% in the 1930s)[15] and the severely depressed United States. Perhaps it is more sensible to compare the recent single-digit contractions in output with interwar Britain. Forget for the moment the darker observations of J.B. Priestley about 'sooty dismal little towns' and 'fortress-like cities' in the stricken regions, and recall that this was also a land peppered (as one social history recounts) with mutually owned working men's clubs with large numbers of attached associations – 'bowls, angling and picnic clubs . . . Oddfellows or Buffaloes' – and special rooms where 'officials of the unions or the co-ops, or local councillors drank'.[16] Besides, the Depression comparison is arguably over-egged, even for the UK. For the slide of 1929 represented a dive in a British economy that was already stagnant. Stiff interest rate rises and extraordinary retrenchment[17] had snuffed out the brief post-First World War boom so decisively that the UK was stuck with, to use John Maynard Keynes' phrase, 'the dragging conditions of semi-slump' for much of the next two decades.[18] This time, by contrast, at least we enjoyed a boom before the bust.

If you really want to cheer yourself up, though, forget about recent *changes* to national income and concentrate instead on just *how much* national income there is. Ceaseless technological advance since the Depression has steadily cashed-in as growth. Over 80 years, this has gradually worked a miracle, roughly quadrupling output. The graphs overleaf provide the long view, cutting through the busts as well as the booms and charting the inexorable rise in income which has prevailed in both the UK and the US. The data is fully adjusted for inflation, and indeed for population growth, because this is national income per head. Look closely, and you can just about spot wobbles connected with the world wars and America's Great Depression. But presented in this way, none of the downturns in either country appears as anything much more than a ripple on a great rising wave. The Great Recession is definitely visible at the ends of both the British and the American series, but in neither case does it look like anything to get excited about. After all, the real action here does not lie in the slight difference between 2010 and 2007, but in the utter contrast between incomes in either of those years and those prevailing at any point of the 1920s or 1930s. If, for example, we compare the peak year of 2007 with 1929, then British incomes had grown to stand at 470% of their pre-Depression peak, while those in the US had risen to stand at 550% of 1929 levels. In the face of these sorts of numbers – and these sorts of charts – any talk of 'hard times' suddenly sounds hyperbolic.

Statistics and charts aside, is all this supposed progress meaningful? Growth works slow-motion magic: it is hard to spot while it is happening, and is more easily grasped at a distance. Let's consider how technology transformed the reach of artificial light in the century

Onwards and upwards together: the inexorable growth of real GDP per head in:

(a) the UK

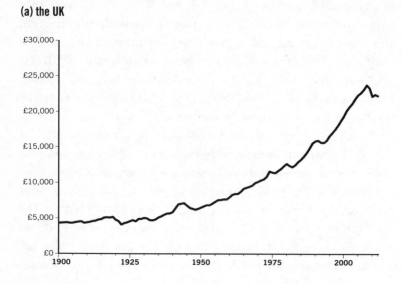

(b) the United States

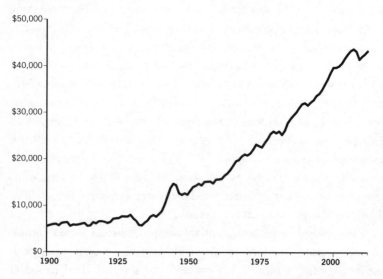

Source: MeasuringWorth, 2013.[19] UK figures are in 2008 pounds; US in 2005 dollars.

before the Great Depression. Back in 1835, the typical overworked and underfed individual would have had to spend a full extra hour labouring for every ten hours that he wished to keep a single candle alight after sundown over the week, a cost that inhibited reading among even the literate minority (and that explains the old expression about an activity not being 'worth the candle'). But after a century of filamentary innovation, by 1930 a glimmer of light equivalent to one candle could be sustained over ten hours for the cost of something like five seconds' work. So it gradually became possible to attain enlightenment in the dark hours without fretting about the cost, a development with profound social consequences.[20]

No more profound, however, than the marvels wrought between the Depression and our own time: from the green revolution in agricultural yields to the deployment of robots in manufacturing; from polymers that make cut-price packaging to molecules that battle malignancies; from endless home entertainment to instant communication with anyone anywhere. The result? In terms of consumer goods and services, we really are much better off on average. A relatively modestly paid worker can today embark on a flight that would have bankrupted someone far higher up the wage range at the time of the Depression – and that's before we even consider the transformation in the chances of surviving the trip!

For any who remain doubtful that growth bears a relation to human welfare, we can go even further back, to the early Industrial Revolution. At that time, Thomas De Quincey was admittedly guessing when he ventured that a quarter of all human misery was toothache; but thanks to progress in dentistry – and our ability to afford it – no one would make the same guess today.

All this growth, then, is real money; it *should* be able to offer society real protection against hard times. As the world slid towards the abyss in 1930, Keynes took a brief break from peering over the edge and looked forward instead, to the 'Economic Possibilities for Our Grandchildren'.[21] He correctly predicted how much magic technology would work, and then suggested that there might come a point when getting richer would 'no longer [be] of high social importance'.

It has always been said that the most valuable things are those that money can't buy. Keynes' essentially accurate long-range forecast prompts the thought that we might already have reached a pass where we can afford to protect the things that really matter – things like mental health, family and community – from the vicissitudes of the business cycle. With national income so high by any historical standard, we are left with a question that holds few terrors: How big a deal is it when a rich society gets a bit poorer?

Hopes of a heartening answer draw support from a wealthy society that has experienced dragging semi-slump in our own time – the curious case of Japan. Supposed 'hard times' have gone on for so long, and there have been so many twists, that it is tricky to date them with precision. The causes remain contentious, but Japan has made a habit of recession for a long time now, and whereas real national income before 1991 was expected to grow by about 3% annually, since then it has barely averaged 1%.[22] The cumulative effect is huge: by 2013, real GDP was fully one-third less than it would have been if pre-1991 growth rates had somehow been maintained.[23]

In 1995 – a few years after stagnation became entrenched – Japanese society faced the Great Hanshin earthquake. It killed over 5,000 people, damaged over 100,000 buildings, chiefly in Kobe, and a fumbling response from Tokyo made matters worse. But then civil society, not previously reckoned to be much of a force in Japan, stepped forward to pick up the pieces – literally and metaphorically. By some estimates, over a million volunteers lent a hand, and eye-witnesses spoke in awed terms of how citizens 'organized themselves with military precision and stormed the city'.[24] This came to be seen as a turning point: by 2004, an American-educated academic based in Tokyo could write that, while Japan had lost 'a system and a fortune, it found improved life style' thanks to 'a quiet transformation . . . extending and reinvigorating its stunted civil society'.[25]

On the economic front, the bad news for Japan just kept coming. After 2008, the familiar steady stagnation was compounded as the Great Recession briefly knocked 10% off GDP, a sharper immediate contraction than in either Britain or the US.[26] In March 2011, just as the nation was sinking into its second post-Lehman dip, *real* disaster struck. Some 43 miles out to sea, the Tōhoku earthquake rumbled into life, unleashing a tsunami that would claim 15,833 lives, deprive millions of electricity and trigger a Level 7 meltdown in the Fukushima nuclear power plant.[27] Prime Minister Naoto Kan pronounced it the 'toughest and most difficult crisis for Japan' since the Second World War. This was a moment to remember that there is more to life than money. But how would two decades of 'hard times' condition the community's response? Recall Michael Lewis' description of recessionary Greek society as 'a collection of atomized particles' – and shudder.

Japan, however, is not Greece. For the most part, the citizenry in the disaster-hit regions did not fight their way onto crowded trains, but either queued at the station in an orderly manner or kept calm and carried on. Then there were the 'Fukushima Fifty': the citizens (in reality far more than 50) who braved the radioactive front line to extinguish the flames in the failed nuclear plant. The ranks of the paid emergency workers were swelled by volunteers, most particularly senior citizens. Many were determined to remain anonymous, but a few were prepared to explain their thinking, including Yasuteru Yamada, who told Reuters that, at the age of 72, 'I will be dead before [the] cancer gets me'.[28] Seasoned observers of Japan warn against dismissing the societal problems of stagnation too readily; poverty and inequality have risen, and although still rare, homelessness is more evident than it used to be.[29] But in the midst of a serious slump, an atomic emergency revealed the antithesis of an atomised society.

There is little doubt that a long record of earlier growth is one of the things that has helped Japan weather hard times well. In this 'rich society that got a bit poorer', the marginal things that were cut back on were less important, and sometimes barely noticeable. Visiting in 2011, a *Guardian* reporter observed: 'it is easy to visit its cities and completely miss out the fact that it has . . . been weathering an economic crisis'.[30] Financial journalist Eamonn Fingleton has lived in Japan since 1985. He wrote in the *Atlantic* that, after some 20 years of supposed stagnation,

Anyone who visits Japan . . . is struck by the obvious affluence even among average citizens . . . The Japanese boast the world's most advanced cell phones . . . Japan's already long life expectancy has increased by nearly two years. Its internet connections are some of the world's fastest.

The wealth of the nation is such, he reasoned, that the great stagnation could almost be a statistical artefact – or a mercantilist ruse to understate the true growth of the nation.[31]

So maybe it will all turn out fine for Britain and America, too. As comparably affluent societies, can we not likewise hope to come through similarly unscathed? Should we count our blessings that we are not facing a Tōhoku-style emergency, but still have faith that, faced with something similar, we would answer it with Japanese-style resolve? An economic downturn, after all, is not a war; a financial tsunami is very different from the real thing. No one needs to die. It's only money.

If we regard the Anglo-Saxon landscape from 30,000 feet up, it might – perhaps – be possible to sustain such comforting thoughts. For example, a two-decade decline in overall crime rates continues in both the UK and the US.[32] Pundits have advanced some quirky theories for the new-found lawfulness, ranging from the legalisation of abortion to the elimination of leaded petrol;[33] but a determined optimist could say that the failure of crime to pick up when the economy slides is not that surprising, because it really is not that big a deal when an affluent community faces a squeeze. The same determined optimist could glance loftily down at average life expectancy statistics: the slow retreat of the Grim Reaper towards later life continues apace; a drop in mortality in slump-stricken 2009 pushed deaths in England and Wales below the half-million mark for the first time in modern history, just as one report summed up the American data with the headline 'US death rate falls for 10th straight year'.[34]

Perhaps, our determined optimist might say – using that dread phrase from financial history – it really is *different this time*: different because we are now wealthy enough to protect ourselves against destitution and despair.

But the sanguine view from the sky cannot survive descent into the communities bearing the brunt. Talk to 'Winston' about his meticulous planning of the week's food ('I've been asked a thousand times how can you survive on £10 a week? Well a lot of rice, a lot of pulses, a lot of pasta and some egg' – a challenge made all the harder because 'I don't have a cooker') and all the cheery chatter about technology shielding society suddenly sounds like complacency.

Nor is it exclusively the poorest of the poor, such as 'Winston', who dismiss the sanguine story about the slump – or indeed the emerging recovery. In December 2013, after three solid quarters of growth in all the UK data, an ICM poll found that while Britons did accept that the economy was recovering, by a crushing 70% to 26% margin they also insisted that they were seeing no personal benefit from this at all.[35]

Earlier the same year, YouGov had asked Britons and Americans for their views on a proposition, the rejection of which would indicate truly interminable pessimism: 'our children's generation will [eventually] end up enjoying a better standard of living than our generation, just as our generation has mostly been better off than our parents'. The wording sums up the story of generational advance that has been the pattern since the Industrial Revolution, and fits with the stories we all hear about our own families – tales of parents and grandparents having experienced privations unimaginable to the young generation. Yet in 2013, only 15% of citizens in the famously optimistic American Republic were inclined to accept this claim, as against 65% who feared that the old pattern of progress would be upended. In recession-hit Britain, the 64:19 split was almost as gloomy.[36] Something, then, would appear to be breaking the spell of growth's slow magic insofar as the mass of the people are concerned.

Some may be tempted to dismiss the popular majority's view of the slump and recovery as melodramatic – or just plain wrong. They should recall that for those without empathy, even the catastrophe of 1930s America could be brushed off as nothing to worry about. Thanks to the intervening century of economic growth, the hungry 1930s did not bring the sort of mass starvation witnessed in the hungry 1840s. Whereas in days gone by hard times had been synonymous with

famine and early graves, in the United States of the 1930s many went
without gasoline rather than bread, and a drop in traffic accidents
actually pushed the mortality rate down.[37] There was enough ambiguity in the patchy crime data from the era[38] for a right-wing romantic
like Ronald Reagan to be able to get away with looking back and
claiming 'we had possibly the lowest crime rate in our history at a time
when poverty was most widespread'.[39] And as the likes of Steinbeck's
Joads were making their terrified trek from the Dustbowl to the West,
there were those who said that they could not truly be poor because
they were driving in trucks. Indeed, in 1931 President Hoover himself
told a journalist: 'Nobody is actually starving . . . The hobos, for
example, are better fed than they have ever been.'[40]

With *average* incomes far higher than in the distant past, one would
indeed hope that we would be better able to keep destitution and
hunger at bay. People will not look back on our era – in a description
applied to Marienthal – as the time 'when men ate dogs'.[41]And yet
averages are compressed statistics, which can conceal more than they
reveal. For all the riches of our age, the reality that will unfold in the
coming pages is that the Great Recession has indeed proved to be a
great disruption for Anglo-Saxon societies, albeit one that disrupts in
a different – a more selective – manner to the great storm that ravaged
America in the 1930s.

Given the great economic divide that has developed over the past
third of a century (a division the next chapter turns to), instead of
the familiar 'economic storm' a more fitting metaphor would be a
tornado – something which tears through a city, destroying some
blocks while leaving others almost untouched.

2

All in it together?

I signed up for food stamps 'cause I needed them, I needed to eat . . .
Men don't mess with food stamps until they really need it, really need
the help. So I gave it a try.
Leroy Armstrong, 48, Fort Myers, Florida, talking to the
New York Times[1]

As well as *The Road to Wigan Pier*, George Orwell also wrote *Coming Up for Air* during the 1930s. This is the tale of a disgruntled insurance man, George Bowling, who resents his era not because there is too little work, but rather because there is too much house-building going on for the good of the countryside. The slump may have affected just about everybody in Marienthal, but that was one small village; in larger and more complex societies, things are never so uniform. Much of southern England fared reasonably well in the 1930s, with something of a boom in new light-manufacturing industries.

There were similar differences within the United States. Thus it was that – in his second inaugural speech – President Roosevelt spoke not only of the 'forgotten one-third of a nation', denied education and opportunity and 'condemned to live in the pall of disaster', but also of citizens for whom wealth was being translated 'into a volume of human comforts hitherto unknown'.[2]

There is, then, nothing new in the idea that hard times hit unevenly – biting in different ways in different towns, and even in different homes. This time, however, the great gulf in conditions that opened up between different parts of the population *before* the slump has, as we shall see, warped every element of the social response. After a third of a century in which the egalitarian assumptions of the post-war settlement have slowly rotted under the surface, the financial tide is going out and exposing a society defined by division. While the previous chapter emphasised the great gain in *average* income since the Great Depression, this one digs down into the distribution and asks what different individuals are getting. Dramatic changes in relative economic fortunes, we will argue, have conspired to make times that much harder.

Faith in the affluence that has been born of industrial progress inspires some to argue that there is no longer any abject hardship in modern society. The Queen's husband, Prince Philip, once caused a great stir by suggesting that there was no longer absolute poverty in modern Britain – and, although it was a characteristically bumbled intervention, on a generous reading of his words you can see what he was trying to get at.[3] His point was the same as that of right-wing think tanks in the US, which dismiss official definitions of 'poor' as 'promoted by politicians and political activists' and disconnected from living conditions. The Heritage Foundation, for example, goes to great lengths to shower the debate with all manner of statistics – from Vitamin C consumption levels, to rates of ownership of DVD players and incidence of what they call 'stunted growth' – in order to demonstrate that the problems facing America's poor in the twenty-first century are often very different from those facing the impoverished in Bangladesh or Niger.[4]

That is undoubtedly true, and there is no disputing the importance of so-called *absolute poverty*. It is likewise true that the problems of poor Americans and poor Britons today are often different from those faced by their predecessors in the 1930s or earlier. For whereas virtually all of the English working-class family budgets recorded a century ago in *Round About a Pound a Week* were consumed by necessities such as rent, food and functional clothing, today, with the subsequent rise in average incomes, there is indeed more often expenditure on things not strictly required for survival.[5] If hard times in today's rich societies only mean reduced outlays on non-essential items, then one might imagine that society should be better able to weather the economic storm.

The dividing line between essential and non-essential expenditure is, however, not as sharp as the likes of the Heritage Foundation would have us believe. For an explanation of why, we turn not to Keynes or Marx, but to an authority whose name is often claimed by the free-market Right: Adam Smith, writing in *The Wealth of Nations*.

> By necessaries I understand, not only the commodities which are indispensably necessary for the support of life, but whatever the custom of the country renders it indecent for creditable people, even of the lowest order, to be without. A linen shirt, for example, is, strictly speaking, not a necessary of life. The Greeks and Romans lived . . . very comfortably, though they had no linen. But in the present times . . . a creditable day-labourer would be ashamed to appear in public without a linen shirt, the want of which would be supposed to denote that disgraceful degree of poverty.

Linen is thus rendered essential for Smith, not because of nature, but by 'the established rules of decency'.[6]

Here, then, we have the father of invisible-hand economics recognising that the conditions required to avoid serious hardship are not fixed for all time, but are rather something that depends on the community, the standards – and, by implication, the average affluence – of the day. As social animals, people left too far behind their fellows in material terms will be ashamed and excluded, and so will be unable to flourish. In our own time, the theoretical implications of this insight have been developed by scholars such as Amartya Sen, through the so-called 'capability approach' to welfare economics.[7] And in fact, over the last several decades, burgeoning evidence of a connection between a lowly relative social standing and life-threatening illnesses has suggested that there might be *physical* consequences of relative deprivation, further blurring the boundary between social necessities and the pre-conditions of physical health.[8]

Crunching the results of 170,000 YouGov market-research interviews conducted in late 2011, just as the UK labour market hit rock bottom, underlines how relative economic standing has a bearing on every aspect of social life.[9] Choose any indicator of economic advantage you like, and then choose any supposedly non-pecuniary aspect of life, and the same connection keeps popping up in the data:

- Family? Some 73% of outright home owners feel positive about relations with family – 12 percentage points more than tenants in social housing.
- Friendship? Around 59% of those in the higher (so-called 'ABC1') occupational grades feel good about relations with friends – 6 percentage points more than people in more routine ('C2DE') lines of work.
- Sex? Only 35% of people with the lowliest school qualifications feel optimistic about their romantic life, as against 47% of Master's graduates.

The detailed data reveals an even clearer social gradient, because respondents with middling indicators of class reliably have intermediate optimism scores.[10] Similar social gradients govern individuals' feelings about the metaphorical health of their neighbourhoods and the literal health of their own bodies.[11]

All these statistics would appear to bear out Smith's concern with relative poverty. But intriguing as it is to hear a pillar of the Scottish Enlightenment explain the cost – the 'toll' – of feeling cut-off (or 'indecent') by deprivation, the point is more poignantly made by those on whom it is biting today. In talking to hard-pressed people in contemporary Britain – whether black or white, old or young, from Edinburgh in the north, to London in the south – we found an overwhelming fear of 'losing face' through poverty, with several explaining how this fear would cause them to cut themselves off from social contact. At the less extreme end of the scale, we heard from 'Laura', a bright but broke 25-year-old student from a Newcastle family whose fortunes were doomed during her infancy, when her father lost his job in the steel works. Studying in institutions where wealthy youngsters abound, she talked of her dread when her friends proposed nights out in flashy bars, where she knew 'I wouldn't be able to afford a single drink . . . I was literally the only one in the group that couldn't, and that's embarrassment.' This embarrassment left her fearing that she would 'be the one ruining the evening by going "Oh, can we not go there"'. And so, 'on occasion, I made excuses – I was like, "Oh, I've got an essay due in tomorrow"' – and she would slip off for an evening alone. Her experience of being relatively strapped for cash is nothing unusual: it is the sort of experience that all but the most privileged of people are likely to have at some time or other in life – and yet it is an experience that temporarily cut her off.

Fewer of us, however, have experienced the dread that grips 'Moira' – unemployed and unhappy, in Hornchurch, Essex – whenever she heads for the supermarket. This fragile, stick-thin 60-year-old only stopped working to dedicate herself to the care of her ageing mother, then found it impossible to land a new job after the old lady died. Today, as she scrambles around for things to sell on eBay, she is haunted by shame: 'I wouldn't want anybody else to know my situation because it would seem embarrassing.' But she feels it most intensely when it is time to get in the groceries. 'When you go out shopping for food', she explains, 'and people are filling up their trollies and you think . . . I *mustn't* get [caught out at] the till because, if I haven't got enough money, that would be terrible; so I always make sure that I have added it all properly in my head.' Being caught short at the counter would not cause such intense worry to someone who did not live with gnawing anxiety about being exposed as poor; but for 'Moira', nerves and feelings are frailer.

As indeed they are for unemployed 'Winston', whom we heard from in Chapter 1. His large Caribbean family has always bonded over barbecued food: 'Granddad's got Jerk chicken, I've got spicy lamb, we've all got different things we know how to do, and we do it with a passion.' Or at least, it always did until hard times hit. These days, 'I try to distance myself when there is a family function because I cannot carry my weight like I used to.' It is not that he fears that the rest of his family would fail to feed him if he turned up, or even that he is unable to rustle up a little something to stick on the grill for himself. Rather, it is that he cannot bear his family seeing that he is no longer able to turn up 'with a big pot of seasoned meat' as he used to – a relative shortcoming to be sure, but one that leaves him absolutely starved of family company. Nobody with a heart can listen to a man in the prime of life, cutting himself off from beloved relations like this, and fail to understand that – whatever the progress of industry might do to average living standards – a human being will never flourish if he feels too poor to take part.

That reality means that the effect of hard times is bound to depend on whether the economic pain is shared around, or whether instead it is concentrated on particular individuals. The shortcomings of the sanguine story about technological progress automatically shielding society now become plain. As national income falls away in a recession, somebody is going to have to get poorer; and even if all incomes remain high by historical standards, if the fortunes of some sink faster than others, then that is going to hurt. Thus growth on its own will not do the business of protecting society from a slump. Fortunately, growth is not the only thing that is different from the Depression; these days, we also have institutions that are supposed to put a check on how far individuals can slide.

Meagre and meanly administered as it can be, there is an awful lot more social security to cushion the blow than there was in the pre-welfare-state 1930s. The UK did have unemployment benefits at that time, but they came attached to a stringent and despised means test, and covered only particular categories of working men. All told, it was a very long way from the comprehensive cradle-to-grave safety net introduced after 1945 – an operation on about half the scale.[12] And in the United States of the early 1930s there was simply no federally organised social insurance at all – Roosevelt created it only *in response* to the Great Depression, reportedly describing his ambitions using the famous 'cradle-to-grave' phrase shortly before signing the Social Security Act into law in 1935, two years into the recovery.[13]

The existence of such financial support for the most vulnerable undoubtedly makes a difference, as unemployed 'Winston' himself accepts: 'I am grateful for the fact I've got a safety net . . . I'm not homeless at the moment which I am very grateful for.' To the extent that social security (or 'welfare') can make up for wages that disappear in a slump, it ought to take the roughest edges off hard times for individuals, and contain the societal fall-out – although, of course, a great deal depends on how high the benefit floor is set.

Going into the Great Recession, the British system provided for more such smoothing than did the American. To compare benefit rates across borders, one needs to cut through complex differences in national rules. The rich countries' think tank, the OECD, does so by averaging across a range of different scenarios that an unemployed worker might face, and then asking how much of his or her wage will typically get replaced. With top-ups like housing included, for a childless Briton this summary 'net replacement rate' stood at 51% on the eve of the storm, implying that he or she would receive benefits of about half the average wage. This put the UK roughly in line (albeit on the low side) with continental nations such as France and Germany, where in both cases the figure stood at 56%. America, however, is another country: the same rate there stood at just 27% – in other words, being without a job cost the average worker in the average situation three-quarters of his or her income.[14] Even if it is better to lose three-quarters than to lose everything – as most of those laid-off in the American Depression were doomed to undergo – falling into a safety net that is three-quarters of the way down to the ground represents a frightening drop.

The apparatus of social security should kick in automatically to provide economic shelter in a slump. The extent to which it actually does so can be powerfully affected by the government of the day. In the first phase of the Great Recession, certain decisions in London and Washington suggested that the lessons of history had been learnt. During the Depression, Britain's second Labour government had split over a claimed need to cut the elementary unemployment benefits; some of its ministers went on to serve in the National Government, which did precisely that in 1931. At the trough of the big dip in 2009, by contrast, Britain's then Labour government took a proactive decision to increase all benefits and tax credits by a little, even though the cost of living was actually falling at the time. This raised the safety net a touch, which – coupled with shrinking banks and a few tax rises that targeted the rich – duly ensured that the first bout of British pain was fairly shared, as is illustrated by the Institute for Fiscal Studies data that is charted below. During the first year when there was a serious squeeze on family incomes, then – believe it or not – the British rich took much of the pain, and income inequality actually declined.

What about the reputedly harsher United States? Well there, too, the immediate response to recession was not in fact to cut benefits in the manner of 1930s Britain, but rather to provide a little relief by easing up the rules. One of the chief reasons why American welfare is

Fairly shared pain during the British recession's first phase

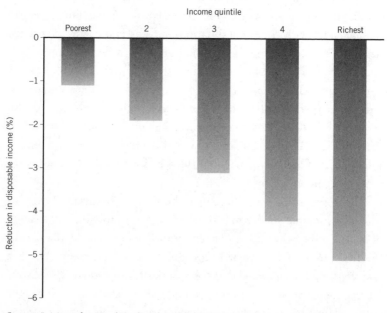

Source: Institute for Fiscal Studies.[15] Data for 2010/11, the first year that the slump's effect was evident in household incomes.

less generous than Europe's is the strict time limits on payments, including unemployment compensation, which is typically available for only 26 weeks. But there were several initiatives from mid-2008 to temporarily extend the term limit, which soon provided additional cover of up to an extra 33 weeks in the most depressed states. This much happened under President Bush, who opposed efforts to create jobs through spending on infrastructure, but nonetheless proved, by signing these moves into law, that he was not quite the reincarnation of Herbert Hoover.[16] The following year, the new president, Barack Obama, championed a stimulus bill that added more expansive coverage again, so that victims of the recession in the worst-hit states could receive 99 weeks of benefits.[17] Thus, by 2010 the same OECD net summary replacement ratio, which had stood at just 27% in 2007, was up to 38%, implying that instead of losing nearly three-quarters of his or her income, the typical unemployed worker was losing something less than two-thirds.[18]

These were modest moves, but they were moves in the right direction. Consequently, in both the US and Britain there was rising redistribution through the state, which somewhat protected the poor: American disposable incomes did not immediately become any more unequal as the economy shrank.[19] For a brief moment early on in the recession, then, it really might have appeared that the great lesson of the past – about weathering hard times collectively, and not allowing a slump to push anyone too far behind – had been absorbed. Even if the slow magic of growth was not in itself enough to shield society from hard times, might it not combine with social security to provide effective shelter?

It sounds a plausible enough suggestion – until you recall the troubling testimony of recessionary victims such as 'Moira' and 'Winston'. A combination of wealth and welfare *might* have allowed society to muddle through in one piece, were it not for what happened next in public policy (covered in Chapter 8) – and what came before. For those one or two years of fairly shared pain at the start of the slump came after a whole generation during which inequality had run out of control. In considering average incomes in the previous chapter, we found that a longer-term perspective allowed for a more sanguine reading of the recent dip; in reviewing the changing distribution of income, by contrast, the long view only serves to strengthen the case for panic. For it is only when we factor in how the poor of Britain and America have been squeezed over the decades that we finally reveal how exposed they were when the storm hit.

Joseph Stiglitz has documented how, since the late 1970s, the United States has steadily lapsed into a new gilded age.[20] The rise in economic inequality in Britain, which used to be more equal financially, is if anything more dramatic.[21] The social geographer Danny Dorling has plotted the arc of shifting income shares back over the course of a century. He concludes that Britain was steadily levelling out from 1910 right through to the later 1970s, but that this trend was then thrown into such dramatic reverse that the income gap has returned to widths unseen since the Blitz of 1940.[22] Three score years and ten separate the People's Budget of 1909 and Margaret Thatcher's arrival in Downing Street; in the three decades after 1979, roughly two-thirds of that life-time's-worth of levelling was undone. The immediate financial pain during the recessionary slide might have been widely shared, but more significant than any marginal change during the first year or two of the slump was the extraordinary skewing of income during the long run-up to the bust.

Using data from the Congressional Budget Office, the chart opposite records what happened to American real disposable incomes, of different levels, over the three decades before the Great Recession. It reveals a slant across the population: the rich got richer faster – with, for example, well-to-do families (the 'Richest below top 1%' bar) having typically seen incomes climb by two-thirds (65%) over this period, compared to an average advance of only one-third (35%) for families in the middle-income bracket. And progress for the poorest was only half of that at the middle – just 18% – and only a fraction of the advances at the upper end. The biggest gulf of all is between the fortunes of the seriously rich and the rest: the top 1% saw their incomes nearly triple in real terms, with a rise of 275%.

The rich and the rest: growth in American disposable incomes before the bust, 1979–2007

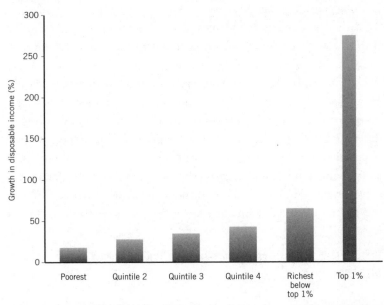

Source: Congressional Budget Office.[23] Figures refer to mean income within each bracket.

We can plot a very similar chart for Great Britain, drawing on the data used for the official poverty statistics (see graph overleaf). There are slight technical differences with the US data,[24] so don't worry too much about comparing exact percentages – concentrate on the chart's strikingly similar shape. Once again, we see the relentless slant across the population, with less of an advance being enjoyed by each successively poorer bracket, so that the gains for the poorest of all are little more than one-third of those for the most prosperous fifth below the top 1%. Once again, however, we see that the greatest gulf is between the very richest and the rest – with Britain's top 1% having more than quadrupled their income on this calculation.

We have checked these extraordinary findings against other income definitions and sources. While the magnitudes bob around a little – so that growth sometimes looks slightly less and sometimes slightly more

skewed – the same basic picture remains.[25] However you cut it, for a
long time before the bust, Britain and America were two societies
growing apart together.

With this skewing of incomes across the range, we can see why
Britons and Americans at the lower end of the scale were falling relatively further behind – and thus feeling poorer – as the decades before
the bust rolled by. There is an important contrast with pre-stagnation
Japan here. Although the Asian country's inequality statistics have
become a matter of controversy – with different surveys pointing in
different directions and with an income gap that does appear to have
widened very recently – a careful like-for-like analysis of the most
recent comparable data suggests that, well into the 2000s, Japan was
considerably more equal than Britain, let alone America.[26] While
downturn followed downturn in Japan, few of its citizens had started

**The rich and the rest: growth in disposable British incomes before the bust,
1978–2008**

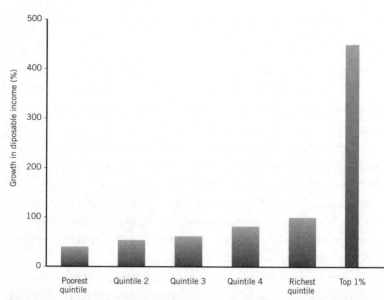

Source: Households Below Average Income data, maintained by the Institute for Fiscal
Studies.[27] Figures refer to the mid-point of each bracket.

out feeling as exposed as the Anglo-Saxon poor. Having become slowly deprived *relative* to their fellows over so many years, Britons and Americans at the bottom of the pile were not well placed to absorb an additional squeeze on their living standards – even if this was briefly widely shared.

Yes, those early recessionary efforts at redistribution did shield the vulnerable from bearing the full brunt of the collapse in the labour market. Nudging up benefits at a time of falling stock prices was enough to prevent the poor from becoming relatively poorer, an important achievement of sorts for both countries.[28] But move from relative poverty rates to the more familiar currencies of pounds and dollars, and the additional handouts were not for long sufficient to make up for pay packets that disappeared in the bust. Regardless of what was happening at the top end, the hard fact was that low incomes were falling: the rich were getting poorer *and* the poor were getting poorer. That was a fairer pattern than it might have been, but it was nonetheless a pattern bound to hurt the poor more, because of the 30 years that had gone before. As the long stagnation in living standards at the bottom end gave way to the big squeeze after 2008, it was not relative but absolute want that edged back into view.

During the so-called 'bubble years', the number of Americans below the official poverty line had already been edging up, from 32 million in 2000 to 37 million in 2007. This was a shocking indictment, since this official tally captures essentially an absolute measure of hardship – one that should be easy to flatter during a boom, simply by throwing the poor a few crumbs from the rich man's table.[29] When hard times officially kicked in, the numbers jumped again – to 46 million by 2010. In other words, in what remains by far the biggest and most powerful economy in the world, more than one citizen in seven is officially poor. The figure stuck stubbornly at 46 million right through 2011 and 2012, and the latest data available in November 2013 still shows no sign of any recovery.[30]

At first blush, the British poverty figures look much more reassuring – for both before and immediately after the crash. Over the decade before the credit crunch (between 1996/97 and 2006/07) the overall proportion of people stuck below any feasible absolute breadline declined by between 1 and 13 percentage points, depending on the exact line used. Remarkably, this progress initially survived the Great Recession: all the indicators remained stable (or even saw a further modest reduction) through to 2009/10.[31] But even by then, a closer reading of the data starts to reveal pain in parts of the community. Poor children and pensioners had benefited substantially from targeted anti-poverty drives under the governments of Tony Blair and Gordon Brown; but if we strip these groups out and concentrate on childless adults, then rising absolute hardship was evident as soon as the slump hit.[32]

The real trouble, though, concerns what happened next. Absolute poverty suddenly started to soar across the UK as a whole, with around 2 million extra people affected in just two years after 2009/10.[33] Looking ahead to years when austerity will bite even harder, the Institute for Fiscal Studies forecasts additional rises in absolute poverty on much the same scale, with another 1.5 million people set to be affected.[34] It is as if Britain's poor weathered the great storm in surprisingly good shape, only to be soaked by the great floods that followed. A technical recovery may be under way in the UK, but for those at the bottom of the heap, the hard times are only beginning.

On both sides of the Atlantic, then, the figures starkly expose how, after long years of stagnant living standards, hard times have made the poor absolutely poorer (albeit, in Britain's case, after something of a delay). Worse, there are two powerful reasons for thinking that these headline figures could be understating the true poverty problem.

The first big reason is particularly important in the UK: housing costs. The miserable post-1970s growth in low incomes recorded on the previous charts is, in fact, an overestimate of the progress in actual living standards, due to the rocketing rents that have faced poor communities over these years. Averaging over the 30 years to 2008 – three decades during which UK national income almost precisely doubled[35] – incomes for the bottom fifth of the population *after housing costs* inched up by only a fraction of a per cent each year.[36] And among those segments of the population that were neglected by public policy, all progress now melts away. Taking housing into account, in the years immediately *before* the bust, the best part of a million Britons in the 'childless, working-age' category had sunk below the breadline and into absolute poverty.[37]

Housing costs are, of course, a concern in America, too; the sharp downturn in property values from 2007 did, however, show at least some sign of filtering through to rents by 2010.[38] By contrast, in southern England and particularly London – after the briefest of interruptions – house prices resumed their remorseless climb, assisted by big money fleeing the eurozone. And rents kept rising in parallel. For all the riches of the capital, once housing is allowed for, the latest official figures reveal that inner London has a poverty rate that is half as high again as the UK as a whole.[39] 'Maria', a Portuguese single mother we spoke to in the capital, graphically explains why. She works full time for a salary of £21,000, close to the median female full-timer's £23,000 wage, which means: 'Net per month, I get £1,400; my rent is £1,385.' She lives in a flat in unfashionable Cricklewood, five miles out of London's centre, and yet without state support her full-time toil would leave her with £15 to survive on each month; the childcare she needs during the school holidays is £28 a day. Right across the UK, the effect of housing on poverty is profound – for lower-earners, the humblest homes strain the limits of affordability in unfashionable Midlands cities, a hundred miles from the capital.[40]

The second big reason why the grim headline statistics understate the true position applies with equal force on both sides of the Atlantic: debt. In 2007–08, the world gradually woke up to the fact that it was not so much playing 'pass the parcel' as 'pass the parcel-bomb' with repackaged IOUs. Before that, debt – or 'credit', as it was more often called in those days – was all the rage. On the hazy assumption that an endless boom would somehow allow all bills to be settled in the end, banks were only too willing to lend. On the lazy (but under-standable) assumption that bankers lending the money must know what they were doing, millions of ordinary Americans and Britons snapped it up. Home owners remortgaged to spend a presumed capital gain, and even those without houses enjoyed easy access to unsecured credit.

In retrospect, the swelling of balance of payments deficits on both sides of the Atlantic indicated societies living beyond their means; the US current account, for example, shifted from virtual equilibrium in 1991 to a deficit of $400 billion in 2000, before ballooning to $800 billion in 2006.[41] As the personal savings rate plunged to 1%, so-called 'household leverage' – the ratio of debt to disposable income, a ratio that historically is no more than two-thirds – reached an all-time American high of 130% in 2007. In the boom-time UK, the household saving ratio was at one point officially estimated to have turned *negative*; although the statistic was later revised to the margins of positive territory, for all practical purposes it had hit the floor.[42]

These scary statistics are economy-wide averages across all income groups, but the worst eventual consequences of living 'on tick' did not fall evenly between them – they were concentrated at the bottom of the heap. In the appraisal of Nobel Laureate Joseph Stiglitz, American banks engaged not merely in reckless lending, but in 'predatory lending, taking advantage of the least-educated and financially unsophisticated . . . by selling them costly mortgages and hiding details of the fees in the fine print'.[43] The results of the same sort of practices are now evident in Britain as well, where, Sir John Hills' thorough new review of the evidence asserts: 'All the sources agree that a quarter or more of households have no, or negative, net financial assets.' His own analysis suggests that by 2005, the poorest tenth had non-mortgage debt exceeding £6,000, tripling (in real terms) the figure of £1,900 that had applied just a decade before.[44]

We will return to the long post-bust shadow cast by boom-time lending in Chapter 7. But even during the so-called 'good times', the burden of simply maintaining such substantial debt eats into the notionally 'disposable' income of many a poor family, such as the disabled and unwaged couple we spoke to in Luton, 'Stephanie' and 'Martin'. They now need to find £200 every month merely to service unexceptional personal debt of £7,000. Making the minimum payments on that total – a debt which, they insist, owes as much to cumulative interest and bank charges as to the original spending – eats up one-sixth of the money that these very sick people (he has advanced cancer; she has lost a leg) have for everything they need. Their case is far from exceptional: it involves a credit card with ordinary terms. Others we spoke to, including unemployed 'Moira' in Essex, had fallen prey to the super-high-interest payday lenders, and were often left trapped in a seemingly unbreakable cycle of borrowing money to pay off unaffordable borrowing.

In line with conventional measures of poverty, this chapter focuses on ongoing *flows* of income, rather than financial *stocks* (such as debts and savings). The burden of debt and the lack of anything to fall back on obviously intensify the experience of hardship, however. And to the extent that interest payments eat up disposable income, they effectively push up poverty, too. The way debt feeds back into the distribution of disposable income is stark: on the basis of Bank of England analysis, the Resolution Foundation recently reported that the poorest British borrowers were spending nearly half (47%) of their income on repayments, compared to a mere 9% of income consumed by repayments among the richest debtors.[45] If the official figures were somehow adjusted to reflect such repayments – as they arguably should be – then all the dismal numbers we have reviewed would be worse.[46]

To grasp what the unfolding rise in absolute poverty actually means, let us again hear first from Adam Smith: 'Custom . . . has rendered leather shoes a necessary of life in England. The poorest creditable person, of either sex, would be ashamed to appear in public without them.' He contrasted this with the position in Scotland (where, for some reason, shoes were deemed necessary for men but not women!) and poorer France, where there was no disgrace in anyone going barefoot.[47] Well, if proper shoes were a necessity in eighteenth-century England, they are still not something that poor families caught up in the twenty-first century's Great Recession can afford to take for granted. Without prompting, four of the cash-strapped Britons we spoke to volunteered the purchase of shoes for themselves or their children as a concern. Working-class student 'Laura' was one; she described her own footwear as 'just like full of holes', adding that 'at the moment it's okay because it's summer and it's not as rainy'. She naturally hopes things will pick up financially before winter sets in.

There is one thing that nobody in eighteenth-century Scotland, England or France could have regarded as anything other than a necessity: food. And yet, more than two centuries later, a soaring number of Americans are nowadays relying on 'supplemental nutritional assistance' (food stamps) to fill their bellies – up from 26 million in 2007 to 48 million in March 2013. The fact that this figure is very similar to the number of people below the official poverty line strengthens the sense that those official figures are getting at something meaningful.[48] While it is, of course, true that eighteenth-century peasants would have been absolutely worse off than many of today's poor – there was no supplemental nutritional assistance in the pre-industrial past – there is nonetheless evidence of really serious contemporary hardship right at the bottom of the American pile. Some energetic digging by the *New York Times* revealed that during the slump something like 6 million Americans (a non-trivial one in every 50) had *no reported income at all* other than their food stamps.[49]

Reporting from around Cape Coral, Florida, where both the property bubble and the subsequent bust were particularly dramatic, the newspaper spoke to Leroy Armstrong, an African American with a scarred face and a proud expression, who, at the top of this chapter, described his hunger-induced move to claim food stamps. The reporters also heard from Isabel Bermudez, a pretty but wearied mother of two, who rose from a drug-addled home in the Bronx to trade Sunshine State apartments for an income of $180,000 a year, before losing all her cash income and being left with nothing but her monthly $320 in nutritional assistance, without which 'I wouldn't be able to feed my children'. They also learnt how Rhonda Navarro, a 'cancer patient with a young son', kept her family hydrated and clean after her water was cut off – she 'ran a hose from an outdoor spigot that was still working into the shower stall'. And then there was 22-year-old Rex Britton, who had come to the area for a job that had since disappeared and was now – in his own estimation – kept from starvation by his stamps; he raised funds for other outlays by selling his blood.[50]

For all of these American people, food stamps represent a lifeline that is often absent in the least-developed countries of the world. Yet Isabel Bermudez nonetheless speaks of waking up 'without enough food to get through the day'. It would seem perverse to deny that all these families are enduring absolute hardship, and indeed struggling for survival.

For all the miracles of modern medicine, among one of the main groups of poor in the US – educational dropouts – a recent epidemiological analysis concludes that 'life expectancies' are 'not much better than those of all adults in the 1950s and 1960s'.[51] Some of this alarming lack of progress over half a century may reflect the fact that school dropouts, rarer than they once were, are now more concentrated at the bottom of the heap. But with evidence emerging that life expectancy in substantial sub-strata of American society has actually been slipping backwards – something that ordinarily only happens in times of epidemic or war – the possibility that poverty, whether through direct or indirect means, might be killing increasing numbers of people in the United States is no longer so easy to dismiss.[52]

In the UK, too, where poverty is somewhat lower on like-for-like indicators, there were nonetheless striking and persistent health inequalities even before austerity-induced penury took hold. As it begins to bite, the analysis and efforts of big charities suggest a powerful effect upon food and shelter – the pre-requisites of physical well-being. In a large-scale 2013 survey for the Children's Society, more than half of the youngsters who judged their own families as hard-up said that their home was too cold last winter, and one-quarter said that their dwellings suffered from mould or damp.[53] In 2012, Save the Children, a charity that normally focuses on the developing world, launched an unprecedented campaign about hardship in the UK. And in 2013, the Red Cross announced that – for the first time in nearly 70 years – it would start handing out food in Britain.[54]

Almost all the cash-strapped Britons we spoke to talked about cutting back on food. At the less-deprived end of the scale, one single mother ('Denise' from London) spoke of arranging to go shopping with a friend, so that they could share 'two-for-one' offers – sensible

planning for a woman who claims that she 'often' skips meals
and subsists on sandwiches, in order to ensure that her two-year-old
daughter receives all the food she needs.

The words of others were more chilling: 27-year-old 'Nick', from
depressed Nottingham, has been unemployed since he got out of
prison a couple of years ago and now looks back nostalgically on the
square meals he used to have 'inside' ('The food is nice in there . . . it
should be nice out here and bad in there, but it's not. It's the opposite
way round. It's good in there and it's horrible out here'). 'Moira', who
feels such anxiety at the supermarket check-out, revealed that she had
'gone down a dress size'. But even that is nothing compared to 'Kirsty'
in Edinburgh, who was briefly out on the streets and 'went from a size
12 to a size 6 in two months' because 'I was not eating'. These days she
is at least housed, with her daughter and the daughter's father; but in
order to keep the child fed, mum gets by on 'one meal a day', while
dad 'lives on a box of cereal for maybe three days'.

Finally, we return to unemployed 'Winston', who has previously
worked as a chef and does like to cook, but currently has only £10 a
week after bills to cover not only ingredients, but anything else he may
need. His case is not so exceptional – the *Guardian* recently found an
unemployed man in Liverpool who explained in some detail how he
tried to restrict his food shopping to £2 a week[55] – but 'Winston'
certainly feels it is taking its toll. He was asked about the future: 'I
probably, if my life continues like this, I don't know I'll probably get
some disease in five or six years if I'm like this because of . . . malnu-
trition . . . I'm either going to be here or I'm not.' Perhaps that is
hyperbolic – no doubt 'Winston' gets more calories than many of the
unemployed did in the Dust Bowl of the 1930s; but he is very likely
unable to get the full range of nutrients that he needs.

As foodbanks open up in Britain at a rate of three per week,[56] there
is statistical as well as anecdotal evidence to suggest that food
purchases have recently been pared right back. Using the official
data on expenditure that is used to calculate inflation, an Institute for
Fiscal Studies (IFS) analysis reveals that overall spending on eating
was squeezed during the Great Recession, as in no other recent

downturn.[57] This is exclusively food consumed at home (leisurely outlay in cafés and restaurants is classified separately), and is part of a downward trend in non-durable spending – a trend that seems to be relatively sharper in poorer parts of the community.[58]

Another IFS report focused on changes in eating habits since the recession. It was based on a second, independent source of data on grocery shopping, and concluded that in sum Britons are eating less, and eating less well. In particular, they are substituting processed foods for fruit and vegetables, with the result that summary indicators of nutritional quality have shown a definite drop. Worse, many of these adverse trends have actually accelerated after the end of the technical recession, as public austerity began to bite in earnest.[59]

With hard times demonstrably taking their toll on poor people's diet, the sanguine suggestion that the slow magic of growth could shield the most vulnerable from the vicissitudes of a modern economy finally collapses entirely. As the chill of winter began to bite in late 2013, a former Conservative prime minister warned that rising fuel bills would soon force many people to choose between 'heating and eating'.[60] This hardship is proving so stark because – long before the bust – so many people had grown to be relatively deprived. After all those decades when the gains from growth were grabbed by those at the top, this recession has come to resemble the Depression-era Labour party poster, in which men from different points on the social scale are perched on different rungs of a ladder that disappears into deep water.[61] The fellow in the cloth cap on the bottom rung, already up to his neck in water, reacts with alarm as the top-hatted chap, several steps up, calls on everyone to move down a rung.

The rising inequality over the decades captured in this chapter's charts reflects myriad causes: squeezed benefits for the poor (to which we return in Chapter 8), an increasing share of US national income accruing as profits, and also changes in family structures, such as the rising proportion of children being raised by single parents. But perhaps most important of all are the questions of what work is available and what that work pays. Chapter 4 turns to the latter, but we must first consider those with no work at all.

3

Mapping the black stuff

Each day I go to the job centre and look online as well. I've had two
interviews but I didn't get either job. You don't even get a call back
most of the time . . . [T]hey think you're not the right kind of person.
Joel O'Loughlan, 18, from Toxteth, Liverpool, describing life in the
dole queue to the *Guardian*[1]

The husband in family household No. 467 in Marienthal used to be
an upbeat sort of chap. When the worst happened and he fell unemployed, his first response was to fire off 130 job applications. It was
only after the failure of all 130 to elicit a single response that he
reached the point where, as he told the Austrian sociologists, these
days he stayed in bed all morning in order to save on heating.[2]

The Marienthal study logged the effect of unemployment on everything from children's experiences of Christmas to the tendency of their
parents to argue. In the United States of the same era, Mirra Komarovsky
talked to workless families and heard jobless husbands say that 'a man
isn't a man without work', while their wives complained that their
menfolk somehow seemed smaller now.[3] Roosevelt, meanwhile, was
speaking of 'the grim problem of existence' facing the unemployed as
the most pressing dimension of the economic emergency engulfing his
country,[4] just as mass worklessness in Germany was conspiring to put
the fate of a continent in the hands of an Austrian-born corporal.

Every concerned commentator since Orwell – who described the 'deadening, debilitating effect' of worklessness, and the numbing experience of seeing 'a skilled man running to seed, year after year, in utter, hopeless idleness'[5] – has regarded enforced idleness as the primary poison to flow from a slump. The wider public grasps its malign significance, too. As mass unemployment returned to haunt Britain in the early 1980s, Alan Bleasdale's television series *Boys from the Blackstuff* – which concerned the travails of workless Liverpudlians – became an instant and unexpected hit for the BBC. Our interviews with cash-strapped Britons, both the employed and the unemployed, underline the continuing strength of a working-class work ethic, which makes a job so important in building up an identity – and its loss so liable to smash one down.

Working mother 'Kate' from Mansfield says her job is hardly worth the effort financially, but insists that it is a question of inspiring 'hopes and dreams' in her children, giving them 'a sense of who you are, and what you're capable of and human beings are capable of'. Strong words – but no stronger than others we heard direct from the dole queue, where those we spoke to emphasised that they had a record of work dating back to their teens. They stressed, too, the variety of what they had done previously – and would be happy to do in future. From 'Winston' ('I was a car chauffeur, I've been a showroom supervisor, I've done ambulance work, I've done youth work . . . From a cook to a taekwondo instructor. The only thing I haven't been is a zoologist') to 60-year-old 'Moira' ('I'm just looking for *any* sort of work') and 27-year-old 'Nick', who claimed to have submitted ten fruitless applications within the last fortnight alone.

We found the same ethic among incapacity benefit claimants, who are sometimes discussed as workers who have just given up. 'Martin' in Luton claims that, before cancer caught up with him, he 'was working seven days a week, twelve hours a day'. 'Norma', originally from Bradford, has lived a peripatetic life, dominated since youth by brittle bones, which continually ache and frequently fracture, and which finally rendered her unable to work – though this was not for want of a disposition to try. When her fourth child was about three days old, she recalls organising a part-time job: 'The midwife would come in, do what she had to, and then I would go to work from twelve to half past five. I was still in my maternity clothes.'

Most people desperately want to work, which is why – in popular imagination and in experience – joblessness is *the* defining feature of hard times. If you can contain it, there should be a chance of limiting the lash of the storm. That is, almost certainly, a big part of the explanation for how Japan avoided societal collapse: through repeated recessions over the past two decades, the unemployment rate has never reached 6%. That means it has never reached even half of the 12% rate that had taken hold across the depressed eurozone in 2013.[6] Whereas in Europe the recession is hammering this large minority, the disappearance of Japanese output has never been dealt with by meting out mass redundancy notices. Instead, stagnation has been absorbed by squeezing incomes all round.

But the American and British economies have not, traditionally, muddled through with the same shared sacrifice. At the nadir of the Great Depression in the US, nearly one worker in four was out of a job, with an all-civilian workforce unemployment rate of 23% in 1932, around twice as bad as the dreadful current European position.[7] In the decades between the wars, unemployment in Britain actually averaged over 10%, peaking far above that in 1930–32.[8] For much of the 1980s and (briefly) the 1990s as well, UK unemployment again exceeded 10%. The economic historian Timothy Hatton has written of the UK: 'in the interwar period [it] was indeed a bit more severe than it has been since 1973, but not by much'.[9] Thus in Britain it was not merely in the distant days of the hunger marches, but also much more recently that joblessness has seemed an endemic rather than an epidemic phenomenon.

So history did not portend well for the Anglo-Saxon societies facing the greatest recession of modern times; and yet – exactly as with incomes – the employment statistics do provide some grounds for comfort, just so long as one concentrates on overall averages, and not on the specific effect on particular communities.

In the United States, the greatest of all recent recessions certainly hit pretty hard, although not as hard as one would have expected. As

GDP tumbled by around 5% after 2007, the unemployment rate rose very much in proportion, by around 5 percentage points – from just under 5% in 2010 to 10% at the worst point in autumn 2009. It was a desperate situation by Japanese standards. But, though dire, the rate – which subsequently slipped back to below 8% by late 2012 – was no worse than it had been in the early 1980s, when a smaller (2–3%) knock to national income was sufficient to add 5 points to unemployment. Back then, the arrival of hard times seemed to result in workers being thrown onto the scrapheap in disproportionate numbers; not so this time around.

If enforced idleness is the biggest threat to communities during hard times, then the end of the American tendency to 'over-fire' represents a societal silver lining to the economic cloud. And in the UK, against all expectations, that lining shimmers through more brightly. Unemployment had averaged a touch over 5% in the two years before Lehman Brothers toppled. With a 7 percentage point fall in GDP, the experience of the 1980s and 1990s pointed to a rise in joblessness of the order of 10 percentage points, to take the rate up to about 15%. But as things turned out, the unemployment rate peaked at a shade over 8%. If we factor in a growing population, the total number of jobs only ever declined by about 2%, one-third of the fall in national income.[10] As of mid-2013, while the UK was still churning out 2% less in the way of goods and services than it had done in 2008, the total number of employed had actually reached a record high. For whatever reason, each chunk of lost output would now seem to be translating into far fewer lost jobs.

Is there something funny going on? Could the figures somehow have been fiddled? Britain has a history of this sort of thing: approaching a million people a year were signed off onto various incapacity benefits in the early 1990s, at a time when Whitehall was desperate to keep the dole queues down.[11] Britain's Trades Union Congress recently published analysis claiming that, on top of the 2.5 million who are technically unemployed, another 2.25 million do not have a job but would like one.[12] The most instructive check on the figures is to transcend the tally of individuals classed as 'unemployed' (a designation that can be affected not only by trickery, but also by early retirement, expanding universities, and the evolving role of women) and look instead at the overall employment rate.

Judged on this metric, the US once again emerges as having endured a bad, though not a truly depressionary recession, with a decline in the proportion of working-age adults in employment from about 72% at the peak to 67% at the trough – again a decline that is very much in keeping with the overall contraction of the economy.[13] In the UK, however, this most inclusive gauge of the jobs market once again paints a rosier picture – compared not only to America, but also to British history.

The graph opposite tracks the profile of the UK's employment recession in exactly the same way as the first chart in Chapter 1 tracked the output recession. Looked at this way, the recent British slump suddenly appears to be something less than great. The 2–3 point dip in the overall employment rate is revealed as scarcely half the fall of the 1990s, never mind the 1980s. Exactly as with the output chart, duration is as important as depth. The graph shows the extraordinary length of the 'jobs recessions' of the 1980s and 1990s, both of which knocked employment rates for a decade – long into what working Britain regarded as the recovery. This time the labour market still has not fully recovered from the knock, but, five years on, it is more than halfway there, with the improvement appearing to acclerate in early 2014. One would have to go back to the 1970s – to a time when a dole queue of a million and an unemployment rate of 5% were regarded as temporary aberrations – to find a milder employment recession.

So far, so heartening; but – exactly as we found with the data on incomes – reassuring averages can conceal frightening variation. The first thing to do in plotting the course of the economic tornado is to establish where the unemployment is in Anglo-American society. We will do so by delving into 40 years of exhaustive data on both sides of the Atlantic. Britain's chancellor, George Osborne, likes to claim that 'we're all in this together'; but look across any dimension you like – race, sex, age or class – and you see that some of us are very much more equal than others wherever joblessness is concerned.

Labouring on: UK employment held up better after 2008 than in previous slumps

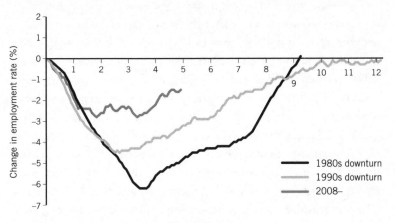

Years from start

Source: Authors' calculation from official data. 'Downturns' are dated here by employment rather than output decline.[14]

Some more than others

Hard times are harder when they compound an underlying pattern – that was true even in the 1930s, particularly in Britain. Ever since the late nineteenth century, northern mills, Glasgow shipyards and Welsh steelworks had been struggling against foreign competition, most particularly from the US and Germany.[15] When the Depression came, it provided the occasion (but not the root cause) for the great shake-out of these old staple industries. It is similarly true today that those who have been consigned to the dole queue are disproportionately those sorts of workers in those sorts of posts that have been steadily falling out of favour with employers since well before the slump.

For a long time 'learn to earn' has been the cheery mantra of public policy, while that slogan's gloomy converse – if you haven't studied, there's an increasing chance you won't work either – has remained implicit. But that is what the data shows, as the charts over the page illustrate. For Britain and America alike, the two graphs record unemployment rates among school dropouts and the college-educated (whom we call 'graduates' for short).[16] Unemployment for the drop-outs is always higher in both our countries. Education is closely linked to social class, and the fact that there is a gap of some sort here is neither surprising nor new: even in 1931, the male UK unemployment rate among relatively well-educated clerical workers was 6%; among skilled and semi-skilled manual workers 12%; and among unskilled workers 22%.[17] But in contemporary America, the extra unemployment suffered by the unqualified is reliably substantial. This 'dropout penalty' – the gap between the two lines on the graph – approaches 10 percentage points in a typical year.[18] In modern Britain, it started out much smaller (2–3 percentage points in the 1970s), but has since drifted upwards and now stands permanently at 5 points or more – so there is a steady structural deterioration in fortunes for the dropouts.

More dramatic than any gradual evolution of disadvantage over the decades, however, is what happens every time recession hits. In bad years for the jobs market, the charts both show that unemployment rises further and faster for the less-schooled, while graduate employment is typically steadier. In really bad years for the American jobs market (like 1983 or 2008), the dropout penalty soars to 14 points or more. In every successive recession in Britain – look at 1981, 1991, or 2008 – a dropout penalty that is no more than 5 points in the good years suddenly spikes to 8 or 9 percentage points. The American penalties appear higher, but don't worry too much about that: differences in the education systems mean that the distinction between the sorts of people caught by our 'dropout' and 'graduate' categories is sharper in the US.[19] The real point, which applies equally across both countries, is that a pre-existing class divide is *always* inflamed by hard times. The dropouts, who are less employable even during the good times, are also reliably the first out on their ears when the downturn arrives.

Remember that what we are talking about here is not the absolute unemployment problem (which will obviously get worse as the economy slides), but rather a measure of the *relative* unemployment problem that one group has when measured against another. If hard times hit equally, everyone's unemployment rate would go up by the same amount; the dropout penalty might exist, but it would not

Class divide: unemployment rates for 'dropouts' and 'graduates' in:

(a) the UK

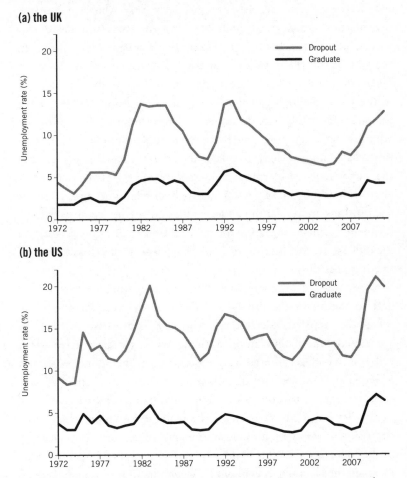

(b) the US

Source: Yaojun Li's analysis of General Household Survey, Labour Force Survey and Current Population Survey.[20]

increase. As it is, though, the differential effects are large – larger perhaps than the currency of percentage points makes plain: the 14 point dropout penalty in the US in 2010 meant that an individual dropout was fully *three times* more likely than a graduate to be unemployed. A difference on this scale is powerful evidence of the economic tornado having cut a narrow swathe.

But the path of destruction has, perhaps, been getting a little broader over recent decades – as becomes clear when we consider the intermediate category (not shown on the charts) of those who successfully pass school exams, but fail to progress to college. In the gale of the 1980s, O-levels or equivalent (the old English exams taken at around age 16) were enough to provide substantial protection in the UK – unemployment for this middling group was more like that for graduates than dropouts.[21] In the slump of the 1990s, by contrast, the unemployment rate among this same middling educational category was closer to that of the entirely unqualified.[22] Exactly the same trend of increased vulnerability for the semi-educated is at work in the United States. Whereas high-school graduates always used to look more like the college-educated than dropouts in terms of unemployment, in 2010 – for the first time in our 40-year series – the jobless rate for this intermediate group was just as close to that of the dropouts.[23]

Now, over these decades educational participation has been rising, and so the increasing difficulties of the moderately qualified may reflect the fact that able students who might once have successfully completed school and stopped there, will nowadays more often progress to college. Alternatively, the apparently dwindling protection afforded by intermediate qualifications might suggest that, in our collective resolve to study for longer, individual efforts are cancelling each other out, with the exam passes required for employment security rising in step with average attainment. Either way, the squeezing of the educational middle in the jobs market mirrors broader developments in the US and UK economies, where the well-to-do are increasingly pitted against the rest.

Nowadays a degree is needed for real security – and even then, to be fully effective it has to be a degree that was earned several years ago, as many recent graduates know to their cost. As of spring 2012, over half of the youngest American graduates (aged under 25) were reportedly either working in jobs for which they were overqualified, or else not working at all.[24] The British media, meanwhile, has been replete with stories of youngsters like 24-year-old 'Camilla', whose first-class literature degree, unpaid work and extra part-time study had – as of summer 2012 – failed to yield anything more than a string of rejection letters from the publishing firms that she longed to work for. She told the *Guardian*'s 'graduate without a future' series that she 'can no longer dream', and she spoke of a society that had 'forgotten how to hope'. There is no doubt that the written contracts of student loans are investing the unwritten social contract of 'learn to earn' with a new urgency.

Desperate as graduate unemployment can be, however, it is neither as common nor, crucially, as enduring as it is for the unqualified young. When I contacted 'Camilla' again in 2013, I was pleased to discover that she was now not merely gainfully employed, but working for one of the UK's leading publishing houses.[25] Before discussing the generational unemployment divide, it is important to register that the gravest trials of youth are still reserved for the poorer young, for whom the familiar problems of not leaving school with the right pieces of paper have been compounded. With that caveat noted, let us consider the overall gulf between the old and young. David Willetts is a member of a coalition government whose policies line up squarely on the side of the 'greys' in the age wars, but as a writer he has amassed a wealth of data which – he claims – demonstrates how the baby boomers have accumulated money and opportunity at the expense of their children, in his book, *The Pinch*.[26] The unemployment data supports the Willetts hypothesis in one important sense, for a stark and unprecedented chasm has indeed emerged between the cohorts.

Back in the 1930s, writes Timothy Hatton, 'unskilled jobs were abundant for young workers' – albeit jobs that were too often snatched away by penny-pinching employers when the youngster turned 21 and so commanded adult rates of pay.[27] More generally, the pattern of that time – when physical fitness was more important for many more positions than it is now – was for 'workers over the age of 50' to be 'unemployed and for longer periods than younger workers'.[28] If it was better to be young than old during the Great Depression, then during the long post-war boom, age made little difference. Two generations ago, British youth, for example, were no more likely to be unemployed than anyone else – which is to say, not likely at all.[29]

But, as the next figure shows, each successive slump since the 1970s has hit young Britons harder – and they never quite recover. Compared with their elders, Britain's young now suffer *more than twice* the unemployment of the over-35s. In leaving so many youngsters with nothing useful to do, the UK is in line with far too much of Europe. Some continental countries fare better, such as Germany, with its famed vocational training and apprenticeship system; others, like Spain, fare far worse: youth unemployment there actually exceeds 50%.[30] But the shocking youth unemployment peaks in Britain shown in the graph – peaks of 20% or more – are, if anything, an underestimation of the true tally. For there are also considerable numbers of British youngsters who are not classified as unemployed, even though they are neither working nor studying. Some will have health problems; others will have family commitments; but many of these so-called NEETs – not in education, employment or training – can be thought of as jobseekers who have grown so discouraged that they have given up on the seeking. As of mid-2013, it was officially estimated that about 900,000 (some 15% of the entire age cohort) were NEETs; while a big chunk of these cases would also show up as unemployed, a substantial proportion would not.[31]

All told, then, there are an awful lot of young Britons with nothing useful to do. In America, it is also somewhat tougher for youngsters to find work, but until recently (as the lower graph on the next page shows) the US always managed to avoid turning recessionary dramas into European-style youth unemployment crises. Even narrowly defined to ignore the UK's NEET problem, the UK chart shows that British youth unemployment has exceeded 20% in three successive slumps, a shameful threshold not breached on the American chart. Let us crudely define the 'youth penalty' as the gap between the two lines on the chart; this widened to 14 points in Britain's early 1990s slump, whereas the same measure of relative disadvantage was then only 8 points in America. The Great Recession has, however, hammered America's young harder than any storm of the recent past, with the

Misspent youth: unemployment rates for mature and young workers in:

(a) the UK

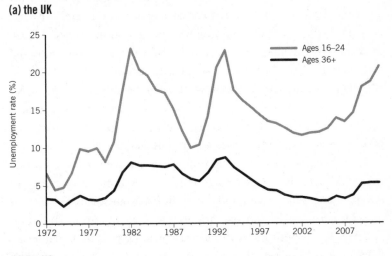

(b) the US

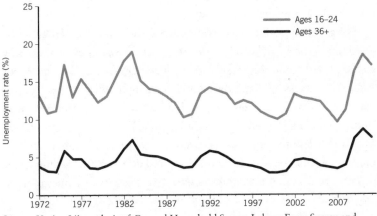

Source: Yaojun Li's analysis of General Household Survey, Labour Force Survey and Current Population Survey.[32]

unemployment rate among young people approaching 20% in 2010, just as the youth penalty burst into double digits. For all the differences in the way its economy is run, the graph suggests that America cannot bank on remaining immune from a European-style youth problem next time the storm hits.

In the case of gender, too, each cyclical ebb and flow reinforces a deeper tide. The feminisation of the workforce goes back at least 40 years. Theories abound as to what has driven this great societal change – from the political (second-wave feminism in the 1970s), through to the demographic (delayed child-rearing after the Pill) and the technological (the value of supposedly feminine communication skills in a post-industrial economy). Judging the merits of these explanations is beyond the scope of this book: the basic point is that male *employment* rates in both the UK and the US have been declining relative to the female rates over four full decades.[33]

Now, because the traditional housewife was deemed to be outside the workforce, this great change is not fully captured by narrower *unemployment* definitions and data. But if businesses answer cyclical dips by cutting back on operations that are anyway in structural decline, then – with the world already moving towards a feminised workforce – recessions will trigger more of a shake-out in male-dominated sectors. And indeed, this is exactly what is witnessed in the UK and the US unemployment statistics.

The graph opposite concentrates on America and reveals that, in the good times, there is relatively little difference in unemployment rates by gender. Every time the skies darken, however, they darken more for men. The excess of male over female unemployment – i.e. the gap between the two lines – has increased in each of the last three American slumps, widening to about 2 percentage points during the slumps of the early 1980s and the early 1990s. Even the mini-recession that followed the bursting of the dotcom bubble around 2001 created a mini 'male penalty' of about 1 point. And when the Great Recession came, another, larger range of layoffs pushed it up to 3 points in 2008 and 2009.

The pattern is strikingly similar for the UK. The only twist in Britain, where the 'male penalty' peaked at 2 points in 2009, is that the gap narrowed before the labour market recovered, falling back to below a single percentage point in 2012. This is most likely because – as the contraction of private industry was followed by public-sector retrenchment – layoffs among the state's workforce fell disproportionately on women. The female headcount has dropped by

The sex factor: male unemployment rises further in every US slump

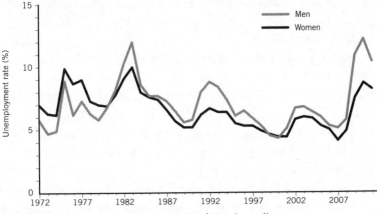

Source: Yaojun Li's analysis of the Current Population Survey.[34]

around 150,000 more than the male payroll in local government alone, a straightforward reflection of the prevalence of women workers in the public sector.[35] This is an important post-recessionary twist, which unions and campaigners legitimately emphasise. But despite female-unfriendly austerity, as of 2013 both the absolute number and the unemployment rate remain higher for men than for women.

Whereas men are traditionally the advantaged sex on just about every measure except unemployment, others who endure excess joblessness – black people, immigrants and dwellers in dead-end towns – start out at the bottom of the heap. From the outset, members of each of these groups have a permanent penalty in the jobs market, and they then see it greatly inflamed by recession. Let us consider race first. The excess unemployment of African Americans is familiar – a chronic, structural blight. In the four decades of data shown on the lower (US) panel of the figure overleaf, the African American 'penalty' – crudely defined, once again, as the gap between the lines – is rarely less than a substantial 5 points.[36] Hard times invariably make matters worse – not just in absolute terms, but relative to the rest of the population. In the depressed year of 1983, for example, the penalty approached 12 points. The Great Recession has had a similar effect, although, encouragingly, in the age of the first black president the penalty is not quite as large, always remaining in single figures.

The black community in Britain is very different. It consists largely of post-war immigrants and their children; indeed, many were originally drawn to the country by the promise of work in the years after the Second World War. The upper chart opposite shows that, back in the lost world of the 1970s, British blacks had almost as much work as British whites. But when hard times came in the early 1980s and 1990s, they suffered in hugely disproportionate numbers – a case of last in, first out, perhaps. The racial penalty (which in the 1970s was, if anything, smaller than in the US) soared to almost 20 points in depressed 1993. This really is a 'hard times' phenomenon: when recovery comes, the gap between the lines always closes up again, at least much of the way. But whenever the storm hits, severe punishment is meted out afresh: during the Great Recession the penalty doubled to 11 points.

The most frightening explanation would be that a deep, latent prejudice on the part of British employers reveals itself as soon as hard times require decisions about whom to fire. But it is too crude to assume that the race gap must reflect discrimination. It could occur, for example, because minorities are more concentrated in depressed regions; or because black workers happen to be concentrated in industries that are particularly exposed to the vicissitudes of world trade. There are, then, plenty of potential explanations besides simple prejudice, although it has to be said that Yaojun Li's analytical work tests some of these comforting theories and finds that they have little explanatory power.[37] For his part, Joel O'Loughlan, whom we quoted at the top of the chapter, was clear about what he thought was going on, telling the *Guardian*: 'Being black definitely makes it harder. Sometimes if you're going to a job [the employers] look at you like "you're not going to work here" . . . it feels like more than bad luck.'[38]

While racial prejudice undoubtedly plays a part in explaining the exceptional vulnerability of black Britons to hard times, there is clear evidence from field tests of discrimination that other ethnic minorities suffer too. Certain Asian-origin communities, such as Pakistanis, have

Race to the bottom? Unemployment rates for black and white workers in:

(a) the UK

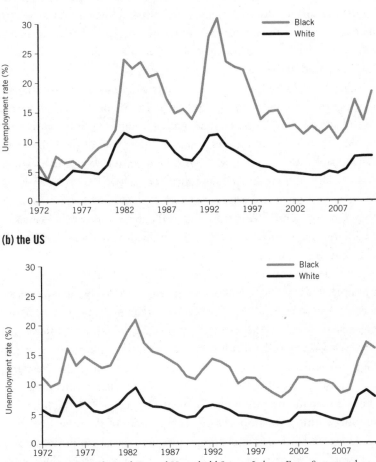

(b) the US

Source: Yaojun Li's analysis of General Household Survey, Labour Force Survey and Current Population Survey.[39]

tended to fare just as badly in British slumps, if not worse.[40] The mill jobs that drew people from the mountains of Azad Kashmir to the green and grey valleys of England's North disappeared soon after they arrived. The people stayed and mostly found alternative work, but it turned out to be the type of work that always disappears with the bubble. A look at the fortunes of American Hispanics – arguably a better comparator than African Americans, since they are often migrants or the children of migrants – only underlines how badly British minorities do. Yes, there is a 'Hispanic penalty', and yes, it increases in hard times. But even in the worst years, it is never much more than 5 points – a fraction of the penalty that minorities have often endured in the UK.[41]

The British labour market, then, really would seem to have a peculiar genius for concentrating cyclical pain. While the US is vastly unequal in so many respects, it also has a tradition of jobless workers upping sticks – a tradition encapsulated in the fables of the 1930s Dust Bowl dislocation, and one reaffirmed by quantitative research, which has established that Americans move almost twice as frequently as Britons, and often move farther, too.[42] Perhaps this helps to spread things around a little. Americans may talk about a 'rust belt recession' or a 'Dixie depression', but the regional divides are, in fact, rarely all that marked – and they never endure.

Our detailed analysis over four decades of data suggests, for example, that in the manufacturing-heavy US Midwest unemployment did jump by a couple of points more than in the north-east in the great shake-outs of the early 1980s and 2008/09.[43] The differences, however, were not sustained: over the years, the rank ordering of the four vast census regions – the Northeast, the Midwest, the West and the South – has often changed. By summer 2013, official figures showed that the overall unemployment rate in each of the four was running within a fraction of a percentage point of the others.[44]

Things are different in Britain, where (as the chart opposite shows) the North invariably has a bit more unemployment than the South; every passing recession exacerbates this difference. The regional dimension of previous recessions is familiar, particularly that of the early 1980s, when so many northern mills and factories closed. But during the recent recession, too, the North–South gap (the 'Northern penalty', if you will) was at least 2 points. Although this is not a penalty on the same scale as that paid by the uneducated and the racial minorities, it is nonetheless substantial. The gap between the prosperous South and the British periphery (defined as Wales, Scotland and England's far North-East; not shown in the figure) is, if anything, more marked than the regional gap in the graph, and has certainly tended to persist for longer into the recoveries. With new analysis of official data revealing that most of the recent growth has been concentrated in London and the South-East, there is little reason to expect this recovery to be any different.[45]

For the sake of simplicity, we have concentrated on straightforward *descriptive* unemployment rates, but we would refer readers who are interested to the analytical paper that underpins this chapter, which deploys a range of regression techniques to assess whether the various 'penalties' that we have described could explain each other away (as would theoretically happen, for example, if the higher unemployment rates of black people turned out to be driven by their having fewer qualifications). Suffice to say here that pretty well all the penalties that we describe turn out to remain statistically significant once potentially confounding factors have been adjusted for. Indeed, the paper also confirms the specific tendency of recessions to inflame such penalties.[46]

All the statistics we have examined demonstrate that we are not all 'in it together' where unemployment is concerned; rather it is a

Northern exposure: regional unemployment rates in Britain

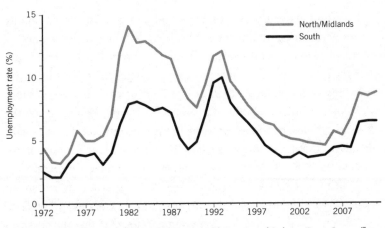

Source: Yaojun Li's analysis of General Household Survey and Labour Force Survey.[47]

problem that blights some much more than others. Not all the numbers point to worsening inequality in the jobs market, it is true; for example, while still substantial, the disadvantage faced by ethnic minorities appears to be somewhat less marked in the Great Recession than in the downturns of the 1980s and 1990s. But to the extent that the core class divide is picked up by education, it has tended to become acute – and to disadvantage more of the spectrum – from one slump to the next.

In describing the extraordinary concentration of worklessness in particular pockets of our communities, we have relied in this chapter on straightforward tallies. But within this remarkable quantitative concentration there is a further clustering of individuals who experience more prolonged joblessness. This can be viewed as a qualitative concentration, because there are powerful reasons to regard the suffering of the long-term unemployed as more intense. After a spell on a decent wage, a short period of income 'poverty' may be easy enough to endure: furniture, clothes and cars bought before redundancy will see to that. It is when these things begin to wear out or break down that penury starts to bite – and that is before we get to the cumulative psychological toll of endless months with nothing to do. The idea of unemployment as a progressive disease is nothing new: the Marienthal researchers classified families as they moved, in stages, from being 'unbroken' to 'resigned', and finally so broken as to be 'apathetic'.[48]

This more damaging, longer-term joblessness reliably rises rapidly during hard times, and also tends to keep on rising after unemployment as a whole has turned the corner.[49] In summer 2013, over a year after the peak in the unemployment rate, official UK figures were still recording a continuing climb in the numbers of citizens stuck without work for more than 12 and 24 months.[50] After the experience of the 1980s and 1990s, depressed parts of Britain are only too familiar with the misery that these statistics entail. By contrast, in the United States – a country that is known more for innovation in job creation and less for industrial sclerosis – rocketing rates of long-term unemployment were a disturbing novelty of the recent slump. As early as spring 2010, the Bureau of Labor Statistics was issuing statements that the numbers being condemned to months on end without any work were breaking all records – records that went right back to 1948.[51] The Great Recession, in other words, was producing prolonged unemployment on a scale not witnessed in America since the Depression – one powerful argument for invoking the 1930s comparison.

At this stage, it almost goes without saying that, just as with unemployment as a whole, this most virulent strain of joblessness is unevenly spread: long-term unemployment is another blight which hammers some communities more than others. It seems plausible that societies which neglected so many of their citizens during the good times might be particularly prone to throw them to the dogs in hard times. That connection between employment and education – a powerful indicator of class – especially suggests a cleavage that will compound the great income divide. We do not pretend to have identified any mechanism linking underlying inequality in the UK and the US with the extraordinary concentrations of unemployment that their labour markets throw up in hard times. But the thought that there might be a connection is encouraged by reports from elsewhere in the world. The tendency for unemployment to be concentrated in poor communities, and even on particular homes, is shared with other English-speaking countries, such as Australia – countries which have embraced the Anglo-American approach to doing business over recent decades, and shared in the attendant rise in economic inequality.[52]

This chapter has examined fifty shades of disadvantage. But the grimmest picture of all emerges when all the penalties – colour, region, sex and low education – hang around a single young neck. In early 2012, an outright majority of young, black British men were jobless. Young, black and hailing from Toxteth in the depressed North, everything 18-year-old Joel O'Loughlan said at the top of the chapter is borne out by the statistics we have reviewed. Average employment rates are certainly better than they might have been; but that is little comfort for those who do not enjoy average opportunity in America and Britain. You can make as many applications and send in as many CVs as you like, but – as Joel says – it may do no good at all, if 'you're not the right kind of person'.[53]

Toil and trouble

If you happen to fall out of line, or your manager thinks you have not done very well that week . . . your hours just get cut – you feel like you are just at the beck and call of the people above you . . . you start to feel a bit bullied.

Zahera Gabriel Abraham, 30, mother and former shop worker, speaking to the *Guardian*[1]

Unemployment may be unevenly spread, but the Anglo-Saxon economies are suffering from a good deal less of it than might have been expected, after a slump on the Great Recession's scale. With overall joblessness of 7–8% in summer 2013, the UK and the US could glance with some smugness at the European continent, which has half as much unemployment again on average, and in places twice as much.

Neoliberals will not be slow to draw their conclusion: that the red-in-tooth-and-claw capitalism that Britain and America are known for is not only more efficient, but kinder as well. As for the inequality highlighted in Chapter 2, if this flows from flexible markets that are protecting jobs in hard times, then the neoliberal message will be: learn to live with it. If unemployment is the chief depressionary problem, then – they will say – the short cut to societal ruin is to subvert the dispersion in pay that the sound operation of these markets dictates.

This 'sclerotic eurozone versus dynamic Anglozone' story is glib. From the structural problems of the Continent's single currency to London and Washington's enthusiasm for heavy state intervention to save the banks, one could pick holes in the twin caricatures going way beyond our scope. In tracing the path of the economic tornado through society, however, it is worth pausing to ask how far the damage is truly concentrated on the relatively small number of British and American jobless. Mapping unemployment has shown beyond doubt that this recession has been very bad news for ethnic minorities, the unqualified and the young. But is the flipside of this concentration that the tornado is cutting a narrow swathe of destruction and sparing other parts of town?

The evidence from Marienthal concerned the unique damage done by enforced idleness, and in past recessions – including Britain's Depression[2] – prices have lagged behind wages, with the result that if you're in a job, you're OK. But after a third of a century in which the pay gap has widened into a chasm, and gnawing job insecurity has developed into a hyperventilating anxiety, it ain't necessarily so . . . The old divide separating fortunate workers who have clung to their jobs from benighted workless souls is not what it was. Poverty pay has blurred the line, while changes to terms and conditions have eaten into the very concept of a 'secure job' for the least-lucky employees in these economies. We will consider both halves of this later in the chapter. But first of all it is as well to consider the fundamental question: the changing nature of the work that needs to be done. For, we shall see, the very latest research is suggesting a close connection between the sorts of jobs that exist in an economy and the reach of the recessionary damage.

The American and British jobs markets have both steadily moved towards an hourglass aspect, with a widening bulge of employment at both the top and the bottom, but a narrowing of opportunity in the middle. For a long time now, mechanisation and computerisation have whittled away at the skilled manufacturing and clerical jobs that traditionally supported the middle station in life. While this change could be profoundly disruptive for individuals reliant on such lines of work, it always used to feel like part of a broader story of progress – for the old jobs being lost were chiefly replaced by new professional posts elsewhere in the economy. During the years *before* the bust, however, something in America changed. The familiar disappearance of positions for clerks and skilled machinists was no longer being matched mainly by new posts in management or accountancy, but instead by low-grade jobs in cleaning, cooking and caring.

A weakness for nostalgia would make it easy to rush to a 'lost golden age' conclusion on the basis of anecdote, but hard data from America really does bear the verdict out. One recent study exploited US census data to grade all jobs by skill and pay systematically. It confirmed that a pattern of polarisation is taking hold. Back in the 1980s, it found that there was a linear relationship between skill level and job growth (or shrinkage): the lowest-grade posts disappeared fastest; those a bit further up the range shrank more slowly; while skilled positions proliferated. That is the traditional story of progress. Around the late 1990s, however, instead of this steady slope across the skills range, the data reveals something more like a U shape – with middling jobs disappearing, and new posts emerging at both the top and the bottom end. Finally, during the (proclaimed) boom of the noughties, the U gave way to a slide and the *only* net growth in American jobs was found at the bottom of the range.[3]

When hard times arrived, instead of job growth, job destruction became the order of the day – and this, too, worked to hollow out the middle. Over 2009–10, the numbers of highly paid American professionals (0% change), managers (–1%) and technicians (+2%) were all essentially unchanged. So too – at the other end of the scale – were the low-paid categories, including food preparation and cleaning (0%) and security (+2%); low-paid posts in caring actually grew (+5%). Over the same two recessionary years, however, the middling occupational categories fell off a cliff: sales jobs were down 7%, office admin posts by 8%, and manufacturing operative jobs by a full 15%.[4] Looking ahead, Washington's official projections imply that the proliferation of bottom-end jobs will continue deep into the recovery. Five of the Bureau of Labor Statistics' top six 'occupations with the largest job growth' between 2010 and 2020 pay less than the median; four – including retail attendants, personal care and fast food – typically pay over one-third less.[5]

The Great Recession has revealed the same polarising force at work in the UK. First, the slump hit those sectors that traditionally provided better-paid working-class jobs disproportionately hard. Compared with an overall decline in total jobs of about 2% between June 2008 and June 2009, there was a shake-out of 8% of manufacturing jobs, and of 4% of posts in construction.[6] In the technical recovery that got under way soon after that, overall jobs growth of a little less than 3% has again been skewed to the detriment of construction, which continued to contract – down 11% between June 2009 and March 2013. There is still room at the top; in the well-paid 'professional and technical' sector, posts rose by an impressive 11%; and there is simultaneous skewing towards the poorly paid accommodation and food sector (up 5%).[7] It is the middle that has been squeezed.

The chart below (based on Institute for Employment Research modelling) illustrates economists' best guess as to where British jobs will come from in the years through to 2020, and suggests that exactly the same polarising trends will continue for many years.[8]

Missing middle: projected gain/loss of UK jobs, 2010–20

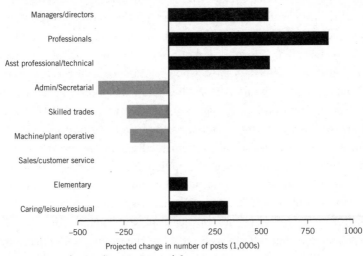

Types of British Jobs Growth

Source: Institute for Employment Research.[9]

This depressing picture raises two questions. First, why have the Anglo-Saxon economies developed a tendency to produce low-grade jobs? Second, what are the implications for workers in a recession? Let us take the second of these first, for it is the more straightforward to answer. (We return to the first and more fundamental question at the end of the chapter.) Workers in low-skill sectors are always likely to be more vulnerable in hard times. When expertise and experience are unimportant, the unemployed become a potential substitute for existing staff; and where bosses have invested neither time nor money in their employees, they can more credibly threaten to make that ruthless swap.

These are two powerful reasons to expect lengthening dole queues to weaken the bargaining position of workers in such sectors. And indeed, with more low-end jobs around, wages have become *much* more sensitive to unemployment. Using regression analysis on UK data, the respected labour market experts Paul Gregg and Stephen Machin find that whereas 'a doubling of unemployment at any point in the period between 1986 and 2002' would have driven down wages by 7%, in more recent years the same proportional rise would 'push typical pay down by 12%'.[10] That amounts to a serious intensification of hard times – as experienced not by the traditional jobless victims, but by people who have remained in employment.

This nasty spillover from redundancy notices onto workers who kept their jobs is most marked at the bottom of the scale – and in the US it is stark. The Bureau of Labor Statistics keeps track of America's working poor, defined as those who spend the bulk of the year in the labour force, but who nonetheless live below the poverty line: the 2010 tally of 10.5 million was the highest since records began, in 1987.[11] One study concluded: 'during . . . the Great Recession, the bottom of the US earnings distribution has fallen dramatically . . . In terms of earnings, the bottom 20 percent of the US population has never done so poorly, relative to the median, during the whole postwar period.'[12] The *only* reason this did not produce an immediate surge in inequality in family incomes, the same paper notes, was rising government redistribution; redistribution that reflects such moves as the extension in unemployment compensation that we reported on in Chapter 2.

The underlying dynamics of the American labour market are frightening – and the position of low-wage Britain is little better. The real value of the UK minimum wage sunk by 6% between 2009 and 2012, and was continuing to sink into 2014, when – a year ahead of an election – Chancellor Osborne started to show some interest in addressing the drift.[13] The number of employees paid within 25 pence of the minimum has soared (at nearly 8% in 2012, it was double the proportion a decade before), and the proportion of *permanent* minimum wage-earners found at the pay floor – those stuck there for at least five years – has climbed from just below 12% in 2005 to just above 17% in 2012.[14] There are, then, more people earning less – and for longer. The UK poverty figures always used to report a cast-iron link with worklessness; but the latest numbers record that a child officially classed as poor is now almost twice as likely to come from a working than from a workless home.[15] The problems of deprivation in hard times are no longer the exclusive preserve of the jobless.

The many and the few

With low wage rates having been pushed further down by recession, it is evident that our economic tornado is tearing a wider strip through society than the unemployment numbers on their own would suggest. We will return in the coming chapters to the question of whether the low-paid share in the misery and isolation of the unemployed, but it is already evident that they are sharing the financial pain. The next question is: just how far up the scale have hard times bitten? Recall those charts in Chapter 2, showing 30 years of skewed income gains concentrated right at the top. Over the past two decades, something above *three-fifths* of *all* the gains of American growth have been grabbed by the top 1%.[16] With this extraordinary concentration of prosperity, could it be that hard times have in fact befallen not some luckless minority, but most of the community?

In the US, which has been seriously unequal for longer, stuck wages for both the middling and the poor had slowly become an established fact of life long before the recession. In the post-war years from 1948 through to 1973, the value of what the typical worker was producing ('labour productivity') and the average wage he or she took home, rose exactly in proportion, at 2.8% a year: workers were gaining in line with the fruits of their efforts. Since that year of the first oil shock, there has not been any dearth of ingenuity – labour productivity has continued to rise by a very similar 2.6% a year. The big difference concerns wages, which have subsequently climbed by only 0.6% annually at the median.[17] That implies that the typical employee has now been missing out on something like three-quarters of the extra prosperity that America has been generating over 40 years.

The graph below captures this great divergence for male workers, for whom it has been most acute. While overall American output has roughly doubled since the 1970s, mostly because of rising productivity, that the figure shows that the pay of the man in the middle, the median male worker, has barely budged. The woman in the middle has not fared quite so badly, but her modest progress has certainly not made up for the difficulties of the men: typical working-age *household* incomes in 2010 were stuck at the levels of the late 1980s.[18]

Growth that got grabbed: US productivity and median male wages

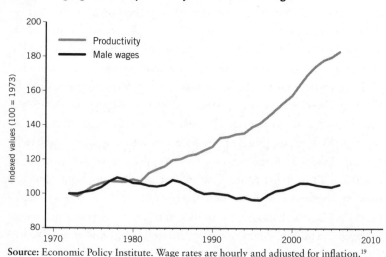

Source: Economic Policy Institute. Wage rates are hourly and adjusted for inflation.[19]

This grim picture is not the product of interpretations or definitions: tinker with the composition of remuneration – by adding in pensions or healthcare, for instance – and it does not brighten.[20]

The old story of a rising tide lifting all boats has simply ceased to apply. Gradually, this supremely important fact has sunk in, and it now causes concern and debate in forums from White House seminars downwards. The UK has sunk into the same pattern of reward-free growth only more recently, around the turn of the century, and so it is less discussed – or, at least, it was until wage stagnation gave way to outright pay cuts in the slump.

Typical real wages in Britain have now been stuck for a dozen years, since well before the recession: the chart below shows how median full-time pay *stopped rising soon after 2000* – right in the heart of the boom. Growth was supposed to be our great insurance policy against hard times; but even before the storm hit, it had ceased to deliver for the working majority. The figure then also shows how, after years of stagnation, typical wages fell off a cliff around the 2008 crisis. Worse still, as the dotted line shows, there is no expectation that recovery will

Growth that stopped during the boom: median full-time UK wages

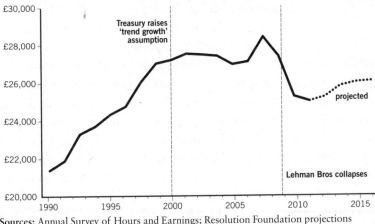

Sources: Annual Survey of Hours and Earnings; Resolution Foundation projections from 2012 onwards.[21]

help: even if the UK economy rolls along the path that officialdom predicts, middling pay packets at the end of the present decade will be lighter than at the start of the last. Our chart includes women as well as men; if we singled out men, the recent picture would be even worse.

For poor people to be left behind as average incomes rise is nothing new in the Anglo-Saxon economies; but – in Britain at least – for stagnation to have set in at the middle like this, and at the height of a so-called boom, is something disturbing and different. In the light of the great growth grab by the top 1%, it is worth checking whether it is not merely the lowly and modestly-paid who have been squeezed, but also those who might previously have thought themselves to be perfectly comfortable.

The chart opposite shows how British real weekly wages have grown since 1979 at different parts of the spectrum: one-tenth of the way up from the bottom (where we might find, say, a burger flipper); the middle (a mechanic, perhaps); and nine-tenths of the way up towards the top (think of a briefcase-toting middle manager). The fanning-out of the fortunes of the three in the run-up to the millennium is as expected: by 2002 the middle manager had secured nearly 67% more real pay than in 1979, the mechanic 40%, and the burger flipper just 16%. But what happens next is quite new.

For all three come several years of sluggish growth or stagnation, followed by an outright dive once the recession hits. The combined effect is that *real wages at all three levels have declined over a full decade*. For the super-rich, things have played out differently: the crunch briefly bit hard on bonuses, yet by 2012 campaigners could leaf through FTSE 100 reports and calculate that top executive pay was again rising by 12% annually, which can hardly be called prolonged stagnation.[22] But right across the range (save perhaps for that elite, which begins somewhere well into the top 10%), the dawn of the century brought economic stagnation, followed by economic decline.

This is a remarkable finding, which reflects declining hours of work in the downturn, as well as a squeeze on hourly rates (unlike the previous graph, this figure includes part-timers). Decisions about exactly how to crunch the data, and particularly how to adjust for inflation, affect how much progress (or not) is recorded over the longer term.[23] But, whichever way the calculations are done, the blunt fact remains: British workers at all three stations in life have less in their pay packets than a decade ago.

We reported in Chapter 1 that, right into 2013, a majority of voters still expected hard times to drag on indefinitely into the future. Looking at this chart, it no longer seems like they were indulging in melodrama. They appear to have been faithfully reflecting on their economic experience over a dozen years or more.

A little caution is needed before jumping to the conclusion that *everybody* has been getting poorer for years. Family fortunes depend not only on wage rates, but also on how many people work and how much – and the slowly rising tide of female participation continued right up until the bust. Government transfers, such as tax credits, can also top-up inadequate pay (as they did for much of the noughties in the UK). Taking everything together, the graphs in Chapter 2 recorded income growth before the recession which, though heavily skewed against the poor, was generally positive. But as wages went from stagnation to outright decline after 2008/09, hours of work were also

The forward march of labour halted? Real wage growth in the UK since 1979

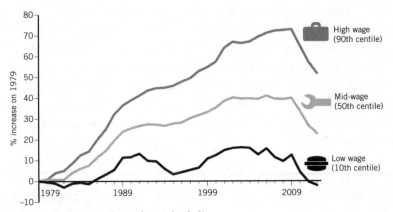

Source: P. Gregg, S. Machin and M. Salgado.[24]

squeezed. Finally, amid Britain's general austerity after 2010, tax credits were subjected to swingeing cut-backs.[25] Once all of this is factored in, it is not merely individual earnings, but also *household* incomes for great chunks of Britain, that are now set for two lost decades.[26]

It is never good for anybody's morale to endure a pay cut; and – as we have seen – cuts in real pay are exactly what ordinary workers have been getting right across the range.[27] It may not be pleasant, but does it really matter in an affluent society? To repeat the question that underlay Chapter 1: why should a bit of a squeeze spell misery and dislocation in a society that remains wealthy by any historical standard? After all, we have been discussing pressure on above-average pay packets, where the question of penury really does not arise. As for relative poverty, it is hardly plausible for *most* people to be getting poorer in relation to the community. Even if the richest 1% pushed everybody else below the arithmetic average, with the other 99% all in the same boat they could hardly be called socially excluded. So in terms of the mechanisms we identified in Chapter 2 as likely to translate recession into serious hardship, the big squeeze looks like something that a rich society might shrug off.

Aside from being poor relative to the majority of one's fellows, however, we can distinguish a second notion of relative impoverishment that might have wide application, and cause widespread hurt, in a sharp recession: namely, being impoverished relative to one's expectations and (closely related) to one's past. Divorce lawyers have long claimed that clients deserve to be maintained 'in the style to which they have become accustomed'. More recently, behavioural psychologists have theorised that expectations are 'anchored' in experience – and have observed that people will go to far greater lengths to avoid dashing such expectations than they would to achieve a comparable gain.[28] The Mancunian band James summed up the thought as well as anyone in its line: 'If I hadn't seen such riches, I could live with being poor.'

We have seen that Japanese society has come through hard times relatively well; here – perhaps – we get a clue as to why. While Japan's cumulative 'losses' from not growing as fast as in the past were huge, they were also largely notional – measured against a counterfactual world of prosperity that never arrived. Throughout most of the so-called 'lost decade' of the 1990s, Japan was not actually shrinking, but was merely growing very slowly. Had Japanese living standards suddenly been sharply reduced – albeit from giddy heights by any historical standard – there might have been more pain.

Marie Antoinette earned notoriety for (supposedly) making the absurd suggestion that stricken peasants rioting over bread prices could eat cake instead. But after a century and a half of industrial progress, in the depths of the American Depression, a woman really could feel poverty keenly because she was suddenly unable to afford cake as before. The wife of an unemployed man explained to Mirra Komarovsky that this was precisely why she nowadays cut herself off. She no longer asked friends round to the house, she said, because 'the least you can offer is a cup of coffee and a piece of cake, and even that costs money'.[29] Fast-forwarding to the twenty-first century, many of us have grown to expect not merely to consume coffee and cake, but to do so in a café. One cash-strapped British woman we spoke to talked about blowing £5 she doesn't really have on a cappuccino and a cupcake in Costa; she recognises that it would be cheaper to have coffee at home, but she does it, she says, because she would otherwise feel 'like I wasn't quite good enough'.

All the recession-hit families that we spoke to made similar points about the difficulty of giving up things they had grown used to – and not just those worst hit. Consider 'Kate' from depressed Mansfield in England's East Midlands, who works in the public sector, advising families that are poorer than her own on how to get back to work. Together with her husband, who brings in a similarly steady but modest income of £20,000, she is raising four children. Having accepted a pay cut as an alternative to redundancy, she struggles with childcare bills that leave her with – she says, after detailing a plausible list of her regular outgoings – a mere £30 a month to play with. To be sure, she still runs her car and has satellite television – things that working-class women in the past would not have had.

Nor indeed would they have had the one thing that she now says she misses most:

> You know, before, we did enjoy a meal out once a week, and it were just a time where everybody could relax and they've not got to worry about cleaning up and washing the pots . . . a really nice time that we got to talk and find out what's happening in each other's lives . . . I struggle with that, really, because I do miss that time.

The Grapes of Wrath this is not; but listening to her, it feels too dismissive to deny that she is enduring hard times in her own way.

With wages squeezed across the range, here is a potentially plausible argument for the recession taking a psychological and social toll that stretches far and wide. Our economic tornado is suddenly looking as though it might, after all, be more of an all-out storm. Up until now, however, we have been focusing only on *amounts* that workers are typically paid. Just as important is the confidence (or lack of it) that employees have about work and wages showing up at all. If squeezed pay applies across the range in the Anglo-American labour market, insecurity is the second great blight to befall people in hard times – and it is a problem that very decidedly affects some more than others.

The swelling ranks of the employed but exposed

'Your hours of work will be advised by the visitor manager and will be dependent upon the requirements.' Thus ran the defining line in one of the increasingly common 'zero-hours' contracts written during the 2009 recession – agreements of 'employment' that provide no guarantee of work whatsoever. The only thing that marked out *this* zero-hours contract, which was obtained by the *Guardian*, was that the employer happened to be Buckingham Palace.[30] This footloose form of hiring is now accepted as normal at the heart of the British establishment: in 2013, it was the turn of the Palace of Westminster to advertise for zero-hours workers – specifically for zero-hours reporters for *Hansard*, the official parliamentary record.[31]

Zero-hours contracts, which gave rise to a brief row in the British media in 2013, are an important issue in themselves. Staff 'employed' in this way can be contractually obliged to keep themselves available by refusing all offers of work elsewhere, though they have no guarantee about what shifts and wages they can expect. They are also symptomatic of wider developments across the American as well as the British labour market. For the structural problem in the Anglo-Saxon economies is not only low wages, but also nagging doubts about what wages there are to be earned. With hard times, a once-hidden casualisation has emerged into plain view.

That wider approach is something that has advanced very much in parallel on the two sides of the Atlantic (though if anything, to a greater extent in the US than in Britain). It has come about through a whole range of institutional developments. One of the most notable has been the weakening of trade union power. There has been a dramatic fall-off in union coverage in the US, unmatched in any comparable country bar one – Britain, where the decline has actually been greater.[32]

The corporate practices of competitive tendering at home and international outsourcing abroad have likewise advanced in the UK and US together, and the thrust of policy has worked to reinforce this drift. The OECD rankings of employment protection legislation confirm that minimally regulated labour is something that marks out the 'Anglo-Saxons' – not just the UK and the US, incidentally, but other English-speaking countries, too.[33]

The rich countries' think tank collects information on everything from statutory payoffs to time limits on unfair dismissal claims, and constructs these into metrics of regulatory protection. Across most dimensions, the OECD ranks America close to the bottom of the table of its 34 members (frequently actually bottom); Britain is generally only a place or two higher than the US.[34] Reviewing the shielding of permanent staff from being singled out for the sack, the OECD comments: 'the US stands out as the least regulated country'.[35] The relatively minimal rights of this sort enjoyed by British and American workers are in marked contrast to the stronger protections enjoyed in

France and Germany.[36] Britain and the US offer more typical protection against collective redundancies, but the light-touch (and sometimes non-existent) regulation of fixed-term contractors and agency workers reinforces the caricature of the Anglo-Saxon labour market as a realm where bosses are free to do as they will.[37]

Of course, flexibility to hire and fire at will does not *necessarily* mean that workers will end up more insecure. After all, the avowed basis of the flexible labour market agenda is to give employers confidence to take on more workers. Where businesses are rendered unviable by onerous regulation then, in the end, all workers will feel the chill; protection for people in permanent jobs would then come at the expense of those with less-secure work or no job at all. The all-important question is how far the famous Anglo-Saxon flexibilities are being exploited; there is mounting evidence that the answer is 'a great deal more in hard times'.

The ranks of the employed but exposed have been a political concern ever since Herbert Hoover unwisely brushed aside concern about America's semi-occupied workers with the boast that 'many people have left their jobs for the more profitable one of selling apples' on street corners.[38] While there is no perfect measure of such 'workers on the fringe', Washington keeps official tabs on a measure of labour market 'marginalisation' which goes much wider than unemployment proper. The graph opposite shows the so-called 'U6' unemployment measure, which includes with the workless 'all persons marginally attached to the labor force', plus those working part time who would rather be doing full-time hours.[39] As the chart shows, the combined total of the unemployed and such 'marginalised' workers peaked at around 17% – more than one worker in every six – at the trough of the recession.

This broader indicator of 'underemployment' affects many more workers than are technically classed as unemployed. And 'marginalisation' is yet another hard-times phenomenon. Unemployment proper rose by 5 percentage points between mid-2007 and late 2009, whereas this broader measure of dislocation shot up by nearly twice as much – about 9 points. The proportion of Americans stuck in the grey area, somewhere between proper work and the black stuff of outright unemployment, roughly doubled between the height of the bubble and the depths of the bust.[40]

So the American picture is one of discouragement, unemployment and *underemployment* all increasing in tandem, and the British picture is no different. The great under-reported fact of the UK recession is that the million who were newly consigned to the dole were joined by another near-million of newly underemployed – those who, official figures record, would snap up a 40-hour week, if only it were there to be had. The growth of this group was one of those retrospectively worrying trends that pre-dated the recession proper. But back in the most buoyant years for the labour market, in the mid-2000s, the number of unwilling part-timers was no more than 600,000;[41] by mid-2013, this total had swelled to 1.4 million, a figure that continued to rise, even as unemployment proper declined through that year.[42]

To give a truer picture of unused human potential in the labour market, the former Bank of England rate-setter, David Blanchflower, has – together with David Bell – devised a new index of UK underemployment, which looks at the proportion of hours actually worked, as

Beyond the fringe: the proportion of 'marginalised' workers grew by more than unemployment

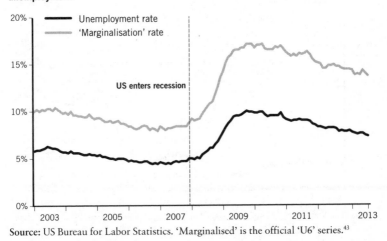

Source: US Bureau for Labor Statistics. 'Marginalised' is the official 'U6' series.[43]

against those that employees would like to work at current pay rates. Carefully designed to avoid exaggeration, this measure subtracts those hours that (often older) unwilling full-timers would voluntarily give up. Before the slump, the two groups – those keen for more work and those keen for less – were of comparable size, and so approximately cancelled each other out, bringing underemployment into rough line with unemployment. Since the storm hit, however – as the graph below shows – underemployment has soared further and stayed higher for longer than unemployment conventionally defined.

In both countries, then, those relatively flattering headline unemployment figures are understating the waste of human potential and the lash of hard times. In the US, a Pew Center survey put all the pieces together – hours cuts, outright pay cuts, spells out of work and so on – and calculated that an outright majority (55%) of the workforce had been directly hit by one or other of these things during the downturn.[44] The effect on American and British families and their finances is exactly what one would imagine. In summer 2012, the *Guardian* spoke to 28-year-old Nicola Probert and 30-year-old Tony Hodge. They live in Bristol with two sons, four-year-old Finlay and

Timed out: 'underemployment' grew by more than unemployment in the UK

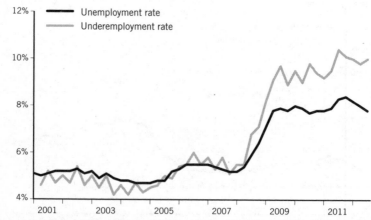

Source: D. Bell and D. Blanchflower. 'Underemployment' is hours actually worked as a share of desired hours.[45]

baby Bobbie. Tony's hours in the building trade had become too erratic to be sure of meeting the bills. Just before the baby came, they found themselves unable to pay the rent, and so had to move back in with Nicola's father. She describes this retrograde step as necessary but 'horrendous', and explained how just 'a few years ago' Tony could rely on topping up his hours of building with nightshifts in a warehouse. In slumpish 2012, however, 'the work just isn't there'.[46]

On top of the problem of insufficient hours comes the problem of insufficient security, which often affects the same people. The British government's figures show hundreds of thousands stuck on short-term contracts because they cannot land anything more secure; by the dawn of 2013 their number had virtually doubled since the recession began.[47] In the United States, the incidence of one particularly insecure form of work – being hired through a 'temporary help' agency – has doubled over a longer timeframe.[48] The familiar defence of such 'no-strings' arrangements is, of course, that any job is better than none – that the important thing for a worker's future is to get a foot in the door. That is often true, but not always: data from Detroit's welfare-to-work programme has been used to demonstrate that 'temporary-help' placements do not improve, and may actually diminish, subsequent earnings and employment outcomes.[49]

Definitive overall statistics on the rise of insecurity are elusive – there are so many different footloose arrangements, and any figures depend on classifying contractual arrangements which workers and firms are frequently hazy about. The rumbling row over zero-hours contracts in Britain is a case in point. Published estimates range from the official 250,000 (which relies on workers knowing to tick the 'zero-hours' box) through to a plausible 1 million, and hyped-up claims of 5.5 million.[50] Whatever the true figure, two things can be said for certain. First, this is a number that has been rocketing in hard times: during summer 2013 the official estimates were revised upwards, and have now climbed by 75% since 2008.[51] Second, the rawest zero-hours deals encapsulate all the insecurity of the Anglo-Saxon labour market.

Unless the work comes in regularly for a prolonged period – and managers can manoeuvre to ensure that it never quite does – zero-hours staff can be left with no sick pay and no holiday.[52] They can have difficulty not only in budgeting for bills or obtaining a mortgage, but even in renting a flat, since landlords often want evidence of a regular pay cheque. Employers get a hired hand when they need it, without any obligation to pay for one when it is not required. This provides very valuable flexibility, and their representatives make great play of the fact that there is notional flexibility for staff as well. But there is little give in the arrangement for cash-strapped workers, who – in order to grab such pay cheques as they can – must arrange their lives so that they can drop everything when a shift crops up. Union leaders talk of winding 'the clock back to the bad old days of people standing at the factory gates, waiting to be picked for a day's work'.[53] The same point is more powerfully made by the dozens of zero-hours workers them-selves who spoke to the *Guardian* (mostly on condition of anonymity) about making ends meet when pay is not merely low, but is entirely uncertain.[54]

For all the talk of flexibility, the first theme to emerge from the staff at the sharp end was that their time belonged to somebody else. The more fortunate 'zero workers' operated to rotas that might be published a week or so in advance; the less fortunate spoke of being 'regularly' called in the middle of a day and asked: 'Can you come to work now?' There was an expectation that they would be ready to switch shifts, in the words of one worker, 'at the drop of a hat'. The big fear of one graduate in her thirties – who was required to buy and wash her own uniform – was of her phone battery running out: if she missed the manager's evening call, 'I might only get a few hours' the next day. The implications for family and volunteering commitments have none of the mystery of the social withdrawal of Marienthal's unemployed: if your time out of work is, in effect, the company's, then how on earth can you commit to anyone besides your boss?

A second theme to emerge from the *Guardian* reportage was of workplaces characterised by bullying and bickering. An employee of the Tate museums' (outsourced) cafés, describes 'fighting for hours' with fellow workers, to the point where she was 'coming into work even when I felt sick', for fear that to do otherwise would be seen as shirking and would lead to 'the worst shifts and lowest hours'. At the beginning of this chapter, we quoted a 30-year-old shop worker with a child to support, Zahera Gabriel Abraham, talking about feeling bullied. Eventually, after suffering panic attacks, she walked out.

The dystopic ideal of an economy run solely by the bosses, for the exclusive benefit of the bosses, shines through in the words of one 30-year-old man employed by a pub chain in London:

> Our bar operates on the basis that they want more staff available than they actually need, so that they can always call on people when they suddenly get busy, but the business wants absolutely no responsibility to ensure you make the money you need to live on in return.

Even when an evening's work actually begins, he insists, there is no guarantee that it will finish: 'Throughout shifts, managers are constantly trying to gauge how few staff they can get away with. If you're not totally pushed and struggling to keep up, someone will get sent home.'

Within this culture of utterly commoditised labour, it is no surprise to discover that the sort of hardship and insecurity more often associated with the unemployed sometimes sets in. The variation in a cinema attendant's reported hours – bobbing around from 30 one week to 10 the next – makes it all but impossible to plan for the bills. A 49-year-old care worker, once steadily employed by the council, found her management first taken over by a charitable organisation, which then paved the way for a 'private company' that introduced zero-hours working. She was, she says, 'devastated' because the disciplined budgeting she had always done 'just isn't possible on these contracts . . . all of a sudden any sort of security is taken away from you'. With no sense of what is affordable, prudence is reduced to curtailing regular commitments – something she did by severing her internet connection. A case study, then, in how modern employment practices are conspiring to induce citizens to cut themselves off from the modern world.

So how far does such a commodification of labour extend up the scale? If one looks narrowly at contractual arrangements, the answer might appear to be 'an awfully long way'. The *Financial Times* recently highlighted the way in which increasing numbers of highly skilled medics working in Britain's health service were operating on zero-hours contracts.[55] That is one way to describe the 'staff banks' in which the work of some radiologists, psychiatrists, heart specialists and others is organised; and yet it is doubtful whether many hospital consultants are fretting about having the gas cut off. Even among the British nurses who work in such 'banks', a majority told their trade union that they were satisfied with work patterns a few years ago.[56] The crucial point is that nurses are workers with specialist training, who can ordinarily rely on finding a buyer for their services; that means there is bargaining power on both sides. Further still up the wage range there is also scope to build up savings and thereby cope with any variation in pay. A large proportion of 'on-demand contractors' sell IT expertise and professional consultancy services for high hourly rates; it is a fair guess that few of them lie awake at night worrying about the household bills.[57]

The serious insecurity is reserved for those at the bottom of the heap. Even before unpredictable shifts bite, the average hourly rate of 'zero workers' is 40% lower than for the population as a whole.[58] It is not mere rhetoric to say that the line between the unemployed and these ultra-casualised workers is blurred. A significant proportion of zero-hours workers in the UK – 18% – really are jobseekers, in the sense that they are 'actively seeking' alternative work or extra hours.[59] Prompted by a harsh benefit regime, the long-standing pattern in hard times has been to cycle between low-grade work and unemployment.[60] Today, as zero-hour contracts lead to volatile pay, the rules governing the knock-on effect on benefit entitlement are fiendish and imperfectly observed, which heightens the overall anxiety by reducing the efficacy of the safety net. And all this is happening just as clinical evidence is emerging to suggest a link between insecure work and heart disease.[61]

◆ ◆ ◆

In this chapter we have seen how stagnant pay for the majority in Britain and America has been compounded by insecure hours and terms for a large and luckless minority. It is a miserable picture, and it should dispel any complacency derived from the relatively flattering headline unemployment statistics. It is also a picture that is closely related to the tendency – which, as we have seen, pre-dates the recession – for the US and the UK to produce low-grade posts of the sort where terms and conditions are particularly susceptible to hard times. The nagging deeper question remains, however: why did this tendency arise in the first place?

The conventional way that economists think through questions about the sectors that wax and wane in different countries is to start with each nation's productive potential (the so-called 'supply side'), and then to factor in the context of global markets. Poor education of less-academic students, for example, might reduce productive potential in industrial sectors that require workers of great skill, and increase 'comparative advantage' in lower-paying industries. Policy recommendations will then focus on doing something about education and training, so that more people can eventually secure a chance to be more productive – and hence to command better wages – in the face of changes to the underlying 'fundamentals' of technology and trade.

Many such stories can be told; some have power, and orthodox recommendations of this sort are worthy enough. But the assumption that vast differences in relative rewards exclusively flow from 'unbuckable' market forces is awry: the reality is that inequality in terms and conditions can become self-reinforcing. Where the market *is allowed* to determine that some human beings are worth vastly less than others, and when public policy tolerates workers being used and discarded like disposable kit, then social habits change. The routine retaining of house servants by moderately well-off families in early twentieth-century England was one facet of pre-war inequality; the subsequent disappearance of live-in domestics went along with the great levelling that gathered pace with the war. Likewise, the relatively trivial cost to the letter-writing classes of Edwardian England of employing unskilled postmen made it viable to run multiple mail deliveries each day, so that correspondence could bounce back and forth across London several times between sunrise and sunset, as the Sherlock Holmes stories attest.[62] By mid-century, however, with workers' wages higher, London businessmen had to make do with twice-daily deliveries.

If the tale of the great levelling of the first two-thirds of the twentieth century can be illustrated by the delivery of letters, the delivery of pizzas makes the point about the great divergence since the 1970s. During the 1980s, some people came to feel that their time was too valuable to cook; others became desperate to do so for modest reward. The result was a mushrooming of restaurants and takeaways. At some point in the 1990s, the selfsame takeaways began offering home delivery, a proposition that made sound business sense: on the one hand, there were more customers who could afford to pay to save a quick trip, while on the other – at the opposite end of the scale – there were more workers who would accept the miserable wages available for making the journey.

As well as using more cheap labour when it is readily available, employers might also come to use it with *less care* – investing less in raising the output of their staff. This is where those self-reinforcing dynamics really kick in. In the US between the 1970s and the 1990s, for example, employers invested far less in kit to raise the output of lowly workers than did their counterparts in West Germany, where institutions pushed up low pay to the point where firms' minds were focused on how to get more bang for their Mark.[63] Across a wider set of countries, too, a free-for-all in hiring and firing has been shown to be associated with diminished productivity.[64] A recent reform in Italy underlines the point: the deregulation of traditional restrictions was undertaken with the aim of stimulating a temporary jobs boom; however, the details were botched and the most notable consequence has been reduced capital investment and productivity.[65] And if orthodox microeconomic theory is correct, this lower productivity will soon feed back into lower pay and worse terms.

Moving from analysis to anecdote, it is possible to see the dynamics of casualisation at work in all sorts of corners of business. Consider, for example, the market for car washing in Britain. Back in the 1980s, drive-in mechanised car washes were spreading, and the expectation would surely have been that they would be ubiquitous by now. Instead, however, there are more and more places where motorists can drop off their cars to be cleaned using more traditional means – the elbow grease of cheap labour. These manual car washes are sometimes branded 'American-style', an explicit nod to the import of low-wage business models.

In working Britain and America, we have seen that hard times extend well beyond the unemployed in terms of pay packets and insecurity. The financial misery has spread far and wide. It is time to ask whether the same is true of human unhappiness as well.

Anxious individuals, unhappy homes

This is the worst point in my entire life, if I'm truthful.
'Winston', 47, from Stanmore

During springtime 2012, Europe was replete with gruesome tales of economic ruin breaking the human spirit. Giuseppe Campaniello was a self-employed bricklayer in Bologna until he became a non-employed bricklayer who could not pay his debts. Unable to see his way through, he marched to the tax office in March 2012 and cremated himself.[1] A thousand miles to the south-east, just a few days later a retired pharmacist, Dimitris Christoulas, shot himself in Athens' Syntagma Square, leaving a note about how government retrenchments had ruined his livelihood.[2]

Terrible as such anecdotes are, it is hard to know whether they are reported and retold because they sit atop some grim tide or rather because they are so exceptional. Those inclined to look on the bright side will insist, first, that the Anglo-Saxon economies were never in the same sort of mess as the eurozone's stricken south, and further, that all those decades of technical progress should have provided the human heart with a sturdy shield against passing recession. They will say that it should be perfectly possible to weather a passing storm with a smile, before getting back to business as usual. Others, however, will take as their starting point the psychological depression and the half-days in bed recorded in Marienthal. They will reason that, even in a rich society, shattered expectations, insecurity and want of purpose will convert economic into psychological depression.

The contention of this chapter is twofold: first, that if we examine the landscape from 30,000 feet up, then the *average* effect on individuals' well-being is not shattering; but, second, if we dive down and inspect the data for those who have been directly affected by the slump, then the picture changes. If not the grapes of wrath, then at least the grapes of despair are swelling. We will return to the extreme (though mercifully relatively rare) question of suicide. The more instructive starting point is general well-being.

Unhappy days

Touring a battered nation in 1932, Franklin Roosevelt's appearances were accompanied by his campaign song, 'Happy Days Are Here Again'.[3] Talking about 'happiness', a rather lightweight term in English, might have seemed inappropriate, almost grating, amid so much suffering. And yet the last-minute choice of tune proved a great success, providing the Democratic party with its unofficial anthem for many years. For the reality is that economic conditions and feelings of happiness are closely connected.

Some scoffed when psychologists started gauging trends in mood simply by asking people how cheery they felt. But Richard Layard's book *Happiness* compiled burgeoning scholarly evidence of how self-rated scores correlate closely to all sorts of things, including health, brain activity and the perceptions of others.[4] The underlying technical literature has nailed a connection between self-rated well-being and heart rate, blood pressure, responses to stress and even the duration of authentic so-called 'Duchenne' smiles.[5] Her Majesty's government has been sufficiently persuaded of the importance of this well-being data to start collating official figures.[6] The first results revealed more intriguing correlations: Blackpool, the seaside town with England's lowest subjective happiness score, is also the place where most anti-depressant prescriptions are written.[7] Self-rated well-being is, then, increasingly accepted as telling us something meaningful.

In the United States of recent years, Gallup has been collating well-being data in quantity on an exceptionally regular basis – for its daily poll. This allows us to track a detailed path through the American recession with particular confidence. Looking across the population as a whole, the average satisfaction scores in this data lend support to a sanguine reading of the slump: the data tracks a little ripple of misery that arrived with the recession, but that very soon washes away.[8] This fits with the so-called 'setpoint theory' of happiness, according to which expectations rise and fall automatically in line with the resources available. While the economy is booming, this tendency of the psyche to reset in line with rising affluence is known as the 'hedonic treadmill', since it demands that we acquire the extra stuff churned out by the economy simply to stand still in happiness terms.[9] In general, that is a real bar to our enjoyment of the extra leisure that Keynes envisaged for future generations.[10] In hard times, however, it could just be that the silver lining of this dark cloud shimmers through. Expectations adjust downward with income, and so, in no time at all – indeed, before the economy has even bottomed out – happiness starts bouncing back.

So far, so reassuring. But if we separate those without work from those who held onto it, we catch our first glimpse of more concentrated pain. The graph opposite shows the substantial 'happiness hit' suffered by the American unemployed: between April 2008 and February 2009, their average life satisfaction scores dropped by one-sixth, more than double the shorter-lived dip for working Americans.

Less-regular Eurobarometer data for the UK reveals the same pattern: a small overall recessionary dip in well-being but a thumping great drop for the unemployed – with a decline of well over 10 percentage points in the proportion of the jobless describing themselves as satisfied with their lives.[11] The one twist in the British story is that something of a happiness 'double dip' is evident in 2011, just as the economy sank into a second period of stagnation. Between June 2011 and November of the same year, when unemployment finally peaked, there was a 5 percentage point drop in the overall proportion of Britons satisfied, and an 18 point drop for the workless.[12] This fresh spike in misery, once again concentrated on the unemployed, just when Britain's abortive initial recovery in 2010 was petering out, reinforces the sense of a strong connection between the economy and well-being.

In Britain, then, as in America, the data reveals that economic hard times dampened spirits a little for everybody, but the big squeeze on pay packets (which, as we saw in the last chapter, was shared across most of the workforce) does not seem to have done serious damage to average well-being scores across the population as a whole. For those who were laid off, however, it is a different story. In both countries, the unemployed were more miserable to begin with, got relatively even more miserable as the slump hit, and took longer to recover from their misery.[13] Perhaps it is no surprise to find that, in the luckless parts of town, our economic tornado is blowing harder.

But if the depressionary dive among the unemployed supports a bleak interpretation of the slump, doesn't the speed of the bounceback point to a more sanguine reading? Look again at the graph. The

How happiness sank with the American economy

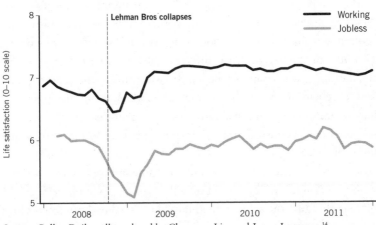

Source: Gallup Daily poll, analysed by Chaeyoon Lim and James Laurence.[14]

misery of the jobless lingers a little longer than that of the employed, but their spirits nonetheless appear to start lifting before the economy does – barely a year into the recession. Their well-being may not quite be at boom-time levels in early 2012, but it appears to have got most of the way back. It may be comforting to imagine that people were getting used to unemployment and learning to live with it tolerably, and the data might be picking up some of that.

Sadly, statistical fog is clouding the picture. 'The unemployed' is, after all, a category whose composition is changing rapidly over this time. We have seen, for example, that the slump has landed many more youngsters in the dole queue. Typically, they will have better health than the older jobless, and will also often never have had a secure pay cheque before – or known the anguish of having one snatched away. As the slump ground on, changes of this sort may have lent a crocodile smile to these happiness figures.

The way through the haze is to isolate *particular individuals* who have been thrown out of work, and then trace their personal happiness trajectory. Do this through repeated interviews, of the sort conducted for America's Faith Matters tracking dataset, and you firmly establish that redundancy lands a hard *and enduring* blow.[15] While Faith Matters records that the well-being scores of the continually employed are remarkably steady between interviews in (pre-slump) 2006 and (post-slump) 2011, a great gulf opens up with Americans who ended up out of work. A full two years after the economic trough, this gap stood at nearly 2 full points on this data's 1–10 life satisfaction scale. A difference of this order indicates a very substantial effect (compare the gap between those who report 'poor' and 'excellent' health in the same dataset, which is only 1.6 points).[16] Statisticians might caution against assuming that this must be because we care more about our jobs than even our health, but that is one plausible reading.

Can the big happiness dip among the unemployed be brushed off with a confounding story about downbeat sorts of people getting laid off? No, because the same individuals who ended up both jobless and depressed originally reported life satisfaction scores within half a point of those whose posts survived the recession.[17] Could we be exaggerating the pain of redundancy, by neglecting things like ill-health, which might make someone a soft target for the sack, at the same time as predicting misery unrelated to the economy? Again, we can demonstrate that this objection does not stand up, through our final check – sweeping regression analysis factoring in age, race, education, number of friends, health and more.[18] After controlling for all of this, the effect in the US remains not only large, but also statistically significant (that is, too large to be explained by any quirk of the survey sampling).

The gist of these results – remarkably stable average life satisfaction for the continually employed, and sharply declining satisfaction for those shunted out of work – also emerges on the other side of the Atlantic, in the British Household Panel Survey.[19] For the UK, although we have slightly different demographic information, we can again allow for all the obvious confounding factors, and doing so only serves again to confirm a large and significant effect. The message conveyed by the numbers is greatly reinforced by what we found when speaking to individuals without work. At the top of the chapter, we quoted unemployed 'Winston' – an outgoing man who would be the optimistic type in easier circumstances – saying he was enduring the 'worst point' in his 'entire life'.

Other data sources confirm a savage psychological toll as unemployment drags on. One American tracking survey of around 500 jobless individuals who, as of March 2010, had been out of work for over six months, bore out the deepening psychological costs: for instance, nearly two-thirds (63%) were suffering from lost or disturbed sleep. And whereas only a minority of the original unemployed sample in 2009 had described themselves as 'depressed', 'anxious' or 'helpless', among those 500 or so who remained unemployed by the following March, all three of these attributes had become majority propositions.[20]

There can, then, be little doubt that mental health is suffering in the eye of the economic storm, along the path of which redundancy notices are served. But how far does the damage extend? If we examine how the misery of a lay-off ricochets through a family and community, we get the impression of damage concentrated in a very narrow zone. In our American tracking data (after controlling for all those potentially confounding factors) we find that a personal move into redundancy is associated with a big 1.4 hit on the 1–10 life satisfaction scale.[21] This shrinks dramatically to an average hit of just 0.4 when redundancy is experienced vicariously, through an immediate family member. For richer, for poorer, a couple's finances may be intertwined; not so, it seems, their life satisfaction. As for close friends and relatives beyond the walls of the home, the raw data suggests that they muster a little empathy (a happiness hit of 0.2), but the statistical analysis suggests that this apparent hurt is not in fact meaningfully different from zero.

All of this encourages what we might call a 'Marienthal reading' of recession – an unemployment-specific story. For while we have seen that there was no dramatic decline in life satisfaction across the wider population, redundancies really did convert economic into psychological depression. That is a grim verdict indeed for the least lucky minority; but with unemployment in Britain and America running at only 7–8% in 2013, it suggests relatively restricted ruin. After everything we have learnt about insecure and inadequately paid employment, however, it would seem wise to poke behind those reassuring average happiness scores for the more exposed parts of the working population. Might unpaid bills be getting settled with despair across a rather wider swathe of society?

Anxiety, far and wide

If the language of happiness does not lend itself to our times, the language of anxiety surely does. Insecure pay, usurious loans and inadequate savings: these things have formed the day-to-day worries of much more of the population than just the unemployed. Having already established that hard times are *not* hammering the happiness of the workforce as a whole, we ought to consider whether some individuals with jobs are nonetheless somehow being singled out. One obvious potential channel is the insecure employment that we described in Chapter 4; another is debt. One British study, using pre-recession tracking data, found that – back in the good times – the presence of consumer debt reliably imposed a psychological toll.[22] Wielding plastic to settle every account has gone out of fashion; but if you do require debt or refinance, it will be harder to find in today's environment, and will come on punishing terms.

There are, then, good reasons to be fearful, and these emerged as major themes in discussions with cash-strapped Britons, whether or not they were unemployed. The breadth of the pall of anxiety cast across daily lives was striking. Some families volunteered 'darkest fears' relating to major life events: financing old age was one common concern ('Whoops! Don't want to think about that, it's too scary, because it is terrifying', said one man); a 50-year-old woman feared being 'made homeless'; a younger one felt spooked by the thought of starting a family ('just thoughts like having a child, how on earth would you have enough money?'). Other anxieties were more familiar budgetary strains of the middle order: 'gas and electricity', an 'essential' car packing up, or being 'literally haunted' by the fridge breaking down.[23] Other 'darkest fears' again concerned outlays that should be relatively small even in the context of a low budget, but which are difficult to deal with since they crop up unexpectedly. One telling example came from a mother in Scotland, who desperately needed £25 for birth certificate copies to secure her son a nursery place that might allow her to work. She fears she will not be able to find the cash.

As for unemployed 'Winston', he answered the 'darkest fears' question: 'My water rates really frighten me.' It is striking that the most necessary, predictable and cheapest of all the utilities should be the one that worries him most. In his own estimation at least, however, his troubles are less to do with being unemployed as such, and more to do with being desperately poor: 'Losing a job is nothing, compared to what I'm going through right now, because I am on the breadline.'

The anxiety of the workless was, perhaps, somewhat more marked in our interviews, but there was little difference between them and the working poor in the sorts of things that stirred fear – those dramatic words about homelessness and being haunted by broken fridges came from case studies of people in work. All this suggests that serious anxiety may be gripping the more weather-beaten sections of the workforce. The next question is whether there is any sign of that in the hard data.

David Blanchflower and David Bell, the same economists who devised the UK 'underemployment' index examined in the previous chapter, have directly explored the psychological toll on those working Britons who are bearing the most severe brunt: people forced to work part time. First, on the basis of the Labour Force Survey (which yields the official unemployment figures), the pair established that under-employed workers who wish they could get more hours are significantly more prone to depression.[24] More recently, they exploited the Annual Population Survey – the dataset that is being refined to include David Cameron's well-being metrics – to pinpoint how the underem-ployed are faring according to the prime minister's new gauges. Whether the question is happiness, satisfaction, anxiety or feeling life is worthwhile, the raw figures show that unwilling part-timers score badly. While the readings are not as dire as the scores for the jobless (for whom such maladies have been documented since Marienthal), the unwilling part-timers are actually closer to the unemployed than to full-timers in the happiness and satisfaction stakes.[25] Blanchflower and Bell's detailed regression analysis confirms these patterns, and suggests a negative underemployment effect that – depending on the particular measure – inflicts anything between one-third and two-thirds of the pain of being unemployed for up to a year.[26]

The suffering of the underemployed, then, looks as if it might be something like half as intense as that of the unemployed proper. But the underemployed are not the only vulnerable part of the workforce: there are also the low-paid and the insecure, groups that may be quite large (Chapter 4). With so many people potentially affected, and through such varied channels, it is impossible to identify all the poten-tial victims in advance. So instead, we gauge the reach of the tornado's ruin in a different way: by analysing the statistical sadness of the unemployed into its constituent parts, and asking which of these parts are liable to be shared with downtrodden workers. More specifically, we will split out the general effects of low income and economic anxiety, to reach a residual that can only be explained by enforced idleness itself.

To produce this calculus of despair, we again perform regression analysis. But this time, along with all the demographic details, we successively factor in the various channels through which misery might flow after redundancy. The most obvious such channel is reduced income. But controlling for this barely dents the direct power of joblessness to cause hurt: this adjustment reduces the strength of the statistical connection between unemployment and falling life satisfaction (in the jargon, 'the coefficient') by only about 15% in Britain, and by less than 4% in the US.[27] That fits with those reassuring average satisfaction scores that applied to the workforce as a whole over the course of the recession, and confirms that the big squeeze on incomes does not, on its own, mete out anything like the misery of mass unemployment.

Moving from income to insecurity, *fear* of being (or remaining) without work is another statistically significant variable that we can factor into the American analysis, as is change in 'financial satisfaction'. Since the latter is added in after already allowing for reduced income, it should instead capture *feelings* – resentment at being unfairly squeezed, anxiety about paying bills – that are likely to be shared with workers on bad terms and conditions. Factor these feelings into the US analysis, and the residual decline in satisfaction for the unemployed is now appreciably smaller – around a third of the misery is explained away. The British data also allows us to control for a broad measure of the sense of being able to manage financially – or not.[28] Again, such feelings turn out to be more powerful than hard currency: after financial anxiety and income are both factored into the British analysis, around half the total misery of the workless in the UK is explained away. That still leaves half, of course, that we haven't explained – the specific direct psychological cost of lacking gainful employment. We might think of this residual as the Marienthal effect.

Coincidentally, perhaps, this final result – of insecurity and hardship driving around half the total misery of the unemployed – fits

neatly with the picture produced by Blanchflower and Bell in relation
to the underemployed. To sum things up very crudely, it is starting to
look as if something like half the misery of the jobless might relate to
the particular curse of having nothing gainful to do, whereas the other
half might relate to financial anxieties, which might well be shared
with the working insecure.

A unique cross-country polling experiment, conducted by YouGov
in spring 2013, provides a final way to chart the uneven shadow of
worry that befalls the population in hard times. A representative
sample of citizens across not only Britain and the US, but also France
and Germany, were asked both about how they had been affected by
the slump and about how other aspects of their lives had changed –
including anxiety.[29] Large majorities claimed to have been substantially affected by 'the economic problems in [their own] country' over
'the last several years' – 57%, 64% and 54% in Britain, the US and
Germany, respectively, with the higher proportion of 80% in France (a
country where something in the culture reliably produces downbeat
results in life satisfaction surveys).[30] Later, the respondents were asked
if they were 'more likely . . . to feel anxious' today than five years ago.

Among Britons as a whole, 57% reported feeling anxious more
often than they did several years ago, as against 39% who report that
pangs of panic are just as rare (or rarer) than before. Now, this is a
recall question – where nostalgia could cloud the picture – so it is as
well not to place too much weight on these absolute proportions. But
so long as such distortions are not restricted to people with a particular experience of recession (and there is no reason to think that they
would be), then any *differences* in the rise in anxiety should be meaningful. And, as the figure opposite illustrates, these differences are
very interesting – implying an exceptionally close connection between
rising anxiety and experience of the slump.

Only 21% of those who claim to have come through the recession
virtually unscathed report feeling more anxious these days. That
proportion rises in steps for those who have been 'not much' affected
and affected 'a fair amount', to peak at a startling 82% among those
who claim to have been affected by the slump 'a great deal'. This

graduated link between experience of recession and rising anxiety is very much in keeping with the emerging picture of an economic storm that lashes some communities savagely, shakes others up a bit, and leaves others again largely untouched. Consider the sheer variety of things that can make people worry, many of which – from troubled romances to turbulent teenage kids – have nothing to do with the economy, and the apparent connection between economic exposure and psychological insecurity looks remarkably close.

Might there be an alternative explanation? Could it not simply be that certain (melodramatic) personalities are inclined to report both being battered by the slump *and* rising anxiety? Perhaps, but if the apparent link between hard times and anxiety merely reflected differences between personality types, then the same connection should surely apply across national borders. Yet the same super-strong link is not found everywhere. It *is* found in the US, but – as the graph overleaf reveals – the connection is less clear in France, where

The link between recession exposure and rising anxiety in the UK

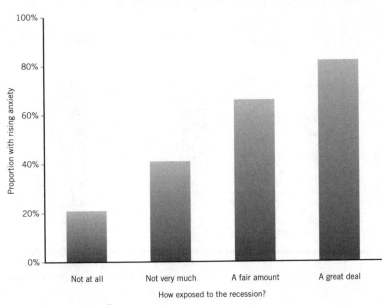

Source: YouGov (2013).[31]

stronger institutional protection for workers and more generous social benefits arguably provide more of an economic shelter.[32]

The points here are subtle. To keep things manageable, our self-reported measure of recession exposure is now simplified into just two categories: the *slump-hit* (those who claim to have been affected a 'great deal' or 'a fair amount' by recession) and the *slump-proof* (those who say they are 'not much' or 'not at all' affected). Different national cultures may encourage citizens to put a brave face on things or else let off steam when responding to surveys, and this may distort the absolute numbers who report rising anxiety.[33] So let us concentrate instead on the more solid *relative* results – the gap between the slump-hit and the slump-proof groups within each country.

In the US, 60% of the slump-hit group report rising anxiety, compared to 26% of the slump-proof – a difference of 34 percentage points. In the UK, the gap is almost as large – 30 percentage points.

An Anglo-Saxon anxiety gap? Worry was concentrated on slump-hit Britons and Americans in 2013, but recession had less bearing in France

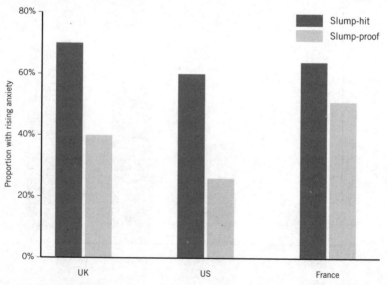

Source: YouGov (2013).[34]

In Germany (not shown) the gap is somewhat smaller, at 22 points. And in France – where 64% of the slump-hit report rising anxiety, as against 51% of the slump-proof – the 13 percentage point anxiety gap is smaller still. So economic misfortune, as one would always expect, still has some bearing in France. But it is nothing like as powerful.

During the Depression, Roosevelt said that America had 'nothing to fear but fear itself'. In drawing our investigation into individual well-being to a close, we can conclude that fear has cast a wide shadow over the contemporary US and UK, too. Our data suggests that perhaps half of the woes of the unemployed stem from some malady specific to being without work, but the other half comes from anxieties shared with others who are badly battered by recession. We have seen nothing to suggest that the large 'prosperous but pinched' group has endured a serious happiness hit; indeed, they can hardly have done so, given that the average figures show the well-being of the workforce as a whole bouncing back rapidly. But with the more seriously squeezed – the poorly paid and, most particularly, the insecurely employed – it is another story. They really do share in a good deal of the pain of hard times. It cannot be assumed that any old dead-end job can be relied upon to keep spirits up.

Ending it all

The ruined former financier tottering off the edge of a Wall Street skyscraper is an iconic image of the Great Depression. And indeed – in the UK as well as the US – the great slump of the 1930s coincided with a visible spike in the overall suicide rate, as is confirmed by a glance at the figure overleaf, which records suicides in both countries between 1920 and 2010. The hard fact of more people taking their own lives in hard times is tougher to shrug off than vaguer claims about well-being: it is one reason why the Depression of the 1930s is remembered as a human tragedy. The timing of the suicide spike does not in itself prove economic causation; but analysts digging down into the American data *have* found support for such a direct connection:

individual states with more bank failures witnessed a larger spike in suicides than those with fewer.[35]

During our more recent hard times, the same sort of morbid statistical association has emerged in stricken southern Europe; in Greece, for example, male suicides were up 20% between 2007 and 2009.[36] Italy's uniquely specific recording system (which includes contextual detail, such as any information left in suicide notes) officially logs deaths labelled suicide 'due to economic reasons': while suicides attributable to other causes have remained flat, suicides of this sort jumped by around 50% between 2007 and 2009.[37]

By contrast, in neither Britain nor America does the chart reveal any contemporary spike visible to the naked eye. Since the Second World War, suicide rates have often risen and fallen substantially for reasons completely unrelated to the economic cycle: in England and Wales, for example, research has pinpointed such diverse underlying drivers as the phasing-out of toxic so-called 'town' gas, the fashion for easy-to-overdose-on barbiturates, and the later trend towards safer sleeping pills, such as Valium.[38] Maybe back in the poorer days of the

A visible suicide spike in 1930s Britain and America, but not after 2008

Source: Siobhan McAndrew's analysis of various data derived from official records.[39]

Great Depression things were different; but looking at this graph in isolation, it is hard to imagine that more recent overall trends in suicides have been driven by the ebb or flow of the financial tide.

This might seem like an important bit of evidence, suggesting that we should not get too exercised about all the troubling data on well-being for the less fortunate parts of the population. Once again, however, there is a danger of complacency. For one thing, it may take time for misery born of a slump to build to a point where the thought of suicide arises, and our long-term series of data only goes through to 2010. While there was no rise at all in the English and Welsh suicide rate recorded up until then, the latest UK-wide data *does* show a considerable spike (around 10% of the pre-recessionary baseline) in 2011, the very year that Britain's unemployment peaked.[40] And in the US, the graph obscures the dynamics, because suicide – always influenced by many things besides the economy – happened already to be on the rise. But the rate of that American increase has stepped up substantially – enough to account for nearly 5,000 excess deaths, according to one estimate.[41]

Those thousands of extra deaths should not be ignored or belittled – even if they are not significant enough to dramatically alter the overall rate. They indicate desperate pain on the part of those most severely hit by the slump. Once again, the fairly reassuring averages conceal more than they reveal. For the recent changes in the number of suicides are by no means equally distributed – there *has* been a relative rise in the number of people doing away with themselves in the communities most hit by hard times. A recent statistical analysis by David Stuckler and colleagues has shown an increased concentration of (particularly) men ending their own lives in precisely those English regions that have witnessed the sharpest rise in joblessness.[42]

This morbid result fits only too naturally with grim memories of Marienthal and everything we have learnt about the distribution of anxiety in our own time. And indeed, despite the famous reports of fallen financiers, the same concentrated pattern of citizens ending it all almost certainly applied in the American Depression, too. Moneymen taking their own lives hit the headlines, but documented cases are few and far between. J.K. Galbraith trawled the monthly suicide statistics and found that they undermined any direct association with the Wall Street Crash, as opposed to with the wider slump that followed. Both October (when the crash got going in earnest) and November 1929 were actually low suicide months.[43] The suicides came later, in step with the truly unbearable suffering – which did not concern great boom-time riches suddenly vanishing, but rather when the familiar grind of making ends meet for the lowly was intensified by recessionary anxiety over how to earn any sort of wage at all.

This is a grind that can narrow horizons until no future is visible at all. It came through loud and clear in the words of one cash-strapped British couple we spoke to. 'If it wasn't for our two children and our granddaughter, I think I'd top myself', said the woman. Her words might have been dismissed as hyperbole, had her husband not calmly added: 'We haven't got a future, really.'

Torn asunder?

We have seen evidence that many (though by no means all) are hurting from the hard times in our affluent Anglo-Saxon societies; but for a smaller minority, the pain is excruciating. Muddling through a miserable period is never going to be easy, but there is a better chance of doing so if you are blessed with a supportive and stable home life. The family provides the oldest form of economic shelter: long before anyone talked of 'cradle to grave' welfare states, families pooled resources and risks to nurture the young, care for the old and rescue the destitute. If hard times weaken family life, therefore, they do not merely take a direct psychological toll, but also increase economic exposure.

Should we expect broke homes to become broken homes? 'Not necessarily' is the message from most of the research and reports from the 1930s. In her classic study of unemployed men in the American Depression, Mirra Komarovsky uncovered much desperation; but she nonetheless found that a majority of families continued to hang together, and on traditional lines, with 44 of her 59 cases reporting no change in the standing of the man within his home.[44] Touring the depressed North of England in the same years, George Orwell wrote that things were 'more normal than one really has the right to expect. Families are impoverished, but the family system has not broken down.'[45] Even in Marienthal, with social withdrawal and psychological depression all around, when the researchers set about categorising households, no more than 7% were put in the 'broken' bracket, where 'family life begins to disintegrate'.[46]

The sense of the robustness of the family unit in the 1930s is reinforced by the most obvious statistical gauge of its health: the divorce rate. As the graph overleaf shows, the great shift in US divorce rates over the past hundred years seems to have been driven by things unrelated to the economic cycle: the Second World War, which sent all those GIs overseas; then again during the 1970s, the decade when implicit social strictures and explicit legal rules about divorce were both being liberalised. Look more closely, however, and you can in fact spot a Great Depression effect – but not in the expected direction. Divorce rates actually fell quite substantially, bottoming out along with the economy in 1932–33. In the UK at this time, too, a strong underlying upward trend in divorce was briefly arrested – a dip of around 10% between 1928 and 1930 was not reversed until 1933, by which time the British (unlike the American) recovery was well under way.[47]

All this history might seem to suggest that families respond to a great impoverishing storm by huddling close. Turning to more recent trends, although the chief impression gleaned from the graph is a downward drift in divorce ever since the early 1980s which is unrelated to the economy, the most recent numbers allow determined optimists to spot a Depression-style drop once again. Although on a chart that covers the best part of a century it is hard to pick out the section between the last full year of American growth (2006) and the trough of 2009, the rate does edge down by about 5%, before recovering weakly with the economy. Thus one cheerfully-minded analyst wrote in the depths of the downturn: 'many couples appear to be developing a new appreciation for the economic and social support that marriage can provide in tough times'.[48]

Weathering the storm together? US divorces fell in the Depression

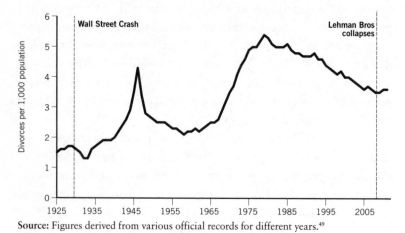

Source: Figures derived from various official records for different years.[49]

Such naïve hopes come crashing down with the briefest delve behind the headline numbers. The drop in the US divorce rate during the Great Depression almost certainly reflected growing difficulties in paying the legal fees and moving-out costs, rather than anything else. One woman quoted in Komarovsky's study of unemployed American families stated quite explicitly that if she had the money she would probably get a divorce.[50] That is exactly what many couples did, just as soon as resources allowed. The chart records how the divorce rate bounced back along with (and more decisively than) the US economy after 1933. The real lesson of history, then, is that we are seeing divorce delayed.

In the UK in our own times, where the divorce rate also fell appreciably (if briefly) in 2009,[51] the family counselling charity Relate reports seeing more couples whose difficulties flow from squabbles over money.[52] That this is not leading to more separations, it suggests, is only because these same strains often render prohibitive the cost of moving into two separate houses, with two mortgages or rents to pay. The cautious official statisticians of Whitehall suspect the same thing; alongside the latest divorce figures, they note that the recessionary drop-off is 'consistent with the theory that recession is associated with an increased risk of divorce, but with a delayed impact . . . perhaps reflecting a couple's wait for an economic recovery to lift the value of their assets'. That is what happened, they warn, the year after the last British slump lifted in the early 1990s.[53] Back in the 1930s, hard times condemned unhappy families to sit things out in their own way in unhappy homes. Behind the comforting illusion of slightly declining divorce rates, the shrewdest bet is that exactly the same thing has happened again.

Moreover, the divorce data is far more misleading today than in the Great Depression. With the growth of co-habitation, there are now many more families whose rupture will never register in any official statistics; and, particularly in the US, these are very often the same families that have been hardest hit by the slump. For the dwindling rates of marriage have not been uniform – the decline has been sharpest in economically vulnerable communities.

The proportion of white American women who are married has dropped from 67% in 1960 to 53% in 2011. This is a substantial decline of 14 percentage points, but is as nothing compared to the 30-plus point decline among their black counterparts over the same period.[54] Meanwhile, Pew Center analysis suggests that marriage rates have been dropping off roughly twice as fast among less-educated members of younger cohorts, as among their peers with a college education.[55] Thus the recession's principal victims, such as African Americans and school dropouts, are disproportionately without wedding rings today. Those seemingly reassuring divorce statistics become even less meaningful.

We need somehow to get a handle on the quality, rather than the quantity, of relationships. Individual stories may allow us to do that more effectively than statistics. While few of Komarovsky's 59 Depression-era families headed for the divorce courts, in several of them resentment born of outside economic circumstance ended up being turned inwards, into the home – a process that one un-employed man summed up eloquently: 'My ears have become sharper . . . I take things to heart which before I wouldn't have heard.'[56]

Komarovsky documented many homes where the Depression's asymmetric psychological impact (an asymmetry which this chapter has reconfirmed in contemporary data) created great tension, including one household where a previously benign husband now passed his days 'brooding' indoors, unable to stand his wife 'remaining so light-hearted' while he was 'worrying so'. For her part, this wife responded with contempt for his character and disdain for his body ('he knows that his advances are rebuffed now when they would not have been before hard times'). This is only one of a number of cases in which Komarovsky documented a deleterious effect on a couple's sex life.[57]

Occasionally, there was husband-on-wife violence; more often there was resentment that cut both ways. Fast-forwarding to the shadow of the Great Recession in contemporary Britain, we find plenty more of that. We spoke to one struggling British couple who had to rely on benefits. They appeared to remain close, but asked whether their circumstances made them argue more often these days the wife replied: 'Definitely . . . sometimes it is quite tense in here'. Such resentment can easily build to a point where a relationship is slowly doomed. 'John', a heavily indebted but employed man, was married when we first interviewed him, but was separated (though *not* divorced) the next time we spoke. He was asked whether hard times had played a part: 'Yeah . . . definitely . . . absolutely', he said. Although the relationship had been facing deeper problems, family finances were 'always there in the mix'. Out-of-work scaffolder 'Jamal', a 41-year-old with two daughters, is blunter about what hard times did for his last relationship: 'We split up because of arguments [that] were about money.'

Of course, the spousal relationship is not the only one that financial hardship can subvert. Tracking the children of the Depression over the course of their lives, Glen Elder established how the slump could sometimes work to knock down parental authority and foist premature responsibility on the shoulders of the young.[58] Komarovsky documented a collapse in the standing of unemployed fathers particularly in the eyes of their adolescent offspring – something that some fathers met with depressed resignation, and others with violence.[59] Moving back to the present, harsh parenting has just been reconfirmed as a selective response to hard times. This comes in a new American analysis of the Fragile Families Survey, which concluded that deteriorating economic conditions lead some, though certainly not all, cash-strapped mothers to hit or shout at their children more often.[60]

Unhealthy filial relations, whether in the Depression or our own times, are characterised by a retreat from frankness. Unafraid of her father but desperately unhappy with his conduct towards her siblings, one teenage girl nonetheless told the Komarovsky study that she remained 'quiet so as not to stir up trouble'.[61] We heard several contemporary echoes of unhealthy secrets. The same 'John' who said that financial strain had played a part in his recent separation, offered a particularly telling example of this. It slowly emerged during a conversation with his two teenage children . . .

Both of them were studying history and languages. It was for precisely such students that the school had laid on a trip the previous year. However, 'Neither of them even asked if they could go . . . they didn't even raise it.' The trip only came to light at all because one of them had mentioned the recent clumsiness of a fellow pupil, who it then transpired had required surgery after getting 'his hand stuck in a revolving door'. This had happened in a great scene that involved the emergency services and a wall being taken down. 'I said, "Oh, I didn't hear about that", and they said, "Well, they were in Germany" . . . The whole thing came out that there was a trip to Berlin, [but] I just let it lie. If I had said that to them, they would have been embarrassed about not having even mentioned it.' John's real sadness was: 'To know that they'd let that cat out of the bag, when they so painfully concealed it for six months . . . I just thought, "Let it go, just let it go".'

It is, then, not hard to find anecdotal evidence of hardship pushing people towards secrets and lies, and it is easy enough to imagine that this might boil over into stress-induced arguments. Hard data in this area is scarce. Just as with anxiety, however, we can exploit YouGov's cross-national polling to investigate the connection between economic trouble and domestic strife. As with anxiety, people's recall of whether they now 'row more with family and others' than in the past may be imperfect; and, again, there may be cultural differences in willingness to open up about bickering. But, for all the caveats, the headline differences are intriguing: 24% of Americans and 25% of Britons admit to arguing more these days, compared to 19% in France and 16% in Germany.

If the gap between the US and the continentals here might be put down to American openness and European reticence, the differences in variation *within* each country are less easily explained away. In the Anglo-Saxon countries, exposure to recession appears to get converted into more arguments. The figure below shows, for example, that Britons who have been hit by the slump are *more than twice as likely* as their compatriots who escaped the recession to report rowing more these days: there is a 17 percentage point gap in the argument stakes between the slump-hit and the slump-proof. The same pattern holds in the US, which has a 15 point gap. But at 9 percentage points, the

Anglo-Saxon arguments: slump-hit Britons and Americans report rowing more than slump-hit continentals

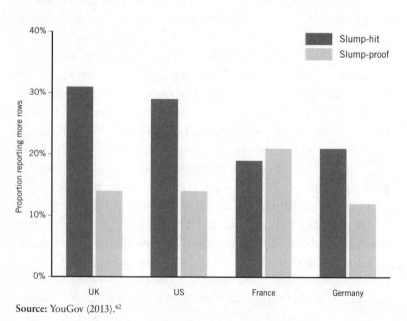

German gap is smaller; and in France, a gap of –2 percentage points indicates no meaningful recession effect at all.

The parallel with the results on anxiety – we have already shown a super-strong link between anxiety and exposure to the recession in the UK and US that was not matched on the Continent – is striking. Again, one question that raises its head is whether the Continent's labour market and other social protections might be sheltering families from the storm.

Another question to emerge is whether the long decades during which poorer British and American families trailed ever further behind has done something to their ability to weather the storm intact. The plummeting rate of marriage in poorer parts of society could simply be a reflection of a growing difficulty in paying the rising cost of weddings, in which case it may not be too much to worry about. A more chilling interpretation is that dwindling expectations of life have somehow diminished the appetite for commitment – something that could leave families frailer in the face of hard times.

The propensity of a wedding ceremony to *cause* a stronger union is doubtful and disputed; but in both the UK and the US there is powerful evidence that the decision to marry does, on average, *indicate* a more stable relationship. Research on parenting, undertaken for another strand of the Harvard–Manchester consortium which produced the *Hard Times* analysis, explored the probability of children living with both parents at the age of five, and established that cohabiting families are more fragile than married ones, especially in the US.[63]

There is a growing proportion of single-adult households in Anglo-Saxon societies. Such families have less scope to pool risks and share resources than the bigger families of hard times past. And to the extent that a failure to marry betrays a fading willingness to commit within impoverished communities, more individuals within them will be left braving the storm in effective isolation.

◆ ◆ ◆

Some accused David Cameron of waffling when – back in the good times – he talked of measuring and maximising 'general well-being'; but that did not make his ambition wrong. Sadly, you don't have to be materialistic to appreciate that hard economic times retard the pursuit of happiness in Britain and America, both directly and by straining an individual's closest relationships.

For the story of life satisfaction is another story of inequality. Anxiety lurks over a good portion of society, often pouring into unhappy homes. But the full dose of recessionary misery was reserved for the small fraction that get laid off. In terms of our tornado image, it is starting to look as if there is a very definite path of concentrated destruction that follows the trail of redundancy notices. At the same time the walls get badly shaken across a much wider area of town, while the more salubrious suburbs carry on much as before.

This chapter has highlighted misery *within* the home. The next will examine the dangers of alienation beyond it – dangers highlighted back in the 1930s by Komarovsky, who heard unemployed families complaining about the expense of socialising, the shame of not fitting in, and, above all, the desire not to be snubbed. She concluded that these things had together 'reduced the social life of the family'.[64] It is time to ask whether hard times have, once again, turned unhappy homes into an archipelago of lonely islands.

The small society

Every door I've knocked on to get help for my family and myself has been closed.
Isabel Bermudez, 42, from Cape Coral, Florida, talking to the
New York Times[1]

In 2008, as the financial world slid over the edge, presidential candidate Barack Obama, a former community organiser, told a nation that it was 'not about me' but about 'We'. America's way out of its hole, he implied, was to come together. Two years later, David Cameron was elected British prime minister on a platform that mixed stern words about the need for economic retrenchment with the sunnier promise of a great wave of volunteering to smooth the rough edges off hard times. We could not afford the big state, was his claim, but we could do without it, thanks to the 'Big Society'. The feasibility of the community coming together to shield itself from hard times inevitably depends on people's willingness to lend a hand. Was there a latent spirit of pulling together in the face of adversity that could be tapped, as it was (or so the folk memory insists) amid the hardships of Britain's Second World War? Or would the proliferation of anxiety breed insularity, as it did in depressed Marienthal?

The answers to such questions determine a nation's resilience to recession – and perhaps its political stability too. Alexis de Tocqueville was the first to suggest a connection between America's popular form of government and the great 'tumult' of civic organisational energy there, which he said 'stunned the visitor'.[2] Since the mid-twentieth century, political scholars have hunted more systematically for the roots of democratic health in civic organisations. Fifty years ago, Gabriel Almond and Sidney Verba published *The Civic Culture*, which noted the dense voluntary undergrowth in Anglo-Saxon societies and argued that this left democratic life there in better stead than in other countries, such as Germany or Mexico. A quarter of a century later, cross-national comparisons continued to put the United States top of the world's volunteering table.[3] In the more immediate run-up to the slump, however, things were not looking so good.

From the 1990s onward, the ties of community – or, in the jargon, 'social capital' – have been shown to bear on everything from the safety of the streets to the life expectancy of the people who live along them.[4] The idea that social networks have value is commonsensical at one level; but the formalisation of this insight within sociology has had results just as radical as those of the new science of happiness. Pubs, Alcoholics Anonymous branches and everything in between are these days tallied as a measure of how tight-knit a community is. Just as the value of this traditional asset of American society was coming into view, however, Robert Putnam's *Bowling Alone* charted the decline of countless forms of civic association in the later decades of the twentieth century, and forced a country to ask whether it was squandering this great inheritance. In the UK, by contrast, there has been less analysis and less concern – the most sweeping academic review of the data concluded that 'aggregate levels of social capital have not declined to an appreciable extent in Britain over the post-war years'.[5] This chapter, however, will find signs that hard times have landed a very particular blow on community life in the UK.

The first place to look for a sense of how associational life is faring is in those community organisations, scattered the length and breadth of the country, through which (it might be hoped) people do good in bad times. The British evidence here is grim. Both the number of volunteers and the level of their commitment slid with the economy. Volunteering had been edging up before the boom, before plateauing in the middle of the first decade of the twenty-first century, with something close to half of all adults formally involved in community life. In 2005, around 44% of English and Welsh citizens offered some form of unpaid help to some organisation or other, and the ambition of getting half the country involved would not have seemed fanciful. But then the Great Recession came, and the proportion – which had already edged down to 42% by early 2008 – sunk to 37% two years later.[6] Meanwhile, among the remaining volunteers, the average time being donated declined.

Take the two halves of this dismal equation together – fewer volunteers plus volunteers who put in fewer hours – and the picture truly darkens. The chart overleaf considers the population as a whole, volunteers and non-volunteers alike. It shows that between the third quarter of 2008 (when the financial crisis was getting going in earnest) and the second quarter of 2010, the average commitment fell by a full hour, from 3 hours 10 minutes to 2 hours 10 minutes.[7] Since this is a whole-population figure, and so includes many people who never have and probably never will volunteer, this is a dramatic change. All the more so, as we have strictly capped the time contribution of the most enthusiastic do-gooders, in order to limit their influence on the overall averages; if we ease this constraint, the total decline becomes sharper still.[8]

The quarter-by-quarter results suggest a particularly close connection with the economy, with an especially sharp decline taking hold from the financially catastrophic third quarter of 2008. But it is also true that these quarterly results bob about somewhat, and so it is as well to lay a smoothing trend line (which we have done in grey) over the more volatile quarterly series, which is plotted in black. But even looking at this, we can still see an overall recessionary drop-off of at least half an hour. The *only* comfort is that the final couple of individual quarterly data-points suggest that by early 2011 the decline had levelled off.

Our grim findings come from the Citizenship Survey of England and Wales, which has itself since fallen victim to hard times, cancelled as part of government cuts and then partially replaced, in a singularly

The small society: volunteering dives with the British economy

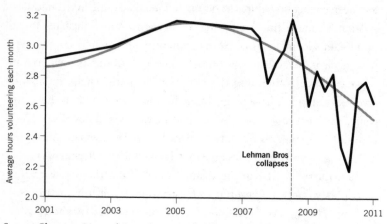

Source: Chaeyoon Lim and James Laurence's analysis of the Citizenship Survey.[9]

messy U-turn.[10] But the gist of the results are emphatically confirmed by other indicators collected during the recent slump. A regular poll for the respected Hansard Society inquired specifically about 'voluntary work' and recorded a drop-off of a full one-third between 2009 and 2011, as hard times ground on.[11]

Why should this be? The employment figures, after all, tell us that there were suddenly 2 million extra Britons who unexpectedly had more time than they would like on their hands, whether they were under- or unemployed. Why was this time not being donated? One sticking point might have been the financial costs of volunteering – typically modest costs that might go almost unnoticed during good times but which are keenly felt when families start experiencing the squeeze. Back in the American Depression of the 1930s, Komarovsky found many who had stopped attending church owing to financially related concerns: a number of men who dreaded not being able to contribute to the collection plate, women who were ashamed to turn up in ragged clothes, and one lady who said she was 'heartbroken' at having had to cease attending 'because she couldn't afford the carfare'.[12] In the depressed Britain of 2012, 'Mike', a leading light in the Safe Anchor Trust, a Yorkshire charity that lays on boating trips for disadvantaged youngsters, told me that finding volunteers to provide lifts to and from the barges has become more difficult because of increasing concern about the price of fuel – a definite echo of that old 'carfare' worry.

Another practical problem – perhaps more of an issue today than in hard times of the past – might be the insecure or unpredictable work shifts, which (as we saw in Chapter 4) have become more common, and which, inevitably, make community life harder to plan. 'Mike' told me that Safe Anchor has one 22-year-old volunteer who exudes enthusiasm, but who has been unable to pre-commit over most of the past two years because of his zero-hours contract with a major high-street retailer: 'he's always keen, but you never know in advance which days he is going to be able to do'. The Scout Association, which currently has tens of thousands of youngsters stuck on its waiting list, as adult volunteering fails to keep pace with burgeoning youthful demand, has registered similar problems in certain areas. Roles that would once have been filled by a single individual are now sometimes split several ways, as Scout groups solicit help on an as-and-when basis, rather than assuming that they can rely on a weekly commit-ment. Twenty-nine-year-old 'Heather', one of four volunteers who share a single Scout leader role in Manchester, reckons that 'the demands and pressures of modern life mean it's harder for people to find time'. Her analysis seems hard to square with recessionary under-employment, until you factor in the insecurity issue. The big dip in overall volunteering immediately after 2008 suggests she is not wrong.[13]

Another possible problem, however, could be that – much as in Marienthal – recession-hit Britons were simply struggling to find the motivation to get involved. Asked why she had stopped doing some-thing or other, Marienthal's 'Frau S' told the researchers: 'God knows, we have other problems these days.'[14] We will return to the dark hypothesis of unfocused despair that those vague words suggest.

Up until now in this book, we have found many more parallels than distinctions between the two sides of the Atlantic. But when it comes to formal involvement in the community, the evidence points in different directions. In the US, the best available data suggests that the Great Recession did not produce any substantial decline in organised volunteering. Ever since 2002, the Current Population Survey (CPS) – a 60,000-sample operation run by the Census Bureau and used, among other things, to calculate the unemployment rate – has been asking about 'activities for which people are not paid . . . through or for an organization', and a remarkably steady 26–28% have always indicated participation.[15] There was a *slight* dip to the bottom end of that very narrow range in 2006; but as that was at the height of the bubble, it can hardly be blamed on hard times. Since the recession took hold, the CPS has suggested that the proportion of Americans who are volunteering has not moved one iota. We also checked the follow-up question for those who did volunteer, about how many hours they put in. Again, there was 'no evidence' of any change.[16]

One smaller survey *did* find evidence of reduced American civic activity in the depths of the big dip of 2009, and there was passing interest in the idea that the US could be suffering from a 'civic foreclosure'. But by 2012, the National Conference on Citizenship (which had commissioned that survey) was instead emphasising the larger and more reassuring CPS data and reporting that volunteering among Americans had 'hit a five year high'.[17] The best bet is that there was in reality no 'civic foreclosure' in relation to America's formal volunteering at all; and if there was, then it certainly proved very short-lived.

Two centuries after de Tocqueville described a people who 'are forever forming associations',[18] it thus appears that the great economic gale has blown across America without making a dent in the propensity to volunteer. The contrast with Britain makes this puzzling, all the more so since the scholarly literature has found no strong relationship between individual values and volunteering,[19] ruling out a story of an optimistic American culture somehow forging characters more determined to 'keep calm and carry on' in the face of adversity.

What the literature suggests *is* important for volunteering is being nudged into getting involved through pre-existing personal or organisational ties.[20] Any attempt to explain the very different effect of the slump on organised do-gooding in Britain and America is somewhat speculative, but the insight that networks beget networks invites two important thoughts. First, a 'civic infrastructure' – both organisationally and in terms of retaining a critical mass of volunteers – is likely to be important in maintaining civic engagement at a time when motivation could ebb. Even if community life has withered in America over recent decades, the US started off with more of it than Britain; Americans during the post-war era were 10 percentage points more likely than Britons to be in voluntary associations, and were twice as likely to have been an officer in these.[21] Worn-out as it may be, this form of infrastructure – like any other – yields benefits for many decades, and perhaps America's 'joining tradition' has continued to help its communities to weather hard times.

Second, the transatlantic difference in religious involvement could make a difference – not because of what people believe, but because of religion's capacity to bring people together. Around three times as many Americans as Britons claim to attend church regularly.[22] Robert Putnam's recent work suggests that religion appears to be a kind of bulwark of civil society in the US.[23] It may be that the intermittent difficulties of the British Scouting movement in finding enough leaders to work with young would-be members are inflamed because wouldbe volunteers were, until very recently, expected to identify a faith to which they belong, and yet very many Britons have no religion to declare. (In 2013, when there were reportedly 38,000 youngsters on Scout waiting lists, the movement eventually decided to introduce the option of a non-religious pledge.)[24] Things are different in the US. Americans' faith, Putnam has found, has proved resilient in the face of the Great Recession, which had remarkably little impact on religiosity, even among those hardest hit. Religiously rooted social networks facilitate civic engagement and good neighbourliness. At both the organisational and the individual level, American religiosity makes civil society more robust, including in the face of economic gales.[25]

For both spiritual and temporal reasons, then, the United States may have a sturdier civic infrastructure to uphold formal community engagement in hard times. With Britain lacking the same support structures, we have seen that organised volunteering fell away with the economy. The one remaining potential comfort for the UK is that the dismal statistics we have reviewed could be more about British disorganisation than any hardening of hearts. We have already referred to the possibility that the drop-off in involvement or volunteering with formal organisations might be a case of people scrimping (for example, on travel or on club subscriptions) on account of the big squeeze. If so, the British people might be making up for this formal withdrawal by continuing to support their immediate communities through informal networks of kindness – by helping friends of friends, say, or simply lending a neighbour a hand.

Fortunately, we have excellent information on the full range of good deeds that Britons report doing: the Citizenship Survey asked about everything, from shopping for an old man next door to babysitting for a toddler down the road.[26] Unfortunately, what this rich data demonstrates is that 'volunteering' of this informal stripe actually fell away *somewhat more steeply* than the formal variety after 2008, with the proportion of citizens indicating that they gave someone a hand at least once a year diving by over 10 percentage points by 2010.[27] More frequent informal helpers (who lent a hand at least once a month) also fell away more rapidly than more frequent volunteers.[28]

Exactly as with formal volunteering, we also have data on how much time continuing 'helpers' put in. The average time spent informally 'helping' across the whole population (see the graph opposite) reflects this as well as the increasing number who are doing no helping at all. In results that echo those for formal volunteering, we can see that the overall average monthly commitment falls by as much as an hour over the duration of the slump; in the second quarter of 2008, Britons typically helped for 3 hours 7 minutes a month; by the beginning of 2010 that had fallen to 2 hours 8 minutes.

Again, we have applied cautious adjustments to reduce the influence on the overall average of the minority who devote most time to caring for others; again, the decline would look even bigger with this restriction eased.[29] Once again, too, we should be wary of putting too much weight on the ups and downs in individual quarters, and so it is as well to consider the slope of a line of best fit. But again, we can see in this overall trend a definite drop of more than half an hour, which this time is particularly concentrated in the most recessionary quarters. The big drop-off in helping in England and Wales came during 2009, just as unemployment soared; in their hour of need, luckless Britons discovered not more, but less spontaneous compassion.

The maximum quarter-on-quarter recessionary decline in both the formal and informal volunteering series is around a third: 31% in both cases. That certainly sounds substantial, but how much of this is down to the volatility of the quarterly data? As a final precaution, we thus disregard this data entirely and concentrate on changes between whole years. And regarding informal help, we are *still* left with a reduction of about a quarter.[30] When social statistics move rapidly by that sort of margin, it is reliably a Big Deal. It is equivalent, for instance, to the proportion of total vote share that the Conservatives mislaid between 1992 and their landslide defeat in 1997 – the defeat that reduced them from a party of government to a parliamentary rump. A particularly alarming contrast is with the economy

The kindness crunch: 'informal volunteering' dives with the British economy

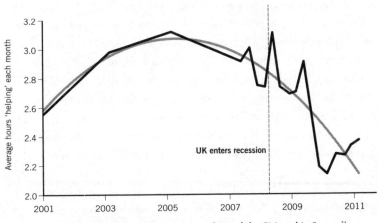

Source: Chaeyoon Lim and James Laurence's analysis of the Citizenship Survey.[31]

itself, which contracted by a good deal less than one-tenth. By this measure, the UK's social recession was considerably larger than its financial one.

In the face of recession, then, Britons responded by hunkering down in their own homes, with their own concerns. Just what would be the wider social effects of that? The *combined* reduction in formal and informal volunteering across the whole population, as measured on the most cautious possible basis, dropped by just short of an hour a month – 56 minutes – between 2007 and 2010/11.[32] That represents a drop-off of just under two minutes (110 seconds to be precise) every single day for every adult in the country – more if we discount the frail and elderly, who will necessarily be more often helped than helpers.[33] If that does not sound like much, consider that two minutes is time enough to help a blind man across the road and back, or to make an old lady a cup of tea. Imagine the difference it would make if every adult in the country did something like that, day in, day out. And now imagine the damage to the community if every one of them suddenly stopped. If the Big Society has any meaning at all, then what unfolded in the immediate face of the recession was its very antithesis.

Why did this happen? Since informal volunteering does not rely on organised clubs, with subscriptions to pay, the decline there cannot be put down to financial scrimping. Rather, it appears that – like 'Frau S' in Marienthal – Britons facing hard times have been shrugging their shoulders and, with a world-weary sigh, deciding that they have 'other problems these days'. This suggests a deeper malaise than a rusty civic infrastructure of outmoded social clubs: it indicates that hard times in some way affected the collective psyche. Our detailed analysis suggests that dwindling trust – specifically trust in one's neighbours – may have played a big part in this (among those who harbour suspicions about other families nearby, there was less engagement to begin with, plus a sharper drop-off during the recession), although trust is not the whole story.[34] The words of individual Britons who now get less involved than they once did may shed more light than any statistical test on exactly how it was that community life came to wither away in the downturn.

With his experience of working with youngsters, it is not hard to tell that unemployed 'Winston' still regards himself as a 'people person' at heart: 'Since my youth-work days, I like bringing people together, I like doing diverse things, I like working outside the box as I've said.' One would not know it, however, from the way he passes his days at the moment: 'I don't get involved; I don't even put myself out there.' The only half-explanation he offers for this change is that 'where I live, I'm not happy with my accommodation. I have no balcony so I'm always in my house.' But no architectural omission can account for a withdrawal so complete that, as he emphasises, apart from the odd dealing with his immediate neighbours, 'I don't get involved in *any* sort of way.' This is 'Frau S' all over again.

Others also told us all about how they had withdrawn – but, just like 'Winston', they struggled to explain quite why. Workless mother 'Kirsty' in Scotland used to volunteer with disabled children 'for three hours' at a time, taking them swimming; she also did 'volunteering with another group called the Rock Trust, and that was maybe a couple of times a week'. Nowadays, however, she has no such formal involvement, and – much more worrying – no informal network of any kind. Asked if she has any close friends, she answers 'No, apart from my grandparents'; she reports being too 'nervous' to strike up conversations in the park. She has no social life, but feels some solidaristic connection with a neighbour (whom she speaks to only rarely), since she knows that this neighbour also struggles, 'because she came to ask to borrow some milk or sugar, and I have done the same'. Pressed to recall any help she might have received, 'Kirsty' fondly recalls that this neighbour 'filled a cup up to the top for me, which was really nice'. Perhaps this former volunteer's expectations of her community have now reached a pass where she fears that a request for milk would be met with a glass half-empty.

It was much the same with 55-year-old 'Norma', an intelligent but troubled disabled woman, who had 'volunteered over the years', including for Citizens' Advice. But something changed not long after the economy collapsed: 'I have not done anything for about two years . . . it drives me mental, stir crazy.' Did she have any friends or family she could turn to if she needed help? 'At the moment, I am on my own, kind of thing.'

Unlike with formal volunteering, where American civic traditions and organisations may play some special protective role, the US is not immune to the sort of generalised malaise affecting 'Winston' and 'Kirsty'. The limited data available suggests that there were also significant problems with 'helping' on the other side of the Atlantic, too. While detailed information on 'informal volunteering' has not been consistently collated in the way that it has in Britain, since the recession took its serious turn in autumn 2008 the Current Population Survey has asked about the regularity with which people trade favours with their neighbours. Between 2008 and 2010, the proportion of Americans who *never* house-sit, lend milk or anything else rose from just under 42% to just over 44%.[35]

The question is differently worded, is restricted to neighbours, and has only been asked since the slump was well under way, and so there is real analytical difficulty in comparing the 2–3 percentage point shift on this metric with the apparently larger slide in England and Wales. The American change does, however, turn out to be statistically significant, which is to say large enough for us to be satisfied that it must be real. The detail of the data further supports the impression of a genuine drop.[36] And the timing reinforces the impression that the recession has something to do with it; the decline was concentrated in those quarters of the year when the US economy was weakening most.

It is also supported by a second piece of American evidence, which looks at the problem the other way round – by asking people not about whether they have helped out, but instead about whether they themselves feel they have someone to turn to if necessary. Since 2008, the Gallup Daily Poll (which we used in Chapter 5 to track the big picture on life satisfaction) has been asking people whether they could rely on relatives or friends if they were in trouble. Now, to be sure, this could be a gauge of mood, or of people's *feelings* about whom they could turn to, rather than anything more objective. But with family included on this measure, one might expect it to be relatively recession-proof: brothers, sisters and parents, after all, really shouldn't disappear just because GDP takes a dive. And yet, as this question was asked hundreds of times during the recession, the indicator saw a definite and substantial fall of around 5–6 percentage points, from a high of close to 88% in early 2008 to a low of just above 82% at the worst point of the recession, in mid-2009.[37] Thus grim feelings like those of Isabel Bermudez in Florida – who, at the top of the chapter, talks of having doors slammed in her family's face – may not be quite as rare as those heartening US statistics on formal volunteering had suggested. Hard times appear to have left Americans, just like the British, sorely short of fellowship.

So far we have been describing the frailty of British and American society *as a whole*, using statistical averages. But after everything we have learnt about the skewed distribution of unemployment, insecure work and other worries during hard times, it is imperative to ask whether all communities are suffering, or whether the damage is, once again, concentrated on the least lucky neighbourhoods and homes. Our rich British dataset allows us to do so.

The first and most obvious question is whether Britain's 'social recession' can be accounted for by the withdrawal from the community of those individuals who have been directly lashed by the financial storm. Intriguingly, the answer is 'no'. Adjusting the quarterly Citizenship Survey data to allow for the rising proportion of individual unemployed people in the sample over the duration of the slump does not materially affect our results. Nor does allowing for household income. So the idea that the big squeeze on pay is directly reducing people's ability to get stuck into community life falls away as an explanation for the volunteering collapse.[38]

It does not follow, however, that we have finally identified a social malady that befalls the nation equally – far from it. It is simply that the economic tornado rages across downtrodden neighbourhoods as a whole, rather than singling out individual homes. There is underlying variation in volunteering rates across the English regions, with people in the depressed North-East least likely to get involved. Furthermore, *changing* unemployment rates across different regions can account for a great deal of the downward recessionary drift in informal 'help';

across more slump-hit regions the exchange of favours fell away more.[39]

The depressed ecology of Britain's poor communities is thrown into sharper relief when we explore how volunteering rates changed across individual boroughs and villages with differing prosperity. The UK government scores all English 'wards' (small, administrative units of about 5,000 residents) using an all-encompassing deprivation index, on the basis of things like employment, income and crime.[40] The latest release is for 2007, before the downturn, so by factoring this measure into our analysis we are exploring the frailty of communities that was not so much caused as *exposed* by the Great Recession. But – as the figure opposite reveals – that frailty is very marked indeed.

For people in richer communities, the recessionary drop-off in formal volunteering rates was a mere blip (from 42% to 41%), the 1 percentage point decline recorded in the graph opposite shown by statistical tests to be indistinguishable from no change at all. It looks as if the prosperous shire towns of southern England might, after all, be blessed with something like the civic infrastructure which we suggested might have pulled American volunteering through the storm. But in poorer communities, where there was already considerably less volunteering, it is a different story. The probability of someone getting involved there drops from 36% to 30%, a 6 percentage point drop-off, which is significant. A pre-existing volunteering gap between rich and poor towns therefore doubled in size. All these results are after controlling for individual characteristics, including unemployment, so what they imply is that a wide shadow was somehow cast over poorer neighbourhoods as a whole.

With informal helping it is a similar story, although the overall drop-off is sharper and there are significant changes for both sorts of neighbourhood this time. For the prosperous shires and suburbs, the decline of 10 points is substantial and significant, but considerably smaller than the 15 point drop in impoverished inner cities. Poor neighbours' dwindling trust in each other is one part of this story, but – as more detailed analysis suggests – it cannot fully explain the difference.[41] It would seem that, over and above the toll that the slump took on trust in poor towns, there was some wider, 'ecological' effect – almost as if whole neighbourhoods forgot how to hope.

The Great Recession stifled spontaneous kindness right across England, but did so more aggressively in the communities that *started out* poor. Some element of speculation is inescapably involved in explaining why. Increasingly insecure work in poor towns, which cannot be easily identified and controlled for in the same way as unemployment, could be a big part of this tale: it may cause people to become withdrawn, or it could make it harder for them to commit their time. But however the link works, it would appear that the reckoning for those long decades in which the Barnsleys, the Liverpools and the Nottinghams were left behind economically finally arrived in the wake of the Great Recession. Social ties that had very gradually frayed in such places proved especially susceptible to hard times. And these, of course, are the very boroughs where people have often got nothing apart from each other.

Hard streets: volunteering fell further in poor communities, 2008–10

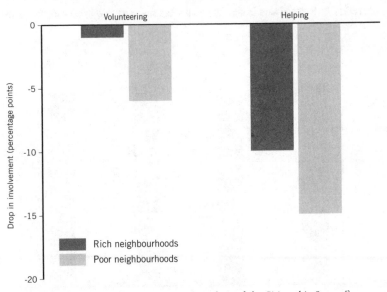

Source: Chaeyoon Lim and James Laurence's analysis of the Citizenship Survey.[42]

We do not have the data to allow us to perform the same community-based analysis for the United States. But, just as with anxiety and family arguments (Chapter 5), we can turn to YouGov's 2013 cross-national polling to get some sort of handle on *who* has suffered from the 'social recession'. Across four countries, the survey asked respondents whether they were 'more likely or less likely to . . . get involved with social and community groups' than a few years ago. Again, we need to enter the usual caveats about recall-based questions and differing national dispositions towards surveys: the *absolute* proportion claiming to be less involved in each country will not tell us anything definitive. Again, however, there is no obvious reason why such biases should discriminate on grounds of economic fortune within each country, and so the *relative* changes within each nation should be interesting.

Just as with anxiety and family arguments, we find a strong differential between the slump-hit and the slump-proof in both

Club class: Britons and Americans who escaped the slump stuck with community groups

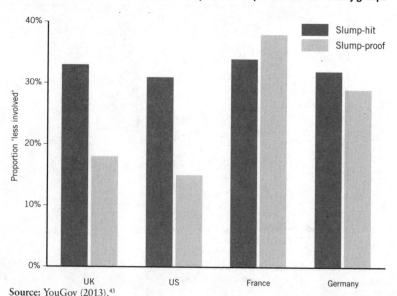

Source: YouGov (2013).[43]

Britain and America – a gap that simply does not apply in the continental countries. The chart on the previous page shows that, in both Britain and the US, those who say they were personally affected by the downturn are roughly *twice as likely* as their compatriots who say they emerged from the slump unscathed to report that nowadays they get less involved with community groups. In neither France nor Germany, by contrast, does direct experience of the recession produce a material participation gap.

We have seen that in Britain at least, there was no 'burst of neighbouring' in the grim economic years after 2008, but rather a shrivelling of society. In America, stronger civic traditions and structures appear to have deflected certain sorts of damage to organised community life, but the spontaneous giving and taking which *ought* to make everybody feel supported through daily life appears to have fallen away in the US, too. We have demonstrated beyond doubt that in England poorer communities took the hardest knock; in the US – for which we do not have the same data – we suggest more tentatively that those hardest hit by the recession do seem to have suffered more pain. As no such division is at all visible in either France or Germany, it looks very much as though 'community' is yet another dimension of life in the Anglo-Saxon economies through which the tornado tore a distinctly selective path.

The shrivelling of society after 2008 was unambiguously a 'hard times' phenomenon: the timing plainly points that way, as does the *differential* decline across regions and the hammering of poorer boroughs.[44] Given that there will one day be another big slump, there is a need for serious thinking about how economic recession might be met with the sort of real big society that could offer meaningful protection, instead of with a frail community that falls away with national income. The particular collapse in volunteering and 'helping' in those neighbourhoods that had fallen behind in the good times is especially instructive in starting to think about how this might be done.

But, as recession gives way to proclaimed recovery, shouldn't the economic link mean that community life picks up in parallel with

GDP? Indeed, in the US, where recovery got under way sooner, the decline in the Gallup poll tracker response about 'having someone to count on' was substantially reversed as a slow recovery gathered pace during 2011.[45] And in the UK in early 2013, as the economy chugged back to half-life, David Cameron boasted in the House of Commons that his cut-price replacement for the Citizenship Survey was finally suggesting that 'volunteering was up'.[46]

So it did, and the apparent improvement in England was sharp, although with only a few quarters of data available from a new survey that inevitably introduced a certain discontinuity, the prime minister might be well advised not to crow too soon. The fact that the sharp rise in formal volunteering reported in the first lot of quarterly data (which included the volunteer-propelled 2012 London Olympics) fell back somewhat in the second quarter invites further caution.[47] Nonetheless, amid a financial recovery, it seems entirely plausible that the social fabric is also on the mend. The expectation must surely be that, as the economy continues to heal, so too will wounded communities. Or must it?

The troubling answer from the very latest analysis – set out in the next chapter – is that, while the social wounds in many places may indeed already be healing nicely, for the towns and streets that were hardest hit, instead of healing, these wounds may harden into lasting social scars.

The long shadow

I'm just almost accepting that I don't feel like I will ever own a house. I just don't think that's attainable.
'Laura', 25, from Newcastle, a student with impeccable qualifications but from a poor family

Some time in the 1980s, economists learnt a new word: 'hysteresis'. It came from engineering, but it sounded like 'history', and the big idea was that *the past matters*. Real historians would wryly point out that only an economist could consider it a revelation that what has gone before will affect where things end up. But social science often assumes that the world gravitates towards some pre-ordained equilibrium, so 'path dependency' is an important insight – the most immediate application for which was hard times.[1] Workers who initially lost their jobs *purely* because of the slump in the early 1980s nonetheless often remained unemployed even once recovery came. Why? Skills had rusted, confidence had waned and suspicions had risen in the minds of employers. In sum, the immediate blow of redundancy had knocked people off the track they were previously coasting along, and onto a low road in life.

The ability of recessions to take an enduring toll may only have been recognised in economic theory in the last generation, but it has long been familiar to students of the Great Depression. James Elder, who spent a lifetime tracking survivors of that time, explained to the American journalist Don Peck that, even decades into America's post-war boom, the ageing men who had suffered economically during the 1930s tended to come across as 'beaten and withdrawn – lacking ambition, direction and confidence in themselves'.[2] In this chapter, we will search for early signs that the Great Recession will cast a similarly long shadow – and we will ask whether it is likely to lead not merely to enduring penury and worklessness, but also to protracted despair and isolation.

Class action

The last few chapters have been concerned with the non-pecuniary maladies that flow from finances. Before we evaluate the slump's enduring social legacy, we must briefly return to material matters, and consider for how long the financial hit is likely to be felt, and by whom.

As we reported in Chapter 4, right across the wage range (apart from the very top) Britons and Americans have experienced a long squeeze on pay that did not begin with – but was greatly intensified by – the slump that began in earnest in 2008. To recap: in the United States, the income of middling households has already been stuck for a quarter of a century; and official UK projections imply that typical real disposable income will advance not one jot between 1998 and 2018. Indeed, the latest forecasts available in autumn 2013 suggest that the median real British wage in 2017 will still be £3,400 less than at the pre-recession peak. This fall is so substantial that *even if* the sort of decent wage growth enjoyed in the distant past resumed now, the typical worker would not make up the recessionary losses until the mid-2020s.[3]

Even considered in isolation, this is a very long shadow – not one but two lost decades. It implies that the old assumption that living standards will tend to rise steadily, year in and year out – the post-Enlightenment presumption of progress in day-to-day life – has been put on hold. The upcoming cohort cannot assume that they will have more material opportunities than their parents. The story that we have all told ourselves about our own families – about each generation avoiding hardships that were inescapable to the last – has ceased to apply for the first time since the last great slump and the greater war that followed it.

Stuck wages, however, are not the end of the matter; cut-backs in workplace benefits and the legacy of boom-time debts intensify the squeeze on the working majority and inflame fears for the future. Across the UK workforce in 2012, official figures recorded fewer staff paying into occupational pensions than at any time since the 1950s.[4] Meaningful provision for old age was once a standard part of the deal with most jobs; these days pensions are less generous, and most of those that remain operate as a punt on the stock market, and so provide little security. With greater life expectancy comes more old age to plan for, but the signal from business is that workers are on their own.

The dismantling of defined benefit (i.e. guaranteed) company pensions in the US was accomplished longer ago, but there is a contemporary transatlantic parallel with health insurance. It used to be a standard perk, but in 2012 the Employee Benefits Research Institute reported that coverage was dwindling, dropping by around 5 percentage points since the early noughties.[5] President Obama's healthcare reforms might arrest this drift. On the UK pension front, a new government scheme to enrol employees in (decidedly modest) workplace schemes may also have some effect. Both these reforms, however, are going against the grain of a corporate culture whose drift is to provide staff with less protection against the contingencies of life.

In relation to debt, the real shadow was, of course, cast by the excesses of the boom years, rather than by the eventual bust. Indeed, after the long recessionary years, in which families have cut back on spending and interest rates have been kept extremely low, household liabilities are now appreciably smaller than they were; but the burden of debt relative to stagnant incomes – a ratio which, in the UK, stood at around 140% in 2013 – remains high by any historical standard.[6] Despite the rock-bottom official borrowing rates, 3.6 million UK households continue to spend more than a quarter of gross income on debt repayments.[7] This is no doubt a symptom of tight post-crunch credit conditions, which – on both sides of the Atlantic – restrict the flexibility of debtors (other than those with exceptional earnings or substantial collateral) to take advantage of the official policy of easy money.

Just because vulnerable borrowers are denied the full benefits of this policy, however, it does not follow that they will be spared the full pain when rates eventually rise. Growth in incomes will eventually return, but assuming it is once again skewed towards the better-off, an early increase in official lending rates of even a single percentage point beyond market expectations would leave 7% of British households with outstanding debt in the perilous position where repayments gobble up over half of gross income by 2017. That is about a million homes – actually *more* than at the peak of the bubble, a full decade after it burst.[8]

To see the full effect on household balance sheets, however, the repayment of debt needs to be considered alongside the reduction in wealth precipitated by the crash. This was large, particularly for ordinary families. One early American analysis estimated that whereas the wealth of high-income households (who might have a wide range of investments) had dipped by 12% in the recession, that of middle-income families (whose money is likely to be tied up in bricks and mortar) had fallen by 23%. Losses were larger still for black (30%) and especially Hispanic families (52%), who were perhaps most often at the sharp end of sub-prime.[9]

In Britain, where shares fell much further than property prices, the initial impact was probably felt more keenly towards the top end; but a recovering stock market and a widening North–South gap in property prices have since ridden to the rescue of the rich. Comparing Bank of England analysis of the distribution of 'net worth' (i.e. the value of assets less debts) for 2005 and 2012 reveals that – when the build-up to the crisis, the crisis itself and the aftermath are all considered together – roughly the bottom three-quarters of households have fallen back, while the top quarter or so have moved ahead.[10]

It is starting to look, then, as if the effect of the Great Recession might have been to compound 30 years of rising inequality in the flow of income (i.e. what people earn) with a fresh opening-up in the gulf between the rich and poor in terms of assets and liabilities – inequality in what families are worth. Take this new skewing of assets, *together* with the stagnant pay, the insecure working terms and inadequate fringe benefits, and you finally start to grasp the true force of recent hard times – a force with the power to turn some of our deepest social tides.

Historians joke about phrases that can confidently be applied to any time or place, and 'a newly ascendant middle class' is one such. Within just two years of 2008, however, Pew Center polling suggested a 5 percentage point drop-off in the proportion of Americans describing themselves as middle or upper-middle class, from 72% to 68%.[11] The surest marker of the 'ascendant middle class' truism has been, for as long as anyone can remember, the rising rate of owner occupation on both sides of the Atlantic. Every sociological cliché – from the withering of old communities to the passing of deference – has been explained in terms of greater owner occupation. The subsequent souring of the dream of home ownership in the recession was initially starkest in the US; the four-fold spike in foreclosures between 2006 and 2009 was far in excess of any other recent recession.[12] The latest Census Bureau data shows American home ownership rates, which had peaked at 69% in 2005, falling back to 65% in 2013, a figure that marches the middle classes back to a point at which they last stood in 1995.[13]

In the UK – where the political rhetoric of the property-owning democracy has trickled down the generations, from Noel Skelton to Eden and on to Macmillan and Cameron – a mix of pragmatic forbearance and low mortgage rates prevented a full rerun of the early 1990s, when mass repossessions were such a feature of the downturn.[14] Yet, because high British house prices have held up as pay has been squeezed, it now looks as if the turning tide against home ownership could be even more marked than in the US. Already by the time of the census in 2011, home ownership was down 5 percentage points on the last nationwide count in 2001, the first such decline in a century.[15] Looking ahead, the National Housing Federation projects that the 73% of the English population that lived in owner-occupied housing in 2001 will fall to just 64% in 2021, returning the statistic to where it stood in the first days of Margaret Thatcher's 'right to buy'.[16]

When John Prescott, the seaman turned deputy prime minister, made headlines in the 1990s by revealing that (surprise, surprise!) with his MP's salary he no longer lived a working-class life, he was widely misquoted as having said 'We're all middle class now'. In fact, he remained far too mindful of Britain's social divisions to have made such a claim; but the misattribution stuck because it seemed somehow to capture the spirit of the times and – so he told me – the message that parts of the Labour high command were trying to put across.[17] The promise that the great bulk of society could be on its way up at the same time was always questionable (and indeed questioned); but half a generation ago it had sufficient credibility to be regarded as winning political rhetoric. Today, in an era when the ranks of the squeezed, the scared and the insecure are so swollen, it would lack any plausibility and fail to gain traction.

On both sides of the Atlantic, 2013 has seen the publication of soul-searching tomes with emotive titles about the dwindling opportunities of ordinary families: George Packer's *The Unwinding* in the US and David Boyle's *Broke: Who killed the middle classes?* in the UK.[18] The big squeeze is engendering a mood of pessimism, and there are some good reasons to fear that widely shared financial problems *could* yet spill over into aspects of family and community life in the years ahead.

Data that tracked British families over several years before the bust suggests that unsustainable housing commitments (of the sort that will proliferate if interest rates rise) adversely affect well-being and mental health.[19] In American tracking data, meanwhile, the presence of consumer debt has been shown to predict marital conflict five years later,[20] and to reduce marital satisfaction.[21] The same US data also suggests that financial arguments have a tendency to play out in particularly nasty ways, with disagreements over money being 'among the consistent top predictors of conflict tactics, including using heated arguments more frequently than calm discussion'.[22] Post-recessionary problems with money, then, could yet pollute the things that money is not supposed to be able to buy, and across a broad swathe of society.

But most of these *potentially* dangerous legacies for middle Britain and middle America remain just that – contingent problems that will arise, for example, in the event of a surge in borrowing costs.

For the moment, it is important to acknowledge that there are many millions of people paying off pre-credit-crunch mortgages, whose repayments have taken an unanticipated dive with official interest rates; for some of them, this more than compensates for the steady erosion of salaries by inflation. Recall the impression of calmness in the big picture on well-being (Chapter 5): for the majority in stable employment, overall life satisfaction bounced back pretty quickly from the recession. The middle class as a whole is *not* in crisis, even if it is feeling the pinch. The bulk of Britons and Americans have settled into being a bit poorer – and a bit less bourgeois, a bit less aspirational – with relative contentment, perhaps because of a feeling that (nearly) everybody is in it together.

The really serious trouble remains in store not for the majority of families, who are suffering from one aspect or another of the big squeeze, but for the unlucky minority being hammered on every front at the same time. Intriguing new work by Jacob Hacker and colleagues underlines the point. It exploits a large bespoke survey on economic security, carried out in waves just before and just after the Great Recession, to assess the range of risks facing Americans – risks regarding work, health, family and wealth. It concludes: 'Insecurity – whether measured in terms of worries or actual economic shocks – is far greater for racial minorities, households with limited education and lower-income households.'[23] That conclusion certainly fits with what we have found in relation to the *immediate* effects of the slump on employment, well-being and community life, and it is pertinent to ask whether these same groups will bear the lasting scars. The initial storm damage was, of course, heavily concentrated on the jobless (to whom we will return) but the young also emerged as an especially wind-beaten element of society. So let us ask first whether the slump's marked effect on them is set to endure.

The young: dreams in the deep freeze

We opened the chapter with 'Laura' explaining why she would never own a home. For a young woman who has already notched up one first-class degree and who is currently enrolled on a Master's course, which paves the way into a secure profession, it would once have seemed a ludicrously gloomy view. Not any more, however. We have seen how home ownership is falling out of fashion across the population as a whole, and this is one trend that is heavily concentrated on the young. Among the under-35s on low-to-middling pay in the UK, the proportion of home-buyers dropped from over 50% to under 30% in just eight years, through to 2011. This is a reduction of seismic proportions.[24]

The huge deposits demanded by lenders after the crunch obviously play a part in the immediate difficulty: it would now take a typical British saver on modest pay 22 years to build up a deposit, compared to a mere three years a generation ago.[25] A new government scheme, Help to Buy, is supposed to help out on this front by providing finance for part of the deposit, but it may only succeed in inflaming the root problem: the sheer level of house prices in the UK.

Youth unemployment obviously destroys all hope of home-buying for a substantial minority; just as important, however, is the ongoing pay squeeze on youngsters who do find work. For those like 'Laura', from working-class families that could never help out with the vast sums involved in buying a property, the consequences of wage stagnation are especially stark. And all the more so because the big squeeze on them looks set to continue into the foreseeable future. Evidence is emerging to suggest that young people pay a *lifetime* price for coming of age in a slump – a true 'hysteresis' effect. The message is that if you slip on that crucial first step on the career ladder – as many of those entering the labour market during a slump are doomed to do – you could spend a lifetime struggling to catch up.

The economist Lisa Kahn followed a decade's worth of college leavers using America's best-established tracking survey, and found 'large negative wage effects' for those cohorts that graduated in years with fewer jobs. These effects persisted throughout the two decades that followed, and remained even after meticulous adjustment for potential feedbacks between economic conditions and the timing and place of graduation.[26] Compared to boom-time graduates, the pay of recessionary college completers emerges as anything from 20% to 1% lower over the long years of the study. And Kahn's detailed econometrics suggest that these numbers should be regarded as lower-bound estimates of the scale of the scar. Other studies point in the same direction: a lasting depressive effect on pay for those whose first brush with the labour market is during hard times.[27]

Furthermore, Kahn finds, 'cohorts who graduate in worse national economies are in lower-level occupations', and they remain stuck in low-grade jobs for longer.[28] Indeed, herein lies the mechanism that results in recession graduates being hammered for so long. In times marked out by caution and a shortage of opportunities, young workers shift between jobs less often, and that in turn means fewer chances to secure the pay rises and training that characterise the first working decade of luckier generations. All told, Kahn sums up, the effects of 'graduating from college in a bad economy are large, negative and persistent'.

So much for graduates. Taking account of everything we have learnt about the bottom end of the labour market, how much worse are the prospects of those who do not graduate, but simply drop out of education and into hard times? We do not know of any comparable long-range tracking studies, but the testimony of young men – such as former prisoner 'Nick', whom we spoke to in Nottingham, with his ten fruitless job applications in a fortnight – answers the question. As do the tales told by student 'Laura' of going home and meeting up with old schoolfriends who never made it out of deprived parts of town, like the Byker Wall estate. One girl 'messed around in her teens, but then, at 19 or 20 . . . decided "actually, you know what, I don't want to live on benefits, I want to go out and get a job"'. By then, however, as Laura explains, 'it was *too late*. She was trying to get a job in a pub, but because the pubs can employ 14-year-olds and pay them £3.00 an hour they are not going to employ someone at 20 who needs the minimum wage; she didn't have any experience on her CV, so it was just getting thrown out.' Eighty years ago, one unemployed man told Mirra Komarovsky: 'It's awful to be old and discarded at 40.'[29] How, then, to describe the fate of a young woman who lives in an economy that regards her as 'past it' at half that age?

Of course, the better-off – and even the middling – part of the rising cohort will not fare as dismally as that young woman from Byker Wall. But with home ownership out of reach, and those grim wage effects that extend indefinitely even for graduates, the great bulk of the rising generation will be saddled with hard times for a while to come. In the US, in particular, the recession only compounds the stagnation in middling wages that has now dragged on for half a lifetime. The *early* American baby boomers were the last cohort that could typically expect to enjoy higher living standards at any given age than the cohort that came before them.[30] In depressed Britain in 2011/12, the average adult slogs right through into his or her early forties and still lives with lower disposable income than the (substantially retired) cohort aged 60–65.[31] And whereas those workers who are today coming up to retirement age experienced positive wage growth over most of their careers, their children have now been getting slowly but steadily poorer for several straight years.

Consider the many burdens on young shoulders – the interrupted CVs, inadequate pensions, the student debt – then throw in the disproportionate growth of jobs in dead-end sectors, and it is not hard to see how the brave hopes of youth could give way to despair. Is that happening? Ipsos MORI provides intriguing evidence of growing pessimism. Using an experientially grounded variant of the question about whether the next generation will fare better than the last (it actually asks individuals whether their own generation is 'on course to fare or has already fared' better than their parents), the pollster finds a striking gap between four British cohorts: people born before or during the war; the 'boomers', defined as post-war babies who arrived in the world before 1965; Gen X, which runs from then until 1982; and Gen Y, which follows after that.

The figure below shows that the oldest cohort retains a striking confidence about life having got better; this confidence remains pretty strong among the 'boomers', but then declines sharply for the Gen Xers and, more particularly, for Gen Y. While it is true that there are still more optimists than pessimists in Gen Y (roughly today's twenty-somethings), the proportions (about 4:3) are fairly balanced, whereas among the oldest there is an emphatic 8:1 majority who believe that they are living better than their parents ever did. And growing economic pessimism among the young appears to go hand-in-hand with a deficit in those attitudes that foster a strong society, in particular trust. Other Ipsos MORI figures suggest a large – and seemingly growing – gulf between the cohorts on the question of faith in 'the

Growing pains: views of successive British cohorts on their own living standards relative to those of their parents

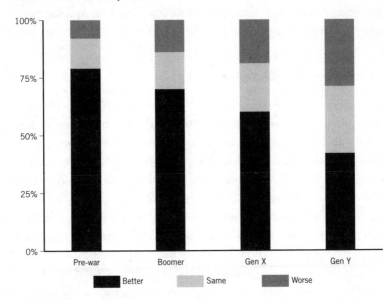

Source: Ipsos MORI.[32]

man or woman in the street' to 'tell the truth'. Back in 2007, such faith was already weaker among the young: 45% of Gen Y had faith in a passing stranger, compared to 53% of baby boomers. By 2013, however, this 8 percentage point gap had widened to 24 points.[33]

We do not have the same data for the United States, but YouGov's cross-country polling provides one or two indicators that point the same way. More of the young (57%) than the old (42%), for example, believe that 'the best jobs are always filled by those from the wealthiest families' – a little flicker, perhaps, of a fading faith in the American dream.[34]

Aristotle thought that youth was 'easily deceived, because it is quick to hope'. In today's hard times, the young would have to be deceived to an outlandish extent to avoid noticing the myriad disadvantages that have befallen them, and that look set to dog them in the years ahead. The polling, however, confirms that they have noticed – they are 'quick to hope' no longer, and instead have decidedly bleaker expectations of the future than their elders. In the light of everything we have learnt, there seems little prospect of this generational gloom gap being reversed any time soon. Both the experience and the expectations of the younger generation have darkened.

The unemployed: blood on the tracks

For a generation now, economists have understood that unemployment does not merely cause immediate financial pain, but can also leave scars that remain even after a new job is found. Forgone training opportunities, bosses' prejudice against gaps in CVs, and bad habits acquired on the dole can all dog those made redundant well into a recovery – and dent earnings even after they eventually find a new job. To this established understanding we wish to add an additional contention: that being knocked off the tracks leads not just to enduring loss of earning power, but to enduring misery and isolation, too.

Rutgers analysis of Americans who were unemployed in 2009 but had found new work by 2010 confirmed a persistent *economic* price had been paid: a clear majority (55%) had swallowed a pay cut, and in nearly half of these cases (26% of the total) it was a substantial pay reduction of more than one-fifth. One-third (33%) had taken a hit on non-salary benefits (such as pensions and healthcare) and a significant minority (15%) were working fewer hours than before.[35] Alongside these material sacrifices, the survey contained definite warning signs of enduring anxiety: a majority of these newly re-employed workers (59%) feared for the security of their new jobs. They were fully three times more likely than the workforce as a whole to report being dissatisfied with the sort of work they were doing.[36]

It is not hard to imagine redundancy imposing psychological wounds that will not heal quickly in these circumstances. For one thing, there is the pain of the downward mobility highlighted in the Rutgers survey; for another, there is the hurt of having been rejected by an employer, typically through no fault of one's own. A third factor, which could be just as important, is the shattering of one's sense of identity, to the extent that this is bound up with a particular type of work. All of these themes also emerge in conversation with Britons at the sharp end.

Workless 41-year-old 'Jamal', from the Isle of Dogs in East London, told us of his frustration at the job centre's disregard for his years of experience, and its failure to understand the sort of work that he does – and, by extension, who he is. 'I am a scaffolder/bricklayer,' he explains, 'and they were just giving me jobs like portering and working at a hospital. Do you know what I mean?' The feeling of being shunted into the wrong sort of work can be greatly intensified by thoughtless words from others. The sociologist Valerie Walkerdine examined what happened after the 'Steeltown' works in Wales shut up shop. She spoke to people who found being pushed into the wrong sort of work just as destructive to their identity as being shunted out of work in the first place. She recorded terrible testimony from a man whose pride was shattered when he lost out on the chance to wear the traditional donkey jacket of the foundry and instead had to don the red cap of the pizza delivery driver – and was then ridiculed by friends and family for doing so. His stepfather would ignore him in the street; his brothers would refuse him a lift; even his mother weighed in to explain how the uniform and the job were embarrassing everyone.[37]

So the *potential* for psychological scarring is certainly there; but encouragingly, our British data suggests that it is the exception rather than the rule. On the seven-point life satisfaction scale used by the British Household Panel Survey (incorporated into the broader Understanding Society study for the most recent years), people who were employed in both 2006/07 and 2010/11 but had experienced worklessness in between reported just a 0.1 point drop in satisfaction, from an average score of 5.1 to 5.0. This is an insubstantial change, and less than a quarter of the slide experienced by those who had fallen into ongoing unemployment.[38] These results are not quirks of the years we have compared: a quick glance at earlier years of the same tracking data reveals a contrast that is, if anything, even sharper between the recovery of the newly re-employed and the ongoing misery of the continuously unemployed.[39]

In America, by contrast, it looks as if the pain of redundancy is no passing pang: those thrown onto the scrapheap remain substantially more miserable than their peers, even after they have moved back into a job. In the Faith Matters tracking data (which uses a 1–10 point satisfaction scale) the decline among the newly re-employed workers between 2006 and 2010 comes in at 1.1 points, strikingly close to the fall of 1.2 points by those laid-off workers who remained unemployed.[40] This persistent misery on the part of America's newly re-employed cannot easily be explained by anything other than their disrupted experience of work. No decline in satisfaction was gripping wider society over these years; among the continually employed the score stood absolutely still between these two years.

The contrasting well-being of the newly re-employed in Britain and America is one of the most important transatlantic differences we have discovered. The data does not in itself *prove* why things should be so different, but there is one fairly obvious place to look for answers: the welfare state and associated labour market protections. As we have emphasised, flexible labour markets are very much a shared Anglo-American approach, but it is an approach that has gone further in the US, where there are more jobs with less protection. Taking minimum wage rates as an example of how much less, at autumn 2013 rates and currency conversions, the UK pay floor of £6.31 an hour is worth $9.78, considerably more than the federal minimum of $7.25 an hour that applies in the US, even though it is the richer country. When there is so far to fall economically between different jobs, simply finding new work may not so easily heal the scars of unemployment.

As for social security, in Chapter 2 we considered the OECD summary statistics, which showed that, whereas a typical unemployed British worker might expect to replace half his wages with various benefits, in the US the expectation would be more like a third or a quarter. There is not simply more money, but also a little more breathing space allowed in the UK. The rules are far from lax: the rates of the main unemployment benefit have been frozen in real terms since the 1970s, and payment has been made conditional on progressively more requirements ever since 1986.[41] But there are other significant British benefits, particularly for families with children, which come without the same strings attached. And while contributory (i.e. insurance-based) benefits are time-limited in both countries, another crucial difference is that in the UK the underlying safety net of means-tested benefits is available indefinitely, at least for those searching widely for work. That removes the threat of destitution, and so – whatever the strict notional obligations[42] – reduces the pressure to take an inappropriate job.

The recent drift of British welfare is pushing British social security in a remorselessly American direction, a dismaying trend to which we return in the next chapter. But analysis of scarring is necessarily retrospective, and so our data does not reflect the latest finger-jabbing strictures imposed on people looking for work. But the breathing space that the British system has traditionally provided in searching for work offers the most plausible explanation for why the psychological wounds of redundancy appear to heal after new work is found. In the United States, by contrast, even with a new job secured, all too often the wounds of redundancy morph into the scars of dead-end employment.

Moving from individual misery to a second important consequence of redundancy – withering involvement in the wider community – we uncover striking scars on both sides of the Atlantic. Taking Britain first, we can use the National Child Development Survey (NCDS) – a large British tracking survey that has followed the fortunes of every British individual born in a single week in March 1958 – to see how being laid off affects social engagement years after the event. The results are disturbing.

After controlling for the extent to which individuals participated in their youth, and also for myriad factors that may make someone a soft target for redundancy *and* reduce social involvement (e.g. family circumstances, IQ and original line of work), we establish that having been laid off *at any point* between the ages of 33 and 50 reduces the chances of someone volunteering at age 50 by 23%, relative to that person's peers.[43] Those made redundant in their thirties and forties are likewise 33% less likely to get involved with political protests or meetings, and 18% less likely to enjoy membership of civil or social groups, such as charitable or neighbourhood organisations.[44] All of these effects are statistically significant – that is, too powerful to be explained away by any random variation in the data.[45]

For the US, we do not have a nationally representative sample; but we do have information on around 10,000 people – a randomly selected third of all those who graduated from Wisconsin high schools in 1957. These people were mostly born in 1939/40, and the Wisconsin Longitudinal Survey has kept tabs on them ever since. With school dropouts excluded (by virtue of the sample's composition), and with a largely white cohort in one of America's more socially cohesive corners, the prospects of recovering from redundancy in community terms should be relatively bright among this group.[46] Again we adjust for potentially confounding factors, such as IQ and parental social class.[47] But again we discover that, for people laid off *at any point* between the ages of 35 and 53 (the ages here differ from those in the British analysis purely because of differences in the point at which respondents were interviewed), social and civic membership at age 53 is depressed by a statistically significant 29%, while the likelihood of involvement in sport and leisure clubs is 32% lower than among peers.[48] Years or even decades after being laid off, Americans who have been made redundant are indeed 'bowling alone'.

The next question is *why* we witness this enduring damage. Sociologists ever since Durkheim have suggested that working life helps to integrate people into the community more widely.[49] Some social organisations, from sports teams to choirs, are expressly linked to workplaces: so, lose your job and you are almost certainly cut off from these. Recall, however, that we are concerned with more lasting damage – damage that persists even for people who have found new work. There are multiple potential mechanisms. Two obvious candidates are: first, the downward mobility that can follow redundancy; and, second, the strain on (or break-up of) families. A third candidate, which – in the light of what we have already learnt – we might expect to apply more in the US, is enduring misery. A hard knock that operates through any of these channels – reduced status, divorce or a depressive turn – could well encourage people to hunker down and withdraw from voluntary commitments.

None of these mechanisms, however, can explain more than a small sliver of the persistent damage that we have witnessed. Controlling for the full range of these mediators – using indicators of family breakdown, economic position and 'psychological malaise' – weakens the link between redundancy and reduced community involvement by a mere fraction.[50] When it comes to membership of civic and social groups, for example, we can explain away only a third (31%) of the American scarring, and much less than that (13%) in the UK.[51] Clearly, the lasting damage that redundancy is doing to social lives is operating in some more distinctive way.

To see how being shunted out of a job actually shunts people out of civic life for years on end, we need first to recall the familiar idea of a career 'ladder' – an everyday idea that has found strong empirical support in the economics literature.[52] A good job allows us to build up earnings, status and security into early middle age, when things stabilise before we ease towards retirement. Although less familiar, it turns out that exactly the same pattern operates over the years in a healthy *citizenship career*, as depicted schematically in the graph overleaf. Half a century ago, the American sociologist Harold Wilensky was already describing 'participation careers' that paralleled and were 'linked to cycles of . . . work'.[53] Volunteering, group membership and much more have since been repeatedly shown to follow a pattern of starting low in one's early twenties and then steadily building to plateau, and perhaps decline, in later middle age.[54]

To be sure, different individual civic activities will assume different life-cycle trajectories: involvement with sports clubs will harness the energies of youth; PTAs the duties of parenthood; and professional associations the esteem of a well-established career. But consider the overall extent of engagement across the spectrum of community life, and you get the pattern shown. Campaigning teenagers and volunteering grannies will provide exceptions, of course, but most of us are destined to tread this sort of path through our community life – unless, of course, something knocks us off it. And that something could very well be hard times.

Get knocked off this 'citizenship career path' before middle age, at a stage when community participation would otherwise still be rising, and not only does civic involvement take an immediate hit, but – by being severed from the societal prompts and pressures that would otherwise draw you further into civic involvement – you actually end

Joining up while growing up: typical civic activity over the age range

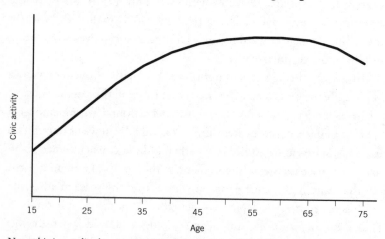

Note: this is a stylised representation of the findings of a whole series of studies.[55]

up *progressively* more cut off relative to your peers. For the reality is that so-called social capital is sticky stuff: if you're tangled up within a network, deeper involvement is likely; if you're outside it, it is not.

The point is best made with real data. We start by separating out individuals who have been made redundant at different stages of life, since – if the 'knocked off the path' explanation is important – we should expect most of the damage to be done to those who are laid off at ages when civic involvement would otherwise still have been developing. And this is exactly what we see. If we split up our UK data by the age at which redundancy occurred, the statistical connection with reduced civic and social membership at age 50 becomes almost twice as powerful among those laid-off before middle age; at the same time, however, the connection virtually disappears for those laid-off later on.[56] This is a remarkable result because it implies that the progressive process of scarring is such that the damage done actually intensifies over time – that is, more recent redundancies are doing less damage than those that took place longer ago.

The chart overleaf, which uses the British data, illustrates how this works. When a youngish individual is laid off, there is no immediate retreat from the social sphere. Rather, she initially parts company with her contemporaries only in terms of her failure to get *more* involved – by *not* enlisting in a PTA or a trade union at a time when her contemporaries will be doing so. Thus the effect is not at first dramatic, but her 'participation career' has been cut short. She ends up less networked than she otherwise would be in her forties and fifties, and also gets more isolated more quickly once engagement starts dwindling in later middle age.

Crunching our American data likewise reveals that redundancy in the earlier stages of working life explains all of the overall scarring effect that we found, and we can draw a very similar graph (overleaf) for the US. Three differences need to be noted. First, largely because of the more inclusive definition of civic/social organisations in the American data (which includes, for example, professional associations), the absolute percentages are now much higher. Second, as a result of the timing of the various waves of the panel survey, we have

Life-cycle sentence (a): how redundancy cuts short the 'participation careers' of Britons laid off before age 42

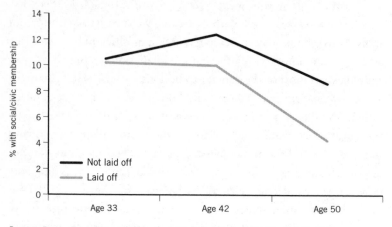

Source: James Laurence and Chaeyoon Lim's analysis of the National Child Development Survey.[57]

to define 'middle age' as older (age 53) here. Third, because of the earlier birth date of the Wisconsin cohort, we are able to track these individuals further through their lives. But for all these caveats, we can see in the figure opposite that the basic picture is the same. Americans who end up being laid off are not initially any less likely to be involved in community groups than are their peers. As the years go by, however, a substantial gulf in participation opens up – 8 percentage points by age 53. And this gap persists to some degree into older age.

The only apparent difference with the story in Britain is that by the time of the final observation, in the US the difference is narrowing rather than widening, which could very well reflect nothing more than the fact that we have followed these American individuals further through life. These results place a nagging question mark over those reassuring overall trends in US formal volunteering that we documented in Chapter 6; with scarring that surfaces as slowly as this, it could be that we are yet to see the Great Recession's real effect.

Intriguingly, it turns out that it is the fact of being laid off – the dashing of expectations – that does the damage, rather than the

Life-cycle sentence (b): how redundancy cuts short the 'participation careers' of Americans laid off before age 53

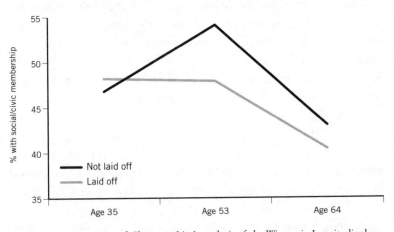

Source: James Laurence and Chaeyoon Lim's analysis of the Wisconsin Longitudinal Survey.[58]

experience of unemployment in other circumstances (say, after college or after having had a child).[59] This detail is suggestive of the particular dangers of the social contract unravelling. Every child is raised to believe that if you work hard, you will do OK. When a job disappears for reasons that are unrelated to how well it was being done, a grievance against the world can develop which does not quickly disappear: middle-aged folk who have been laid off at *any point* are appreciably less trusting than their peers.[60] And at the same time, we have seen that they hunker down, joining fewer groups and volunteering less – with the dismal result that, having been knocked onto a different track in life, these isolating differences do not diminish, but can actually grow with time.

All the grim results we have presented are after adjusting for the various disadvantages that those made redundant tend to start out with (poorer education and so on). But there will, of course, be considerable variation in the number of redundancies across different communities. Consequently – in common with every other social pathology we have considered – the scars imposed on the social fabric will affect less prosperous communities more than others. The last chapter suggested that the British appetite for doing things together had shrivelled along with the economy in 2008; but it also reported – on the basis of the latest nationwide data – that the corner might finally have been turned. The upshot of this chapter's analysis, however, is that in the more depressed regions of both Britain and America, sick roots will long lurk beneath green shoots.

The withering of spontaneous kindness in the face of recession (as charted in the previous chapter) was frightening enough. It was suggested that two societies – both once admired for their civility – had tended to atomise in the face of hard times. The added insight that redundancy can knock people onto a life-long path that leads towards a more isolated future darkens the picture still further. The implication is that the grip of hard times will be felt for many years after the pink pages of the *Financial Times* hail a recovery.

Future generations: your children will be next

The greatest comfort in hard times ought to be the thought of better days ahead – and most especially the thought of a better future for our children. We have seen that the immediate faith in renewed prosperity has been tested by a full decade (or, in the American case, by several decades) in which the incomes of ordinary people have failed to grow with the economy. We have learnt, too, of the particularly grim prospects for today's young adults. But what of the more distant horizon? Perhaps the faith that might still pull society through austere times is the faith that the *next* generation of youngsters can – as they mature – cast off individual family hardship and the shared experience of economic depression, and somehow get ahead.

Certainly, this seems to be the hope that our politicians are banking on. Barack Obama, David Cameron and Gordon Brown have all waxed lyrical about increased social mobility, the idea known – in less jargon-laden times – as the 'ladder of opportunity'. The rhetoric is used loosely, to refer to subtly different ideals. Sometimes, the point made is simply that every individual should get a fair roll of the dice – with the logical (if unspoken) implication that, as more people climb the ladders, so more should slide down the snakes. Sometimes the thought expressed is the unalloyed hope that more of the next generation will somehow be able to get on. The research has something to say about both these things, and it has been attracting a great deal of attention on both sides of the Atlantic – because things have not been looking too good on the upward mobility front.

Before we even get to the question of how the slump is stifling opportunities for today's children, there are the dismal underlying dynamics of the last several decades to consider. In the post-war era, the great shift from an industrial to a service economy, and the attendant proliferation of middle-management positions, turned many a blue collar white, on both sides of the Atlantic. In Britain, at least, there is hard data to show that this enabled aggregate upward movement on the social schema. Such mobility, however, slowed after the great transformation gave way to a post-industrial steady state,[61] and in time a boom in bottom-end jobs followed. As for movements in and out of *relative* economic brackets – where steps up and down must inevitably cancel out one another overall – one widely cited analysis suggests that fewer Gen Xers (born in 1970) than baby boomers (born in 1958) have risen from the station in life that they started from.[62] It is true that there are other measures, and some show stability rather than worsening sclerosis;[63] but – given Britain's traditional image as a class-bound society – it is disappointing indeed that there is no evidence of the old hierarchies loosening their grip.

As for the US, the belief in the possibility of upward mobility is almost a foundational myth – a point underlined by the fact that the same idea is sometimes referred to as the 'American dream'. But the current administration in Washington is at pains to point out that the celebrated possibility of a young man or woman making it from log cabin to White House are today frighteningly remote. In a 2012 speech, the chairman of Barack Obama's Council of Economic Advisers, Alan Krueger, set out the statistics and observed frankly that the correlation (i.e. the statistical connection) of 0.5 between parental income and the earning power of the child in adulthood was 'remarkably similar to the correlation that Sir Francis Galton found between parents' height and their children's height over 100 years ago'. To illuminate the power of the link, he encouraged his audience to think about the relative stature of father–son pairs that they knew:

> The chance of a person who was born to a family in the bottom 10 percent of the income distribution rising to the top 10 percent as an adult is about the same as the chance [of] a dad who is 5'6" tall having a son who grows up to be over 6'1" tall. It happens, but not often.[64]

Through an innovation he christened the 'Great Gatsby Curve', Krueger also attempted to nail one particular lie – peddled by, among others, Nick Clegg, the Liberal Democrat deputy prime minister in Britain's Coalition – that rough justice about who gets what today will be righted by equal opportunities for the future.[65] The Great Gatsby Curve (in reality more of a straight line) traces the connection across different countries between, on the one hand, historic inequality, and on the other, class rigidity. The former is measured by a summary statistic (the Gini coefficient) of the gap in household incomes in 1985; the latter by the strength of the link between what a father earns and what his son goes on to bring home – the so-called 'elasticity' of intergenerational income. The graph opposite plots the two things together and reveals that, in countries where income is more unequally spread, the next generation enjoys less mobility; it also shows that Britain is a rare western country where opportunities are almost as unequal as in the US.

To understand how the relationship works, think of a wealthy parent (who has enjoyed bumper pay rises over several decades) stumping up for a Master's course or professional training for his son that will, in time, secure him a good living. Then think of a bright young woman with working-class parents who would love to help, but whose long years of stagnant pay preclude any possibility of making the same investment.

One problem with the use of social mobility metrics in public policy is that, as a phenomenon that plays out over entire generations, it can only ever be observed deep in the rear-view mirror: the earning power of the children of the 1980s and 1990s is only now starting to be seen. For the type of politician who is intensely relaxed about privilege, there is little possibility of being held to account, and therein lies the attraction. But today's administration in Washington seems genuinely concerned, and – on the basis of what has happened to the dispersion of American family incomes since the 1980s – hazards a guess at where social mobility is headed.

Krueger's analysis (now prominently displayed in an interactive on the White House website) suggests that rising inequality will further shrivel the possibilities of opportunity in America, prospectively pushing the link between parental and child earnings up from an 'elasticity' score just short of 0.5 to one just short of 0.6. This is highlighted in the chart, with the label 'US (projected)'.[66]

From generation to generation: unequal parents breed kids with unequal chances

Source: Estimates of intergenerational elasticity collated by Miles Corak; Gini coefficients from OECD.[67]

With even the White House effectively warning that an already class-bound American society is set to seize up further, rising mobility is looking like a decidedly over-optimistic answer to hard times in the US. There has also been debate during the downturn about dismantling class barriers in Britain, but it has been disproportionately taken up with questions about access to a few top jobs and colleges. That might seem weird in the light of all we have learnt about the concentration of disadvantage at the bottom of society during the slump; but one only needs to look at what has been happening in British public life to understand why.

If the American dream is about boys born in log cabins making it to the White House, it is Henry VI's dreams for Eton that are the mark of modern Britain. As of 2013, the prime minister, the next king but one, the Archbishop of Canterbury, the chief whip, the chief of staff at No. 10 Downing Street and the chief economic adviser at No. 11 all attended this same boys-only school, where fees are currently £32,000 a year. That summer, when David Cameron moved to 'broaden his circle' with new policy advisers, it was to two more Etonians that he turned.[68]

Yet if we cast such gripes aside, and take the concerns about social mobility at face value, then the priority must surely be to tackle social sclerosis at the bottom of the heap. And in the aftermath of the biggest slump in living memory, the single most pressing priority would have to be to ensure that unemployment does not become an inherited curse. In both the UK and the United States, however, our new analysis of long-range tracking data reveals that worklessness is precisely that: a child raised in a home where the parents experience a big gap between jobs is herself more likely to end up without work.

This effect can be seen by focusing on girls. Girls are worth singling out because they can be pushed off course in two ways: by following an unfortunate parental example of unemployment, or by getting pregnant and themselves becoming parents too young. Low expectations of the world of work can encourage them to embark on either of these routes, both of which will lead them away from whatever bright prospects they may have had. The figure opposite looks at British and American girls raised by working parents and those from workless homes. For the UK, the data is from the same 1958 cohort study (the National Child Development Survey) that we used in the analysis of scarring in civic life; for the US, however, we exploit a different, nation-wide sample of people born a few years later, in the early 1960s, from the National Longitudinal Survey of Youth. While these Britons and Americans were all born into the very different post-war world of full employment, the young women of this generation had their early experience of work in the decidedly 'hard times' context of the early 1980s labour market.

Taking the UK data first, British girls raised in 'workless homes'[69] spent on average 14% more of their total time as young adults without a job than did their peers from working homes; between the ages of 16 and 29 that adds up to a difference of about 1 year 10 months. In the United States, the effect is similar, or in fact a little greater: girls from

Like father, like daughter: young women from workless homes spend more of young adulthood out of work

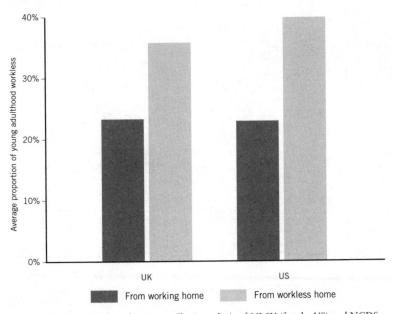

Source: Paul Gregg and Lindsey Macmillan's analysis of NLSY (for the US) and NCDS (for the UK).[70]

workless homes spent some 17% more of their young adulthood workless than the rest of their cohort; between the ages of 16 and 29 that adds up to a little over two additional years. The total proportion of this phase of their lives that these American women spent without work was nearly 40%, or just over five years.

Not all of that time without work need necessarily have been wasted; some of it might reflect study, or a positive decision to have children. It is thus also important to consider unemployment more narrowly, as it is a more reliable indicator of wasted time. And it is an especially instructive indicator in the case of young men, who are less likely to drop out of the labour force because of parenthood. In the figure below all the proportions are now lower, largely because we are using this narrower criterion. But the gap between young men coming from homes of different sorts is just as marked as for young women. In

The 'hard times' inheritance: young men with jobless parents spend more of their own time unemployed

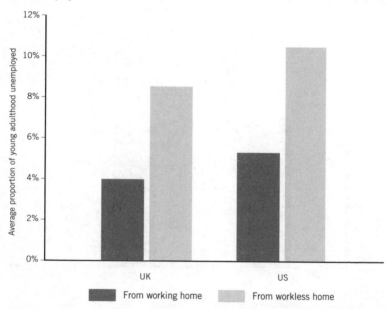

Source: Paul Gregg and Lindsey Macmillan's analysis of NLSY (for the US) and NCDS (for the UK).[71]

both countries, the proportion of young adulthood spent unemployed is roughly twice as high for those who grew up in workless homes: in Britain, such young men spent 4.5% more of their total time workless than did their peers; in the US, there was a similar gap of 5.1%.

How robust are these results? All the effects we report are statistically significant (i.e. inexplicable by sampling variation). Beyond that, the general finding of heritability is rock solid in this data. It applies however the problem is framed – whether we look only at jobless fathers or at single mothers, too; at sons or at daughters; and whether we focus on unemployment narrowly defined or worklessness more generally. For every permutation examined, those who grow up in workless homes are both substantially and statistically significantly more likely to end up without gainful employment themselves.[72]

The strongest remaining potential objection is that, in this data concerning British and American baby boomers, the results could flow from some distinct facet of one particular cohort. But consideration of another (younger) British generation – Gen Xers – using a second tracking survey merely reinforces the results.[73] However the calculation is done for this younger cohort, the penalty for having been raised workless is always on a par with, and sometimes greater than, the penalty suffered by the 'boomer' generation.

The heritability of joblessness, then, is hard to dispute. Unlike many of the maladies we have uncovered, there will be no need to persuade the political Right that this problem exists. Indeed, if anything the tendency is to exaggerate it – to suggest that the poor live in a parallel culture with different norms, something that Ronald Reagan implied when he summoned up the bogeywoman of the 'Welfare Queen' during his unsuccessful tilt for the White House in 1976.[74] And in the UK of today, Work and Pensions Secretary Iain Duncan Smith has spoken of whole communities in which nobody in three generations has worked. These are overblown and misleading claims.[75] They also wrongly imply that there are places so permanently downtrodden and marginalised that hard times can come and go without making much difference. The reality, as was laid bare in Chapter 3, is that downtrodden groups' chances of working are invariably *more* susceptible to the cycle than the chances of anyone else. Consideration of how the heritability of unemployment is affected by depressed labour markets reinforces the message that the economic cycle counts for an awful lot where the children of disadvantaged homes are concerned.

For, like ethnic minorities and school dropouts, the children of the unemployed turn out to be one more group that gets thrown out on its ear more quickly when the economy turns downward. The simplest way to see this is to examine the proportion of booming and of slumpish years that people from different backgrounds spend without work. Taking the British baby boomers first, the sons of unemployed fathers were always less likely to be gainfully employed: we find that, in a typical year, they spent on average about 10% of their time without work, 5 percentage points more than young men from working homes. In slumps, like the great shake-out of the early 1980s, everybody spends more time without work. But whereas the average proportion of time that young men from working homes passed without work rose by only 3 points (up from about 5% to about 8%), for those whose fathers had also gone without work, the already higher proportion of the year spent jobless shot up by *twice as much*, to peak at over 20%.[76]

In the UK, it would seem, hard times chiefly get visited upon those whose parents also experienced them. We find the same pattern in the US, where the early 1980s recession added around 5 points to the proportion of the year that men from working homes spent jobless, but around 7 points in the case of the already disadvantaged group, whose fathers had previously been without a job. In the early 1990s downturn, too, the proportion of time that these disadvantaged men spent without work again soared by 7–8 points, while for the luckier group whose fathers had always been employed, worklessness rose by no more than a couple of points.[77]

The heartening corollary of all these gloomy statistics about the divisive effect of recession is that, *contra* the underclass thesis, strong recoveries ought to do most for the employment prospects of those from workless homes. Far from these people being beyond the reach of the business cycle, economic conditions – for good or ill – are most important for their prospects. Drilling down into the variation across towns and cities further confirms that, more than anything, it is the health of the local labour market that determines the prospects of the children of the unemployed. In a boom year in, say, Surrey, in Britain's stockbroker belt, our analysis suggests that a young man with a jobless father faces no penalty at all; a similar young man, however, is hit hard in a bad year in depressed Blaenau Gwent in Wales – doomed to spend 30% more of his total time jobless than a friend from a working home. In the United States, the strength of the link between workless fathers and workless sons turns out to be three times more powerful in a good year in, say, Bismarck, North Dakota, where unemployment is low, than in the middle of a slump in stricken Stockton, California.[78]

All this is yet another way of demonstrating the selective path of destruction taken by the economic tornado: when hard times re-appear, they will tend to hit those same clans who have previously suffered from the effects of recessions past. Our final challenge in this chapter is to figure out why. The political Right likes to emphasise endemic as opposed to epidemic worklessness because this fits with its view that the root cause of the problem is a sprawling welfare system, whose good intentions have grown warped. Within the supposedly stifling grip of social security, as the so-called 'welfare dependency' theory holds, parents are seduced into idle ways, and their offspring are culturally conditioned by this poor example during their youth, before falling prey to the same temptation to 'slob about' on the sofa when they grow up.

The facts we have uncovered thus far do not fit well with this story. If there really were a problematic culture of dependency, this would be a deep structural problem, beyond the reach of the comings and goings of the cycle; and yet we have learnt that the swings of the economy are, in fact, *especially* important for the children of the unemployed.

Furthermore, if excessive social security were indeed the root cause, one would expect to see less hereditary worklessness in the US. For social security there has always been less comprehensive: married mothers have never had general recourse to income support, and the meagre assistance available to lone parents has long been tied to stiff work-search requirements (requirements that have only very recently been partially mimicked in the UK).[79] And yet, a look back at the last couple of graphs suggests that the cast-iron link between growing up in a jobless home and ending up without work is at least as marked in America as it is in Britain. It is a fair summary of the exhaustive underlying statistical analysis to say that there is no meaningful difference in the power of the heritability effect on the two sides of the Atlantic.[80] One of Mr Duncan Smith's Conservative predecessors in the early 1990s, Peter Lilley, damned 'young ladies who get pregnant just to jump the housing list';[81] but if there is a culture of inherited worklessness, it applies just as much to American young ladies, who have few expectations of public housing or other state help. The familiar 'welfare dependency' tale explains nothing at all.

If supposedly generous British benefits are not to blame, then what is? The marked variation in inherited disadvantage between different local labour markets might be taken as implying that more willingness to clamber onto the coach – or, in the famous phrase of 1980s Britain, to 'get on yer bike' – would help. Once again, however, the easy theory falls flat when we glance across the Atlantic. Americans *do* move about much more, and yet, as we have seen, they inherit at least as much disadvantage.[82] That can only be because the real damage is done not across sink estates or dead-end towns, but *within* demoralised homes. It is there that the bad habits and stunted aspirations are formed; they in turn determine (among other things) the course of education.

One logical possibility is that the underlying abilities or dispositions of the sorts of parents who end up unemployed might inculcate disadvantage within the family, irrespective of whether they work or not. In line with what we learnt in Chapter 3, for example, it is very likely that unemployed parents will have less education; and it could be that a lack of learning, rather than a lack of work, renders them less effective in fostering the attitudes that will eventually help their children secure and hold down a job. An interesting theory, but one that the data knocks flat: adjusting for such underlying factors explains at most one-third of the disadvantage that gets passed on.[83] This is not a story of predictable things happening to the usual sorts of people, any more than it is a story of lavish benefits or the culture of dead-end towns. None of these stories can account for why the booming and busting of the economy matters as much as it does.

Instead, it seems as though an unemployed dad puts something in his child's backpack that weighs him down wherever he goes – and especially in hard times. Lessons learnt earlier on in this book offer insight into how this works. In a depressed labour market, where opportunities are scarcer, self-belief and optimism probably count for more. Fathers rendered psychologically depressed by unemployment (a danger that Chapter 5 laid bare) are not well placed to inculcate these dispositions. Another likely mechanism is the severing of parental social networks – something else that (as we have established) can be a marked and enduring consequence of redundancy. This matters for the next generation because of the well-documented reality that many young people find their jobs through such networks: one American male in five finds his job through older men in the family.[84] When jobs are scarce, they become precious, and so are especially likely to be dished out to friends and relatives – and thus the direct link between a parent's place of work and a child's opportunity is indeed demonstrably stronger in hard times.[85]

The most intense disadvantage faced by the children of the workless is not passed on through any financial channel, then. Having an unemployed father would not induce 'rational economic man' to sprawl on the sofa. Rather, it is a tale of psychological frailty and corroded social networks – a story that would have been all too familiar to the children of Marienthal. And in unequal societies like Britain and especially America, where unemployment so often leads to hardship, exclusion and misery, it would be rash to bet against this story being played out again and again.

The specific risk that youngsters from workless homes will end up unemployed themselves is, we believe, beyond argument. But what about the prospects for the offspring of those who are struggling through in low-grade work? As we saw in Chapter 4, with the casualisation of contracts, the line separating the working and the workless is not what it was in the Anglo-Saxon economies. We learnt, too, that – looking a long way ahead, far into the recovery – projections for employment growth suggest that those middling jobs and skilled trades which traditionally provided a step up from the bottom will likely remain hard to come by.

If today's children of janitors and cleaners are to get ahead, then, for most of them at least, there is probably only one route open: education. Not all the signs are bad here; in particular, the significant extra resources and attention devoted to schooling poor children around the turn of the century in Britain appear to have paid dividends. By 2008, the old cast-iron link between parental income and exam results finally appeared to be rusting;[86] and in 2010, for the first time in the long expansion of higher education, most of the extra places were being grabbed by children from poor homes.[87] But English university fees have since been sharply increased, and – more recently – the increased maintenance bursaries for poorer students that Coalition Liberal Democrats had initially secured to compensate for the higher fees have themselves been earmarked for cut-backs. Put everything together, and it cannot be assumed that the benign trends in access to college before the slump will continue.[88] The latest estimates from the United States suggest that the average student borrower is graduating with debts of $26,600, a figure that fuels the ongoing rumbles about college finances reaching crisis point.[89]

Faced with this sort of daunting financial calculation in hard times, young people will be particularly influenced by the advice of their family. In unequal societies, such as Britain and America, some parents are far better placed than others to give the right advice. Among all the poor and unemployed Britons we spoke to, we found a strong commitment to coaching children to better themselves. In several, however, we found advice that more privileged parents would regard as hopelessly outdated. Workless scaffolder 'Jamal', for example, tells his daughter that she would be 'better off getting experience' first, before dashing off to university. Unemployed 'Winston', a committed parent, says he will impress upon his young son the importance of acquiring 'a manual skill' as opposed to just mental skills, 'because those things you can take anywhere in the world'. It is an understandable belief, but one that is hard to sustain in the face of the projections we have looked at for the pattern of jobs growth in the coming recovery.

Earlier on in our Harvard–Manchester collaboration, interviews were also conducted with working-class families in America about their aspirations for their children, and the way that they guided them through the end of compulsory schooling.[90] Anxiety about how to foot college fees was ubiquitous, but the determination to ensure that they somehow got paid, and the faith that the investment would pay off in the end, were heavily influenced by parents' own experience of working life.

We can illustrate the point by peeking within just one home in Kensington, Philadelphia. When interviewed, father 'Pete' was content enough with his work as a despatcher at the fire department; by contrast his wife 'Sally', who had once started training in New York to be a gemologist, had effectively been forced to give up work, and all hopes of a career, when overwhelmed by the demands of motherhood.

Whereas 'Pete' was gung-ho about the future of their 'smart' teenage son 'George' ('I told him . . . you've got to start planning for college *now*'), 'Sally' sounded a despondent note about the prospects of anyone from their part of town. With one working parent and one who has given up work, 'George' might be OK. But to see how the mechanisms of social sclerosis start to grind, just imagine what would have become of his prospects if his father had been made redundant and had become similarly pessimistic. Hard times are visiting precisely this sort of story on homes across the economy. The effects will not quickly fade.

This chapter has established the enduring effect of hard times on the hopes, the happiness and the community life of poorer homes. To continue our extended meteorological metaphor, it is as if a passing rainstorm has set off the gradual corrosion of those beams and girders that previously supported ambitions and social structures in the disadvantaged parts of town.

A tale of two tragedies

The storm has blown just as hard as it did in the 1930s, but this
time the weak have been shielded . . . Individual men and women have
been able to turn in their hour of need to a community which shows
some compassion.

These are not words that anyone who has reached this stage of this
book would utter about our own hard times. They were, in fact, used
by British politician Michael Foot in connection with the economic
ravages of an earlier decade, in an address to the voters of Ebbw Vale
in 1979.[1] The societal shielding that he referred to was the product of
reforms he had witnessed in his political youth. These reforms were
inspired by the best-selling, welfare-state-shaping Beveridge Report,
which, though published in wartime a decade on from the trough, was
arguably the delayed distillation of the lessons Britain drew from the
Great Depression. When that same crisis first deepened in the US, the
governor of New York and future president, Franklin Roosevelt,
summoned the state legislature not only to demand financial relief for
the poor, but also to set out a new philosophical basis for providing it:

In broad terms I assert that modern society, acting through its
government, owes the definite obligation to prevent the . . . dire

want of any of its fellow men and women who try to maintain themselves but cannot . . . not as a matter of charity but as a matter of social duty.[2]

For all Foot's hopes, however, there was to be no return to the spirit of Beveridge, or indeed Roosevelt, in 1979. Instead, Margaret Thatcher swept into Downing Street in the British election of that year, before Foot himself went on to lead the Labour party into oblivion at the ballot boxes in 1983 – the moment that finally buried a post-war settlement founded on that ideal of compassion in the hour of need. Between these two British elections, a third had taken place across the Atlantic and brought Ronald Reagan to power.

The drift of the next 30 years is familiar. Of course, there are important and distinct qualifications to be made about particular policies on either side of the ocean, but there is a good deal of truth in the common caricature of the post-1980s age as an era of deregulation, deunionisation and the squeezing, freezing and dismantling of various post-war social protections.[3] The programme of the New Right was controversial at every pass; but it won sufficient victories and became sufficiently associated with the perception of prosperity for it to survive, in modified form, after the partisan pendulum finally swung away from its instigators. We have seen how inequality surged to the point where the real incomes of very many stagnated; and yet, for enough of the people, enough of the time, living standards did rise. For the rest – all those Americans, and latterly Britons as well, whose pay packets did not share in the proceeds of growth – there was a burgeoning range of options for credit.

Anglo-American societies did not always seem healthy: Robert Putnam's *Bowling Alone* recorded the withering of American community life, and the new science of happiness suggested that the rising average wealth of society was doing little to reduce the misery quotient. But the political mainstream regarded these insights as quirky caveats attached to more general principles about the unique efficacy of running things on individualistic lines. The great inflation of the 1970s had, after all, exposed Foot's old order as bankrupt, and so – like the

Cold War before it, and the British Empire before that – the New Right's 'post-post-war' settlement had slowly developed an air of permanence by the time the slump arrived.

And then, one might have imagined, everything would have changed. After all, the last time the economic gale had hit with such force, the eventual political result was that New Deal agenda (and its delayed British equivalent) of building shared shelters and levelling society a little. At the same time, government had embraced a responsibility to provide jobs – implicitly, through American New Deal make-work schemes from 1933 onwards, and explicitly, in Britain's 1944 Employment White Paper.[4] The approach had reflected the understanding that the right way for society to weather the storm was for the community to come together, to pool resources and risk.

The evidence we have reviewed about the human consequences of hard times renew and reinvigorate this old argument. For direct impoverishment brought on by recession is compounded by the knock-on effects of financial anxiety on individual well-being, family and community life; the imperative of avoiding enduring societal damage further strengthens the case for shielding the vulnerable in their hour of need. We have shown that the minimalist American welfare state offers none of the supposed protection against an inherited dependency culture, and yet does allow the blow of redundancy to fester into an enduring scar. One might, then, have hoped that any politician worth his or her salt would be scrambling to update and apply the great risk-pooling principles of the mid-twentieth century. That, however, is very far from what we have had. In certain respects, it has felt instead as if policy has returned to 1929/30.

It is important not to exaggerate here. The world has *not* experienced an economic collapse on the scale of America's Great Depression, and this is largely because certain important economic lessons have been learnt – in particular, the imperative of avoiding deflation, if needs be by cutting interest rates to zero and printing money. In relation to the fiscal aspect of policy, too – where the state's direct role in pump-priming demand and redistributing resources bears more directly on our societal concerns – certain technical lessons have also been learnt, though these have been absorbed much more falteringly.[5] It is the great social and political lesson of the 1930s warning of the perils of throwing the vulnerable to the dogs, that has been forgotten.

Both Britain and America have ended up leaving the victims of hard times out in the cold; but they have done so because of very different decisions taken at very different times. We must acknowledge that the narratives diverge, and so consider the two sides of the Atlantic separately here. Very crudely, the United States erred through the gradual demolition of shared societal shelters in the years *before* the storm hit, but then made at least some sort of effort at a collective clean-up of the worst of the rubble. The UK, by contrast, fell into the slump with much better support structures in place; it is in the *aftermath* that it has made a fetish of knocking them down. We will consider these sorry tales in turn.

American neglect

Remember the sanguine interpretation of the slump that we encountered in Chapter 1 – the reading that stated that recessions were no more than passing ripples on a tide of prosperity? This prosperity ultimately flowed from technology, and was – so the argument ran – steadily doing away with real poverty. At one distant time this was the optimistic creed of centrist America, but for several decades before the bust, public policy was actively working to ensure that the rising economic tide did *not* lift all boats.

A simple, if very crude, way to make the point is to examine one public policy that is targeted at those at the bottom of the heap: the minimum wage. The graph overleaf adjusts for purely inflationary price rises over the decades since the end of the Second World War, but makes no allowance for relativities with other workers, or indeed for the tripling of national output per head over this time. This is the *real* wage rate – a straightforward gauge of how much actual stuff you can buy with the proceeds of an hour of low-paid labour. It is clear that most of the movement has been downward since it peaked at (in today's terms) somewhere over $10 an hour in 1968. It was eaten away by inflation during the Reagan years, falling to a real rate of just over $6 – a real minimum wage last seen in the mid-1950s. The steady march of inflation soon ate up small subsequent increases, and in 2006 it fell as low as $5.87, a federally licensed rate of poverty pay not seen since the 1940s. It is true that the rate was subsequently nudged up, and in his 2013 State of the Union address, President Obama proposed that it should rise again, although the instant dismissal of the idea by Republican House Speaker John Boehner revealed the likely insurmountable obstacles in the way of it becoming law.[6] The president returned to the theme in 2014, but as things stand, the minimum wage remains well below the $8.46 real rate that prevailed in 1956 – bang in the middle of the Eisenhower era.

Economic conservatives would argue that we are meandering a long way from the cause and the consequences of hard times. They would point out (reasonably) that minimum wage rates tell us little about poverty, unless we also consider how many people are paid them,[7] and would insist (more dubiously) that any higher minimum wage would have deepened the downturn, by pricing people out of jobs. But the real point of the story about what Washington allowed to happen to the minimum wage is what it betrays about the official attitude to poverty since the 1970s. Withholding from the smallest pay

The rise and fall of the US minimum wage since the Second World War

Source: Minimum wage rates from US Department of Labor, deflated by CPI from MeasuringWorth.[8]

packets all the benefit of the last 60 years of economic growth indicates a malign passivity towards the lowliest living standards – an attitude that has prevailed ever since Ronald Reagan shrugged off the activism of the 1960s with the claim 'we fought a war on poverty, and poverty won'.[9] Such defeatism has gone on to infect the range of public policy.

Ever since the 1970s, the real value of the American safety net, such as it was – always strictly limited to families with children – was allowed to sag steadily as prices rose, losing as much as 40% of its purchasing power by the mid-1990s.[10] The most devastating damage, however, was done with the welfare 'reform' legislation signed by President Clinton in 1996. Smugly hailed in Washington as a triumph of bipartisan co-operation, the Personal Responsibility and Work Opportunity Reconciliation Act ended the idea of welfare as an entitlement: it cut claims off cold after two years and imposed a cumulative *lifetime* limit of five years on multiple claims. Having established that hard times tend to hammer the same people – the black, the unschooled and so on – in repeated recessions, the impoverishing potential effect of a lifetime restriction ought to be plain. Just as significantly, the Act replaced federally funded income support with cash-limited block grants, which states were much freer to administer (or, in many cases, maladminister) as they saw fit. Some have added shin-kicking requirements (for example, for people to apply for dozens of jobs that they had no chance of getting), in order to discourage poor families from claiming the inadequate help that remains.[11]

Within the ludicrously narrow criterion that Washington set – reducing the number of people being helped (or, in the parlance, 'on the welfare rolls') – the legislation was bound to be the triumph it proved.[12] The number of families on welfare duly fell from a peak of 5.1 million in 1994 to just over 1.6 million in June 2008, and at first this appeared to be at least in large part because more people were getting jobs. But a report for the British government, on experience of work-related conditions for benefits around the world, cited a large number of academic studies of the American reforms, *all* of which suggest that the combined effect of America's late-1990s boom and more generous tax credits were more important for employment than the new welfare rules.[13] Just how much more important would become plain over the course of the Great Recession, which suddenly pushed the labour market participation of lone parents back by a decade, and their actual employment rates back further still.[14] In the words of one non-partisan think tank concerned with California (admittedly a state that has been hard hit, but also the most populous state in the Union), 'in just three years, the downturn erased *all* of the employment gains that single mothers made following the implementation of welfare reform'.[15]

Turning from employment to poverty, the structural damage wrought by the 1990s reforms was initially disguised by the booming economy at the end of that decade, because most – though by no means all – of those denied help could find some sort of work instead. As the comprehensive review of the pre-recession American evidence for the British government observes, even at this time only a minority of those who left the welfare rolls had year-round employment or basic entitlements such as sick pay.[16] Striking proportions of welfare leavers, preliminary Census Bureau analysis found, ended up working as cleaners, janitors and household servants.[17] Here, perhaps, the destruction of welfare entitlements was playing its part in reordering the American world of work, bringing it in line with newly unequal underlying realities. But, even with the economy still humming, a significant minority of at least 10% of 'leavers' (the precise figure depends on the particular study) disappeared from the system, and ended up reporting no earnings whatsoever.

With the ultimate safety net withdrawn – and OECD tables showing a cold zero for the proportion of a low wage that a long-term unemployed family can get replaced, compared with a British figure of 56% – the thought of job loss became more frightening.[18] Then the great storm arrived. Jobs disappeared, and the poor of America found that they suddenly had something more than fear itself to worry about: namely, penury. We described the official statistics in Chapter 2, but to recap: the number of Americans below Washington's own official breadline (31 million in 2000) surged to 46 million in the hard times of 2010 – and the latest figures available suggest that this is exactly where that figure remains. Of course, not all of this rise in poverty was about

Temporary Assistance for Needy Families strictures and time limits; but they did play a role in making hard times harder, and several studies have found that they bite disproportionately on school drop-outs and African Americans.[19] The tendency of the private economy to hammer such groups in the recession was thus not ameliorated, but rather redoubled by the thrust of public policy.

So how do all these American families both without work and denied welfare survive? Sheila Zedlewski and her colleagues interviewed nearly a hundred extremely poor families who had fallen through the widening holes in the US safety net *before* the recession. They discovered shame, deprivation, chronically untreated health problems and occasional homelessness. It is fair to say that things were pretty bad. Sometimes, however, a mix of support from relatives (which most of the families enjoyed to some extent) and casual work for friends and relatives, such as babysitting, allowed them to get by.[20]

After the recession, however, a separate study by Kristin Seefeldt found that both the family handouts and the casual work lifelines were fraying.[21] Interviewing poor or vulnerable African American single mothers in Detroit, Seefeldt found some women like 'Tamara', who was increasingly reluctant to ask relatives for help in hard times (because 'everybody's in the same boat as me') and others like 'Carol', who had discovered that there was no longer any point asking – her mother, who used to help out, had now told her bluntly: 'I ain't got no money for you.' Previous opportunities for informal work – cooking, hair-braiding and childcare – also diminished with the recession. The emerging response to extreme poverty in hard times is, as Seefeldt emphasises, not really a sustainable strategy at all: it is to fund some everyday living costs through credit and to evade others by systematic underpayment of bills; and then – when the debt collectors come calling – to tell them (in the words of 'Adrienne') 'I don't have it right now'.

The most obvious danger of a policy that leaves large numbers with nothing (except perhaps in-kind support, such as food stamps) is immediate material hardship. It is plain, too, that the women who discussed their options for bankruptcy with Seefeldt will bear financial scars for many years into the recovery. As we have seen, such financial pressures translate into anxiety, isolation and strained family relationships. The neglect of the US safety net for decades before the bust ensured that poor and middling Americans were very much on their own when hard times hit. And this very likely contributed to the subsequent recessionary misery and the strains in the social fabric in vulnerable parts of the United States.

The other unfortunate consequence of Washington's 30-year neglect of the American social protection was to doom – or, at least, sorely compromise – far braver efforts made in the immediate aftermath of the Great Recession. Though fairly criticised as inadequate, the American Recovery and Reinvestment Act of 2009 was a big undertaking, pumping something like $800 billion of demand into the economy, complementing the emergency medicines already administered through the bank rescue and ultra-lax monetary policy. All told, by 2012 the most conventional of analysts were calculating that the stimulus from all this active policy had boosted output by 4%, rescuing the economy from the 'recession proper' phase of the downturn, which would otherwise have continued to drag on.[22]

So the stimulus was a very Big Deal, and elements within it – most notably the jobs created in 'shovel-ready' building projects, and the extended unemployment insurance – were targeted at the heart of the social problem. But, after so much dismantling of the anti-poverty infrastructure, no single big bold move was ever going to fix recessionary hardship. All the more so because the inevitable bargaining between various individual power-brokers within the administration and on Capitol Hill, each with their own agenda, conspired to curb the overall size of the stimulus and to warp the priorities within it. Funds were drained from various proposed high-return public investments and job-boosting employment subsidies, as a third of the total available resource was squandered on household tax cuts.[23] These were an unfocused and inefficient way of stoking demand, but they were an option that fitted with the continuing (and decidedly non-Rooseveltian) mood of scepticism about the proper role of government.

All these difficulties came at the height of a crisis, which Obama aide Rahm Emanuel famously insisted must not be allowed to 'go to waste' as an opportunity to do things that could not be done before. Reforming the wasteful inhumanity of America's costly healthcare system had long been an elusive goal for progressives. The passage of a law which, for all its flaws and logistical problems in implementation, should eventually protect an extra 30 million Americans from the fear of being ruined by medical bills, was the one solid example of opportunism that does call Roosevelt to mind.[24]

As the immediate crisis eased, however, the old politics of Washington reasserted itself more aggressively – and so did the dismal thrust of policy pursued over the previous decades. To the extent that Obama could do anything more for the poor in the rest of his first term – and he did achieve some extension of the stimulus – he was forced by the Republicans to trade his efforts for an extension of Bush-era tax cuts for the rich.[25] Not only were these tax cuts the epitome of the very plutocratic politics that had shredded the social safety net in the first place, but they also compromised an important revenue stream that might otherwise have been used to repair it for the future.

Worse was to come, after a faltering recovery picked up and attention turned from the stagnation of the economy as a whole to battered public finances. In 2013 – a point when long-term unemployment remained stubbornly high – a series of states moved to cut new holes in unemployment compensation.[26] While official figures continued to show 4.3 million Americans jobless for more than 26 weeks, the emergency stimulus provision for more extended insurance than that began to come to an end. Then, in states such as North Carolina and Georgia, there was an unprecedented rolling back of the previous nationwide understanding that compensation would always be available for at least those first six months. In the case of North Carolina, the state government also moved to reduce benefit rates in a manner incompatible with the nationwide rules, thereby cutting itself adrift from elements of federal funding, and further shredding the ideal and the practice of national solidarity in hard times.[27]

Meanwhile, the ultimate fall-back of food stamps was cut by around 5% in November 2013, as other special recessionary provisions came to an end, even though recessionary poverty rates persisted.[28] Still not satisfied, Republicans pushed a bill through the House that provided for far deeper cuts, and which would have attached to food stamps the same mix of work tests, block grants and time limits that Washington had long ago applied to cash welfare.[29] Only the president and the Senate stood in the way of hard times bequeathing far hungrier times than we have seen for many decades.

There is a particularly stark long-term danger here: with cut-backs in nutritional support, youngsters will be growing up on less food or food of lower quality. At least some of the eventual costs, in terms of medical treatment and sickness benefits, will probably fall on the community several years down the line. But even disregarding this likely cost to the state, the American economy as a whole would surely stand a better chance of prospering if it had a healthier workforce that was raised on better food. This is not an ideologically charged argument, and it does not feel like it should be a particularly contentious one either. It is an argument which, in slightly modified form, could be applied to various social programmes besides food stamps.

And yet the case for stronger permanent shelters for Americans exposed to the tornado was never really made during the Great Recession. Now, as the recovery is established, those elements of protection that remain are being attacked afresh. The upshot is that the next time an economic storm strikes, the ordinary Americans who are lashed by it will be even more vulnerable than they have proved this time.

British blind panic

Through the initial dip of the Great Recession, believe it or not, the number of poor Britons on the most-quoted measure actually *fell* by the best part of a million.[30] This was something of a statistical artefact, reflecting a fall in a relative breadline, pegged to plunging average incomes. Even so, it indicated fairly shared financial pain, which is why the absolute poverty figures cited in Chapter 2 initially remained stable, rather than rising.

There is more to poverty than money, of course, and – as we have seen – the British economy was run on lines that left many workers insecure. After all those decades of runaway inequality, the underlying extent of deprivation in the UK was greater than in many continental economies, and – as we have also seen – community life proved frail. But for any society in the grip of the biggest slump in living memory to manage to protect low incomes is a notable achievement. For all the UK's (often deserved) reputation for heartless capitalism, the OECD's international comparisons reveal that when the storm hit (between 2007 and 2010) it sheltered its poor better than any other major western country.[31] As the leaders of the world's mightiest economies convened in London in April 2009 to cobble together a G20 response to the slump then gripping the planet, the hosts were doing a better job than most of their guests in sheltering their people from the immediate financial effects of the storm.

Just a few years later, however, in the hard times of 2014, the soothing statistics sound like a dispatch from another country entirely: hard times for the poor have now begun in earnest. Two questions are raised by this twisting tale: Why did poor Britons take so much less of a hit than poor Americans in the first instance? And what has altered since?

Certain emergency decisions played a role in the initial shielding of the British poor – in particular, a small discretionary increase in the benefit safety net in 2009/10 and a parallel insistence on diverting tax rises away from the poor. But this was tinkering around the edges. The biggest transatlantic difference was that the basic architecture of British social security that was in place remained in place when recession hit. Margaret Thatcher fuelled inequality by freezing benefit rates, but – for the most part – had stopped short of cutting outright American-style holes in the safety net.[32] The essential apparatus remained there, ready for use when required. And in places, it was subsequently strengthened. After 1997, the New Labour government of Tony Blair maintained Thatcher's Scrooge-like stance on unemployment benefits, but Blair articulated an ambition to 'end child poverty', and his chancellor, Gordon Brown, followed through by creating a system of family tax credits.[33] These not only topped up inadequate wages, but also made good on some of the losses when there was little or no work to be had. Already by the turn of the century, for parents earning less than the average, the system was much more generous than the equivalent American tax credits.[34] As the boom rolled on, extra resources were repeatedly found to enhance the credits, and thereby improve low-paid parents' effective insurance against both wage cuts and unemployment.

Thus it was that when the recession arrived, a typical British family with children that fell on hard times enjoyed far more immediate protection than its American counterpart – being able to turn to the state to replace roughly 20 extra percentage points of income in the event of redundancy.[35] To see that such a vast gulf in financial support has significant social consequences, it is necessary merely to glance at one of the most fundamental of all statistics for any ageing society: the birth rate. In America, the economic slide ushered in a baby bust, with a substantial 8% decline in the overall birth rate for women aged 15–44.[36] In Britain, where families were more sheltered, there was only a trivial decline in the number of births in 2009, and this was more than offset by large rises in both 2008 and 2010. The big picture showed a continuation of a mini-baby boom that had been evident since the millennium.[37]

It was only after 2010 that a great fit of panic about the public finances set in, and all serious thought of protecting the poor from hard times evaporated. That was, of course, the year that the administration changed, although it is important to acknowledge that what happened next is not reducible to the swing of the political pendulum. The slump had done some serious damage to the state's coffers, which would have to be repaired at some point. The outgoing Labour government had also pencilled in large and unspecified cuts, and – even if the Coalition's austerity economics involved cutting unwisely early – some painful policy choices were eventually inevitable. The recession's victims were never likely to be completely immune from the results.

Had their interests continued to be prioritised, however, they might have escaped disproportionate damage. But things did not turn out that way.

The politics had been pushing in a reactionary direction ever since – at the height of the original financial crisis in 2008 – the then shadow chancellor, George Osborne, stood up at the Conservative party conference and ditched his party's previous promise (then a totem of Tory modernisation) to match Labour's public spending plans. Instead, he conjured up grainy images of stern politicians from hard times past, with a distinctly interwar slogan: 'We will put sound money first.'[38] The early emphasis in the austerity agenda he imposed after taking office in 2010 was on chopping public service spending, particularly public investment, which was roughly halved over the two financial years after 2009/10.[39] As the term of the coalition government wore on, however, the pain was steadily concentrated onto the poor through reductions in social security.

There are more and less frightening ways to describe the scale of these cuts. Right-wing pundits point to numbers suggesting that the welfare budget will continue to rise through to 2017–18. But such soothing statistics rely on a double distortion – flagrant disregard for inflation, and disregard, too, for the rapid demographic change associated with the super-size cohort of baby boomers approaching pension age. This ageing has enormous implications for social security, since pensioners consume rather more than half the total 'welfare budget'. And yet senior citizens, enthusiastic voters in Britain, have been largely exempted from the cuts. The upshot is that virtually all of the £23 billion in annual savings which the Coalition had announced by 2013 has had to come from working-age families – equivalent to about a quarter of all the payments they previously received.[40]

Population growth and other underlying pressures will prevent the actual budget from declining by anything like this proportion.[41] It should also be said that benefits are holding up better in relation to wages, which have themselves been falling. But that notional drop of a quarter is probably the best guide to how it is going to feel for the families on the receiving end.

Not *all* the retrenchments have been trained on the have-nots: the previously universal child benefit has been taken away from high earners. But the great bulk of the Osborne cuts have hit the vulnerable hard. The graphs that the coalition government initially made a point of including in its budget book, which purported to show most of the fiscal burden falling on the richest shoulders, have been relegated to a separate annex – recognition of the reality that they are no longer believed. The data is not wrong as such; it is just very peculiarly edited. Major future benefit cuts are excluded from the charts, while various progressive tax rises announced by the last Labour government are still included. Those inherited tax policies help sustain a claim that the richest are bearing the heaviest burden. But even with all this editing, Whitehall's own numbers now confirm that – right across the rest of the income range – austerity is proving regressive.[42]

Looking ahead, the respected and doggedly non-partisan Institute for Fiscal Studies foresees that the fairly shared squeeze of the recession's initial phase (which we reported in Chapter 2) is set to unwind. It predicts that 'Lower-income groups will fare considerably worse over the post-recession period', with large rises in absolute poverty. 'The key explanation . . . is that those on lower incomes are most affected by the substantial cuts to the welfare budget.'[43] It is, then, the policies of the chancellor who coined the phrase about us 'all being in it together' which are now ensuring that the poor are taking the pain.

The Coalition's lop-sided brand of austerity – roughly 80% cuts in (mostly social) expenditure and only 20% in added taxation – was almost bound to hurt the vulnerable more. Whatever view one takes of the necessity of retrenchment, this balance is obviously a political choice. The sense of the poor being deliberately neglected is reinforced by what happens when the government does have resources to play with. Even in today's cash-strapped Britain, the Treasury always manages to conjure up a little money on Budget day, and on every occasion it has thus far revealed the same priorities: lower petrol duties and higher income tax allowances. The first measure helps those who have cars, but does nothing for those who don't; the second benefits nearly everybody who has work, and almost nobody who doesn't.

Indeed, the annual cost of pursuing these policies, together with a third Osborne project of reducing the main rate of corporation tax, has built up to a point where it more than matches the vast cuts being imposed on benefits.[44] To govern is to choose.

Then, above and beyond all the cuts and associated arguments about financial necessity, there have been deregulatory changes which have been freely chosen, even though they will leave the vulnerable more exposed: the abolition of the Agricultural Wages Board, which used to regulate the pay of farm workers; the imposition of new caps on compensation for unfair dismissal; and a move to bar more recent recruits from protection against being unreasonably laid off. The argument here is that more flexibility will cut costs for employers and thereby encourage the creation of jobs. The Coalition's opponents counter that making it easier to sack people is a perverse way of getting the economy moving, since a frightened workforce will not spend, but will instead keep their wallets closed. We would add that the insecure conditions of Britain's deregulated workforce appear to have played a crucial role in converting the loss of 'mere money' into misery and broken social bonds.

By far the biggest assault on the economic well-being of recession-hit Britons, however, is coming through reduced welfare benefits. The central fact of the cuts sometimes gets missed in the media because of a vast administrative overhaul to merge various payments into a single universal credit, which is taking place in parallel. This move, which has been oversold as the solution to every perversity in social security, in reality offers modest theoretical advantages, and potentially big practical problems.[45] It is a sideshow, and a messy one at that.[46] The real story is the cuts.

The historic scale of what is happening can be seen by comparison with the 1930s. The Labour government split and fell in 1931 because it was unable to agree on a plan to reduce unemployment benefit by 10% (a retrenchment subsequently imposed by the National Government). The rules were tightened up in other ways, too, but with retail prices having dropped by 11% since 1928, this most controversial decision actually amounted to a mere freeze in real terms.[47] By contrast, it is reckoned by the Institute for Fiscal Studies that between 2010 and 2015 the *real* income of an unemployed couple, with three children to support and typical private rent to pay, will fall by well over 10%.[48] And this is a run-of-the-mill family, not one with super-high rents or disabilities; for these the proportional losses can sometimes be considerably greater, as we confirmed in conversation with poor Britons.

The individual measures are coming thick and fast, and we can describe only a fraction of them. The biggest single saving comes from Osborne's move to hold benefits at below the cost of living for several years in a row, capping rises at 1%, irrespective of a rate of inflation that in summer 2013 was running at close to 3%. At the same time as the chancellor was issuing the Bank of England's new governor, Mark Carney, with a new remit recognising the 'need to use unconventional monetary instruments'[49] – coded encouragement for taking more risks with inflation for the sake of recovery – his benefit policy was ensuring that the victims of hard times would be more exposed to higher prices than at any time in recent history. A recipe for social insecurity indeed.

With the important exception of old age, social insurance against all of life's financially testing contingencies is being pared back. Children in larger families are being arbitrarily impoverished through a cap on a household's total benefits. Stiff time limits have been imposed on important payments for the sick. Several of the specific cuts could almost have been designed to inflame the anxiety of the era. The Social Fund – a scheme to provide emergency, low-interest loans to pay an overdue utility bill or to replace a broken bed or cooker – has been shredded, leaving loan sharks to come in and do their worst. A toughened-up assessment process for incapacity benefits – first developed under Labour, but now being accelerated – is giving rise to hundreds of thousands of appeals, which in 40% of cases end with claimants having money restored after months of needless worry.[50]

People who are steadily losing their mobility, their sight or even their lives are left battling with Atos (the private company implementing the test) to save their income.[51] 'Norma', who was originally from Bradford and has a congenital bone disease that means she is in constant pain, told us she is 'very worried' about her own reassessment, not least because she has already seen a son and a daughter who share the same unfortunate genes being classed as 'fit for work'.

According to 'Norma', in the case of her daughter, who 'still has unhealed fractures in her spine', that decision was made because, when asked 'Can you pick up a pen?' she had thought 'We have to be honest' and truthfully answered that yes, she could. Now well into her fifties, 'Norma' left school at a time when 'you didn't have [comprehensive] disability allowance'. As a young woman, she would work and 'when the pain got too bad, I would just take painkillers and cry'. But, frailer today – her fingers are prone to fracture merely from driving – such stoicism is no longer an option. If the assessment goes the wrong way, she says simply, 'I don't know how I will manage. I won't manage.'

The 'reform' of another payment to those with medical issues, Disability Living Allowance (DLA), was rammed through Parliament in terms that were precise about the saving that would be made, but entirely hazy about how it would be achieved. Even the government seems confused about how things will change: in October 2013 it slowed the implementation;[52] and individual claimants have little idea about whether they can expect to keep money that they depended on – a formula for worry if ever there was one.

The sick couple we spoke to in Luton, both dependent on DLA, emphasised what a blow it was to receive letters saying that their eligibility, which they had previously understood was awarded for life, was now going to be reassessed. In the midst of all the other cut-backs, the wife 'Stephanie', an amputee, explained why 'the DLA side of it' was the element that frightened her most. She had 'thought that because of our problems that was *one* thing I didn't have to worry about'. But now it is all being reviewed. If the decision goes against her, she will lose the car she relies on to shuttle her desperately ill husband back and forth to his oncologists and nurses 'two or three times a week'. 'Norma', too, is worried that she could lose her DLA-funded car. She explains bluntly how that would cut her off: 'Without that, I wouldn't get anywhere.'

The sick are not the only section of the population to feel harangued. Partly thanks to toughening regulations, but largely owing to changing mood music, which encourages officials to exploit their existing powers with less mercy, the unemployed are being punished more often. Before the recession, the total number of so-called 'sanctions' – that is, disciplinary docking of benefits, for example for missing a job centre interview – was 'fairly consistent at between 130,000 and 150,000 per year'.[53] After the crash and the Coalition, however, financial punishment rocketed, soon rising to 540,000 cases annually, a four-fold increase that far outstrips the recessionary growth in the benefit caseload.[54] The effect is very often to push the unemployed from stable if grinding hardship into sudden desperation, and then into crisis or debt.

One of the victims is unemployed 'Winston', who told us in Chapter 1 how he budgeted for a week's meals on £10 a week. He reached his current depths of poverty after the job centre sanctioned him just before Christmas 2012 'because I hadn't signed up to the government gateway' scheme. He promptly submitted job-seeking log books and a letter to explain the oversight, but to no avail. 'Winston' is – proudly and remarkably – free of debt, though only, he says, because he was brought up to save for a buffer against rainy days. But 'since I suffered the sanction', he explains, 'I had to use what little money I had saved'. His past thrift no longer offers any protection; he is facing hard times entirely exposed. With the council's housing office and the revenue's child tax credit office in similarly mean-spirited mood to the job centre, he tells Kafkaesque tales of letters going missing between bureaucracies and of the arrival of missives summoning him to appointments on dates that have already passed. He sums up the last six months as time spent 'lost in the department of work and pensions'.

As the retrenchment of private industry in the initial recession was slowly replaced by the public retrenchment of the Coalition's cuts between 2011 and 2013, our analysis of hundreds of thousands of YouGov market research interviews suggests that, while the financial mood of the nation stabilised, the public's feelings about family, friends and community continued to darken.[55] And, in the case of people like 'Winston', the link between such pessimism and the stance of the public authorities is not hard to grasp. Whereas he used to 'cycle into London twice a week . . . [to] go see my son' (whom he otherwise sees only at weekends), his workfare obligations – and his terror of breaching them – now mean that he cannot make the trip.

A wider slice of the population could soon experience such workfare-type requirements, as policy adjusts to the reality that much benefit spending now goes to the working poor. Changes in the pipeline could extend such obligations from the unemployed proper to the underemployed and the low-paid: the government has taken powers to allow it to extend a sanctions regime to the tax credits of poor working families, so that their payments can also be docked if their personal efforts to increase their hours of work or their rate of pay are deemed inadequate.

The greatest single threat to the ties of family and community life is, however, the cutting-back of support for costly housing – support previously available to low-paid workers, as well as the unemployed. The cuts save money by shunting families away from their established neighbourhoods. The dangers are most acute in the capital, where the cost of renting a family house privately is beyond any ordinary wage, and where, for large families, the cuts are compounded by the overall benefit cap. An eminent London School of Economics academic, Tim Leunig (by no means an unthinking critic of the Coalition: he is currently working with the government in an official capacity), calculates that, after essential bills and rent, even in less-fashionable parts of London, this cap could leave children being raised on a third-world-style stipend of 62 pence a day.[56] Obviously, that isn't going to happen, so families will 'up sticks' instead, disrupting their children's education and their social networks.

Single mother 'Pearl', whom we spoke to in London, maintains three children and (somehow) a cheery disposition. She regularly relies on 'my mother and sister . . . cousins and friends' for the substantial practical help that she needs. Nonetheless, she insists that her finances could soon force her to move: 'I was thinking either Luton or Kent, I was thinking Birmingham.' With the destination unknown, the one certainty would appear to be loneliness; and yet, she insists, the only thing holding her back is concern about one daughter's nursery place, a worry that will only apply for few more months.

A socially disruptive exodus of the poor from inner London is picking up speed, but housing benefit cuts are inflicting misery across a wider swathe of Britain as well. One element that we found to be biting widely was the so-called 'bedroom tax', a new requirement on poor social tenants to pay the rent on unoccupied rooms. This hit the headlines in 2013, when a woman left a suicide note blaming the policy, and then again after a UN rapporteur on human rights demanded that the measure be axed.[57]

During an era of difficult choices and poverty, there is a certain technocratic plausibility in the argument that the state simply cannot afford to foot the bill for homes that exceed basic requirements; thus the government insists that there is no 'bedroom tax', but only the withdrawal of 'a spare room subsidy'.

The difficulties, however, arise not with the theory, but with the practice. What counts as a 'spare' room? What about families with children at college? Our sick couple in Luton finally persuaded the council that the husband, who is prone to life-threatening infections, was under doctor's orders to sleep in a separate room; but they still have to scrape together £15 a week for their third bedroom. Of course, they don't truly *need* this third room, but it is tough to move, because their house has been adapted for disability (with accessible showers and so on). Their dilemma is far from unique: in our sample of just two dozen British families, 'Norma', with brittle bones, also faces losing her customised 'wet room' because of a move necessitated by the bedroom tax. In Chapter 2 – in a possible portent of a post-welfare-state British future – we heard about an American cancer patient who had to keep clean with the help of an outdoor spigot. If the showers on offer to the disabled are a good test of civilisation, their flow is running cold.

But 'Stephanie' brushes off all concerns about her customised bathroom and insists 'we would give up this house *willingly* if there was a suitable two-bedroom, one-level'; the problem is that there are no such homes. That illustrates the wider point. Unlike other elements of the welfare state – which have been far better maintained in Britain than the US over the years – social housing has, for several decades, been a forgotten mission. Council house-building fell off a cliff in the mid-1970s and has never recovered. The subsidised sale of social homes to tenants who could afford it followed in the 1980s. And the remaining stock is often ill-configured to today's smaller families. The cumulative result is that there is a dire shortage, with nearly 2 million families nationwide on waiting lists.[58]

The problems here, then, go back much further than 2008; but the crisis and the cuts have brought things to a head. Having lived in the same Essex home for 44 years, since she was a teenager, 60-year-old 'Moira' shudders at the thought of uprooting herself from 'a lovely road' and 'good neighbours . . . who are really nice'. This jobseeker was so desperate to stay that she talked to the council about fostering a child to use the extra bedroom, but they were not keen – and it sounds as if her date with isolation is now getting close.

◆ ◆ ◆

In Britain and the United States, we have seen, public policy has taken very different twists and turns. In both, however, the net effect has been to deny economic shelter to the families who have been battered by the economic storm. Hard times might be fading from the GDP figures, but American poverty remains stubbornly high, and the financial difficulties of Britain's poor are only just beginning. Whereas the expanding state of the 1930s and 1940s proved an agent of salvation to people who had suffered during the Depression, the retrenching state of the 2010s is often regarded as an enemy on both sides of the Atlantic, even by those who have no one else to call on.

Long before the Great Recession produced such a desperate expansion in the need for public assistance, throughout much of the United States – and especially in the South – welfare was provided with a mean spirit that aimed at (and often succeeded in) discouraging people from applying for the help they needed. Stigma and myth were just as important in this as the actual rules. In their pre-recession study of families without earnings or cash support, Sheila Zedlewski and her colleagues heard from a Native American in Alabama who feared that an application for welfare would prompt the state to take away her child; another woman, this time in Virginia, had heard from a friend that if she received public support, her son would be barred from ever seeing his father. But 'rude' case workers, making 'infeasible', 'unreasonable' demands, were another part of the problem; having spoken to the welfare office about their (supposed) work experience programme, one woman reckoned that she would be toiling for '40 hours a week for $137 a month' in benefit, an effective hourly wage rate of less than a dollar.[59]

Another woman again, this time in Mississippi, spoke for all these needy American families: 'I never want to receive a check, 'cause they find some kind of way to mess with you.' Her words – that hostile 'they' for the state, that disdain for any help in the form of a benefit 'check' – betray just how far the US has slid from the Rooseveltian view, quoted at the start of this chapter, that 'modern society, *acting through its government*, owes the definite obligation to prevent . . . dire want'. That ideal, as we have emphasised, has held up better in the United Kingdom, although it is now coming under unprecedented attack there as well.

The effects on those who have no choice but to rely on state payments was described to us in Luton by disabled 'Stephanie' and her sick husband 'Martin'. 'Stephanie' said the time of day she most dreaded was the arrival of the mail: 'It's horrible when you hear the postman come up the path, you don't even see what comes through the letter box . . .' She is interrupted by 'Martin': 'Because if it's a brown envelope . . .' His wife completes the shared thought: '. . . that means a government letter.'

Nobody is thrilled by official correspondence, but so predictable is it for this couple that mail from the 'welfare' state will be a bossy command, a demand for proof or a threat of some sort, that 'Stephanie' can hardly bear 'brown envelope days'. After a lifetime of toil spent fitting aircraft and in primary schools, respectively, 'Martin' and 'Stephanie' have turned to the community in their hour of need. But instead of compassion, they feel they have been shown contempt. 'It's no life really, is it?' reflects 'Martin' on an existence overshadowed by brown envelopes. A few minutes later, 'Stephanie' adds: 'I feel that I'm scum, really.'

American welfare has long been marked out by a mix of shame and petty strictures. The words of this Luton couple suggest that seeking recourse to benefits in Britain is fast becoming a similarly humiliating experience. The Great Depression revealed the need for economic shelters, which were duly built. Just a few years after the biggest slump in living memory, it is a remarkable fact that both the UK and the US are tearing them down. The next chapter asks how democratic politics can have allowed that to happen.

The veil of complacency

*It's turned the society against each other. People are turning against
their neighbours and their friends. But I think it's been done so that
people don't actually stand up.*
'Norma', 55, with brittle bones that preclude work, on how hard times
are dividing Britain's communities

It is never wise to assume that hard times will foster solidarity.
Sometimes they did so in Marienthal, as when a neighbour would
notice hungry children next door and bring them a bowl of soup. But
sometimes impoverished Austrian families would turn on each other.
As the slump wore on, increasing numbers snitched on one another
to the dole office for tiny transgressions, such as busking with a
harmonica while drawing relief.[1] Likewise, at much the same time in
England's industrial North, Orwell reported on 'much spying and
tale-bearing', with one man he knew 'seen feeding his neighbour's
chickens while the neighbour was away' and subsequently being
reported to the authorities for having 'a job feeding chickens'.[2] The
response to hardship can go either way.

Let us consider, first, why a mood of solidarity could rise as the
economy sinks. In a famous thought experiment, the philosopher John
Rawls provided a theoretical underpinning for egalitarian institutions,

with his 'veil of ignorance'.[3] This device imagines prospective citizens debating the best way to run society from behind a 'veil' that blocks their knowledge of the rank that they will occupy within that society. If nobody knows whether they will be born a prince or a pauper, the argument runs, then everybody will surely agree on fair rules that afford the pauper decent protection – just in case it happens to be them. Fear of an economic storm, which can lash anybody, should likewise prove a great leveller – and provide a terrific incentive to co-operate in building shared shelters.

Just listen to Roosevelt's second inaugural – 'we refused to leave the problems of our common welfare to be solved by the winds of chance and the hurricanes of disaster' – and you can hear how the New Deal was deliberately rooted in this sort of argument.[4] The same logic animated Britain's post-war reconstruction.

The 'all in it together' pitch supported not only social insurance and labour market protections, but also the macroeconomic commitment to full employment, which became a settled objective for governments in both the UK and the US until it was dislodged by alarm over the great inflation of the 1970s. Just as with taxes and spending, macroeconomic choices over interest rates and so on will create winners and losers, and the balance of political power between them will bear upon the direction of policy.[5] But monetary policy in the Great Recession has been nothing like as controversial as during the Depression: this time reflationists have carried the day with relative ease in Britain and America, if not continental Europe. Although it is worth noting in passing that 'quantitative easing' has disproportionately boosted the value of assets held by the rich,[6] even this unprecedented aspect of the monetary stance has not proven especially divisive. It thus makes sense for us to concentrate on the fiscal side, and most especially social expenditure and redistribution.

In tracing public opinion on these things, we will concern ourselves not with particular policies or plans (which inevitably evolve over time, and on which many voters will typically have no view), but rather with support for the broad underlying principles of providing for the poor and pooling risk – principles as pertinent today as they were in the hard times of the 1930s.

In repeatedly invoking the twin precedents of Roosevelt and Beveridge, we have implicitly suggested that the same goals could again be pursued with the same political strategy as in their day. That, however, could be seriously misleading: the achievements of these men reflect their times as much as themselves.

Roosevelt was, in the words of his biographer, a 'Hudson River aristocrat, a son of privilege who never depended on a paycheck', and never showed any particularly progressive instincts in his youth.[7] Beveridge was decidedly sceptical about Keynes' great insights, favouring sun spots as an explanation for the economic swings of the past.[8] And his great reforms were implemented by Clement Attlee, an impeccable conservative in everything but politics, obsessed with his old boarding school.[9] These men had many qualities, but they were able to build shelters against hard times only because the mood of their times was receptive. So the pertinent question is how an appeal to solidarity would fare in our own hard and divided times – and there are good reasons to suspect that things may be different.

In those historic years of the 1930s and 1940s, society in both Britain and America was dealing with unique emergencies that threatened nearly everybody. The primitive American opinion polling available from the time confirms a taste for activist government, and strong support for raising the revenue to fund it by taxing the better-off: in 1936, Gallup recorded a 49% to 32% plurality in favour of a levy on income from federal bonds.[10] But, as the political economist Benjamin Friedman has written of the United States in those years:

> This was not a situation in which farmers or industrial workers or small business operators were uniquely unfortunate ... [E]nough Americans from different walks of life saw one another in distress that they may well have felt as if they were now, for practical purposes, part of one large community.[11]

And, he argues in a wider judgement, with dispiriting implications for our own time, this is what made the Great Depression the 'Great Exception' from 'the more general tendency ... for economic stagnation or decline to erode society's tolerance, openness, and democracy'.[12]

As for Britain, it was arguably less economic depression than war – and the threat to the life of the nation that came with it – that awakened a new sense of responsibility for the well-being of fellow citizens, resetting societal mores in a way that facilitated the social democratic settlement that followed. One historian defined 'Mr Attlee's consensus' as 'the new dispensation which began after Dunkirk in 1940'.[13] As well as ushering in a sea change in public opinion, the war readied the tools for 'winning the peace' by putting unprecedented financial and administrative resources at the state's disposal. Yes, as anti-austerity left-wingers always point out in the UK, the British state was saddled with a more burdensome national debt at the time it established the health service than it is today. But the post-war Labour party was also starting out with taxes at record rates and vast, soon-to-be-demobilised armed forces. This combination created unique resources that could be tapped, without the usual electoral problems involved in jacking up taxes.[14]

Such ready resources are not at hand today, and so building shared shelters is going to be more of a political challenge. And all the more so in an unequal society where, as we have documented, the path of the economic tornado is only too predictable. Since the great gulf in incomes opened after the 1970s, experience has demonstrated on three separate occasions that it will be the young, the black and the unschooled that take the serious pain on the employment front. During the recent recession, those selfsame people who feared for their jobs often faced the greatest financial perils imposed by the need to bail out bankrupt family members or (in the US) by medical bills. All of these problems were closely correlated both with each other, and with the basic demographic indicators of disadvantage.[15]

Whether it is individual well-being, family or community life, *all* the evidence we have reviewed points to a storm that has blown with wildly varying intensity in different neighbourhoods. So desolate districts exist side by side with salubrious suburbs where nothing much has changed. The Anglo-Saxon economic divide had steadily widened over long years before the slump; with the Great Recession, this pre-existing economic divide deepened it into a societal schism. And this greatly complicates the politics of rallying the people towards a common response. Citizens in the better-protected communities, who dwell at a safe distance from the path of maximal destruction, may calculate that self-interest lies in supporting immediate tax cuts over Michael Foot's quaint old promise – highlighted at the top of the last chapter – of a community that 'shows some compassion' in hard times. In such circumstances, instead of a veil of ignorance, the fortunate acquire a veil of complacency.

Indeed, the situation gives politicians an opportunity to score points by turning the more fortunate against the hapless – a tactic we have recently seen on both sides of the Atlantic. Just as a fresh tranche of the Coalition's deep social security cuts was starting to bite in April 2013, George Osborne leapt on the case of Mick Philpott, a jobless man who had just been convicted of killing six of his children in a house fire. The case raised, the British chancellor said, 'a question for government and for society about the welfare state, and the taxpayers who pay for the welfare state, subsidising lifestyles like that . . . And I think that debate needs to be had.'[16]

Exactly how tax credits and housing benefit payments persuaded a man to set ablaze a home packed with his slumbering offspring was never explained. And it hardly mattered. For the none-too-subtle intention was to lock in electoral support for further retrenchment by setting those 'taxpayers who pay for the welfare state' against the users of social security, by tainting this huge and disparate group with the evil deeds of a single man.

A YouGov poll provided early evidence that the tactic was working: British voters approved of the chancellor's decision to link the Philpott case with the welfare debate, by 48% to 41%. Yet it succeeded, the detailed data revealed, only by inflaming pre-existing divisions: an overwhelming majority of respondents who felt that the cuts were having 'little impact' on their own lives backed Osborne in making the link; among those voters who reported that they were suffering from the cuts, the plurality felt the chancellor had got it wrong.[17]

Some months before Osborne's remarks, on the other side of the Atlantic the Republican challenger for the White House, Mitt Romney, had unwittingly made explicit the same divisive reasoning that was implicit in the British chancellor's intervention. Seeking election on a platform that sought to knock down such shared economic shelters as remain in America – by simultaneously swinging an axe at death duties for the rich and expenditure programmes for the poor[18] – Romney was caught unawares by a secret recording of a private fund-raising dinner, at which he explained that he was happy to write off very nearly half of the electorate:

> There are 47 percent . . . who are dependent upon government, who believe that they are victims, who believe that government has a responsibility to care for them, who believe that they are entitled to health care, to food, to housing, to you-name-it . . . Our message of low taxes doesn't connect . . . so my job is . . . not to worry about those people.[19]

Right-wing politicians, then, have sensed that the same gale of hard times, which as we have already seen has exerted a divisive social effect, has also polarised opinion; they discern electoral possibilities in rallying the haves against the have-nots. But we should recall that Romney lost. Perhaps, the hopeful progressive will suggest, his calcu-lation was simply awry? At a time when the economy is beset with so much anxiety, shouldn't the ranks of the scared be sufficiently swollen for the logic of the veil of ignorance to be restored?

Certainly, that has sometimes happened in hard times past – and in the much more recent past than the 1930s. When recession hit the US at the start of the 1980s, the immediate impulse was, on balance, for collectivism in social policy. That is not how we remember things, partly because after the inflationary 1970s came a period of conserva-tive ascendency in macroeconomics – high interest rates and conse-quent unemployment came to be regarded as an acceptable levy to pay for price stability, a big break from the post-war years. We remember the early 1980s as a right-wing time, too, because a deeply conservative president, Ronald Reagan, went on to secure re-election in the economic upswing. But a question that was repeatedly asked in the General Social Survey (GSS) – recorded in the graph opposite – shows that the proportion of Americans who supported redistributing (by taxing the wealthy and assisting the poor) rose from 43% in 1980 to 49% in 1984.

Over these same four years of recession and its aftermath, another GSS question recorded strongly rising support for welfare; the proportion believing that too much was being spent on it declined by more than 20 points.[20] If American voters were more resigned to unemployment than they might have been in the 1960s, it did not follow that they were in a mood to abandon those on the receiving end. Yes, Gallup found that 1980s voters were more sceptical about the role of government than their predecessors had been during the Great Depression, and they were also alarmed by the swelling federal deficit. But if cuts were required, American voters in 1983 felt that these should be made in defence (where the balance of opinion was 55% to 35% in favour of cuts) rather than in general 'social programmes' (where the split was 50% to 42% against retrenchment). More specific cuts to 'Medicare, Medicaid and social security' were rejected even more emphatically as ways of tackling the deficit – reductions in these entitlements were rejected by a crushing 82%.[21]

After several years of rising inequality, however, the recession at the start of the 1990s encountered a very different public mood. Support for the same redistribution proposition that had risen in the 1980s now fell sharply; the graph records a fall of 12 percentage points, from 52% to 40% between 1990 and 1994. There was an even sharper decline in support for spending on welfare: the percentage believing that America was providing too much of it more than doubled, from 28% in 1990 to 62% in 1994. Tough talk on 'welfare' from President Clinton and more particularly the Republican party was admittedly beginning to colour the debate, but a hardening of opinion was also evident on a less politically charged GSS question, concerning spending 'on assistance to the poor'. Belief that the government had a responsibility to take care of the less fortunate likewise dwindled.[22] The first

President Bush once promised 'a kinder and gentler nation'; trends in public opinion in the face of the slump that started on his watch suggest that America became anything but.

This pattern of hard times precipitating a less generous mood has continued. By 2010, the last datapoint shown, the 'don't redistribute' line had ticked up 8 percentage points over two recessionary years, rising from 32% in 2008 to 40%. On attitudes towards welfare expenditure, too, the GSS showed yet another swing against state support.[23] After one serious recession in the early 1980s, when economic empathy was the order of the day, America has now suffered two successive downturns during which the prevailing mood has been better characterised as 'the victims are on their own'.

There are many developments that may have affected the appetite for solidarity over these decades: from the evolving anti-welfare rhetoric of political leaders to the slow disappearance of voters who remembered the Great Depression. There is powerful evidence, for example, that a change in tone on the part of the elite can make a difference in particular contexts (a thought to which we will return in the concluding chapter).[24] But the particular possibility we wish to

Harder times: support for redistribution rose in the Reagan recession, but fell during more recent slumps

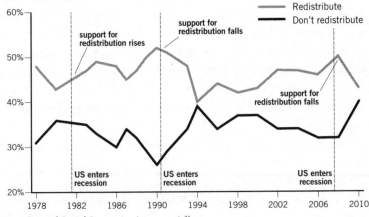

Source: General Social Survey (various years).[25]

explore here is that, in an increasingly polarised economy, with increasingly predictable financial victims, attitudes have polarised too. That is to say, in hard times the exposed are more desperate for help than ever, but the majority – with secure if modestly paying jobs – have come to calculate that it is better to throw their lot in with the haves, than to risk being saddled with tax rises to provide assistance to the have-nots. New analysis allows us to test this hypothesis directly – by peering below average shifts in headline opinion, and investigating whether there have indeed been divergent movements across different parts of the population.

Consider, first, support for a very general progressive proposal: for 'an increase in the funding of government programs for helping the poor and the unemployed with education, training and employment, and social services, even if this would raise your taxes'. Just before the slump hit, in July 2007, 55% of Americans indicated that they would be willing to back this proposal; after the crisis, the figure dropped appreciably, to 47%.[26] That 8 percentage point drop in support for generosity towards recessionary victims is very much in line with the overall drift in opinion that we have already reported.

A recent analysis of this data in the *American Political Science Review*, however, establishes that among individuals whose income had taken a significant hit, or who felt that their own job was increasingly insecure, there was a post-slump majority for such government efforts. Among people who had actually been laid off, the majority was bigger still. Even after adjusting for things like education and age (which turn out not to matter much), as well as partisanship (which certainly does), losing a job is associated with a huge 24 percentage point increase in the probability that someone will support such a programme of training, welfare and job creation for the benefit of the unemployed.[27]

Another new study exploits a special 'insecurity supplement' to the American National Election Studies, and finds that respondents' 'level of worry is associated with their level of support for government action across all the domains'.[28] While the actual knocks that people had suffered in the recession were important in shaping their attitudes,[29] opinion was also being reshaped by fear itself. American anxieties about medical bills, pension cut-backs and the potential need to bail out struggling family members were all combining to encourage support for more active government among the ranks of the scared. In relation to support for government job creation and unemployment benefits, the same study found, economic insecurity was exerting more power even than partisanship or ideology.[30]

At a time when the dole queues were lengthening, these were dramatic and progressive shifts; but they were not sufficient to offset the countervailing swing among the more fortunate and more numerous. Tracking data from the General Social Survey confirms that that while individuals do indeed want 'more redistribution when they experience unemployment or lose household income', among the stably employed, average support for pro-poor social policies sank like a stone as the recent recession dragged on. More specifically, among those who had fallen out of work by 2008, there was a 0.6 increase (on a seven-point scale) in support for redistribution, which was almost exactly matched in the opposing direction by a 0.55 decline in support among those who were fully and stably employed over the course of the subsequent two years.[31]

For a large part of the American population, then, economic anxiety *has* worked to engender progressive radicalism, in just the same way as it did during the Depression; however, there is another – larger – constituency that has leant the other way, and has responded by becoming more doubtful about Washington playing Robin Hood.

The evidence is thus consistent with the idea that, as a society becomes more unequal, different dynamics of opinion kick in – with the logic of the veil of ignorance potentially being discarded in favour of the veil of complacency. The point here is subtle: there is no reason why rising income inequality should in itself undermine the argument for social insurance; it will only do so if the effect is to harden class lines, so that prosperous parts of the electorate believe they will never sink to the point where they would require a state safety net. Why might that happen? First, over time extra income at the higher end allows more people to build a personal safety net in the form of wealth;

and with the average value of personal wealth having grown more rapidly than personal incomes for a third of a century, it is no longer just the rich, but also the moderately affluent who enjoy a substantial private cushion.[32] Second, the flipside of the Anglo-American problem with social mobility (which we reviewed in Chapter 7) is that the well-to-do can be confident that their offspring will do sufficiently well to avoid falling back on the government. Finally, there is the blunt fact of the grossly unequal incidence of redundancy.

Recessionary victims are becoming not merely predictable but almost preordained. There is a parallel here with a policy problem in a very different field: so-called 'genetic discrimination' in healthcare. As science unravels the double DNA helix, it also untangles the mystery about who will need what medical care in future, as many costly cases start to become identifiable in advance. Concern in America that the insurance industry's ability to pool risk would be compromised reached such a pitch that federal legislation was passed.[33] There is no such concern about the undermining of the basis of social insurance against economic risk, but with the same victims being hammered by successive recessions, that might already have happened. If one citizen exposed to Roosevelt's 'hurricanes of disaster' put forward a plan for pooling risk today, a wealthier counterpart might respond that the proposer has nothing to pool. If brutal enough, he might add: 'No insurance policy can protect you against what has already happened – and you already happen to be the wrong sort of person.'

The hunch that the political economy might play out in this dismal way is reinforced by an ingenious study that estimated voters' *desired* level of inequality (from the amounts that they believe people in different sorts of jobs should earn). It established that, in the unequal America of the late 1990s, there was 'a strong, and increasing, polarization of attitudes toward income levelling'.[34] A more recent cross-national study of 20 democracies deploys similar methods and points the same way, suggesting that, as incomes fan out around the world, inequality 'perpetuates itself' as people assume less egalitarian views.[35]

So what about Britain? Just as in the US, the difference in response to successive slumps in the UK proves instructive. But in order to identify this changing cyclical pattern, we must first abstract from a deeper secular tide, which – through booms as well as busts – has been running against the ideal of social security. In the long-running British Social Attitudes (BSA) series, which conducts face-to-face interviews with over 3,000 people every year, one regular question concerns unemployment benefits. As the chart overleaf shows, the responses suggest rising disregard for the needs of the jobless over two decades. When unemployment peaked in 1993, by a crushing 55% to 24% margin, Britons rejected the idea that benefits were 'too high and discouraged work' in favour of the view that they were 'too low and caused hardship'. Eighteen years later, those proportions had been inverted, with 62% taking the harsher view and just 19% expressing concern about poverty in 2011. This sea change in attitudes came even though the main unemployment benefit has been frozen in real terms throughout this long period, and so replaces less pay than it used to.

Although this great general change dominates the chart, it is also possible to discern a more specific reaction to hard times. As unemployment soared by a million between 1990 and 1993, those who believed that excessive benefits were part of the problem fell from 29% to 24%, while there was a similar rise in the proportion who took the contrary view. Other BSA questions from the same years confirm the generous mood: the suspicion that many benefit claimants 'don't really deserve any help' became rarer, dropping off by 4 percentage points;[36] the proportion agreeing that less generous benefits would encourage people 'to stand on their own feet' fell away to much the same extent;[37] and there was a 9 point rise in the proportion favouring tax rises to bolster public services and state benefits.[38]

In the British slump of the 1990s, then, voters tended to become more empathetic – glancing at the luckless and reasoning that 'there, but for the grace of God, go we'. As with the US of the early 1980s, this reality may not accord with the standard memory of the times. This was, after all, an era of Conservative rule; and a government that maintained high interest rates in the face of recession secured re-election in 1992, even as unemployment soared. But, exactly as with the US in the early 1980s, there is a distinction to be drawn between the mood on macroeconomic policy (where the Right continued to make the political running, as it had done since the inflationary 1970s) and the mood on social policy. One interpretation of the data might be that the public had yet to appreciate that the unemployment produced by the hard-line economics was not a threat to everyone equally, but chiefly afflicted those who were already poor.

Another reading, however, is that Britain was simply not yet sufficiently divided to run into the same anti-welfare response to hard times which we have seen kicked in over these years in the (more unequal) US. Now Britain in the early 1990s had, it is true, already experienced the great Thatcherite fanning-out of incomes; the underlying trend in opinion was already probably moving away from economic solidarity. But attitudinal changes take time; besides, on most measures at least, inequality had some way to go before it reached the heights that it scaled at the dawn of the Great Recession.[39] And, sure enough, the reaction to the crisis in 2008 went the other way. The chart shows that there was an immediate 8 percentage point surge in

Hard luck in hard times: feelings towards UK benefits softened in the 1990s slump but hardened after 2008

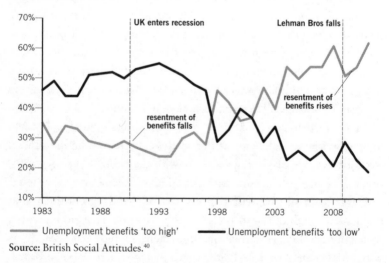

Source: British Social Attitudes.[40]

the proportion believing that excessive benefits breed indolence, from 54% in 2007 to 61% in 2008. The figures subsequently yo-yoed somewhat, but in 2011, as UK unemployment peaked, the view that excessive benefits fostered idleness registered a record score of 62%.

Older adults claiming Jobseeker's Allowance in 2011 were expected to eke out an existence on £67.50 a week, hardly an enticing invitation to stay in bed. Some leftish commentators imagine that the whole rightward drift in sentiment must be the product of poisonous propaganda served up by the media and the political class. And some of it probably is. But isn't it a bit too easy to deride those who court the voters without pausing to consider whether those voters might have opinions themselves? Our investigations suggest an alternative interpretation: that in an increasingly polarised society, where individual prospects become easier to foretell, attitudes towards welfare have polarised along with economic fortunes.

The great divide that has been cut through British opinion by hard times is evident not only in the decades-old British Social Attitudes series, but also in more recent snapshot surveys, designed to establish whether such polarisation is occurring. YouGov polling in spring 2013 separated out those who reported being personally affected by spending cut-backs from those who reported life rolling along as normal. A political chasm divided the two. Among those who claimed to be smarting, a crushing 71% to 19% majority believed that retrenchment was being unfairly implemented, whereas those who had avoided the pain tended, by 49% to 35%, towards the belief that it was being dished out justly. Two political nations also emerged on the pace of austerity: 62% of those afflicted by the cuts said austerity was being implemented too hastily (and only 8% disagreed), whereas 65% of unscathed Britons thought the pace should be maintained or stepped up. On the necessity of cuts, self-identified victims were split down the middle, while those who were avoiding the pain overwhelmingly believed that austerity was unavoidable.[41]

While these numbers suggest that economic divisions are hardening into political cleavages, it is possible that the effect is being exaggerated by voters who dislike the UK's coalition government and so *both* denounce its policies *and* claim to be suffering from them. YouGov's separate cross-country analysis in spring 2013 is less prone to such distortion, for it divided respondents not by experience of government policy, but by how they claim to have fared in the face of general economic problems over several years – problems that pre-dated the Coalition.

Examined this way, the UK's political schism remains. Britons personally affected by the downturn (the same 'slump-hit' category used in Chapters 5 and 6) believe, by a margin of 43% to 35%, that 'the government is being too harsh towards people on benefits'. 'Slump-proof' individuals, by contrast, indicate, by 45% to 26%, that policy 'is not being tough enough'. Parallel differences are found in attitudes towards the role of government (the slump's victims want more redistribution), resentment towards top pay (more marked among those feeling the pinch) and faith that hard work can take poor children to the top (a faith that is faltering among the families ravaged by recession).[42]

The sense that hard times are digging opinion into particularly deep trenches in the UK is reinforced by the fact that nowhere – neither in the United States nor in the other countries asked exactly the same YouGov questions at the same time – did personal experience have such a consistent bearing on attitudes about the roles and responsibility of the state.[43] No doubt parochial politics played a role.

David Cameron had once affected the pragmatic air of Harold Macmillan – a truly moderate, mid-twentieth-century Conservative; but after the storm broke in 2008/09, he sought to persuade the majority who had clung onto their jobs that the gravest danger came from the social welfare state. In the midst of the great crisis of unbridled capitalism, Cameron offered a diagnosis worthy of Barry Goldwater in his heyday, insisting that excessive public spending had 'got us into this mess'. 'Why is our economy broken?' he asked. He then went on to answer himself:

> because government got too big, spent too much and doubled the national debt. Why is our society broken? Because government got too big, did too much and undermined responsibility. Why are our

politics broken? Because government got too big, promised too much and pretended it had all the answers.[44]

As a politician who was then on the way up, David Cameron had a relatively rare opportunity to be listened to, and he might have done something to reshape the thinking of those who had come through the slump on the luckier side of the divide. But if parts of the country were receptive to the pointing of the finger at big government, that also reflected a wider political rule in recessions: people always want somebody or something to blame. A recent analysis of decades of American data, for example, found that rising unemployment rates went along with resentment of the banks and a sense that life isn't fair, and yet at the same time with mistrust in the institutions of government to which previous generations had turned when they wanted to resolve such grievances.[45]

Insofar as a recessionary spirit can be coherently summed up from that, it is less a spirit of Left or Right, than a mood of angry despair. In the UK, the siren call of the far Right continues to resonate more in depressed areas, as can be seen by overlaying a map of unemployment with a chart showing the hotspots of British National Party support.[46] Mercifully, the far Right is not at 1930s strength and is in no position to challenge for power: there are deep societal tides running against racial prejudice in both the UK and the United States.[47] There remains, however, a mood that lends itself to myriad resentments of other sorts.

In talking to cash-strapped Britons, we found that resentment is very often directed with particular intensity at people who by any objective measure are in the same boat. While the polling evidence that we have reviewed suggests that those who have been hit by recession are keener than ever on ameliorative government action of some sort, things get far more contentious when the question turns to *who* should get help. A UK-only YouGov poll in 2012 suggests that, even among households surviving on less than £10,000 a year (the great bulk of which will have some personal benefit entitlement), a full 60% believe there are not merely a few fraudulent or determinedly work-shy benefit claimants, but that there are very many.[48] And while there may be support among the poor for social assistance as a general proposition, as soon as discussion turns to specific proposals to support particular groups, jealousies break out in every direction.

The most familiar resentment – and the one that the UK Coalition has most nakedly inflamed – is the mistrust with which struggling workers regard the unemployed. This was aired by 'Kate' from Mansfield. She expressed it gently, and with some empathy, as she herself remembers having 'no confidence when I were out of work'. Nonetheless, she recalls hearing of 'a young girl who'd got I forget how many children' moaning about money, and thinking, 'Well, hang on a minute . . . in terms of disposable income you've probably got more than me, and you're not working.'

Strikingly, she repeats the politicians' mythical claims of an under-class 'third generation . . . that have always been on benefits', and deploys a bit of rhetoric – 'working families' – used on both sides of the Atlantic to subtly separate the jobless from the rest. Indeed, asked specifically about what the government should do differently, she answered: 'for me it's about . . . being made to feel as though, as a working family, we're not valued as much as someone out of work . . . there's a lot of emphasis on . . . a non-working population'. She added that her 'very tiring battle' is not helped by 'seeing non-working families being able to afford . . . visits to . . . the soft-play areas every week.'

This is precisely the sort of talk that sends shivers down the spines of our sick and unwaged couple in Luton. 'Stephanie' volunteers unprompted: 'I don't like this title that Cameron keeps saying "the hardworking families". We were the hardworking families until the illness took his job!' After so many years of toil, followed by illness, she adds that, when the prime minister speaks in these terms, 'I feel like I'm getting stabbed in the back.'

This resentment on the part of struggling workers – and the associated hurt on the part of the workless – came as no surprise. Less expected, however, are all the other varieties of rivalry that flow between different elements of the downtrodden. Perhaps because of all the 'hardworking families' rhetoric, the unemployed worry that low-waged employees are getting a better deal than they are. Workless 'Moira' from Essex was quite explicit: 'I think you get more help now if you are in work with the government than if you are unemployed.' Moreover, almost all the individuals accepted the media narrative of ubiquitous fiddling of benefits, including unemployed 'Winston': 'Yes, I'll agree that there are people out there abusing the system.' Virtually all, however, thought that this scrounging was only a problem among families claiming different types of benefits from themselves.

Both 'Winston' and 'Jamal' claim Jobseeker's Allowance, and both believe that there is a problem with scroungers, but that this problem really concerns people on incapacity benefits. 'Jamal' insists:

> The *only* people that I can say are [getting a good deal at this time] are [all those] claiming disability that are not disabled . . . I have a couple of mates, the only people I know that are doing well: . . . One's got a bad back, and one's saying he's going a bit loopy . . . There is nothing wrong with either of them.

'Winston' is at pains to stress the dedication of his fellow jobseekers: 'I see people going to the work club and they are just writing, writing, writing' applications and letters. But he harbours suspicions where the sick are concerned:

> A young man I used to work with . . . basically just told me he's got ESA [the rebranded incapacity benefit] . . . so he doesn't really have to go to work . . . He could be getting, from what I understand, up to £100 a week . . . So he is clearing £400 a month without doing anything . . . I'm clearing £240 a month and I'm running backwards and forwards, . . . in a job club, . . . in the work programme twice a week.

Our couple in Luton, who live in the shadow of 'brown-envelope days' and official threats to snatch their money away, would no doubt feel that they have much to tell jobseekers about the reality of living 'on the sick'. But they have equally stern words to hurl in the other direction. When it comes to the unemployed proper, 'Martin' takes a tough line: 'The government could have put their foot down.' He believes it should say to 'these people on Jobseeker's . . . "There's work there, you do it or you lose your money"'. His wife 'Stephanie' agrees and adds that 'a lot' of them 'are lazy'. The quadrupling in the use of punitive sanctions for missing interviews and refusing jobs – punishment that has hit 'Winston' hard – has obviously passed them by. Just as the tightening of the rules on incapacity benefits has escaped the notice of 'Winston'.

There are other divisions as well: private tenants understandably envy the security and lower rent of those on council estates. Small families sometimes resent larger ones – and vice versa. Being dependent on income support did not prevent 'Denise', a single mother of one child in London, complaining about parents 'on benefits [who] have got four or five kids and all their kids have got laptops and the latest iPhones and all that'. By contrast, 'Kirsty', with her family of four in Scotland, argues that benefits are *less* generous for big families: 'you . . . only receive maternity grant for your first child'. She also thinks traditional households are short-changed, by comparison with single mothers: 'I don't understand how they can justify [paying a couple] £30 less' for 'living together'.

We heard a few of the traditional sort of myths and half-truths that have always coloured discussion of welfare: the old belief that the rules are softer for the latest immigrants (in this case Romanians 'with begging children'); the genuine perennial problem of 'the fags and the drink' in some homes; even rumours about 'an alcoholic' who supposedly gets a special payment 'of about £200 a week, and that's to pay for basically bottles of vodka and stuff, so they can drink'. Such tales, however, emerged as scattered individual grumbles; complaints about immigration, drinking and drugs were inconsistent, and certainly no more of a feature than rage against the bankers and the wealthy. The one real constant of resentment was, by contrast, the belief that *other poor people* were somehow getting a much better deal.

Aside from feisty disabled 'Norma', who offered her analysis of 'divide and rule' at the top of the chapter, our only interviewees who offered a wholesale challenge to the overall narrative of welfare scroungers were student 'Laura' (whose own family's experience on benefits leaves her in no doubt: 'I think that's rubbish about them being too generous') and indebted professional 'John'. He dismisses concern about scrounging from people who 'live on social security' with the traditional leftist line: 'Rich people don't pay any tax at all, and what they should pay is ridiculously low anyway . . . [so] . . . you know, who's the scrounger?'

But both 'John' and 'Laura' are exceptionally well educated, and have the intellectual confidence that often comes with that; there was little such talk among our other – more representative – victims of hard times. After so much talk of scroungers, even to ask them for their thoughts on social security put them on the defensive. Disabled 'Stephanie' in Luton said: 'We just feel like we are beggars, sitting there with our hands out.' Few human beings in that frame of mind will have the confidence to round on their accusers; instead the instinct is to acquit oneself by finding someone else to point the finger at.

◆ ◆ ◆

'We are the 99%' is the great slogan of the Occupy protesters. It is a slogan justified by reference to the income distribution statistics, and one that sounds as if it ought to be able to rally a crushing electoral majority. But the numerical prevalence of the squeezed majority is, in fact, a weakness as well as a strength – identities within any 'group' that claims to cover anything like 99% of people are likely to be more defined by divisions than anything else.[49] Yes, 'the 1%' has grabbed the lion's share of growth over many years – and everyone else has a legitimate grievance about that. Beyond that, however, workers plodding along on reasonable (if stagnant) pay may feel as if they have little in common with others enduring serious hard times.

The constituency of the 'squeezed but basically safe' is large, and their overriding concern – to avoid being saddled with big tax bills – means that in both Britain and America the Great Recession has pushed average attitudes about the welfare state rightwards. But – just as we found with well-being scores, volunteering ratios and employment rates – such averages conceal more than they reveal. Large parts of both Britain and America – the parts that have sustained serious damage – are crying out for something like a new New Deal. The economic tornado is not merely dividing social conditions in different communities, it is propelling political opinion in divergent directions, too.

The resulting polarisation of attitudes makes it hard, if not impossible, to build broad coalitions; the deep schism seared through American politics underlines this especially regularly. At least, one might have thought, the radicalising mood of recessionary victims should give progressives something to build on and work with. But even among these victims proper, there is tremendous economic diversity, and this – as our conversations with poor Britons suggest – is conspiring to weaken political ties. The unemployed proper do not feel that they are the same as those who are inactive for other reasons; both are different from part-timers and temps, who in turn are different from each other, and different again from low-paid full-timers. Although we have not conducted the same range of interviews in America, it would be naïve to assume that liberals can rely on any greater solidarity among recessionary victims there.

Up until now, this context of splintering opinion has allowed those who believe that the community is under no obligation to show compassion in hard times to make all the running. Britain's chancellor, who will one day inherit a baronetcy, rallies cash-strapped grafters against workless households whose 'blinds stay shut' in the morning. He speaks of layabouts 'sleeping off a life on benefits',[50] as if the condition of unemployment could somehow be compared to a boozy night out.

It appeared to be a winning strategy, too – or at least it did until he overplayed his hand by cutting tax for the wealthiest 1% in April 2012, which gravely damaged his stock.[51] A few months before Mitt Romney went down to defeat in the US, an older instinct for fairness was stirred in the UK: as austerity ground on in 2013, the latest British Social Attitudes survey revealed a sudden swing back away from the view that blamed unemployment on benefits.[52] During the same year, more UK polling evidence emerged to suggest that the 'bedroom tax' (see Chapter 8) had become increasingly unpopular, even though this is a public expenditure cut that narrowly targets poor families on council estates, and so is something that leaves most voters personally untouched.[53] Wider concern for the minority who have suffered most in the recession has not quite disappeared.

In this chapter, we have argued that there is a connection between inequality and the political response to a downturn – a response that could condemn recessionary victims to hard times for a very long while to come. It is a powerful mechanism, but it is not the only thing that can move public opinion. It is still too soon to assume that all hopes for solidarity are doomed. As well as recapping the many societal fault-lines we have found criss-crossing both Britain and America, our final chapter discusses the sort of response to hard times that just might make a difference – and command support across the divides.

Shelter from the storm

I have put money into the system and my family have put money into the system, it's there for a reason . . .
'Norma', 55, with brittle bones

It is customary for this sort of social-science-meets-public-policy book to close with a little wish-list of novel eye-catching policies – asset-based welfare, 'nudging' pension schemes or happiness classes in schools. My broad-brush suggestions are, by contrast, wearyingly familiar. After everything we have learnt about the battering endured by so much of our society, the agenda that suggests itself can be summed up with a tricolon: jobs, fairer shares and a decent safety net. The lessons distilled from hard times past could be summed up with the same three-part formula, and yet today the latter two-thirds of it are not merely neglected, but (as Chapter 8 described) under active assault. The bewildering post-recessionary consensus appears to be that jobs and growth are best pursued by getting back to Anglo-Saxon business as usual, with all that entails for inequality in security and pay, not to mention – some critical economists add – an in-built volatility that could inflame the risks of further booms and busts.[1] The position raises an urgent question: how on earth to pursue an ideal of economic solidarity that has itself fallen on such hard times?

In the remaining pages, we will recap our main findings and explain why they cry out for that ideal. The need for welfare and labour market policies that can do something about the material hardship we uncovered is evident, but – while the connection might be less obvious – we will also explain why economic solidarity is essential in responding to all our chilling analysis of the 'social recession'. We will deal with the serious, as well as the entirely spurious, economic constraints, and will finally come back to the challenging political picture.

At the outset, though, we need to prise back open an economic debate that has grown narrowed, and remind ourselves that many things that these days seem inevitable are, in fact, the result of deliberate decisions. Britain and America are, as we have hammered home, both very rich countries, by any historical or international standard. As such they have choices. It is, undeniably, a choice to run a public policy that means that a redundancy notice immediately plunges its recipient into poverty. It is a choice, too, to accept rather than challenge the economic gulf that has opened up since the 1970s. And it is a decision, whether actively taken or not, to concede that pursuing skewed growth of the same sort that puffed up the bubble is the only way to go after the bust.

The Cameron conundrum

David Cameron was right: in affluent societies – which Britain and America remained throughout the recession – what *ought* to matter is not GDP, but the ties of community and general well-being. After 80 years of industrial progress, there is no reason why a passing financial storm should instigate any of the misery of Marienthal: we should have been able to shield the things that mattered. Yet using precisely the sort of gauges that Cameron favours (or used to favour), we have uncovered all too much of that misery – not, it is true, across all of society, but across very substantial swathes.

Contemporary Britain and America have not been broken as a whole, as the US was 80 years ago. Saner monetary policy managed to contain overall unemployment. Private affluence, as well as the continued existence of certain social protections, kept certain fears in check, and avoided the mass dislocation that can finally finish off community life. The roads are not blocked by lines of uprooted families, as they were when hapless and hounded 'Okies' such as the Joads fled the Dust Bowl. But we must not be complacent: as poor residents from costly central London boroughs such as Westminster are shunted out to the capital's lower-rent outer-east, it is said that the jibe 'Westies' can be heard whispered around their new homes.[2] Neither the average crime figures nor the overall mortality statistics suggest a drift back to a world where life is 'nasty, brutish and short'. But what of the two less-remembered adjectives that Hobbes applied to life in the state of nature – 'solitary' and 'poor'?

On both of these two final counts, great tracts of contemporary Britain and America are enduring very hard times indeed. When the storm hit, the immediate consequence was soaring unemployment in exactly the same communities that have been battered by all recent recessions (Chapter 3), as well as an explosion in insecurity for those who clung on to low-grade work (Chapter 4). Intriguingly, the recession did *not* immediately widen the pre-existing gulf in incomes (Chapter 2), because automatic redistribution kicked in, while wages were squeezed far and wide. But after long decades in which poor communities had been cut adrift, even before austerity started to concentrate post-recessionary pain on the luckless, the losses at the bottom were that much harder to bear. Coming on top of concentrated joblessness and worsening conditions in low-grade jobs, resurgent penury has left Britons like 'Moira' feeling deep shame, and Americans such as Leroy Armstrong hungry enough to swallow their pride and claim food stamps.

Beyond the material hardship, the recession worked to deepen the great Anglo-American economic divide into a societal schism. While wallets have been squeezed across the wage range, in every other respect our economic tornado has blown with unequal force. Unemployment and insecurity we have mentioned; but in relation to happiness (Chapter 5), community and friendship (Chapter 6), too, we have exhaustively charted the course of a gale that has blown harder on some than on others. We found tentative signs of family life coming under particular strain in recession-battered homes, and unequivocal evidence of highly selective scarring (Chapter 7), which will blight life for many years to come in the towns where redundancy notices were scattered like confetti in 2009. Indeed, we have pinpointed the way in which recessionary victims get bumped onto tracks that lead away from society, and have highlighted knock-on effects that will stifle the opportunities even of children as yet unborn. Through such channels the damage done in hard-hit towns could actually *continue to deepen* even after the recovery is officially complete.

Sometimes we have found a storm that raged harder in Britain; sometimes in the US. At all points, however, we have found 'a social recession' that has discriminated between different parts of the community, hitting the already vulnerable harder in every respect. As the slump slowly fades from the GDP figures, there are many comfortable suburbs where it will soon be forgotten. There are also, however, many less-fortunate places where what is unfolding doesn't feel like a recovery at all – for the very good reason that a savage experience is lingering on.

Although our focus has been on the effect of the recession, throughout our investigations we could not help encountering evidence of problems with roots that stretched back to well before 2008. For all the riches of the millennial years, we found swathes of society that were already sorely exposed by that time. Consider, for example, the steadily rising American rates of absolute poverty over the noughties – rates which all but guaranteed that a downturn would immediately translate into penury. Consider, too, the substantial pre-recession volunteering deficit in Britain's more deprived neighbourhoods, and the long-term trend for a particular plunge in rates of marriage among disadvantaged Americans. All of these things, which emerged over those same decades in which inequality soared, worked to leave more of the vulnerable braving the storm in effective isolation.

It would be going too far to claim that all the real damage was done before the recession, and was merely *revealed* by the downturn: we have seen that the purely recessionary surge in unemployment had profound and unhappy consequences for well-being. But the wider mood of anxiety that defines these hard times undoubtedly has deeper roots. As one recent academic analysis in the US concluded, on the basis of extensive data from both before and after the slump,

> 2009 was not as unusual as one might expect. Many economic worries were already quite common before the downturn began. The Great Recession exposed a broader cross-section of Americans to economic risks, but those risks were very much a part of American economic life even before it hit – and they are certainly still a part of it today.[3]

Similar worries fell upon the shoulders of poorer Britons in boom time; they were weighed down by debt and insecure contracts even before rising unemployment made matters worse. Beveridge's five giants have been replaced by three modern-day demons – anxiety, aimlessness and isolation – and both the first and the last of these demons were stalking poor neighbourhoods long before the slump.

So how have hard times hurt? Not primarily through reductions in absolute levels of income. Though we have seen that serious material deprivation is indeed a reality for the hardest-hit minority, more generally (and despite the overall squeeze on pay packets) there has been no comparably sustained effect on the self-rated life satisfaction of the populace as a whole. Rather, what our exhaustive statistical analysis of the well-being data suggests is, first, that those thrown out of work have taken exactly the hammering in happiness terms that students of Marienthal would have expected; and second, that the working insecure and poor have shared in perhaps half the misery of the jobless.

Anxiety appears to be the channel through which a lot of the unhappiness flows, and it is also important in the withering of community bonds. Just as an unemployed painter told Mirra Komarovsky during the 1930s that he had 'learned to keep people at a distance so as not to get snubbed', so 'Winston' told us in 2013 that these days 'I don't even *put myself out there*', as if getting socially involved was somehow to make oneself exposed. That is how it feels when you drop down in a country that allows blameless people to fall too far. Komarovsky's impoverished painter was quite explicit about that during the Depression: 'I now feel inferior' to the 'well-to-do people' who 'used to be my friends'.[4] Without decent protection for an economy's victims, 80 years of intervening industrial progress count for nothing in addressing such feelings, or the isolation they foster. Until we have an economy that delivers fairer shares and some measure of security across society, such anxiety will never be banished, and – in the face of the next financial storm, whenever that may come – neither 'general well-being' nor community life is going to be safe.

To reiterate, these objectives are the right ones for hard times. Stronger social ties and families would indeed have helped us weather the storm – and perhaps even from a narrow financial perspective. Although it is really a subject for another book, it is worth noting new American analysis suggesting that stronger communities can feed back beneficially into the economy. After adjusting for all the obvious confounding factors, and using serious datasets, the researchers calculate that 'states with high social cohesion suffered from unemployment rates 2 percentage points lower than their less connected and trusting counterparts', during the depths of the downturn.[5] If, as it seems, employers with more faith in, and connections to, their neighbourhood are more inclined to keep workers on, then the pursuit of recovery that disregards the human dimension could actually be self-defeating, while an economy that can foster a strong community may actually draw strength from that in return. In parallel, a plethora of studies are emerging to suggest a link between the pursuit of happiness in the workplace and rising productivity.[6]

All of this sounds like it ought to be grist to Cameron's Big Society mill. And yet we are left with a puzzle: a phrase the British prime minister was once obsessive about is now mostly forgotten by his friends, and written off as 'BS' of another kind by his detractors. For the pertinent question is not whether a strong community and general well-being are desirable, which they invariably are and especially in hard times, but how to go about getting them. Whatever the answer may be, it will not be a politician at a lectern.

Economic insecurity is certainly not the only factor that is material here – culture is undoubtedly important as well. Indeed, we have demonstrated that America's formal community life appears to have been better protected than Britain's during the recession, and we suggested that this is because of different habits and traditions, and could perhaps owe something to the greater social role of American churches. It is a similar story with respect to philanthropy: every opera house or community group seeking support from cash-strapped ministers in Whitehall has, at one time or another, been brushed away with the suggestion that they should try and unlock US-style giving. The differences are real enough – Americans give more and their donations held up better in the slump – but being able to observe this is not the same as being able to emulate it.[7] Culture cannot be bundled up and shipped.

Attempts to create a strong community by edict are doomed, if not absurd. One cannot logically (or so you might think) compel volunteering. But the UK government is getting about as close as is conceptually possible, mandating jobseekers to undertake a variety of unpaid community work as a condition of benefits. This, however, is not producing a kinder or gentler society. The charities receiving the free manpower were already complaining that it is not of the right sort, before the press reported that unwilling 'volunteers' recruited from the dole office to help out with the Queen's jubilee ended up being told to sleep under Blackfriars Bridge the night before the pageant.[8] There could hardly be a more poignant fable of hard times in a dis-United Kingdom.

Money matters

So what are we left with in policy terms? While there are no doubt important specialist interventions to be made in mental health services and in providing support to charities, we have presented a book full of evidence which demonstrates that, in hard times especially, people's propensity to connect and thrive is going to have a lot to do with work, security and the avoidance of poverty. Governments cannot wave a magic wand and secure these things without any cost or risk – otherwise they would have done so already. But they do have hugely important choices to make in all of these areas, just as they did after the Depression.

The first and most obvious lesson, now as then, is to keep the employed to a maximum and the unemployed to a minimum. Our analysis of the well-being data makes it abundantly clear that the jobless are still the worst-hit recessionary victims, and our examination of the scarring effect of redundancy both on future community engagement and on the prospects of the next generation greatly reinforces this familiar reality. The most important of all factors in hard times here is macroeconomic policy. It is for others to debate the details of this, but we can make two very general appeals.

First, do not underestimate the damage that hard times can do. Amid all the uncertainties and risks of bold policy action, plumping for passivity and accepting a year or two of stagnation can appear a seductive option – that is, for example, the calculation that Britain made on the fiscal side. Our research on social scarring, however, suggests that there could be an enduring cost to letting things drift, which will not show up on any public finance spreadsheet in Washington or Whitehall. But, make no mistake, frailer communities and worse mental health will cost the public purse in the end.

Because deep recessions do such damage, it is important to be grateful for one great mercy: the prevailing policy of easy money in both Britain and America. Record low interest rates and liberal use of the printing presses represent one crucial break with the early 1930s, and have allowed both countries to avoid the trap of debt deflation and the wholesale destruction of jobs that has historically come with it. We have not dwelt on this point because the reflationists have mostly carried the day; it is, however, important to register, since undue panic about inflation, or pressure from savers fed up with low returns, could yet force a premature policy shift. The continuing misery of the eurozone illustrates (among other things) the dangers of even a slightly more restrictive monetary policy for jobs. Our research suggests that the knock-on effects of that on European society could be felt for a long time to come.

Second, do not imagine that the relatively reassuring overall employment rates in Britain and America tell the whole story about unemployment in either society. The total number of redundancies may not have been on a truly depressionary scale, but they have fallen so unevenly that on poorer streets you would not know it. At moments during the slump, the most vulnerable of all – such as young, black British males – were more likely to be without work than to be in it. Our analysis adds clarity about who requires attention – youngsters, ethnic minorities and school dropouts – all of whom are easily identifiable groups that well-designed employment programmes should have no difficulty in targeting. Prevention is far preferable to cure, because there is one other group that is seriously disadvantaged in the jobs market: people who have already been laid off. With their morale undermined and isolation more of a risk, they have less chance of hearing of a vacancy or of putting up a confident interview. The best interventions will therefore come before unemployment has got its grip.

Jobs, then, are at the heart of resolving hard times, just as they always were. In the light of what we have learnt, however, it would be wrong to make *jobs of any sort* the limit of the ambition. For we have also seen that Anglo-American working life has become laced with worry. The four-decade squeeze on American pay packets – a squeeze that has also affected Britons for the past dozen years or so – is only the beginning. Closely associated is the proliferation of low-grade work, which holds out few prospects and which (as we explained in Chapter 4) has directly increased the 'recession exposure' of workers who held onto employment. Most disturbing of all, and most directly pertinent to all those societal problems that link back to anxiety, is the spread of insecurity across the bottom end of the workforce – insecurity that intensified during the slump. When pushed to the extreme, as in zero-hours contracts, it is no exaggeration to say that the once-clear line between the employed and the jobless becomes blurred. All of this has played its part in making hard times harder.

And the implication of the long pay squeeze, in particular, is that it was not merely the recent absence of growth that landed so many families in financial difficulty. In turn, that raises doubts about the ability of the present restoration of growth on the old model to achieve widely shared prosperity.

The problems with working life in Anglo-American societies are clear enough; but in economies that have come to be built around cheap and commoditised labour, finding the right policy prescriptions is more difficult. If the United States suddenly legislated a $15 an hour minimum wage it would make great strides on poverty pay; but, in the short run at least, it might also have to live with considerably more unemployment. For social as well as economic reasons, it would be irresponsible in the extreme to pretend that this danger did not exist. Others are far better qualified to advise on the sort of trade-offs involved in this sort of calculation, including radical economists who query whether the costs of regulation really bite as hard as British and American employers claim.[9] As with bigger-picture economic policy, however, on the back of our investigations we can add a few general observations on labour market regulation in hard times.

First, because of the special role that anxiety plays in converting economic into social damage, a priority for regulatory effort should be curtailing practices that exacerbate insecurity. But as evidence about exploitative use of zero-hours contracts built in Britain – contracts which, in the worst cases, involve workers signing away any opportunity to work for other firms, in return for no security – the Coalition consulted not only on taking action, but also on doing nothing.[10]

Second, to the extent that inequality exacerbates anxiety in hard times – through that inflamed fear of falling further – employment protection laws and institutions have a role to play. A recent cross-national analysis of European data on incomes, inequality and employment protection in the *Economic Journal*, a publication ordinarily marked by academic caution and caveat, concluded: 'The results are startling and fairly unambiguous: in countries with strictly regulated labour markets, the distribution of household incomes is significantly more equal than in those countries with flexible labour markets.'[11] In this book we have touched on suggestive evidence of the 'social slump' playing out less divisively in France and Germany than in the UK and the US. Here we can spot an important clue as to why that might be.

An even more obvious way to tame financial insecurity than employment regulation is directly, through the maintenance – or in America's case the creation – of a decent safety net. Theoretical concerns about encouraging idleness are inevitably aired, and there is evidence that prompting benefit claimants to train or search out work can make a difference to employment around the edges. But there is less evidence that rates of benefits matter, and a few easily summarised facts expose such considerations as entirely second order.

First, unemployment is not driven by tweaks to benefit policy; as the Great Recession and every previous downturn has unremittingly demonstrated, what matters far more are the great swings of the macroeconomic cycle. One of the few absolute certainties in social science is that unemployment insurance did not create the mass American unemployment of the 1930s, since Roosevelt only invented it in response! Second, unemployment in Britain was at historic lows during the 1950s and 1960s, when unemployment benefit 'replacement rates' were far higher than today.[12] Finally, as Chapter 3 detailed, during the recent recession overall unemployment rose considerably further in the US than the UK, peaking at 10% rather than 8%, despite the UK's more extensive safety net. Unlike with employment regulation, where there may be serious trade-offs, there is no real 'jobs argument' against countries that start out with inadequate benefits improving their provision.

Two transatlantic comparisons that drop directly from our research renew the argument for better protection. One serious societal problem with the minimal welfare model of the United States came to light: the persistence of deep scarring on the well-being of Americans who were thrown out of work, even *after* they got a new job; such scarring was not found among Britons. At the same time, one claimed advantage fell away: the US system turned out to offer no protection against a 'dependency culture', since we found just as much inherited worklessness in America as in the UK. Threatening benefit recipients with destitution in order to force them to take the first unsuitable job that may come along is thus not so much being 'cruel to be kind', as is often pretended, but simply being cruel.

The serious argument against providing a decent safety net for hard times, if there is one, must be about the cost rather than about jobs. The crass insistence that 'we can no longer afford to support poor families as we once did' is not hard to knock down. Narrowly defined 'welfare' expenditure in the US is now so small, relative to both GDP and the overall federal budget, that decisions at the margin about what to spend it on are plainly a matter of political discretion, as opposed to exogenous economic constraint.[13] In Britain, where non-pension social security represents a fairly substantial 13% of government expenditure, the argument looks a little more tenable.[14] But there is no getting away from the fact that the decision to defend or cut into this expenditure remains a political choice.

Other countries, after all, have done things differently. In Japan, which (Chapter 1 suggested) has held together relatively well as a society through long years of economic stagnation, hard times did not immediately precipitate the same sort of sustained reduction in benefits for the poor and workless that is being embarked on in the Anglo-Saxon world today. It was only after the disappearance of the first 'lost decade', during the 2000s, that certain cuts to lone parent benefits were made and modest workfare-style conditions imposed; and after a change of government in recessionary 2009, important elements of these changes were reversed, while other aspects of the safety net were actually strengthened.[15] Shinzō Abe's government is currently talking tougher on public expenditure and has made some cuts; but – despite a much larger public debt burden than either the US or the UK – it is reportedly treading with some caution on welfare, with the plans to rebalance the books placing more emphasis on sales taxes.[16]

Before we even get onto the important question of taxation, however, or panic about racking up public debt on a Japanese scale, there are all sorts of choices about where to spend public money. The British state, for example, pays for a nuclear deterrent, even though it has no one to point this at. It forks out to keep unprofitable farms in business and to sustain rural railway lines that could be more cheaply replaced with buses. These might be nice things to have; but the decision to put them ahead of a rate of jobseeker's allowance that might prevent redundancy notices becoming a trapdoor into poverty is plainly just that – a decision.

This is not to deny that there *are* real questions about sustaining social security – containing the bill would be a concern for any administration. It is only to dispute *which* questions. If there really have to be cuts, then there ought to be plenty of scope for debating exactly where these should fall, taking careful account of the ability of those on the receiving end to absorb the proposed pain. But there is scant evidence of this sort of deliberation in the choices being made.

It is a particular perversity that the one area of broad 'welfare' expenditure that really does face deep long-term pressures is the one area that has remained most peripheral to the retrenchment debate. American social security for the elderly already consumes incomparably more resources than state payments to anyone else, and Britain's over-60s also receive the lion's share of benefits. In ageing societies, the weight of supporting ever more people – not through passing hard times, but through long and lengthening retirements – is a more serious challenge. The right way to deal with it, though, is by tackling the root cause of this particular problem, and not by laying into state support for other people. With important exceptions for people who grow infirm early, that means accepting that pensionable and normal retirement ages will steadily rise and likely keep rising in line with longer healthy life expectancy. It also means having a hard-headed look at the balance between universal and targeted support for the elderly, and perhaps the pension indexation regime. Far more effort than now needs to be put into supporting people to keep working for longer; the fact that employment rates are still typically measured as a percentage of the under-60s or under-65s, rather than as a proportion of all adults, illustrates the culture shift that is required.

Making strides on this front might, in the end, bring literally millions of extra hands into the Anglo-American workforce. Parallel efforts to provide the right childcare for parents and the right support for disabled employees could eventually enable many more people again to make the move into work.[17] Concentrating on that objective could help shrug off the pervasive pessimism gripping public policy. Likewise, building affordable homes would contain pressure on housing benefits. All this would free up resources to allow the system to do a better job of providing emergency shelter when hard times next hit. But this is not the direction in which the discussion has been heading. We need to face this grim reality squarely, and turn to the final, and most difficult, challenge – changing the terms of a debate that has been veering off to the right.

From polarisation to persuasion

The claim 'Norma' makes at the top of this chapter – that the social security system is 'there for a reason' – should be compelling in hard times, and yet it is falling flat. Just how flat becomes clear in what she said next:

> . . . it just feels like now everything has been taken away, and I'm just waiting for the workhouse to come back to be honest . . . It's like you have to fight to survive. I cannot believe actually that they are doing this. It's hard to get your head round [how] they can get away with doing it.

The despair of beneficiaries of state welfare might be unavoidable if the cuts were simply a matter of financial necessity; but we have argued that there is a considerable element of choice. The argument for cuts to social security in the UK – cuts which are pushing British welfare in a remorselessly American direction – are not sold on purely financial grounds, but rather peddled through stories about scroungers and fraudsters.

Even in the United States, where these days there is little welfare left to shred, the Right continues to play the same old records. During 2012, Republican challenger Mitt Romney picked a running mate,

Paul Ryan, who had only recently proposed ending Medicaid and food stamps as entitlements, by replacing them with cash-limited block grants, on the argument that: 'We don't want to turn the safety net into a hammock that lulls able-bodied people into lives of dependency and complacency.'[18] It is remarkable that such language is no longer used about cash payments that might be misspent, but about programmes to provide food and medicine to poor people in the world's richest economy – and at a time when a huge tide of redundancies has so recently rendered millions penniless through no fault of their own. The Romney campaign went on to whip up a story that regulatory tweaks to workfare made by the Obama administration were tantamount to telling layabouts to relax because 'we'll just send your welfare check'.[19]

The passionate airing of the work ethic that we heard direct from the British dole queue in Chapter 3 *should* be an effective riposte to the layabout myth. As for fraud, it must of course be admitted that, yes, there is indeed fraud in the system, just as there always has been. It must be agreed, too, that this needs to be dealt with. One of the women we spoke to confessed to being a former culprit: 'I did what you call "work on the side". I did some cash-in-hand work.' Even though she pleads that this was during 'times when we didn't have any food', officialdom can never be blasé about this sort of thing. The integrity of the system requires that breaches of the rules are not indulged. But with Whitehall itself estimating that this accounts for no more than 0.7% of the total benefit bill, a little perspective is needed.[20] To have reached a pass (as we have in the UK today) where there is talk about locking up benefit cheats for longer than the average rapist betrays a lack of proportion.[21] There *should* be a commonsensical case for explaining that as well.

One important reason that these points are not getting through is, indubitably, that they are not being made. We have emphasised how hard times in unequal societies can work to frustrate a progressive response, but the dynamics of political opinion cannot be reduced to underlying economic conditions – there are other influences, too. There is powerful evidence that a big part of the lurch to the right on questions of welfare in the UK can be traced to a change in tone on the part of the elite. Analysis of two decades of BSA data suggests that much of the overall drift to the right on redistribution and benefits occurred during the mid-1990s, just as Tony Blair was rewriting the Labour party's traditional 'welfarist' line and allowing Conservative complaints about social security to go unchallenged. Furthermore, the overall swing in opinion was not found across the political spectrum – as might be expected with a generalised cultural shift – but was concentrated among Labour voters, suggesting that they were responding to the changing tone of their own party's leadership.[22]

So a little more nerve on the part of progressive political advocates might do some good. But it is always easy to demand 'more political will', and rarely a complete answer. In Chapter 9, we reviewed both British and American evidence that revealed how divergent social experiences of recession were being transposed into polarised opinion. The scare-mongering crusade against welfare is being fought on fertile territory, reshaped by recession. It has served its purpose in turning the working-but-pinched majority against those with no work at all. And as the recovery takes hold, polarisation could deepen again, because the well-to-do are – quite correctly – far more inclined than the penurious to believe that the sort of expansion that is now picking up is going to work to their personal advantage.[23]

Getting beyond this great division is not going to be easy – especially not in the United States, where deeply ingrained anti-government sentiment so profoundly colours the debate. In YouGov's spring 2013 cross-country polling, large majorities of three-quarters or more in Britain, France and Germany agreed that it was the government's job both to 'help poor children get ahead' and to provide 'a decent minimum income for all'. In hard-times America, by contrast, only 50% of voters agreed with either proposition. In the same polling, 'redistributing across the income range' found favour with narrow majorities in all the European countries, but was endorsed as a legitimate job for government by only 32% of respondents in the US.[24] There is some solace for egalitarian Britons here. There might be a shared Anglo-Saxon way of doing business, but – when it comes to accepting that the corollary of vigorous capitalism must be an expansive government to smooth its rough edges – the British people are firmly in the European rather than the American camp. For progressives in the US, by contrast, these polling numbers merely underline the challenge. The case for fairer shares and a decent safety net is going to have to be made extremely deftly if it is to have any chance of prevailing at the American ballot box. However disgruntled people are with stagnant living standards in a malfunctioning economy, they are not going to accept that a mistrusted government has any business meddling, *unless* that meddling can be shown to be legitimate.

Here reforming Americans and Britons of our own time would do well to learn a lesson from Roosevelt. He was clear-headed about the challenge he faced in pushing through the 1935 Social Security Act, legislation that was originally intended to be more comprehensive than it eventually proved, after sceptical elements of the executive conspired with the legislature to insert various exemptions.[25] So messy compromises were required, and Roosevelt entered into these with steely pragmatism. Most particularly, he grasped the importance of funding the scheme through ear-marked payroll taxes, which the progressive policy 'wonks' of the day sternly warned were deflationary, but which he nonetheless judged to be politically indispensable.

'Those taxes were never a matter of economics', the president would later reflect. 'They were politics all the way through. We put those payroll contributions there so as to give the contributors a legal, moral and political right to collect their pensions and their unemployment benefits.' The payroll tax linked the American safety net to work and contribution, and ensured that working Americans *owned* it. Consequently, perhaps, while broader American welfare has since been savaged, Roosevelt's basic scheme has indeed survived. He was quite right to foresee that 'with those taxes in there, no damn politicians can ever scrap my social security program'.[26]

Compare that with New Labour efforts at redistribution, which did not fuss too much with the question of legitimacy, but just pumped money towards poor families with children – simply by reason of their being poor. It was a noble endeavour, but one that has proved tragically easy to undo in hard times. Gordon Brown even passed an Act of Parliament to enshrine in statute the goal of rescuing youngsters from poverty.[27] That legislation is still sitting there, impotent on the statute book, as the number of poor children sets to rocket. For no legislation can protect a social ambition that was never properly explained, still less sold, to the working majority.

Instead of unlocking a new social settlement, post-recessionary policy is reaffirming the split into two (or more) nations that hard times have revealed, in Britain and America alike. The egoistic logic of opinion that polarises along financial lines could continue to dominate political economy – and yet it does not have to. The challenge is to rescue the economy's hardest-hit victims on a basis that the majority ultimately understands to be in its own interests too. We close with a few thoughts on how this might be done.

These are harsh times as well as hard ones – this is not an era in which every societal split can be wished away, and nor can the mood of resentment. Part of the trick of progressive politics in the coming years is going to be to identify divisions that can be exploited for reformist purposes, instead of meekly accepting those splits which, we have seen, are pitting victim against victim. There is some potential in the 'rich versus the rest' theme, which also has the merit of unlocking important sources of public revenues that might be used to heal social wounds. After 30 years of runaway inequality, there is less truth than there used to be in the old assumption that taxes on the wealthy cannot on their own pay for anything significant.[28] Corporate buccaneers and swindlers are also ripe for attack, just as the great monopolies and cartels of the past proved worthy targets for the progressives of the time. As the 'cost of living' argument rages in the UK, the penurious and the merely pinched have been rallied to common purpose against the energy companies, train operators and private pension providers who are accused of ripping them off.

Orthodox economists will protest that meddling in such markets is an inefficient way to redistribute resources – and sometimes they will have a point. From a political point of view, however, no opportunity to do something practical and popular for the stricken in these hard times can be missed. Suspicion of corporations, also evident in the mood of public anger over the elaborate tax avoidance regimes of various transnationals, reads across into certain arguments about workfare, too.

One of the few retreats on social security that public opinion forced on the British Coalition is instructive in this connection. It came about after reports that unemployed people who had voluntarily agreed to try unpaid work (including shelf-stacking at Tesco) with no guaranteed job prospects were later told they could have their benefits docked if they walked away before completing a full four weeks. As outrage flared, mindful of PR, the big businesses involved denounced the element of compulsion, and ministers removed the link between this work experience scheme and benefit sanctions. The political lesson is that whereas the majority might not like free-riding benefit claimants, they are even less keen on free-loading corporations.[29]

Alongside combativeness, hard-headedness is another important virtue in hard times. There is still a crucial political job to be done in explaining why the sort of economy that Britain and America were running *before* 2008 proved so vulnerable to the great economic and social recession that subsequently unfolded. The brand of capitalism in which hot money is free to chase high returns for minimal commitment has fed underinvestment, and thereby contributed to the downgrading of so many jobs in Britain and the US. Economists are increasingly interested in how the great growth grab by the top 1% has rendered aggregate demand more volatile and less balanced. Joseph Stiglitz writes that it is 'no accident that this crisis, like the Great Depression, was preceded by large increases in inequality'.[30] The steady concentration of spending power in the hands of the rich, for whom outlays are discretionary, increased susceptibility to the great financial mood swing in 2007/08.

After the storm broke, much of ordinary Britain and America was left weighed down by consumer loans that many workers had accrued during the bubble, as they strove to enjoy some small slice of the wealth that their labour was creating for other people. A failure to grasp the battered balance sheet of ordinary homes compromised the policy response, and bequeathed a lacklustre initial recovery.[31] And, arguably, a failure to address the lop-sided pattern of rewards in the Anglo-Saxon economies will increase volatility, and with it the danger of something similar happening again. These sorts of arguments urgently need to escape the economics seminar room and find their way onto the platform of presidential and prime ministerial debates. In the wake of the Great Recession, no argument should resonate more with the majority of ideology-light, pragmatic voters than an analysis suggesting how we can guard against any repeat.

Another important lesson is to go with the grain of the work ethic that we have discovered among the ranks of the scared and the squeezed. Thus far it has been used to pit recessionary victim against victim – and thereby to split communities. How the discourse would change if shelters against economic storms could somehow be built upon foundations in working life. This thought strengthens the case for not relying on state benefits to do all of the sheltering, but also to look towards regulating, rewarding or otherwise nudging employers to do more for their staff on security, as well as pay.

I have heard clever and well-meaning economists half-joke that the minimum wage is 'a means-tested benefit, arbitrarily targeted on hourly wages rather than overall income, and arbitrarily funded through a ring-fenced tax on the employers who keep low-skilled workers off the dole'. There is an economistic way of looking at the world that sees things in that light. This is a vantage point from which it always looks tidier to shelter the vulnerable by raising income support than by telling employers what to do. That is not, however, the way that voters concerned about exploitation by unscrupulous employers see things, and anyone who is actually concerned about getting resources to those lashed by hard times must respect this reality.

In a poll containing many unwelcome messages for the British trade unions that commissioned it, Greenberg Quinlan Rosner established in September 2013 that the public was considerably more concerned about social security supporting work than anything else, including withdrawing money from those who did not deserve it.[32]

That is bad news indeed for any egalitarian foolish enough to allow herself to be painted into a corner of being indifferent as to whether or not people are working; but it also highlights the potential appeal of providing financial support for families that are struggling by on low pay. A closely related implication, which Roosevelt grasped, is that social security tied to contributions is more likely to endure.

It is complex and – from a narrow, anti-poverty view – often wasteful to shower resources on people who sometimes do not need the money because they have 'paid a stamp'. In the end, though, it might be the only way to create a politically sustainable social security. Even though the link between social contributions and social benefits has always been complex and frequently compromised, the same poll-sters, Greenberg Quinlan Rosner, established continuing sympathy for the principle.[33] More than that, by highlighting shared contributions – and a shared desire for security – renewed and suitably modernised social insurance might actually heal some of the divides that we have found being seared through British and American communities.[34] For even if the risks from recession are now hugely skewed to the disadvantage of the already-poor, Middle Britain and Middle America are surely not beyond understanding that bad things can happen to good people. At the very least, state payments made as an earned right would save women like disabled 'Stephanie' from feeling – as we reported – that her family were 'beggars, sitting there with our hands out'. Even on its own, addressing such painful sentiments would do a lot to smooth the very sharpest edges of poverty.

The final wider lesson, which is tough for desiccated political parties in which ambitious and privileged graduates loom so large, is to listen – really listen – to the way in which people discuss hard times. Throughout this book, we have heard the voices of many who are suffering, and have seen how certain policies that possess a certain technical plausibility (such as Britain's 'bedroom tax') unravel with appalling consequences in poor communities. Too many of the elite do not think through the consequences, because – as the decades of income data reported in Chapter 2 make plain – they live in a parallel world, where hard times cannot touch anything of significance.

The old faith in progress is faltering, and not merely because of the scale of the recent recession. It is faltering, too, because so many people had already ceased to see any return from skewed economic growth, and because inequality has wrought a fragile society. In the grievances of the working majority – disgruntled about squeezed pay packets, downgraded jobs and stunted opportunity for their children – there really ought to be an opening for change. Unless it is grasped, we will emerge from the Great Recession doomed to re-create the very errors that brought it into being. Society as a whole might be able to survive that, but it should not be assumed that poor communities could. Having been cut adrift for 35 years, it is tough even to say with any precision when hard times began for them. And, with austerity looming for as far as the eye can see, it is outright impossible to offer them any reassurance about when their hard times will end.

Notes

Foreword to the paperback edition: 'Recovery' 2015

1. John McArthur's story was previously reported on in Shiv Malik, 'DWP orders man to work without pay for company that let him go', *Guardian*, 4 November 2014, at: www.theguardian.com/society/2014/nov/03/dwp-benefits-electrician-work-placement-labour
2. Historic data on prices and earnings collated by the Bank of England, and analysed by the Trade Union Congress, 'UK workers suffering the most severe squeeze in real earnings since Victorian times', 12 October 2014, at: www.tuc.org.uk/economic-issues/labour-market-and-economic-reports/economic-analysis/britain-needs-pay-rise/uk%20
3. Richard Blundell, Claire Crawford and Wenchao Jin, 'Employment composition, hourly wages and the productivity puzzle', *Economic Journal*, 124: 576 (2014), pp. 377–407, nominates 'increased labour supply compared with past recessions' as one of the main potential explanations as to why pay fell so far, and notes that trends in labour supply are 'consistent with recent changes to welfare policy in the UK' (p. 381). Paul Gregg, Steven Machin and Mariña Fernández Salgado, 'Real wages and unemployment in the big squeeze', *Economic Journal*, 124: 576 (2014), pp. 408–32, acknowledges 'increased pressure to take low-wage work' among benefit claimants as an 'obvious possibility' for explaining the increased 'substitutability' of existing workers within the bottom third of the wage distribution (p. 428).
4. Carl Emmerson, Paul Johnson and Helen Miller (eds), *The IFS Green Budget 2014*, Institute for Fiscal Studies, London, 2014, Chapter 6, at: www.ifs.org.uk/budgets/gb2014/gb2014_ch6.pdf, esp. Table 6.2, p. 139.
5. ibid., Table 6.11, p. 140.
6. Abi Adams and Peter Levell, *Measuring Poverty When Inflation Varies Across Households*, Joseph Rowntree Foundation, York, 2014, Figures 12 and 13, p. 25.
7. Paolo De Agostini, John Hills and Holly Sutherland, *Were We Really All In It Together? The distributional effects of the UK Coalition government's tax-benefit policy changes*, Social Policy in a Cold Climate: Working Paper No. 10, LSE, London, 2014, at: http://sticerd.lse.ac.uk/dps/case/spcc/wp10.pdf
8. Office for Budget Responsibility, *Welfare Trends Report*, London, 2014, at: http://budgetresponsibility.org.uk/wordpress/docs/Welfare_trends_report_2014_dn2B.pdf
9. Office for National Statistics, *UK Labour Markets, November 2014*, at: www.ons.gov.uk/ons/dcp171778_381416.pdf

10. Office for National Statistics, *People in Employment Reporting a Zero-hours Contract, August 2014*, at: www.ons.gov.uk/ons/dcp171766_373757.pdf

11. Office for National Statistics, *Self-employed Workers in the UK – 2014*, at: www.ons.gov.uk/ons/dcp171776_374941.pdf

12. Data from the *Community Life Survey, 2013 to 2014*, at: www.gov.uk/government/statistics/community-life-survey-2013-to-2014-data

13. Chris Belfied, Jonathan Cribb, Andrew Hood and Robert Joyce, *Living Standards, Poverty and Inequality in the UK: 2014*, Institute for Fiscal Studies, London, 2014; at: www.ifs.org.uk/uploads/publications/comms/r96.pdf, pp. 52–3, 87–8, 105–8.

14. Erzsébet Bukodi, John H. Goldthorpe, Lorraine Waller and Jouni Huha, 'The mobility problem in Britain: New findings from the analysis of birth cohort data', *British Journal of Sociology* (print edn forthcoming, 2014), doi: 10.1111/1468-4446.12096.

15. A. Park, C. Bryson and J. Curtice (eds), *British Social Attitudes 31*, NatCen Social Research, London, 2014; at: www.bsa-31.natcen.ac.uk/downloads.aspx, pp. 101, 121 and 110–12.

16. Robert E. Lucas, 'The industrial revolution: Past and future', *Federal Reserve Bank of Minneapolis: Annual Report 2003*, 2004, at: www.minneapolisfed.org/publications_papers/pub_display.cfm?id=3333, pp. 5–20.

Introduction

1. Marie Jahoda, Paul F. Lazarsfeld and Hans Zeisel, *Marienthal: The sociography of an unemployed community*, Transaction Publishers, New Brunswick, NJ, 2002 [1933].

2. ibid., p. 70.

3. John Steinbeck, *The Grapes of Wrath*, Pan Books, London, 1975 [1939], p. 369.

4. Every country with any sort of stake in global trading felt some effect, though not every country fell into technical recession. The most obvious exception among the developed economies was Australia – it experienced a brief contraction, but bounced back so rapidly that it is generally deemed to have avoided a slump. See 'Australia dodges recession', *Sydney Morning Herald*, 3 June 2009, at: www.smh.com.au/business/australia-dodges-recession-20090603-buyq.html

5. J.K. Galbraith, *The Great Crash*, Penguin/Allen Lane, London, 2007 [1954], p. 85.

6. For an account of Credit-Anstalt's failure and the financial contagion that followed, see Charles H. Feinstein, Peter Temin and Gianni Toniolo, *The European Economy Between the Wars*, Oxford University Press, Oxford, 1997, pp. 107–10.

7. Robert D. Putnam, *Bowling Alone*, Simon & Schuster, New York, 2000, p. 54, Figure 8. The numbers charted are a composite of membership rates across the 32 organisations, defined as a proportion of the pool of potentially eligible members for each organisation, in terms of age, faith, region, etc. – so Hadassah membership is measured as a fraction of all Jewish women, 4-H membership as a proportion of all rural youth, and so on.

8. ibid., p. 54.

9. Mirra Komarovsky, *The Unemployed Man and His Family: Status of the man in fifty-nine families*, AltaMira Press, Walnut Creek, CA, 2004 [1940], pp. 123–4.

10. Putnam, *Bowling Alone*. For PTAs, see Figure 9, p. 57; for professional associations Figure 15, p. 84; and for playing-card sales (which declined from about 54 to 45 packs of cards sold per hundred Americans aged over 14 every year), see Figure 21, p. 103.

11. This selective list of violent threats to orderly democracy at the state level in the US is distilled from Jean Edward Smith, *FDR*, Random House paperback edition, New York, 2008 [2007], p. 290.

12. The number of African Americans recorded as being lynched in these years (not necessarily an exhaustive list) rose from 7 in 1929 to 24 in 1933. From the Tuskegee

University archive, available online at: http://192.203.127.197/archive/bitstream/handle/123456789/511/Lyching%201882%201968.pdf?sequence=1

13. Quoted in Don Peck, *Pinched: How the Great Recession has narrowed our futures and what we can do about it*, Crown, New York, 2011, p. 54.

14. In 2012, the Keep Talking Greece blog reported 'Athens: Soup kitchens close for summer due to shortage of volunteer cooks', at: www.keeptalkinggreece.com/2012/07/02/athens-soup-kitchens-close-for-summer-due-to-shortage-of-volunteer-cooks/ By 2013, the mainstream media picked up on the volunteering drought: Helena Smith, 'Greece's food crisis: Families face going hungry during summer shutdown', *Guardian*, 7 August 2013, at: www.theguardian.com/world/2013/aug/06/greece-food-crisis-summer-austerity

15. Michael Lewis, *Boomerang: The meltdown tour*, Penguin/Allen Lane, London, 2011, p. 82.

16. For Ireland, ibid., pp. 83–131. Quotes from p. 106 and p. 116.

17. Anthony B. Atkinson and Thomas Piketty (eds), *Top Incomes over the Twentieth Century: A contrast between continental European and English-speaking countries*, Oxford University Press, Oxford and New York, 2007.

18. For the main empirical trends, see A.B. Atkinson, Thomas Piketty and Emmanuel Saez, 'Top incomes in the long-run of history', Chapter 13 in Anthony B. Atkinson and Thomas Piketty (eds), *Top Incomes over the Twentieth Century: A global perspective*, Oxford University Press, Oxford and New York, 2010, pp. 664–759. See especially: section 13.3, from p. 678, which demonstrates that the income share of the top 10%, top 1%, top 0.1% and top 0.01% has tended to follow a U-shape of decline followed by rise in all the Anglophone countries. By contrast, in the continental countries – Germany, France, Switzerland and the Netherlands – there is no U; only decline until the 1970s, and then in essence stability. There is some disagreement between data sources about recent trends in Japan, but the historic results quoted here (p. 682) suggest stability, at least until the end of the twentieth century. For an updated précis by the same distinguished team, see Anthony B. Atkinson, Thomas Piketty and Emmanuel Saez, 'Top incomes in the long run of history', *Journal of Economic Literature*, 49:1 (2011), pp. 3–71, at: http://elsa.berkeley.edu/~saez/atkinson-piketty-saezJEL10.pdf

19. Consider, to take one example, regulation on temporary contracts. Of over 30 OECD members ranked, the bottom five places are all English-speaking economies: bottom of all is Canada, then the US, Great Britain, New Zealand and Australia. On many other indicators the US is the lowest ranked of all. See OECD, 'Protecting jobs, enhancing flexibility: A new look at employment protection legislation', in *OECD Employment Outlook 2013*, 2013, pp. 65–126, passim, and Figure 2.9 (p. 92) for temporary contracts in particular, at: http://dx.doi.org/10.1787/empl_outlook-2013-6-en

20. See above references to Atkinson et al. (2010).

21. Jackie Calmes, 'Spotlight fixed on Geithner, a man Obama fought to keep', *New York Times*, 12 November 2011, at: www.nytimes.com/2011/11/13/us/politics/spotlight-fixed-on-geithner-a-man-obama-fought-to-keep.html?pagewanted=all&_r=0

22. Most lending always goes towards individuals' mortgages and financial institutions. But the combined total share of 'manufacturing' and 'other productive businesses' in lending by UK-resident financial institutions fell from 9.7% over the pre-crisis years 1997–2007, to 5.9% over 2008–12. Analysis of official data by the Centre for Research on Socio-Cultural Change at Manchester University for the *Guardian*; Aditya Chakrabortty, 'London's economic boom leaves rest of Britain behind', *Guardian*, 23 October 2013, at: www.theguardian.com/business/2013/oct/23/london-south-east-economic-boom

23. Claire Jones and Chris Giles, 'King warns over surge in asset prices', *Financial Times*, 13 February 2013, at: www.ft.com/cms/s/0/756c4840–75ff–11e2–9891–00144

feabdc0.html#axzz2jt3EgRGf For a fuller explanation and analysis of quantitative easing, see M. Joyce, M. Tong and R. Woods, 'The United Kingdom's quantitative easing policy: Design, operation and impact', *Bank of England Quarterly Bulletin*, 51:3 (2011), pp. 200–12.

24. For a comparison of Chamberlain's and Osborne's rhetoric, see Duncan Weldon, 'UK recession: Have we heard it all before?', *Guardian*, 25 July 2013, at: www.guardian.co.uk/commentisfree/2012/jul/25/uk-recession-george-osborne-neville-chamberlain

25. George Osborne, Budget statement to the House of Commons by the Chancellor of the Exchequer, 22 June 2010.

26. The equivocation here is on the definition of 'recession', always an arbitrary business. One widely used convention (which has no basis in theory) is two successive quarters of negative GDP growth. Though simple, even this is not unambiguous. The latest unrounded official statistics available at September 2013 suggested that Britain's GDP declined for three successive quarters, between Q4 2011 and Q2 2012. Ambiguity arises because the decline in Q1 2012 is so tiny (a meaningless 0.01%) that the Office for National Statistics (ONS) rounds it to zero – which is entirely sensible because much larger declines are frequently revised away. Under this rounding convention and the two-quarters rule, it can thus be said that there was no double dip. But this is misleading, since over these three straight quarters there was no growth and only shrinkage. Indeed, after brief growth coincident with the London Olympics, the economy shrank again, such that negative aggregate growth stretched over five quarters. That certainly sounds like a second recession, and – seeing as the population continued to grow as the economy shrank – it would certainly count as one if we were concerned with GDP per head. More socially significant, and less susceptible to revision than GDP, is the employment rate, which was recovering in spring 2010, but took a second dip in 2011. The balance of evidence, then, suggests that there was a second economic decline after the first signs of recovery in 2010. But to avoid getting dragged into definitional arguments, we avoid using the term 'double dip' and 'second recession' in the remainder of the book.

27. Conversation with the author, London, May 2013.

28. See, for example, Paul Krugman, 'The economic consequences of Mr. Osborne', New York Times Blog, 24 October 2012.

29. Quoted in 'No longer the martyr, it's time for Rudd to lead', *Sydney Morning Herald*, 27 June 2013, at: www.smh.com.au/opinion/politics/no-longer-the-martyr-its-time-for-rudd-to-lead-20130626-2oxt1.html#ixzz2XQKnsiXn

30. On 9 September 2013, as revised GDP figures for the year's second quarter recorded 0.7% growth, George Osborne declared that Britain had 'turned a corner'. His remarks are available on the *Guardian* website at: www.theguardian.com/politics/video/2013/sep/09/george-osborne-economic-recovery-video

31. On the return to property inflation in the UK, see 'UK housing: Building bubbles', *Financial Times*, 13 September 2013, at: www.ft.com/cms/s/3/616d81fe–1ae3–11e3–87da–00144feab7de.html?siteedition=uk&siteedition=uk#axzz2fcVIxyzT On Vince Cable's specific concerns, see George Parker and Kiran Stacey, 'Divisions between Nick Clegg and Vince Cable expose Lib Dem fears', *Financial Times*, 16 September 2013, at: www.ft.com/cms/s/0/ee1815dc–1e31–11e3–85e0–00144feab7de.html#axzz2fcVIxyzT

32. A macroeconomic appraisal of 'expansionary fiscal contraction' is beyond our scope; for a sweeping (if polemical) assessment of the idea of restoring prosperity through retrenchment, see Mark Blyth, *Austerity: The history of a dangerous idea*, Oxford University Press, New York, 2013.

33. Annie Gowen, 'Glenmont neighborhood in Washington suburb has grown closer in the poor economy', *Washington Post*, 4 May 2009, at: www.washingtonpost.com/wp-dyn/content/article/2009/05/03/AR2009050302330.html

Chapter 1: Not quite 1933

1. Gordon Brown, Budget statement to the House of Commons by the Chancellor of the Exchequer, 21 March 2007, at: www.publications.parliament.uk/pa/cm200607/cmhansrd/cm070321/debtext/70321-0004.htm

2. The freezing of the interbank lending market in July 2007 was an important clue that something was amiss, which was widely commented on – although also widely misinterpreted – by financial experts.

3. Niall Ferguson, 'A long shadow', *Financial Times*, 22 September 2008, at: www.ft.com/cms/s/0/aeb88d8a–8800–11dd-b114–0000779fd18c.html#axzz2WahpoyYx

4. One analysis of post-war financial crises estimates that unemployment rises by an average of 7 percentage points, while output falls an average of 9%, the latter taking place over the course of two years; whereas the average 'non-financial' recession lasts less than a year. See Carmen M. Reinhart and Kenneth S. Rogoff, 'The aftermath of financial crises', *American Economic Review*, 99:2 (2009), pp. 466–72, at: www.ems.bbk.ac.uk/for_students/msc_econ/ETA2_EMEC025P/GZrhein.pdf

5. The 2001 census recorded a UK population of 59,113,500, whereas the 2011 census recorded a total of 63,285,100. That implies population growth of around 1.25% a year. The Office for National Statistics is currently revising its estimates for intermediate years, but the last published numbers suggest no appreciable recession effect. By way of comparison, during the 1930s population growth was considerably lower. Estimation is rough, but some official projections – implying growth of around 0.5% in these years – are provided in *Census 1951: Preliminary Report*, at: www.visionofbritain.org.uk/census/SRC_P/1/EW1951PRE

6. We say 'nastiest' rather than 'deepest' as we are factoring in duration as well as depth. Looking at the peak-to-trough fall in GDP alone, we would also have to include the brief downturn of 1957, which is forgotten as it was all over so rapidly.

7. YouGov (2013). Cross-national fieldwork details and results at: http://d25d2506sfb94s.cloudfront.net/cumulus_uploads/document/u7f0cyctl1/YGCam-Archive-results–040413-All-Countries.pdf

8. John Maynard Keynes, *A Treatise on Money*, vol. 2: *The Applied Theory of Money*, Macmillan, London, 1950 [1930], p. 154.

9. Peck, *Pinched*, p. 14.

10. The Federal Reserve Bank of Minneapolis data is at: http://www.minneapolisfed.org/publications_papers/studies/recession_perspective/index.cfm

11. Patrick Butler, 'Britain in nutrition recession as food prices rise and incomes shrink', *Guardian*, 19 November 2012, at: www.guardian.co.uk/society/2012/nov/18/breadline-britain-nutritional-recession-austerity

12. These results come from YouGov's 'recession tracker', a commercial product containing data on 75 questions, which was kindly supplied by the company as a spreadsheet. The results quoted come from Tabs 4, 13 and 40.

13. Real GDP series from the MeasuringWorth website implies a calendar-year-on-calendar-year fall of 26.7%. Louis Johnston and Samuel H. Williamson, 'What was the US GDP then?', at: www.measuringworth.org/usgdp/ MeasuringWorth, which we exploit at several places in the book, is an online resource which provides data refereed by distinguished scholars.

14. Peak-to-trough falls in GDP and industrial output respectively quoted at 30% and 47% in Richard H. Pells, 'Great Depression', for *Encyclopaedia Britannica*, at: www.britannica.com/EBchecked/topic/243118/Great-Depression

15. Feinstein et al., *European Economy Between the Wars*, p. 106, Table 6.3.

16. Ross McKibbin, *Classes and Cultures: England 1918–1951*, Oxford University Press, Oxford, 2000 [1998], p. 185.

17. Public spending was cut by 75% between 1918 and 1920, an extraordinary figure even allowing for the fact that these were years of demobilisation. See Barry Eichengreen, 'The British economy between the wars', in Roderick Floud and Paul Johnson (eds),

The Cambridge Economic History of Modern Britain, vol. 2: *Economic Maturity, 1860–1939*, Cambridge University Press, Cambridge, 2004, p. 322.

18. Robert Skidelsky, *John Maynard Keynes*, vol. 2: *The Economist as Savior, 1920–37*, Penguin Viking, New York, 1995, p. 392.

19. The particular data in these charts was from Louis Johnston and Samuel H. Williamson, 'What was the US GDP then?' and 'What was the UK GDP then?' at: www.measuringworth.org/

20. Authors' calculation from: William D. Nordhaus, 'Do real output and real wage measures capture reality? The history of light suggests not', in Robert J. Gordon and Timothy F. Bresnahan, *The Economics of New Goods*, University of Chicago Press for National Bureau of Economic Research, Chicago, 1997, at: http://papers.nber.org/books/bres96–1/ Page 31 gives a wax candle's emission as 13 lumens; Table 1.4 gives hours of labour at prevailing US wages required to buy 1,000 lumens in different years.

21. John Maynard Keynes, *Essays in Persuasion: The collected writings of John Maynard Keynes*, vol. 9, Cambridge University Press, Cambridge, 1978. The relevant essay is available online: at: www.econ.yale.edu/smith/econ116a/keynes1.pdf

22. In the first 'lost decade', 1991–2000, real growth averaged just 0.5%; over the second, 2000–10, the average was 0.8%. See W.R. Garside, *Japan's Great Stagnation: Forging ahead, falling behind*, Edward Elgar, Cheltenham, 2012, p. 83; Masaaki Shirakawa, 'Deleveraging and growth: Japan's long and winding road', lecture at the London School of Economics, 10 January 2012, at: www.lse.ac.uk/asiaResearchCentre/_files/ShirakawaLectureTranscript.pdf

23. If growth drops from 3% to 1%, then instead of growing to 191.6% of the original year's GDP over 22 years, GDP will grow to only 124.5%, a counterfactual reduction of 35.0%.

24. Bloomberg Business News reporters Andrew Morse and Todd Zaun, quoted in 'The great Hanshin earthquake', Japan Policy Research Institute Occasional Paper No. 2, at: www.jpri.org/publications/occasionalpapers/op2.html

25. Jeff Kingston, *Japan's Quiet Transformation: Social change and civil society in the 21st century*, RoutledgeCurzon, Oxford, 2004, pp. 2–3.

26. The year-on-year decline was more like 7%, but at the trough of the second quarter of 2009 the decline briefly represented a fall of 11.5%, by comparison with the final quarter of 2007. See Table 1 in Japan's Department for National Accounts (GDP, expenditure approach) data at: www.esri.cao.go.jp/jp/sna/data/data_list/sokuhou/files/2013/qe131_2/pdf/jikei_1.pdf

27. The death figures are from the Japanese police report, 'Damage situation and police countermeasures', 11 September 2013, at: www.npa.go.jp/archive/keibi/biki/higaijokyo_e.pdf

28. Kevin Krolicki, 'Japanese retirees ready to risk Fukushima front line', Reuters US edition, 6 June 2011, at: www.reuters.com/article/2011/06/06/japan-fukushima-retirees-idAFL3E7H60ZD20110606

29. On recent trends in poverty and inequality in Japan, see OECD, 'Crisis squeezes income and puts pressure on inequality and poverty: New results from the OECD Income Distribution Database', 2013, at: www.oecd.org/els/soc/OECD2013-Inequality-and-Poverty–8p.pdf

30. Aditya Chakrabortty, 'How will Britain cope with its lost decade? Take a look at Japan', *Guardian*, 6 December 2011, at: www.guardian.co.uk/commentisfree/2011/dec/05/britain-lost-decade-look-japan

31. Eamonn Fingleton, 'The myth of Japan's "lost decade"', *Atlantic*, 26 February 2011.

32. In the UK there was a brief surge in certain property crimes (see Alan Travis, 'Thefts and burglaries on the rise as recession bites', *Guardian*, 24 April 2009, at: www.guardian.co.uk/uk/2009/apr/24/crime-figures-burglary-theft-rise), but – as hard

times wore on – the overall pattern was of continuing decline (Alan Travis, 'Crime in England and Wales falls to lowest level in more than 30 years', *Guardian*, 26 April 2013, at: www.guardian.co.uk/uk/2013/apr/25/uk-crime-falls-official-figures). For an informal survey of the American evidence, which concludes that, despite the downturn, crime rates have continued to decline in six out of seven categories, see Christopher Uggen, 'Crime and the Great Recession', Stanford Center on Poverty and Inequality, 2012, at: www.soc.umn.edu/~uggen/crime_recession.pdf

33. On the 'abortion theory' of crime reduction, see Steven D. Levitt and Stephen J. Dubner, *Freakonomics*, Penguin/Allen Lane, London, 2006, Chapter 4; on the 'lead theory' of crime reduction, see George Monbiot, 'Yes, lead poisoning could really be a cause of violent crime', *Guardian*, 8 January 2013, at: www.guardian.co.uk/commentisfree/2013/jan/07/violent-crime-lead-poisoning-british-export

34. For England and Wales, deaths last totalled less than half a million in 1952, when the population was far smaller. See ONS, *Births and Deaths in England and Wales, 2011 (Final)*, 2012, p. 4, at: www.ons.gov.uk/ons/dcp171778_279934.pdf In the US that same year, the *Science Daily* summed up the official stats: 'US death rate falls for 10th straight year', at: www.sciencedaily.com/releases/2011/03/110319091220.htm The decline in age-adjusted mortality through the Great Recession is charted in Donna L. Hoyert and Jiaquan Xu, 'Deaths: Preliminary data for 2011', *National Vital Statistics Reports*, 61:6 (2012), p. 3, Figure 1, age-adjusted series, at: www.cdc.gov/nchs/data/nvsr/nvsr61/nvsr61_06.pdf

35. Tom Clark, 'Most Britons have felt no benefits from economic recovery, opinion poll finds', *Guardian*, 10 December 2013, at: www.theguardian.com/politics/2013/dec/09/no-gains-economic-recovery-tories-cut-labour-lead-icm-guardian-poll

36. YouGov (2013). Cross-national fieldwork details and results at: http://d25d2506sfb94s.cloudfront.net/cumulus_uploads/document/u7f0cyctl1/YGCam-Archive-results-040413-All-Countries.pdf

37. Overall mortality rates seem to have dropped by about 10% during the Great Depression, most plausibly due to declining mortality on the roads. See David Stuckler and Sanjay Basu, *The Body Economic: Why austerity kills*, Penguin/Allen Lane, London, 2013, pp. 9–11.

38. The FBI only began uniform crime reporting in 1930, and there were discontinuities as more cities were covered and got used to the practice. See Ryan S. Johnson, Shaun Kantor and Price V. Fishback, 'Striking at the roots of crime: The impact of social welfare spending on crime during the Great Depression', National Bureau of Economic Research, 2007, pp. 40–1, at: www.nber.org/papers/w12825

39. Gil Troy, *Morning in America: How Ronald Reagan invented the 1980s*, Princeton University Press, Princeton, NJ, 2005, p. 88.

40. Herbert Hoover's effective dismissal of relative poverty in the Depression struck a callous note, but his emphasis on absolute deprivation was not necessarily cynical; earlier in his career, he had headed Washington's efforts to feed famished Europeans during the First World War, a context in which mass starvation was a real threat. The quote comes from President Hoover's interview with Washington journalist Raymond Clapper on 27 February 1931, quoted in Smith, *FDR*, pp. 286–7.

41. The American writer Robert N. McMurry, quoted in Jahoda et al., *Marienthal*, pp. xxv–xxvi.

Chapter 2: All in it together?

1. Jason DeParle and Robert M Gebeloff, 'Living on nothing but food stamps', *New York Times*, 3 January 2010, at: www.nytimes.com/slideshow/2010/01/03/us/FOODSTAMPS_15.html?_r=0

2. Franklin Roosevelt, Second Inaugural Address, 20 January 1937, at: http://history-matters.gmu.edu/d/5105/

3. Peter Catterall and Virginia Preston, *Contemporary Britain: An annual review 1995*, Ashgate/Dartmouth, Aldershot, 1996, pp. 254–5.
4. Robert Rector, *How Poor are America's Poor? Examining the 'plague' of poverty in America*, Heritage Foundation, Washington, DC, 2007, at: www.heritage.org/research/reports/2007/08/how-poor-are-americas-poor-examining-the-plague-of-poverty-in-america
5. Maud Pember-Reeves, *Round About a Pound a Week*, C. Bell and Son, London, 1914, at: http://archive.org/stream/roundaboutpoundw00reevrich#page/12/mode/2up
6. Adam Smith, *An Inquiry into the Nature and Causes of the Wealth of Nations*, Electronic Classics Series Publications, Hazleton, PA, 2005 [1776], at: www2.hn.psu.edu/faculty/jmanis/adam-smith/wealth-nations.pdf
7. See, for example, Amartya Sen, *Inequality Reexamined*, Oxford University Press, Oxford, 1995.
8. The connection between, for example, low social class and cardiovascular disease is now familiar. But even 20 years ago, a review of other studies showed a consistent association between socio-economic status and cardiovascular disease. George A. Kaplan and Julian E. Keil, 'Socioeconomic factors and cardiovascular disease: A review of the literature', *Circulation: Journal of the American Heart Association*, 88:4 (1993), pp. 1973–98, at: http://circ.ahajournals.org/content/88/4/1973.full.pdf
9. YouGov kindly produced tables for us in six-monthly blocks, based on regular field-work between January 2011 and June 2013. The thrust of the results we report does not change greatly over this period. The fieldwork quoted was undertaken between July and December 2011. The total number of interviews in these months was 172,706; they were carried out online. The figures have been weighted to be representative of all British adults.
10. On the family question, for example, home-buyers with mortgages (71%) and private renters (64%) have intermediate optimism scores, as compared with 73% for outright owners and 61% for social tenants, confirming a consistent social gradient across tenure types, which also applies in relation to positive feelings about relations with friends and the neighbourhood. On the love-life question, between the 35% optimism rating for those with the lowliest school qualifications and the 47% for holders of Master's degrees, the data shows a score of 41% for those with the basic measure of success at secondary school (an O-level pass or equivalent) and 45% for single-degree university graduates.
11. Consider, for example, the respective degree of optimism for Master's graduates and those with lowly certificates of secondary education (CSEs). Only 36% of the latter were optimistic about their own health, compared with 51% of the former. Only 10% of the latter were optimistic about their neighbourhood, compared with 21% of the former. Those with intermediate educational qualifications had intermediate scores on both questions; a similar gradient is evident across housing tenure and occupational grade.
12. Public expenditure on social services rose from 4.9% of GDP in 1920 to more than 10% after 1948. Roger Middleton, *Government versus the Market: The growth of the public sector, economic management and British economic performance, c. 1890–1979*, Edward Elgar, Cheltenham, 1996, pp. 198, 392.
13. In Britain, where the 'cradle to grave' characterisation of universal welfare is more commonly used, it is typically attributed to a broadcast that Winston Churchill made on the Beveridge Report (Winston Churchill, 'A four-year plan for England', BBC broadcast, 21 March 1943, at: www.ibiblio.org/pha/policy/1943/1943–03–21a.html). But according to the memoirs of Roosevelt's labour secretary, Frances Perkins, the president had got there several years earlier, telling her 'across the table', that social security must be: 'Cradle to the grave – from the cradle to the grave everyone ought to be in a social insurance system' (Frances Perkins, *The Roosevelt I Knew*, Viking, New York, 1946, pp. 282–3).

14. OECD figures at: www.oecd.org/els/benefitsandwagesstatistics.htm (updated March 2013). Select 'Gross replacement rates, uneven years 1961–2011' to download spreadsheet, and then Tab 4 'NRR incl SA HB (AW)'.

15. Jonathan Cribb, Robert Joyce and David Phillips, *Living Standards, Poverty and Inequality in the UK: 2012*, Institute for Fiscal Studies, London, 2012, p. 29, Figure 3.2.

16. Republican Party acquiescence in extended unemployment benefits quickly evaporated after the loss of the White House in 2008/09. For an informal overview of the party's evolving stance, see Tom Murse, 'A brief history of unemployment compensation and partisanship', About.Com, 30 July 2010, at: http://usgovinfo.about.com/od/federalbenefitprograms/a/unemployment-benefits-and-partisanship.htm

17. For a detailed account of how unemployment insurance was extended between 2008 and 2012, see Henry S. Farber and Robert G. Valletta, 'Do extended unemployment benefits lengthen unemployment spells? Evidence from recent cycles in the US labor market', National Bureau of Economic Research Working Paper 19048, 2013, pp. 40–1, at: www.nber.org/papers/w19048

18. OECD figures at: www.oecd.org/els/benefitsandwagesstatistics.htm (updated March 2013). Select 'Gross replacement rates, uneven years 1961–2011' to download spreadsheet, and then Tab 4 'NRR incl SA HB (AW)'.

19. The extra redistribution was, of course, due to rising numbers claiming unemployment benefit, as well as to increases in the generosity of it; but there were other progressive tax and benefit changes, too. All told, 'redistribution reached historically high levels in 2010'. See Fabrizio Perri and Joe Steinberg, 'Inequality and redistribution during the great recession', Federal Reserve Bank of Minneapolis Economic Policy Paper, Minneapolis, MN, 2012, at: www.minneapolisfed.org/publications_papers/pub_display.cfm?id=4819

20. Joseph Stiglitz, *The Price of Inequality*, Penguin/Allen Lane, London, 2012.

21. In the UK, the rise in income inequality was sharper than in any other comparable country over the last quarter of the twentieth century, irrespective of whether it is measured in proportional or absolute terms. See P. Gottschald and T. Smeeding, 'Empirical evidence on income inequality in industrial countries', in A.B. Atkinson and F. Bourguignon (eds), *Handbook of Income Distribution*, vol. 1, Elsevier, Amsterdam, 2000, pp. 261–307.

22. D. Dorling, 'Fairness and the changing fortunes of people in Britain', *Journal of the Royal Statistical Society A*, 176:1 (2013), pp. 97–128, at: www.dannydorling.org/?page_id=3597 Dorling's judgements are based on the World Top Income Database.

23. Congressional Budget Office, *Trends in the Distribution of Household Income between 1979 and 2007*, CBO, Washington, DC, 2011, p. x, Summary Figure 1, at: www.cbo.gov/sites/default/files/cbofiles/attachments/10-25-HouseholdIncome.pdf Income is after tax, and before transfers. See Appendix A for more on the way income is defined.

24. Aside from slightly different time periods, the differences are in the way income is defined and averaged. The 'snapshot' nature of the underlying UK data may result in the growth in inequality being overstated if weekly incomes have grown increasingly volatile – see note 46 below for more discussion of this possibility. There is some evidence of this, but certainly not enough to explain away the overall picture: alternative measures based on income recorded in annual tax records also suggest rising inequality.

25. For most countries, the World Top Income Database is the best gauge at the top end. For the US, this implies 194% growth 1979–2007 for the top 1% (mean), so somewhat lower than the 275% recorded on the chart, although this rises to 224% when capital gains are included. The mid-point of the top 0.5% (including capital gains) has risen more modestly (by 115%), but things become more dramatic at the real extreme. On

the same basis, the 99.99th centile – the entry point to the top 1% of the top 1% – has soared by 337%. For the UK, the tax-record-based World Top Income Database numbers are less useful, since there is a discontinuity in 1990, when independent taxation was introduced for husbands and wives. If one disregards this shift from family to individual incomes, the average in the top 1% rose by 212% between 1978 and 2007. Making plausible adjustments for the discontinuity, we estimate a lower bound for growth in mean top incomes in this series of 320%, as compared to the 451% growth shown in our chart. On the other hand, if we had drawn the chart using the same Households Below Average Income (HBAI) data that we actually used, but with a different definition of disposable income – after housing costs are deducted – income growth would appear *more* skewed. The after-housing cost medians are just 20% median growth for the poorest fifth, which rises in steps to 104% for the mid-point of the richest fifth, and to a staggering 502% for the median within the top 1%. One potential issue with the HBAI data is volatility in the underlying weekly 'snapshot' incomes recorded in the Family Resources Survey; see note 46 below for discussion of whether this will exaggerate the rise in overall inequality. But any such distortion is not a problem for the very rich, seeing as their incomes are imputed separately from average tax data. The World Top Income Database is at: http://topincomes.g-mond.parisschoolofeconomics.eu

26. Dimitris Ballas, Danny Dorling, Tomoki Nakaya, Helena Tunstall and Kazumasa Hanaoka, 'Income inequalities in Japan and the UK: A comparative study of two island economies', *Social Policy and Society* (First View article), 2013, pp. 1–15, at: www.dannydorling.org/wp-content/files/dannydorling_publication_id3648.pdf

27. The Institute for Fiscal Studies works with the British government to maintain the Households Below Average Income (HBAI) database, and publishes summary statistics from across the range of the distribution of incomes at: www.ifs.org.uk/fiscalFacts/povertyStats Additional detail on median incomes *within* the top 1% in this data was supplied to the authors by the institute. Income is adjusted for family size and is ranked after taxes but before housing costs are paid. The underlying data for HBAI came from the Family Expenditure Survey for the years before 1993, and from the Family Resources Survey thereafter. Top incomes, which would otherwise be liable to measurement error, are imputed into this data on the basis of income tax data. For the official account of how this is done, see N. Adams, A. Barton, S. Bray, G. Johnson and P. Matejic, *Households Below Average Income: An analysis of the income distribution 1994/95 to 2008/09*, Department for Work and Pensions/Office for National Statistics, London, 2010, Appendix 2, pp. 267–8.

28. The OECD notes stable relative poverty rates for the US and falling relative rates in the UK in its report 'Crisis squeezes income and puts pressure on inequality and poverty: New results from the OECD Income Distribution Database', 2013, p. 6, Figure 7, at: www.oecd.org/els/soc/OECD2013-Inequality-and-Poverty–8p.pdf

29. Poverty in America has traditionally been officially (and somewhat arbitrarily) defined by taking the real cost of a basic diet and tripling it. See Peter Edelman, *So Rich, So Poor*, The New Press, New York, 2012, pp. 26–9.

30. All official figures in this paragraph from the US Census Office, 'Historical Poverty Tables – People', Table 2 (latest available data – 2012), at: www.census.gov/hhes/www/poverty/data/historical/people.html

31. IFS summary statistics at: www.ifs.org.uk/fiscalFacts/povertyStats (see the 'Poverty BHC' (Before Housing Costs) tab for a range of possible fixed poverty lines). There is a marginal discontinuity in the series because after 2001 the figures include Northern Ireland. Across the range of fixed poverty lines shown, the difference between 2006/07 and 2009/10 vary between no change and a 2 percentage point decline.

32. IFS summary statistics: www.ifs.org.uk/fiscalFacts/povertyStats ('Working Age Non-ParentPov.BHC' tab). Across the range of fixed poverty lines shown, there was a rise

in the poverty rate among these childless adults of between 0 and 2 percentage points between 2006/07 and 2009/10.

33. IFS summary statistics: www.ifs.org.uk/fiscalFacts/povertyStats ('Poverty (BHC)' tab). The precise figure depends on the poverty line chosen – with the line fixed at 60% 2010/11 median income (the most widely cited measure), poverty rose by 2.2 million.

34. Fixing an absolute poverty line at 60% of the 2010/11 median income, and looking ahead to 2015/16 on the basis of pre-announced benefit policies and current trends in earnings, the IFS forecasts that the absolute poverty rate will rise by over 4 percentage points for children and by nearly 2 further points for working-age adults. This implies an additional 1.5 million children and working-age adults sinking into absolute hardship. See Jonathan Cribb, Andrew Hood, Robert Joyce and David Phillips, *Living Standards, Poverty and Inequality in the UK: 2013*, Institute for Fiscal Studies, London, 2013, p. 77, Table 4.11 (Before Housing Costs figures).

35. Overall real national income rose from (in 2008 pounds) £694,765 million to £1,433,871 million – so just more than double; on a per-head basis, the rise is from £12,367 to £23,353, which is marginally less than double. See Johnston and Williamson, 'What was the UK GDP then?'

36. IFS summary statistics: www.ifs.org.uk/fiscalFacts/povertyStats These show that incomes at the 10th centile rose 20% in these years, which represents an annualised rise of just over 0.6%.

37. IFS summary statistics: www.ifs.org.uk/fiscalFacts/povertyStats See 'Working Age Non-Parent Poverty AHC' (After Housing Costs) tab. Between 2002 and 2009/10 (the final year *before* the crisis reduced average household incomes), the number of poor individuals in this category rose by between 0.7 million and 0.9 million under all the various fixed poverty lines shown.

38. Of course, the relationship between house prices and housing costs is not automatic for those who are renting rather than buying. During the trough of the American Great Recession rents rose more than general inflation, as many families were forced into rented homes. Ultimately, however, there is some connection between the cost of renting and buying – by 2010, rents were pretty flat. See Ingrid Gould Ellen and Samuel Dastrup, *Housing and the Great Recession*, Stanford Center on Poverty and Inequality, Stanford, CA, 2012, at: http://furmancenter.org/files/publications/HousingandtheGreatRecession.pdf

39. The latest official respective poverty rates (on basis of proportion of all individuals below 60% median After Housing Cost income) are 21% for the UK and 33% for inner London. See Haider Alzubaidi, Jane Carr, Rachel Councell and George Johnson, *Households Below Average Income: An analysis of the income distribution 1994/95–2011/12*, Department for Work and Pensions/Office for National Statistics, 2013, Table 3.6db, at: www.gov.uk/government/uploads/system/uploads/attachment_data/file/206778/full_hbai13.pdf

40. If affordability is defined as spending no more than 35% of net income on rent, then private renting of a bottom-end property (lowest quartile of the local market) is beyond the reach of: 90% of all British working-age households in Islington, inner London; 62% of such households in Guildford, Surrey; and 20% of such households in Coventry in the Midlands. Overall, the Resolution Foundation found that the clear majority of low-to-middle-income working families saddled with unaffordable housing lived away from London and the South East. See Vidhya Alakeson and Giselle Cory, *Home Truths: How affordable is housing for Britain's ordinary families?* Resolution Foundation, London, 2013, Table 10, at: www.resolutionfoundation.org/media/media/downloads/Home_Truths_1.pdf

41. The quoted figures have been rounded. Data obtained from the OECD STAT database at: http://stats.oecd.org/Index.aspx?QueryId=3017# (figures are US dollar converted and seasonally adjusted).

42. US figures quoted from Reuven Glick and Kevin J. Lansing, *Consumers and the Economy*, part 1: *Household Credit and Personal Saving*, Federal Reserve Bank of San Francisco, San Francisco, 2011, at: http://www.frbsf.org/economic-research/publications/economic-letter/2011/january/consumers-economy-household-credit-personal-saving/ The official UK households saving ratio series is at: www.ons.gov.uk/ons/datasets-and-tables/data-selector.html?cdid–RJS&dataset=ukea&table-id=XS1

43. Stiglitz, *Price of Inequality*, p. 191.

44. Analysis of the British Household Panel Survey, in John Hills, Francesca Bastagli, Frank Cowell, Howard Glennerster, Eleni Karagiannaki and Abigail McKnight, *Wealth in the UK: Distribution, accumulation and policy*, Oxford University Press, Oxford, 2013, pp. 28–9, Table 2.6.

45. Matthew Whittaker, *On Borrowed Time? Dealing with household debt in an era of stagnant incomes*, Resolution Foundation, London, 2012, p. 18.

46. We say such an adjustment is 'arguable' because many economists would mistrust a snapshot measure of income or poverty that factored in debt repayments while disregarding the benefit accrued when the money was spent. Such economists, who emphasise individuals' freedom to borrow and save to 'smooth' consumption in line with 'permanent income', also tend to believe it is more instructive to look at expenditure than income data, and so already mistrust traditional poverty measures. For more on such alternative approaches, see Richard Blundell and Ian Preston, 'Consumption inequality and income uncertainty', *Quarterly Journal of Economics*, 113:2 (1998), pp. 603–40. During the 1990s, British empirical analysis of expenditure data had suggested that inequality in living standards might not have risen as sharply as the income figures suggested. See Alissa Goodman and Steven Webb, 'The distribution of UK household expenditure, 1979–92', *Fiscal Studies*, 16:3 (1996), pp. 55–80, at: www.ifs.org.uk/fs/articles/fsgoodman.pdf The most sanguine interpretation of this finding was that incomes were not so much becoming more unequal as more volatile, and that households could use financial markets to smooth things over. To the extent that the credit crunch has left the poor with unaffordable debts, however, the starker rise in income inequality now appears more instructive, and the more modest increased dispersion in household spending less so.

47. Smith, *Wealth of Nations*.

48. Food Research and Action Center, 'SNAP/Food Stamp Participation, March 2013', at: http://frac.org/reports-and-resources/snapfood-stamp-monthly-participation-data/#mar

49. Jason DeParle and Robert M. Gebeloff, 'Living on nothing but food stamps', *New York Times*, 3 January 2010.

50. ibid.

51. S. Jay Olshansky, Toni Antonucci, Lisa Berkman, Robert H. Binstock, Axel Boersch-Supan, John T. Cacioppo, Bruce A. Carnes, Laura L. Carstensen, Linda P. Fried, Dana P. Goldman, James Jackson, Martin Kohli, John Rother, Yuhui Zheng and John Rowe, 'Differences in life expectancy due to race and educational differences are widening, and many may not catch up', *Health Affairs*, 31:8 (2012), pp. 1803–13.

52. Rising mortality among white women who dropped out of school is observed (and partially explained by unemployment and smoking) in Jennifer Karas Montez and Anna Zajacova, 'Explaining the widening education gap in mortality among US white women', *Journal of Health and Social Behavior*, 54:2 (2013), pp. 165–81, at: www.asanet.org/journals/JHSB/Jun13JHSBFeature.pdf

53. Larissa Pople, Laura Rodrigues and Sam Royston, *Through Young Eyes: The Children's Commission on Poverty*, Children's Society, London, 2013, p. 11, at: www.childrenssociety.org.uk//sites/default/files/tcs/poverty_commission_report_final.pdf

54. 'Save the Children launches first poverty campaign in Britain', *Daily Telegraph*, 5 September 2012, at: www.telegraph.co.uk/education/educationnews/9521238/Save-the-Children-launches-first-poverty-campaign-in-Britain.html; 'Red Cross to

distribute food to Britain's poor and hungry', *Guardian*, 11 October 2013, at: www.theguardian.com/uk-news/2013/oct/11/red-cross-to-distribute-food-to-britains-poor-and-hungry

55. Unemployed Liverpudlian Peter Browne, 42, interviewed in Patrick Butler, 'Heat or eat? Or take out a loan, do both, and hope for the best?', *Guardian*, 30 September 2013. Browne reportedly stretches out £2 over a week with 'Packets of noodles for 12p, and tins of spaghetti for 19p'.

56. The Christian charity, the Trussell Trust, operates the majority of British foodbanks. It was almost unheard of before the recession, operating only a handful of banks, but by 2012 it claimed to be feeding 100,000 British mouths, and opening three banks each week as demand grew and as it moves towards its goal of a foodbank in every town. See the charity's press release, at: www.trusselltrust.org/resources/documents/Press/Foodbanks-feed–100,000-in–6-months.pdf

57. Using official data, and adjusting for the rising relative price of food, the Institute for Fiscal Studies estimates that average British spending on food fell by 6.1 percentage points a year through the recession, a 'statistically significant and relatively large' change. In the slumps of the 1980s and 1990s, the same study showed no statistically significant fall in food-spending whatever. See Thomas F. Crossley, Hamish Low and Cormac O'Dea, 'Household consumption through recent recessions', *Fiscal Studies*, 34:2 (2013), pp. 203–29.

58. The fall in non-durable expenditure is nearly 2 percentage points higher in low- than in high-education households. See ibid., p. 224.

59. Rachel Griffith, Martin O'Connell and Kate Smith, 'Food expenditure and nutritional quality over the Great Recession', Institute for Fiscal Studies Briefing Note BN143, 2013, at: www.ifs.org.uk/bns/bn143.pdf

60. 'Sir John Major calls for windfall tax on energy profits', BBC News, 22 October 2013, at: www.bbc.co.uk/news/uk-politics–24621391

61. The poster, from the 1929 election campaign, can be viewed at: www.independentlabour.org.uk/main/wp-content/uploads/2010/07/sacrifice–2.jpg

Chapter 3: Mapping the black stuff

1. James Ball, Dan Milmo and Mark Ferguson, 'Half UK's young black males are unemployed', *Guardian*, 10 March 2012, at: www.guardian.co.uk/society/2012/mar/09/half-uk-young-black-men-unemployed

2. Jahoda et al., *Marienthal*, p. 52.

3. Komarovsky, *The Unemployed Man and His Family*, pp. 132–3.

4. Franklin Roosevelt, First Inaugural Address, 4 March 1933, at: www.bartleby.com/124/pres49.html

5. George Orwell, *The Road to Wigan Pier*, Penguin Books, Harmondsworth, 1962 [1937], pp. 73, 75.

6. Japan's unemployment peaked at 5.4%. See Shirakawa, 'Deleveraging and growth'. Eurozone unemployment in March 2013 hit 12.2%, according to official statistics at: http://epp.eurostat.ec.europa.eu/statistics_explained/index.php/Unemployment_statistics#Unemployment_trends

7. The exact figure was 22.9%. With farming excluded, the rate was higher still – reaching 31.7% of the non-farming workforce in 1932. David R. Weir, 'A century of US unemployment 1890–1990', in Roger L. Ransom, Richard Sutch and Susan B. Carter, *Research in Economic History*, JAI Press, Greenwich, CT, 1992, vol. 14, Table D3, pp. 341–3.

8. Average for 1921–38 was 10.91%. This is the all-workers rate, lower than the more commonly quoted insured-workers rate. Figure taken from Table 13.4 in Timothy J. Hatton, 'Unemployment and the labour market, 1870–1939', in Floud and Johnson, *Cambridge Economic History*, vol. 2, p. 371.

9. Professor Timothy Hatton's notes on his research profile. Available on the Essex University website at: http://privatewww.essex.ac.uk/~hatton/tim_research.htm

10. Official figures for total number in employment from various Labour Market Statistics editions: June 2008 edition, 29.55 million; June 2010 edition, 28.86 million; June 2013 edition, 29.76 million. This implies that there was a 2.3% fall between early 2008 and early 2010, close to the trough on this measure, and that a new peak in employment was reached by 2013.

11. For more detail on how and why incapacity claimant numbers soared in the 1980s and 1990s, see Work and Pensions Select Committee of the House of Commons, *Fourth Report of Parliamentary Session 2002–3*, at: www.publications.parliament.uk/pa/cm200203/cmselect/cmworpen/401/40104.htm

12. '"Total" unemployment in the UK is nearly five million – almost double the official figure', TUC press release, 5 September 2013, at: www.tuc.org.uk/economy/tuc-22565-f0.cfm

13. Overall official employment rates for Britain and America over the course of the Great Recession are charted in 'Mustn't grumble', *The Economist*, 29 September 2012, at: http://www.economist.com/node/21563766

14. Dated this way, most recessions drag on longer – for so long, in fact, that the chart has to truncate the 1990s 'jobs recession'. Official data was supplied on request by the Office for National Statistics.

15. For more on the relative performance of different UK industries at this time, see: Sue Bowden and David M. Higgins, 'British industry in the interwar years', in Floud and Johnson, *Cambridge Economic History*, vol. 2, pp. 374–402, esp. pp. 382–23 for international productivity differentials.

16. 'Graduate' includes those who have completed advanced vocational as well as academic tertiary study. 'Dropout' in Britain is here coded as anyone who failed to secure a pass at O-level/GCSE; American dropouts are simply those who fail to graduate from high school.

17. Mark Thomas, 'Labour market structure and the nature of unemployment in interwar Britain', in B. Eichengreen and T. Hatton (eds), *Interwar Unemployment in International Perspective*, Kluwer Academic Publishers, Dordrecht, Netherlands, 1988, p. 123.

18. The median dropout penalty in this 39-year series is 9.7 percentage points.

19. In particular, the 'dropout' category in Britain covers anyone who fails to secure the equivalent of a pass at O-level/GCSE, even if they have some lower qualifications; this is a broader category than American dropouts – those who fail to graduate from high school.

20. UK data from General Household Survey (GHS) (1972–2005) and Labour Force Survey (LFS) (1983–2011); American data from Current Population Survey throughout (1972–2011). See Yaojun Li, 'Hard times, worklessness and unemployment in Britain and the USA (1972–2011)', Institute for Social Change Working Paper 2013–4, Manchester, 2013, at: www.humanities.manchester.ac.uk/socialchange/publications/working/documents/Ethnicunemploymentandworklessnessunderhardtimesin GBandUSA1972to2011.pdf The data shown in the text is a slightly modified version of the British panel of Figure 9, p. 27. We are grateful to Yaojun Li for supplying it in simplified form.

21. Consider 1985, for example, a year when the 'unemployment penalty' that British dropouts faced compared with graduates was 9.3 percentage points. Yaojun Li's underlying data suggests that the penalty for not attending college (the gap between the college-educated and the intermediate educational group) was only about one third of that, at 3.4 points.

22. In 1992, the 'unemployment penalty' that British dropouts faced was 8.0 percentage points. Yaojun Li's underlying data implies that the penalty for not attending college (the gap between the college-educated and the intermediate group) was approaching two-thirds of that, at 5.2 points.

23. In 2010, in our American data, the 'unemployment penalty' that dropouts faced was 14.0 percentage points. Yaojun Li's underlying data suggests that the penalty for not attending college (the gap between the college-educated and the intermediate educational group) was half of that, 7.1 points. In all previous years high-school graduates without college had less than half the disadvantage of the dropouts.

24. See analysis of official data by the Economic Policy Institute and others for the Associated Press. 'Half of recent college grads underemployed or jobless, analysis says', Associated Press, 23 April 2012, at: www.cleveland.com/business/index. ssf/2012/04/half_of_recent_college_grads_u.html

25. Correspondence with the author, July 2013..

26. David Willetts, *The Pinch: How the baby boomers took their children's future – and why they should give it back*, Atlantic Books, London, 2010.

27. Hatton, 'Unemployment and the labour market, 1870–1939', p. 352.

28. ibid., p. 353.

29. For more on the contrasting fates of the young and the elderly in the Great Depression and the Great Recession in both Europe and the US, see David Runciman, 'Stiffed' (review of *The Occupy Handbook*), *London Review of Books*, 25 October 2012, at: www.lrb.co.uk/v34/n20/david-runciman/stiffed

30. OECD figures for 2012 put the Spanish youth unemployment rate at 53.2%. See OECD, 'Employment and labour markets: Key tables', 2013, Table 2: 'Youth unemployment rate % of youth labour force (15–24)', at: www.oecd-ilibrary.org/ employment/youth-unemployment-rate_20752342-table2

31. Department for Education/ONS, 'NEET Statistics – Quarterly Brief – Quarter 1 2013', 2013, at: www.gov.uk/government/uploads/system/uploads/attachment_data/ file/201104/Quarterly_Brief_NEET_Q1_2013_pdf.pdf For more on the imperfect overlap between the NEET and unemployment categories, see: Jack Britton, Paul Gregg, Lindsey Macmillan and Sam Mitchell, *The Early Bird: Preventing young people becoming a Neet statistic*, University of Bristol Economic Department and CMPO, Bristol, 2011, p. 13. For 18-year-olds, for example, this analysis shows that while 8% of the cohort was both unemployed and out of education/training, a further 6% of the cohort were workless and not doing education/training but not classed as unemployed because they were not actively looking for work.

32. UK data from GHS (1972–2005) and LFS (1983–2011); American data from Current Population Survey throughout (1972–2011). We show a variant of the data in Li, 'Hard times, worklessness and unemployment', p. 21, Figure 3. We are grateful to Yaojun Li for supplying his latest data aggregated across the sexes.

33. The long-term convergence in overall employment rates for the two sexes is visible in the 'worklessness' rather than the 'unemployment' series, which is included – for both the UK and the US – in Li, 'Hard times, worklessness and unemployment', p. 19, Figure 1.

34. This is an updated version of the data in the 'unemployment' US panel of Figure 1, from ibid., p. 19, which was kindly supplied by Yaojun Li.

35. The overall UK gender gap figures quoted here are calculated using the official annual time-series obtained from the ONS on request. On the differential impact of austerity on women's jobs, the female headcount in local government has plunged by 253,600 since 2010, while the number of men in local government jobs is down only 104,700 – according to ONS data published by the Local Government Association. These cuts left 1.43 million women and 452,300 men in local authority jobs. See Katie Allen, 'Public sector austerity measures hitting women hardest', *Guardian*, 2 July 2013, at: www.theguardian.com/business/2013/jul/01/public-sector-austerity-measures-women

36. In a few boom years – 1999 and 2000, and also the immediate run-up to the Great Recession – the penalty fell below 5 points, but never below 4.

37. Li, 'Hard times, worklessness and unemployment', pp. 12–17.

38. James Ball, Dan Milmo and Mark Ferguson, 'Half UK's young black males are unemployed', *Guardian*, 10 March 2012.

39. UK data from GHS (1972–2005) and LFS (1983–2011); American data from Current Population Survey throughout (1972–2011). We show a simplified version of Li, 'Hard times, worklessness and unemployment', p. 23, Figure 5. We are grateful to Yaojun Li for supplying his latest data, aggregated across the sexes.

40. Measured in the same way, the 'penalty' for Pakistanis and Bangladeshis in Britain soared to 24 percentage points in 1984 and 21 points in 1994, although, when this penalty rose again in the more recent recession (by which time the Pakistani element at least was better established) it remained in single figures. See Li, 'Hard times, worklessness and unemployment', p. 23, Figure 5 for the full time-series for all major minorities, disaggregated by sex.

41. Measured in the same way, the 'penalty' for Hispanics peaked at 7 percentage points in 1983, but barring the single recessionary year of 1993 it was never otherwise above 5 points, and before the Great Recession, in 2007, it had slipped below 2 points. The Great Recession has since pushed it up, but only to 4 points. See Li, 'Hard times, worklessness and unemployment', p. 23, Figure 5 for the full time-series for all minorities, disaggregated by sex.

42. Michael Greenwood looks across countries and compares the number of residential moves per year and finds that in the US, 19% of people moved in 1971 and 18% of people moved in 1981. In the UK the corresponding numbers were 12% and 10%, indicating that little more than half as many moved. (See M. Greenwood, 'Internal migration in developed countries', in M. Rosenzweig and O. Stark (eds), *Handbook of Population and Family Economics*, Elsevier, Amsterdam, 1997, pp. 647–720.) People also often move further in the US than in the UK: one study found that for every 1,000 people in the population, the number moving *at least 50 km* each year was 46 in the US but only 15 in the UK (Larry Long, *Migration and Residential Mobility in the United States*, Russell Sage Foundation, Chicago, IL, 1988).

43. See Li, 'Hard times, worklessness and unemployment', p. 25, Figure 7 for full regional time-series of unemployment rates in both countries, for men and women separately.

44. Regional unemployment rates varied from 7.2% in the South to 7.8% in the West. See US Bureau of Labor Statistics, 'Economic news release', Table 1, at: www.bls.gov/news.release/laus.t01.htm

45. Recent growth of Gross Value Added in London and the South East represented 52.2% of that across the UK, according to analysis of official data by the Centre for Research on Socio-Cultural Change at Manchester University, reported in Aditya Chakrabortty, 'London's economic boom leaves rest of Britain behind', *Guardian*, 23 October 2013.

46. Li, 'Hard times, worklessness and unemployment', pp. 12–17.

47. The South comprises the standard government regions: South East, South West and East Anglia, but excludes London, whose labour market is very different. The North/Midlands includes the North West, Yorkshire and Humber, the East and West Midlands, but excludes the far North East, which our analysis lumps in with the peripheral economies of Scotland and Wales. Data for all regions – for both the UK and the US, and for men and women separately – is shown in Li, 'Hard times, worklessness and unemployment', p. 25, Figure 7. Yaojun Li kindly supplied the data aggregated across the sexes on request. The underlying data is from GHS (1972–2005) and LFS (1983–2011).

48. Jahoda et al., *Marienthal*, pp. 45–65; Chapter 6.

49. Paul Gregg and Jonathan Wadsworth, 'Unemployment and inactivity in the 2008–2009 recession', *Economic and Labour Market Review*, 4:8 (2010), p. 45.

50. ONS, 'Labour market statistics: Statistical bulletin, July 2013', Table 9(1), at: www.ons.gov.uk/ons/dcp171778_315111.pdf

51. US Bureau of Labor Statistics, 'Long-term unemployment experience of the jobless', at: www.bls.gov/opub/ils/summary_10_05/long_term_unemployment.htm

52. This pattern of increasingly concentrated unemployment has developed in Australia, about the only rich country to avoid an outright recession after 2008. On spatial concentration of unemployment in lower-income neighbourhoods, see Bob Gregory and Boyd Hunter, 'The macroeconomy and the growth of ghettos of urban poverty in Australia', CEPRD Discussion Paper 325, 1995, at: http://cbe.anu.edu.au/research/papers/ceprdpapers/DP325.pdf On the spread of workless households in Australia, see: Peter Dawkins, Paul Gregg and Rosanna Scutella, 'The growth of jobless households in Australia', *Australian Economic Review*, 35:2 (2002), pp. 133–54. Both papers are cited in: Andrew Leigh, *Battlers and Billionaires: The story of inequality in Australia*, Redback, Collingwood, VIC, 2013.
53. James Ball, Dan Milmo and Mark Ferguson, 'Half UK's young black males are unemployed', *Guardian*, 10 March 2012.

Chapter 4: Toil and trouble

1. Simon Neville, Matthew Taylor, Phillip Inman and Hannah Waldram, 'Zero hours Britain: "I didn't know week to week what I was going to get"', *Guardian*, 31 July 2013, at: www.theguardian.com/business/2013/jul/30/zero-hours-contracts-case-studies
2. Different econometric studies point in different ways about how far rising unemployment pushed down wages in interwar Britain. But such was the fall in prices during the 1929–32 dip that the purchasing power of the average money wage across the economy continued to rise roughly in line with the trend across the economy as a whole. See Hatton, 'Unemployment and the labour market, 1870–1939', pp. 360–6 for a discussion and Figure 13.3A for real-wage data.
3. David Autor, *The Polarization of Job Opportunities in the US Labor Market*, Center for American Progress/Hamilton Project, Washington, DC, 2010, at: www.brookings.edu/~/media/research/files/papers/2010/4/jobs%20autor/04_jobs_autor.pdf
4. ibid., p. 9, Figure 3. Please note, we use slightly simplified descriptions of the occupational categories in the text.
5. US Bureau of Labor Statistics, 'Employment projections: Occupations with the largest job growth', at: www.bls.gov/emp/ep_table_104.htm
6. Authors' calculation from official statistics in ONS, 'Labour market statistics: Statistical bulletin, June 2010', Table 5(2), at: www.ons.gov.uk/ons/rel/lms/labour-market-statistics/lms-june-2010/index.html Official figures used the old 2003 standard industrial classifications at this point.
7. Authors' calculation from comparing official statistics in ONS, 'Labour market statistics: Statistical bulletin, November 2011', Table 6, at: www.ons.gov.uk/ons/dcp171778_241735.pdf and ONS, 'Labour market statistics: Statistical bulletin, June 2013', Table 6, at: www.ons.gov.uk/ons/dcp171778_312067.pdf Official figures used new 2007 standard industrial classifications at this point.
8. Resolution Foundation, *Gaining from Growth*, Resolution Foundation, London, 2012, pp. 114–17.
9. R.A. Wilson and K. Homenidou, *Working Futures 2010–2020: Main Report*, Institute for Employment Research, Coventry, 2012, p. 91, Table 4.4, at: www.ukces.org.uk/assets/ukces/docs/publications/evidence-report–41-working-futures–2010–2020.pdf
10. Paul Gregg and Stephen Machin, *What a Drag: The chilling impact of unemployment on real wages*, Resolution Foundation, London, 2012, at: www.resolutionfoundation.org/media/media/downloads/What_a_drag_1.pdf
11. 'The poor in America: In need of help', *The Economist*, 10 November 2012, at: www.economist.com/news/briefing/21565956-americas-poor-were-little-mentioned-barack-obamas-re-election-campaign-they-deserve

12. Perri and Steinberg, 'Inequality and redistribution'.

13. The 2012 calculation comes from Professor Alan Manning, 'Minimum wage now lower than eight years ago', press release by the London School of Economics, 17 April 2012, at: www.lse.ac.uk/newsAndMedia/news/archives/2012/04/Minimum-Wage-Press-Release.pdf In January 2014, Chancellor Osborne pre-empted the Low Pay Commission review by signalling he wanted a higher minimum wage. Before this, forecasts implied further falls. See James Plunkett and Alex Hurrell, *Fifteen Years Later: A discussion paper on the future of the UK national minimum wage and Low Pay Commission*, Resolution Foundation, London, 2013, p. 25, Figure 11, at: www.resolutionfoundation.org/media/media/downloads/FINAL_Future_of_the_minimum_wage_discussion_paper.pdf

14. Conor D'Arcy and Alex Hurrell, *Minimum Stay: Understanding how long people stay on the minimum wage*, Resolution Foundation, London, 2013, pp. 3, 5, at: www.resolutionfoundation.org/media/media/downloads/Minimum_stay.pdf

15. Of course, children from workless homes (of whom there are far fewer than those whose parents work) are still at greater *individual* risk of poverty. See Cribb et al., *Living Standards, Poverty and Inequality in the UK: 2013*, p. 8.

16. Over the years 1993–2011, the exact proportion of growth accruing to the top 1% was 62%. See Thomas Piketty and Emmanuel Saez, 'Income inequality in the United States, 1913–1998', *Quarterly Journal of Economics*, 118:1 (2003), pp. 1–39. The relevant table, updated to 2011, is published on Emmanuel Saez's website at: http://elsa.berkeley.edu/~saez/#income

17. Jared Bernstein's analysis of US Census Bureau (real median wages) and Bureau of Labor Statistics (labour productivity) data. Presented to the Resolution Foundation in London, 21 November 2011.

18. Jared Bernstein's analysis of US Census Bureau (real median family income) and NBER (output) data. Presented to the Resolution Foundation in London, 21 November 2011.

19. Economic Policy Institute analysis for its State of Working America programme. Data downloadable at: www.epi.org/resources/research_data/state_of_working_america_data/ Select spreadsheet 'Productivity and median and average compensation, 1973–2007'.

20. In 1973–2009 productivity grew by 92.6%, while average hourly wages grew by just 4.3% excluding benefits, or by a marginally less modest 10.3% including such perks. See Larry Mishel and Heidi Shierholz, 'A lost decade, not a burst bubble: The declining living standards of middle-class households in the US and Britain', in Sophia Parker (ed.), *The Squeezed Middle: The pressure on ordinary workers in America and Britain*, Policy Press, Bristol, 2013, pp. 22–3, Figure 1.1.4.

21. Weekly average earnings figures from the Annual Survey of Hours and Earnings up to 2011 (collated and kindly supplied by Resolution Foundation; numbers have been annualised); Resolution Foundation projections based on Office for Budget Responsibility forecasts thereafter.

22. High Pay Centre, *The State of Pay: One year on from the High Pay Commission*, London, 2012, p. 5, at: http://highpaycentre.org/files/state_of_pay.pdf

23. Here we deflate by the Retail Price Index, the traditional inflation measure, because it is available right back to the 1970s. It has recently been criticised for technical deficiencies, which can lead to inflation being overstated. Using the Consumer Price Index (available from 1988) instead, Paul Gregg, Stephen Machin and Mariña Fernández Salgado find that the 10th, 50th and 90th centiles had respectively advanced 21%, 29% and 39% on 1988 wages by 2002, but that these advances then fall back to 10%, 21% and 35% respectively, which implies rounded declines over the 2002–12 decade ranging from 11% of the 1988 baseline at the bottom to 3% at the top. One can also strip out compositional changes, relating to the spread of female workers and part-time work, by examining men in isolation. Professor Machin has previously done so and, by 2011, had found a decade-long decline at all three percentiles.

24. P. Gregg, S. Machin and M. Salgado, 'Real wages and unemployment in the big squeeze', Centre for Economic Performance, London School of Economics, mimeo, 2013. Underlying data is from the New Earnings Survey and the Annual Survey of Hours and Earnings.

25. The Universal Credit reform complicates consistent calculation, but in 2011 Gavin Kelly, director of the Resolution Foundation, totted up cuts of £2.9 billion by 2012–13, which already represented 10% of total tax credit spend. (See Gavin Kelly, 'So who pays?', Resolution Foundation blog, 29 November 2011, at: www.resolutionfoundation. org/blog/2011/Nov/29/so-who-pays/) Subsequently announced policies, such as sub-inflation indexation, have probably added another £1–2 billion of cuts.

26. Applying official estimates for wage growth to low-to-middle-income working households, the Resolution Foundation calculates that average net household income in this group will fall in real terms from £22,800 on the eve of the crash in 2007/08 to £20,000 in 2017/18. That is just below the figure of £20,400 for 1997/98. See Office for Budget Responsibility, *Economic and Fiscal Outlook: December 2012*, p. 9, Table 1.1, at: http://budgetresponsibility.independent.gov.uk/economic-and-fiscal-outlook-december–2012/; Resolution Foundation, *Squeezed Britain, 2013*, London, 2013, pp. 24–5, at: www.resolutionfoundation.org/media/media/downloads/ Resolution-Foundation-Squeezed-Britain–2013_1.pdf

27. We are referring here to 'real' cuts, which occur whenever pay increases more slowly than prices. These are little different in economic theory from outright cuts in money wages, which do occur but are less typical. But the psychology, and hence the politics, could be very different. If people blame 'rising prices' rather than falling wages for their difficulties, they may blame shops (for high prices) or the government (for failing to control inflation), rather than bosses (for having cut pay).

28. Daniel Kahneman and Amos Tversky dominate the relevant literature. One important early paper in which they developed the idea of 'anchoring' (i.e. making decisions with reference to gains and losses from a particular starting point, rather than on the basis of final outcomes) was Amos Tversky and Daniel Kahneman, 'Judgment under uncertainty: Heuristics and biases source', *Science*, NS 185:4157 (1974), pp. 1124–31, at: www.socsci.uci.edu/~bskyrms/bio/readings/tversky_k_heuristics_biases.pdf This developed into the 'prospect theory' of decision making in: D. Kahneman and A. Tversky, 'Prospect theory: An analysis of decision under risk', *Econometrica*, 47:2 (1979), pp. 263–91, at: www.princeton.edu/~kahneman/docs/Publications/prospect_ theory.pdf

29. Komarovsky, *The Unemployed Man and His Family*, p. 124.

30. Simon Neville, Matthew Taylor and Phillip Inman, 'Buckingham Palace uses zero-hours contracts for summer staff', *Guardian*, 31 July 2013, at: www.theguardian.com/ money/2013/jul/30/buckingham-palace-zero-hours-contracts

31. Hannah Kuchler, '"Zero hours" contracts numbers leap', *Financial Times*, 8 April 2013, at: www.ft.com/cms/s/0/ff75254e–9f89–11e2-b4b6–00144feabdc0. html#axzz2av2Ea5Ce

32. Francine Blau and Lawrence Kagh, 'International differences in male wage inequality: Institutional versus market forces', *Journal of Political Economy*, 104:4 (1996), pp. 791–837. Cited in Edelman, *So Rich, So Poor*, p. 169.

33. See OECD, 'Protecting jobs, enhancing flexibility: A new look at employment protection legislation', in *OECD Employment Outlook 2013*, pp. 65–126. The report shows that for 'protection of permanent staff against individual dismissal' (Figure 2.4), the bottom four countries are (starting with the least protected) the US, Canada, Great Britain and New Zealand. On the 'regulation of temporary contracts' (Figure 2.9) it is the same cluster of countries again but in a different order, and this time joined by another Anglo-Saxon nation (Australia) in fifth place.

34. OECD, *OECD Employment Outlook 2013*. See, for example, p. 78 for permanent workers' protection against dismissal: on the six-point scale, the US comes bottom

with zero and the UK scores just over 1 – substantially below the OECD average of 1.6.

35. ibid., pp. 83–4.

36. On a 0–6 scale (where 6 would indicate maximal protection in every respect), the US score for 'protection of permanent staff against individual and collective dismissal' is 0.26, which places it bottom of the table; Britain is in third place, with 1.03. For comparison, the same score for France in 2013 was 2.38 and for Germany 2.87. Data from OECD STAT database, at http://stats.oecd.org Select the theme 'Labour' and then sub-theme 'Employment protection'.

37. OECD, *OECD Employment Outlook 2013*, p. 88, Figure 2.7 reports that the US has no relevant protection for regular fixed-term contractors, whereas – among the majority of countries that do regulate – the UK is the least restrictive. In regulating agency working (p. 90, Figure 2.8), the US and the UK are third and fifth respectively from the bottom of the table.

38. Hoover's own memoirs, quoted in Smith, *FDR*, p. 287.

39. See US Bureau of Labor Statistics, 'Economic news release', Table A–15, at: www.bls. gov/news.release/empsit.t15.htm It defines 'persons marginally attached to the labor force' as those 'who currently are neither working nor looking for work but indicate that they want and are available for a job and have looked for work sometime in the past 12 months'.

40. In fact, the *gap* between the unemployment rate and the U6 marginalisation rate precisely doubled, from 3.6% in March 2007 to 7.2% in November 2009. We qualify the claim, and say 'roughly doubled' only because the denominators for the two series are slightly different, with certain discouraged workers being included in the base of the U6 series.

41. Official statistics reveal that, as late as February–April 2006, the number of workers in this position remained at 620,000. See ONS, 'Labour market statistics: First release, June 2008', Table 3, at: www.ons.gov.uk/ons/rel/lms/labour-market-statistics/june–2008/index.html

42. The exact figure for May–July 2013 was 1.447 million, and this was continuing to rise, up from 1.422 in February–April. See ONS, 'Labour market statistics: Statistical bulletin, September 2013', Table 3, at: www.ons.gov.uk/ons/dcp171778_325094.pdf

43. The 'marginalised' line tracks the official U6 series, accessible at: www.bls.gov/ webapps/legacy/cpsatab15.htm ('Seasonally Adjusted' series) and so includes certain discouraged workers and those forced to work part time owing to the economy. The denominators in the two series differ slightly, as explained in note 40 above.

44. Across those currently working (N = 1,604), Pew found 28% had faced reduced working hours, 23% a pay cut, 12% enforced unpaid leave, and 11% had been forced to switch to part time. Among the workforce as a whole (N = 2,256) 6% were currently underemployed, and 55% had experienced one or other of these problems. Pew Research Center, *A Balance Sheet at 30 Months: How the great recession has changed life in America*, Pew Center, Washington, DC, 2010, p. 1, at: www.pewsocialtrends. org/files/2010/11/759-recession.pdf

45. David N.F. Bell and David G. Blanchflower, 'Underemployment in the UK revisited', *National Institute Economic Review*, 224 (2013), pp. F8–F22.

46. Amelia Hill, 'The hidden poor – in work but sinking, after years without pay rises', *Guardian*, 19 June 2012, at: www.guardian.co.uk/society/2012/jun/18/hidden-poor-years-without-pay-rises

47. Official figures show 360,000 temporary workers who wanted full-time work in February–April 2008 (ONS, 'Labour market statistics: First release: June 2008', Table 3). This had risen to 657,000 in November 2012–January 2013 (ONS, 'Labour market statistics: Statistical Bulletin, June 2013', Table 3).

48. By 2013, 2.7 million staff were now deployed in this footloose manner, compared with half that number in 1993. Bureau of Labor Statistics figures for May 1993 and

May 2013, reported in Ian Brinkley, *Flexibility or Insecurity? Exploring the rise in zero hours contracts*, Work Foundation, London, 2013, at: www.theworkfoundation.com/DownloadPublication/Report/339_Flexibility%20or%20Insecurity%20-%20final.pdf

49. David H. Autor and Susan N. Houseman, 'Do temporary-help jobs improve labor market outcomes for low-skilled workers? Evidence from "Work First"', *American Economic Journal: Applied Economics*, 2:3 (2010), pp. 96–128.

50. On the basis of a survey of around 1,000 employers, the Chartered Institute of Personnel and Development estimates that around 1 million British workers could be on zero-hour contracts. See 'Zero hours contracts more widespread than thought – but only minority of zero hours workers want to work more hours', CIPD press release, 5 August 2013, at: www.cipd.co.uk/pressoffice/press-releases/zero-hours-contracts-more-widespread-thought–050813.aspx On the basis of a less representative survey of its own members, the trade union Unite estimates that around 20% of workers were on zero-hour style arrangements, which produces a whole-workforce figure of 5.5 million. See 'Research uncovers growing zero hour subclass of insecure employment', Unite press release, 8 September 2013, at: www.unitetheunion.org/news/research-uncovers-growing-zero-hour-subclass-of-insecure-employment/

51. John Aglionby, 'ONS increases its estimate of workers on zero hours contracts', *Financial Times*, 1 August 2013, at: www.ft.com/cms/s/0/46b6c682-fa94–11e2-a7aa–00144feabdc0.html#axzz2av2Ea5Ce

52. Such workers will almost certainly not have sick pay or holiday entitlement as part of their contract, and are unlikely to believe that they do. The only equivocation here is that case law indicates that the day-to-day reality of the relationship of employment could confer rights, even if the contract does not. In other words, if a worker took their firm to court, they might be able to secure more rights than they are contracted for. See Doug Pyper and Feargal McGuinness, 'Zero hour contracts', House of Commons Library, Briefing Note SN/BT/6553, 2013, p. 5.

53. Dave Prentis, quoted in Simon Neville, Matthew Taylor and Phillip Inman, 'Buckingham Palace uses zero-hours contracts for summer staff', *Guardian*, 31 July 2013.

54. The cases throughout the following couple of pages are taken from Simon Neville, Matthew Taylor, Phillip Inman and Hannah Waldram, 'Zero hours Britain: "I didn't know week to week what I was going to get"', *Guardian*, 31 July 2013.

55. Hannah Kuchler, 'Employers embrace "zero hours" contracts', *Financial Times*, 8 April 2013.

56. A Royal College of Nursing survey from 2006 reported in Brinkley, *Flexibility or Insecurity?*.

57. The top three occupational groups – managers, professionals, and associate and technical staff – made up 43% of zero-hours contractors in Britain in late 2012, according to Work Foundation analysis of the Labour Force Survey. See ibid.

58. Average hourly rates for zero-hours workers are reported to be just £9, compared to £15 for the population as a whole. See Matthew Pennycook, Giselle Cory and Vidhya Alakeson, *A Matter of Time: The rise of zero-hour contracts*, Resolution Foundation, London, 2013, at: www.resolutionfoundation.org/media/media/downloads/A_Matter_of_Time_-_The_rise_of_zero-hours_contracts_final_1.pdf

59. The same report finds that the comparable figure for other workers is just 7%. See ibid., p. 3.

60. That pattern of cycling between low-paid work and unemployment was already evident at the time of the UK's last recession. See Amanda Gosling, Paul Johnson, Julian McCrae and Gillian Paull, *The Dynamics of Low Pay and Unemployment in Early 1990s Britain*, Institute for Fiscal Studies, London, 1997.

61. One recent study found that job insecurity was associated with a statistically significant 1.42-fold rise in the risk of coronary heart disease, as compared with secure

employment – a result barely changed by adjusting for the underlying health characteristics and behaviours of the insecurely employed. See J.E. Ferrie, M. Kivimäki, M.J.
Shipley, G. Davey Smith and M. Virtanen. 'Job insecurity and incident coronary heart
disease: The Whitehall II prospective cohort study', *Atherosclerosis*, 227:1 (2013), pp.
178–81.

62. London houses could receive mail 12 times a day. See Randall Stross, 'The birth
of cheap communication (and junk mail)', *New York Times*, 20 February 2010,
at: www.nytimes.com/2010/02/21/business/21digi.html?adxnnl=1&adxnnlx=
1267470299-TxuOOpsKkQg6AhS78K9ptg&_r=0

63. W. Koeniger and M. Leonardi, 'Capital deepening and wage differentials: Germany
versus U.E.', *Economic Policy*, 22 (2007), pp. 71–116.

64. M. Elot, J. Boone and J. Van Ours, 'Welfare-improving employment protection',
Economica, 74 (2007), pp. 381–96. This paper stresses a different mechanism, whereby
the absence of labour market protection discourages *workers* from investing efforts in
developing firm-specific skills.

65. Lorenzo Cappellari, Carlo Dell'Aringa and Marco Leonardi, 'Temporary employment, job flows and productivity: A tale of two reforms', *Economic Journal*, 122:562
(2011), pp. F188–F215. See F193–F194 for a description of the reform.

Chapter 5: Anxious individuals, unhappy homes

1. Andrea Vogt, 'Widows of Italian suicide victims make protest march against economic
strife', *Guardian*, 5 May 2012, at: www.theguardian.com/world/2012/may/04/widows-
italian-businessmen-march

2. Helena Smith, 'Greek man shoots himself over debts', *Guardian*, 5 April 2012,
at: www.theguardian.com/world/2012/apr/04/greek-man-shoots-himself-debts?guni=
Article:in%20body%20link

3. The original campaign song 'Anchors Aweigh' was jettisoned at the last minute
at the Democratic convention, after Roosevelt aide Ed Flynn complained that it
sounded like 'a funeral march' and demanded a 'peppy' alternative. See Smith, *FDR*,
p. 268.

4. Richard Layard, *Happiness: Lessons from a new science*, Penguin/Allen Lane,
London, 2005.

5. On the link between 'authentic' smiling and self-rated well-being, see P. Ekman,
R. Davidson and W. Friesen, 'The Duchenne smile: Emotional expression and brain
physiology II', *Journal of Personality and Social Psychology*, 58:2 (1990), pp. 342–53,
at: http://brainimaging.waisman.wisc.edu/publications/1990/the%20duchenne%20
smile.pdf

6. Official updates on well-being statistics now feature on the ONS website, at:
www.ons.gov.uk/ons/guide-method/user-guidance/well-being/index.html

7. On Blackpool's bottom ranking for happiness, see Mark Easton, 'What are the top
five happiest parts of the UK?', BBC News, 24 July 2012, at: www.bbc.co.uk/news/
uk–18973923; on anti-depressants see Mark Easton, 'The north/south divide
on antidepressants', BBC News, 2 August 2012, at: www.bbc.co.uk/news/uk–
19076219

8. On Gallup's 0–10 scale the overall average score fell from 6.9 to 6.4 between February
and November 2008. By January 2009, however, the overall average score was back
at 6.9.

9. Layard, *Happiness*, pp. 49–50.

10. Keynes, 'Economic possibilities for our grandchildren', in *Essays in Persuasion*,
available online at: www.econ.yale.edu/smith/econ116a/keynes1.pdf

11. Rather than a 1–10 life satisfaction score, Eurobarometer asks respondents whether
they are satisfied with their lives on a four-point scale. In the text we concentrate on
the total proportion satisfied, i.e. the proportion 'very' or 'fairly', as against those who

are 'fairly' or 'very' dissatisfied. For the unemployed, the proportion thus satisfied dips from 80% in May 2007 to 68% at the height of the financial crisis (November 2008), a decline of 12 points. For the employed, the drop-off over these months was just 2 points – from 90% to 88%. See Chaeyoon Lim and James Laurence, 'Economic hard times and life satisfaction in the UK and the US', Institute for Social Change Working Paper 2013–3, Manchester, 2013, at: www.humanities.manchester.ac.uk/socialchange/publications/working/documents/JamesLaurenceHardshipandWell-Being.pdf

12. Between June and November 2011, Eurobarometer shows that the overall average proportion of all Britons (including pensioners, who are neither working nor workless) who were 'very' or 'fairly' satisfied dipped from 92% to 87%, very much in line with the trend among the employed. Among the unemployed over these months, the decline was from 79% to 61%.

13. In the British Eurobarometer data, by July 2009, 91% of working Britons were 'very' or 'fairly' satisfied, actually higher than the 90% in May 2007. For the unemployed, the July 2009 score was 76%, still 4 points down on May 2007.

14. The precise Gallup question was: 'Please imagine a ladder with steps numbered from zero at the bottom to 10 at the top. The top of the ladder represents the best possible life for you and the bottom of the ladder represents the worst possible life for you. On which step of the ladder would you say you personally feel you stand at this time?' See Lim and Laurence, 'Economic hard times', p. 7.

15. The original Faith Matters survey was conducted in 2006 on behalf of Harvard University by ICR. The original national survey interviewed roughly 3,100 Americans over the phone about religion as well as social/ political engagement. In subsequent waves, in 2007 and 2011, as many of these respondents as possible were re-contacted and re-interviewed (respectively about two-thirds and one-half of the original total). The original questionnaire can be read online at: http://americangrace.org/RESEARCH/FM2006%20FINAL.pdf For more details, see: Robert D. Putnam and David E. Campbell, *American Grace: How religion divides and unites us*, Simon & Schuster, New York, 2012, pp. 557–62.

16. Figures from the Faith Matters dataset. See Lim and Laurence, 'Economic hard times', p. 13.

17. Claim based on the Faith Matters dataset. See ibid.

18. Full list of controls provided in ibid., p. 18.

19. The British data is presented in ibid., p. 32, Figure 4.

20. Debbie Borie-Holtz, Carl Van Horn and Cliff Zukin, *No End in Sight: The agony of prolonged unemployment*, Rutgers University, New Brunswick, NJ, 2010, Tables 10–12, at: www.heldrich.rutgers.edu/sites/default/files/content/Work_Trends_May_2010_0.pdf

21. Lim and Laurence, 'Economic hard times', pp. 17–18; for coefficients see p. 35, Table 1 (Model 1).

22. S. Brown, K. Taylor and S. Wheatley Price, 'Debt and distress: Evaluating the psychological cost of credit', *Journal of Economic Psychology*, 26:5 (2005), pp. 642–63.

23. Amelia Hill, 'The hidden poor – in work but sinking, after years without pay rises', *Guardian,* 19 June 2012.

24. Depression defined here on the basis of a Labour Force Survey question about various health conditions, including 'depression, bad nerves, or anxiety', which emerges as the condition which most affects approximately 1% of respondents. See D.N.F. Bell and D.G. Blanchflower, 'UK unemployment in the Great Recession', *National Institute Economic Review*, 214 (2010), pp. R3–R25, esp. pp. R17–R19, Table 15, at: www.dartmouth.edu/~blnchflr/papers/Bell-Blanchflower.pdf

25. D.N.F. Bell and D.G. Blanchflower, 'Underemployment in the UK reconsidered', unpublished Working Paper (March 2013 draft), Table 7. The results are quoted by permission of the authors.

26. ibid., Table 8, reports coefficients for part-timers who want to work full time that vary between 33% and 64% of the coefficient for being unemployed for less than 12 months. These results are quoted by permission of the authors.
27. The percentage declines in this paragraph are the proportional drop in the coefficients between successive models 1–3 in Table 1 (US) and Table 2 (UK) of Lim and Laurence, 'Economic hard times', pp. 18–19.
28. The relevant survey question in the British data is: 'How well would you say you yourself are managing financially these days? Would you say you are: Living comfortably; Doing alright; Just about getting by; Finding it quite difficult; Finding it very difficult?'
29. YouGov (2013). Summary results and fieldwork details at: http://d25d2506sfb94s.cloudfront.net/cumulus_uploads/document/u7f0cyctl1/YGCam-Archive-results–040413-All-Countries.pdf
30. Professor Claudia Senik (of the Sorbonne), 'What makes the French so unhappy?', *Financial Times*, 4 April 2013, at: www.ft.com/cms/s/0/07920018–9c8c–11e2-ba3c-00144feabdc0.html#axzz2Y9tCPbof
31. The precise question on recession exposure – which admits the four answers that form the categories on the chart – was: 'Thinking about your life in the last few years: how much, if at all, have you personally been affected by the economic problems in your country in this period?' The question on anxiety was: 'Thinking about your life in the last few years, would you say you are more likely or less likely to . . . feel anxious?', and the chart records the proportion answering 'more likely'. YouGov (2013). Summary results and fieldwork details at: http://d25d2506sfb94s.cloudfront.net/cumulus_uploads/document/u7f0cyctl1/YGCam-Archive-results–040413-All-Countries.pdf Some additional cross-tables provided by YouGov on request.
32. Chapter 4 touched on differences in employment protection between France and the UK and the US. To illustrate the difference in the benefit safety net, consider net replacement rates for a single long-term workless individual, who previously earned the median wage, and who does not qualify for in-kind top-ups. In the US, there is no long-term unemployment compensation – the replacement rate is 0%; meagre UK benefits replace 13% of the lost wage; in France the figure is 22%. OECD figures for 2011, updated March 2013; at: www.oecd.org/els/benefitsandwagesstatistics.htm Select spreadsheet 'For long-term unemployed, 2001–2011'.
33. Indeed, the established French tendency to stress the negative in surveys looks to be having a bearing here. Seeing as the French are especially likely to claim to have been hit by recession, the 'slump-proof' French are a highly select group. And yet – perversely – this minority reports *more* anxiety than their less-select British and American counterparts. This oddity obviously increases the absolute proportion of the French who report rising anxiety in comparison to other countries.
34. Sources and exact question wording given in note 31 above.
35. D. Stuckler, S. Basu, P. Fishback, C. Meissner and M. McKee, 'Banking crises and mortality during the Great Depression: Evidence from the US urban populations, 1929–1937', *Journal of Epidemiology and Community Health*, 66:5 (2012), pp. 410–19, at: www.ncbi.nlm.nih.gov/pubmed/21441177
36. Stuckler and Basu, *The Body Economic*, p. 86.
37. ibid., pp. 110–11 and Figure 7.1.
38. K. Thomas and D. Gunnell, 'Suicide in England and Wales 1861–2007: A time-trends analysis', *International Journal of Epidemiology*, 39:6 (2010), pp. 1464–75, at: http://ije.oxfordjournals.org/content/39/6/1464.full
39. There are certain definitional differences between the two countries. The denominator for both series is total population (all ages). However, in line with national official procedure, the English/Welsh data does not class any deaths of under-15s as intended suicides. Deaths of indeterminate cause that are nowadays officially classified as suicides in the English/Welsh statistics were unavailable before the 1960s, and

so have been excluded throughout. As a result, the numbers here are lower than the contemporary official English suicide rate. The US data covers only 'Death Registration Districts', which excluded much of the country in the early twentieth century, but had achieved 95% coverage by 1930. The US data for 1925–98 is published by the Center for Disease Control (CDC) – 'HIST290: Death rates for selected causes by 10-year age groups, race, and sex: Death Registration States, 1900–32, and United States, 1933–98', at: www.cdc.gov/nchs/nvss/mortality/hist290.htm For years after 1998, we have used CDC 'Fatal injury reports, national and regional, 1999–2010', obtained via CDC's WISQARS database at: www.cdc.gov/injury/wisqars/index.html For England and Wales, data was collated from official records and kindly supplied by Kyla Thomas at the University of Bristol. More detail on this data is provided in Thomas and Gunnell, 'Suicide in England and Wales'.

40. ONS, *Suicides in the United Kingdom, 2011*, at: www.ons.gov.uk/ons/dcp171778_295718.pdf Unlike other figures referred to, this analysis includes Scotland and Northern Ireland. The downloadable data behind Figure 1 reveals that the total number of suicides rose by 12% between 2007 and 2011, from 5,377 to 6,045. Age-specific rates rose by 8% for men and 16% for women in this time, although ONS warns that there are some discontinuities over these years.

41. Stuckler and Basu, *The Body Economic*, p. 12.

42. Ben Barr, David Taylor-Robinson, Alex Scott-Samuel, Martin McKee and David Stuckler, 'Suicides associated with the 2008–10 economic recession in England: Time trend analysis', *British Medical Journal*, 345 (2012), at: www.bmj.com/highwire/filestream/597905/field_highwire_article_pdf/0/bmj.e5142.full.pdf

43. Galbraith, *The Great Crash*, pp. 148–52.

44. Komarovsky, *The Unemployed Man and His Family*, p. xv.

45. Orwell, *The Road to Wigan Pier*, p. 78.

46. Jahoda et al., *Marienthal*, pp. 54–6. Note that slightly different categorical schemas are discussed by the researchers over these pages; the 7% we quote in the text is the proportion of families *broadly* defined as 'broken', and as such are an upper bound.

47. The total number of divorces fell from 4,018 in 1928 to 3,563 in 1930, remaining below 4,000 until 1933, when it rose to 4,042. ONS data, collated in 'Divorce rates data, 1858 to now: How has it changed?', *Guardian* Datablog, at: www.theguardian.com/news/datablog/2010/jan/28/divorce-rates-marriage-ons

48. W. Bradford Wilcox, 'The Great Recession's silver lining?', in Wilcox (ed.), *The State of Our Unions, 2009*, National Marriage Project, University of Virginia and the Institute for American Values, Charlottesville, VA, 2009, p. 16, at: www.stateofourunions.org/2009/SOOU2009.pdf

49. There are various limitations in the available official data, but we have carried out checks to ensure that this does not distort the trends described. In particular, there was a change in the way the information was collected in 2000, which may introduce some discontinuity. Coverage of the states in Vital Statistics is incomplete; in recent data California, Georgia, Hawaii, Indiana, Louisiana and Minnesota are excluded. But nationwide survey-based data suggests a broadly similar overall divorce rate. See Philip N. Cohen, 'Recession and divorce in the United States: Economic conditions and the odds of divorce, 2008–2010', Population Research Center, Baltimore, MD, 2012, at: papers.ccpr.ucla.edu/papers/PWP-MPRC-2012-008/PWP-MPRC-2012-008.pdf Data limitations meant that we had to use divorces per 1,000 of all population to create a long time-series, but divorces per 1,000 married women is arguably more instructive, as it allows for compositional changes (i.e. the declining proportion of married people in the population) which could distort time trends. Where this alternative measure was available, however, we checked against it, and the choice of denominator made little difference to the short-term movements we describe. The numbers for 1925–67 are from US Department of Health, Education and Welfare, '100 years of marriage and divorce statistics United States', *Data from*

the National Vital Statistics System, Rockville, MD, 21:24 (1973), Table 1, at: www.
cdc.gov/nchs/data/series/sr_21/sr21_024.pdf Numbers for 1968–79 are from National
Center for Health Statistics, *Vital Statistics of the United States, 1979*, vol. 3: *Marriage
and Divorce*, Public Health Service, Washington, DC, 1984, Table 2.1, at: www.cdc.
gov/nchs/data/vsus/mgdv79_3.pdf Numbers for 1980–90 are from: Centers for
Disease Control and Prevention, *Monthly Vital Statistics Report*, 43:9 (1995), p. 9.
Numbers for 1990–2000 are collated from Centers for Disease Control and Prevention
(various years) by Pearson's InfoPlease website. Its summary table is at: www.
infoplease.com/ipa/A0005044.html For selected years we verified its figures against
the Centers for Disease Control and Prevention reports directly. From 2000
onwards, we have provided a summary table produced directly by the Centers for
Disease Control and Prevention, at: www.cdc.gov/nchs/nvss/marriage_divorce_
tables.htm

50. Komarovsky, *The Unemployed Man and His Family*, p. 132.
51. The divorce rate (per 1,000 married persons) fell from 12.1 in 2006 to 10.5 in 2009, but
    then bounced back to 11.1 in 2010. Official data, collated in 'Divorce rates data, 1858
    to now: How has it changed?', *Guardian* Datablog.
52. Amelia Hill, 'Trapped: The former couples who can't afford to move on', *Guardian*,
    21 November 2012, at: www.guardian.co.uk/society/2012/nov/20/trapped-couples-
    partners-relationships
53. ONS, 'Divorces in England and Wales – 2011: Statistical bulletin', 2012, p. 4, at: www.
    ons.gov.uk/ons/dcp171778_291750.pdf
54. For black American women the (rounded) decline was from 60% to 28%. All figures
    from National Marriage Project/University of Virginia/Institute for American Values,
    The State of Our Unions, 2012, Charlottesville, VA, 2012, p. 65, Figure 2.
55. The Pew Center analysis suggested there had been a relatively modest 7 percentage
    point drop-off in the marriage rate for college-educated 30-year-olds between 1990
    and 2008, but a 15 point drop-off among those of their peers who finished with study-
    ing at school. See Richard Fry, *The Reversal of the Marriage Gap*, Pew Center,
    Washington, DC, 2010, p. 1, at: www.pewsocialtrends.org/files/2010/11/767-college-
    marriage-gap.pdf
56. Komarovsky, *The Unemployed Man and His Family*, p. 44.
57. ibid., pp. 27–9, 130–3.
58. 'Changes among the offspring of deprived families are consistently in a conservative
    direction, towards traditional values and relationships.' G.H. Elder, *Children of the
    Great Depression*, University of Chicago Press, Chicago and London, 1974, p. 287.
59. Komarovsky, *The Unemployed Man and His Family*, pp. 92–115.
60. The new study's emphasis on the variety of families' response to hardship echoes the
    work of Komarovsky and Elder, but in a twist that would not have occurred to
    Depression-era researchers, the researchers also seek to explain this variation via the
    'DRD2 Taq1A genotype'. See Dohoon Lee, Jeanne Brooks-Gunn, Sara S. McLanahan,
    Daniel Notterman and Irwin Garfinkel, 'The Great Recession, genetic sensitivity,
    and maternal harsh parenting', *Proceedings of the National Academy of Sciences
    of the United States of America: Early edition*, 2013, at: www.pnas.org/content/
    early/2013/07/31/1312398110.full.pdf+html
61. Komarovsky, *The Unemployed Man and His Family*, p. 95.
62. Respondents are grouped as 'slump-proof' or 'slump-hit' on the basis of self-
    appraisal, as explained earlier. The exact recession question wording and links to the
    source are given at note 31 above. This chart is based on the proportion answering
    'more likely' to the question: 'Thinking about your life in the last few years, would
    you say you are more likely or less likely to . . . argue with family and others?'
63. The researchers establish a double-digit percentage point gap in the likelihood of
    married and cohabiting couples living stably together until their child reaches the age
    of five in both countries, but the gap is especially marked in the US. They conclude

that in Britain cohabitation represents a 'poor man's marriage', whereas in the US cohabiting unions are unstable as well as disadvantaged. See Kathleen Kiernan, Sara McLanahan, John Holmes and Melanie Wright, 'Fragile families in the US and UK', Bendheim Thomas Center for Research on Child Well-Being Working Paper WP11–04-FF, Princeton, NJ, 2011, at: http://crcw.princeton.edu/workingpapers/WP11–04-FF.pdf

64. Komarovsky, *The Unemployed Man and His Family*, pp. 123–4.

Chapter 6: The small society

1. Jason DeParle and Robert M. Gebeloff, 'Living on nothing but food stamps', *New York Times*, 3 January 2010.

2. Gabriel A. Almond and Sidney Verba, *The Civic Culture: Political attitudes and democracy in five nations*, Sage, Newbury Park, CA, 1989 [1963], p. 216.

3. For the post-war era, see ibid., Chapter 9 (esp. pp. 216–21) and Chapter 10 (esp. Tables X1–X9). Cross-national tallies of civic engagement typically show the US first and Britain second. In the early 1980s, America remained top of the table, but church membership contributed heavily to explaining much of this pole position. See J.E. Curtis, E.G. Grabb and D.E. Baer, 'Voluntary association membership in fifteen countries: A comparative analysis', *American Sociological Review*, 57 (April 1992), pp. 139–52.

4. On the connection between 'social capital' and crime, see Putnam, *Bowling Alone*, pp. 307–18; on the link between social capital and mortality, see ibid., pp. 329–31.

5. Peter A. Hall, 'Social capital in Britain', *British Journal of Political Science*, 29:3 (1999), pp. 417–61, at: www.abdn.ac.uk/sociology/notes06/Level4/SO4530/Assigned-Readings/Seminar%209.2.pdf

6. The figures quoted for 2008 and 2010 are based on quarterly Citizenship Survey data, quoted in Chaeyoon Lim and James Laurence, 'Doing good when times are bad: Volunteering behaviour in economic hard times', *British Journal of Sociology* (forthcoming, 2014).

7. Laurence and Lim provided this analysis of the Citizenship Survey, which shows that whole-population formal volunteering declines from 3.18 hours in Q3 2008 to 2.18 hours in Q1 2010.

8. To guard against a small number of full-time volunteers skewing the quarterly changes, individual volunteers' time contribution was capped at 40 hours per month – a very restrictive cap. When (on request) James Laurence and Chaeyoon Lim raised the cap to 160 hours, the decline was from 4.11 in Q3 2008 to 2.35 in Q2 2010, a sharper reduction than we report.

9. The Citizenship Survey was originally released on a biannual basis, shifting to a quarterly basis after 2007/08. Something approaching 10,000 adults were included over each year. Respondents were asked to identify groups or organisations to which they had 'given unpaid help' in the last 12 months; if they had given any help, they were asked how much. The data shown is a slight variant of that presented in Lim and Laurence, 'Doing good when times are bad', and was provided by those authors.

10. In January 2011, the Department for Communities and Local Government (DCLG) announced that the Citizenship Survey had been cancelled, with effect from March 2011. See the statement at: www.communities.gov.uk/communities/research/citizenshipsurvey/surveycancellation/ Subsequently, however, it proposed a replacement survey, the Community Life Survey, which began collecting data in Q2 2012/13, and tried to re-establish certain discontinued time-series through use of selected Citizenship Survey questions. Official details at: http://communitylife.cabinetoffice.gov.uk/faq.html

11. Hansard Society, *The Audit of Political Engagement 9: The 2012 Report*, p. 90, at: www.hansardsociety.org.uk/blogs/parliament_and_government/archive/2012/04/27/audit-of-political-engagement–9-part-one.aspx

12. Komarovsky, *The Unemployed Man and His Family*, p. 125.

13. Correspondence via the Scout Association, October 2012.

14. Jahoda et al., *Marienthal*, p. 39.

15. More details about the Current Population Survey at: www.census.gov/cps/methodology/

16. Analysis of the CPS data presented by James Laurence and Chaeyoon Lim at the SCHMI seminar in Sarasota, Florida, March 2012.

17. The 2009 online survey for the National Conference on Citizenship (NCC) only covered selected states. The NCC reported 72% of respondents claiming to have cut back on civic engagement. Based on subjective assessment, this figure was not comparable with the Current Population Survey and – given how many people do no volunteering at all – it strikes us as implausibly large. See NCC, *America's Civic Health Index, 2009: Civic Health in Hard Times*, at: http://ncoc.net/2gp54 In 2012, the NCC's *Volunteering and Civic Life in America 2012* (www.volunteeringinamerica. gov) instead highlighted the CPS data, which suggested that there had been little if any recessionary decline in volunteering.

18. Alexis de Tocqueville, *Democracy in America*, Fontana/HarperCollins, London, 1994 [1840], p. 513.

19. In the context of religion, for example, while faith-based networks are very important, neither the content nor the intensity of personal belief seems to affect volunteering much. See Ram Cnaan, Amy Kasternakis and Robert Wineberg, 'Religious people, religious congregations, and volunteerism in human services: Is there a link?', *Nonprofit and Voluntary Sector Quarterly*, 22:1 (1993), pp. 33–51.

20. Mark A. Musick and John Wilson, *Volunteers: A social profile*, Indiana University Press, Indianapolis, IN, 2008.

21. Almond and Verba, *The Civic Culture*, Table X.1 and Table X.7.

22. A 2010 Gallup survey found that 42% of Americans claimed to attend church weekly or almost weekly, at: www.gallup.com/poll/125999/mississippians-go-church-most-vermonters-least.aspx A 2007 survey for the charity Tearfund found that 14% of English respondents claimed to attend church regularly (at least monthly), at: http://news.bbc.co.uk/1/shared/bsp/hi/pdfs/03_04_07_tearfundchurch.pdf

23. Putnam and Campbell, *American Grace*.

24. For background on the Scout Association's review of its religious pledge, see Cole Moreton, 'Scout Association amends vow to God in bid to appease atheists and other faiths', *Daily Telegraph*, 23 June 2013, at: www.telegraph.co.uk/news/religion/10136888/Scout-Association-amends-vow-to-God-in-bid-to-appease-atheists-and-other-faiths.html On the decision to introduce a non-religious pledge, see Sam Jones, 'New Scouts pledge welcomes non-believers', *Guardian*, 8 October 2013, www.theguardian.com/society/2013/oct/08/scouts-pledge-welcomes-non-believers Scout waiting-list numbers reported in Tracey McVeigh, 'Scouts learn new skills as they set up camp in the UK's inner cities', *Guardian*, 14 October 2013, at: www.theguardian.com/society/2013/oct/13/scouts-skills-inner-cities

25. We are grateful to Professor Putnam for this summary of the relevant implications of his research on religion in personal correspondence.

26. For the full list, see DCLG, *The 2010/11 Citizenship Survey Questionnaire*, p. 30, at: http://webarchive.nationalarchives.gov.uk/20120919132719/http://www.communities.gov.uk/documents/communities/pdf/1703735.pdf

27. Lim and Laurence, 'Doing good when times are bad'.

28. The recessionary drop in the proportion that helped informally more frequently (once a month, rather than once a year) was roughly 6 percentage points between 2007/08 and 2009/10, as against a 2 point drop-off for frequent formal volunteering. See the

final official results of the Citizenship Survey (for England only) at: http://webarchive.nationalarchives.gov.uk/20120919132719/http:/www.communities.gov.uk/publications/corporate/statistics/citizenshipsurveyq4201011

29. In calculating the averages, the cap imposed on an individual's hours of helping was 40 hours a month; raise that to 160 hours and the decline is of 1 hour and 19 minutes between Q1 2008 and Q1 2010. We are grateful to James Laurence and Chaeyoon Lim for supplying this extra analysis.

30. Comparing annualised data for 2007 and for 2010/11, and applying to this less volatile annual data the higher cap of 160 hours' helping a month, average helping drops from 3 hours 15 minutes to 2 hours 25 minutes – a reduction of 25.5%.

31. Citizens count as 'informal volunteers' if they have helped a non-relative in any of the ways suggested by the Citizenship Survey question 'IHlp' over the last 12 months. The data shown is a slight variant of that presented in Lim and Laurence, 'Doing good when times are bad', and was kindly supplied by its authors.

32. This measure is especially cautious because – to limit the effect of outliers – *combined* formal and informal volunteering is now capped at 40 hours, an effective cap of 20 hours for someone heavily involved in both. In addition, using the whole year 2010/11 as our final data point arguably understates the recession effect, as both the economy and rates of helping bounced back somewhat during parts of that year.

33. James Laurence kindly provided this extra analysis of the Citizenship Survey.

34. The effect of trust is explored in: Lim and Laurence, 'Doing good when times are bad', Table II. There is a significant (post-controls) effect on helping, but a particularly marked effect on volunteering; among people who trust their neighbours, there was no formal volunteering decline at all. It is trust in the local neighbourhood that seems to matter – generalised trust in people more widely does not materially affect the results.

35. Lim and Laurence, 'Doing good when times are bad'. The exact Current Population Survey figures (presented by that paper's authors at the SCHMI seminar in Sarasota, Florida, March 2012) are 41.9% in 2008 and 44.4% in 2010.

36. Statistical significance remains, even adjusting for changes in socio-economic factors between different samples. There is also steady downward-shifting between the categories in the frequency with which people claim to help. Analysis of CPS data presented at the SCHMI seminar in Sarasota, Florida, March 2012, by James Laurence and Chaeyoon Lim.

37. Data presented at the SCHMI seminar in Sarasota, Florida, March 2012, by James Laurence and Chaeyoon Lim.

38. All the statistical models – the results of which are reported in Table I of Lim and Laurence, 'Doing good when times are bad' – adjust for personal characteristics, including employment status, and yet the significant decline in volunteering remains. Factoring household income into the modelling, the authors report, yields results that are 'almost identical'.

39. The text here summarises the modelling results (reported in ibid., Table I) in non-technical language and necessarily simplifies matters. Several specific points are wrapped up in this general discussion. First, in the basic 'spline' regressions (which control for individual characteristics, including personal unemployment), all English regions have a positive and significant coefficient for volunteering against the reference of the (high-unemployment) North East. Second, factoring in annual regional unemployment rates, together with a term for the interaction between regional unemployment and the recession period, produces strongly negative coefficients, implying that regions with more unemployment saw a sharper recessionary drop-off in volunteering. Indeed, for informal helping, once regional unemployment rates are factored in like this, the original coefficients for the regions and for the recession period are left with little explanatory power.

40. This is officially known as the Index of Multiple Deprivation; official details about the 2007 release of this index are at: http://webarchive.nationalarchives.gov.uk/20100410180038/http://communities.gov.uk/communities/neighbourhoodrenewal/deprivation/deprivation07/

41. The effect of trust in neighbours is analysed in Lim and Laurence, 'Doing good when times are bad', Table II. After taking trust in neighbours into account, both types of volunteering still declined more in disadvantaged communities than in prosperous ones.

42. Affluence of communities is rated using the Index of Multiple Deprivation (IMD): top quintile wards are ranked as 'rich'; bottom quintile 'poor'. The IMD does not cover Wales, and so results are for England only. The chart records the decline in the predicted probability of an individual volunteering (between Q2 2008 and Q2 2010), as calculated by Lim and Laurence on the basis of modelling which adjusts for various individual-level socio-economic factors. See ibid., Figures II and III.

43. Respondents are grouped as 'slump-proof' or 'slump-hit' on the basis of self-appraisal, as is explained in Chapter 5. This chart is based on the proportion answering 'more likely' to the question: 'Thinking about your life in the last few years, would you say you are more likely or less likely to . . . get involved with social and community groups?'

44. Lim and Laurence, 'Doing good when times are bad'.

45. Gallup data presented at the SCHMI seminar in Sarasota, Florida, March 2012, by James Laurence and Chaeyoon Lim.

46. David Cameron said in response to the leader of the opposition, 'he, like me, will welcome the report this week showing that volunteering is up'. See *Hansard*, 13 February 2013, column 854, at: www.publications.parliament.uk/pa/cm201213/cmhansrd/cm130213/debtext/130213–0001.htm

47. Official results of the Community Life Survey are available on the Cabinet Office website, at: http://communitylife.cabinetoffice.gov.uk/explore-the-data.html Select 'Excel format' files, then Table 12. As of late November 2013, the latest quarter available is Q1 2013. Comparing August–October 2012 with the pooled data covering August 2012–April 2013 suggests that formal volunteering dipped over the year. The results for informal helping over these quarters are more encouraging.

Chapter 7: The long shadow

1. One celebrated early application of the idea was Olivier J. Blanchard and Lawrence H. Summers, 'Hysteresis and the European unemployment problem', *NBER Macroeconomics Annual*, vol. 1, University of Chicago Press, Chicago, 1986, pp. 15–78, at: www.nber.org/chapters/c4245.pdf

2. Peck, *Pinched*, p. 53.

3. Updated forecasts kindly supplied by the Resolution Foundation on request. Based on the official numbers in Office for Budget Responsibility, *Economic and Fiscal Outlook: March 2013*, Table 1.1, at: http://budgetresponsibility.independent.gov.uk/economic-and-fiscal-outlook-march–2013/ The projected decline is from £24,600 in 2005/06 to £21,200 in 2017/18 (2012/13 prices).

4. Jill Insley, 'Number paying into occupational pensions at 54-year low', *Guardian*, 27 October 2011, at: www.theguardian.com/money/2011/oct/27/pensions–50-year-low

5. Workers offered coverage fell from 71.6% to 67.5% of the total between 2002 and 2010; meanwhile take-up dropped from 61.0% to 56.5%. See Paul Fronstein, *Employment-Based Health Benefits: Trends in access and coverage, 1997–2010*, Employee Benefit Research Institute, Washington, DC, 2012, p. 4.

6. Resolution Foundation analysis of various official data by Matthew Whittaker, presented at the Foundation in London, July 2013, at: www.resolutionfoundation.org/publications/closer-edge-prospects-household-debt-repayments-in/

7. Whittaker, *On Borrowed Time?*, p. 4.

8. Matthew Whittaker, 'Closer to the edge?', analysis presented at the Resolution Foundation, London, July 2013, at: www.resolutionfoundation.org/publications/closer-edge-prospects-household-debt-repayments-in/

9. Analysis of the Panel Study of Income Dynamics in Pew Research Center, *Balance Sheet at 30 Months*, p. 34.

10. The Resolution Foundation compares Bank of England/NMG Consulting Surveys for 2005 and 2012, which consider the distribution of home-buyers and renters separately. The pattern of rising 'net worth inequality' is found among both. See Whittaker, *On Borrowed Time?*, Figure 8.

11. Pew Research Center, *Balance Sheet at 30 Months*, p. 6.

12. Ellen and Dastrup, *Housing and the Great Recession*, Figure 6.

13. 'Residential vacancies and homeownership in the second quarter 2013', *US Census Bureau News*, 30 July 2013, at: www.census.gov/housing/hvs/files/currenthvspress.pdf

14. Council of Mortgage Lenders figures show that repossessions peaked at about 75,000 in 1991, but remained below 50,000 throughout the post-2008 recession. See Gary Styles, 'Looking back to the really bad old days', *Mortgage Strategy*, 5 March 2012, at: www.mortgagestrategy.co.uk/analysis/looking-back-at-the-really-bad-old-days/1047392.article

15. 'Home ownership falls for the first time in past century', Office for National Statistics website, 19 April 2013, at: www.ons.gov.uk/ons/rel/census/2011-census-analysis/a-century-of-home-ownership-and-renting-in-england-and-wales/sty-home-ownership.html

16. Figures have been rounded. See 'Housing market in crisis as owner occupation falls', National Housing Federation website, 30 August 2011, at: www.housing.org.uk/media/press-releases/housing-market-in-crisis-as-owner-occupation-rates-fall

17. Conversation with the author, August 2012.

18. George Packer, *The Unwinding: An inner history of the new America*, Faber and Faber, London, 2013; David Boyle, *Broke: Who killed the middle classes?*, Fourth Estate/HarperCollins, London, 2013.

19. M. Taylor, D. Pevalin and J. Todd, 'The psychological costs of unsustainable housing commitments', *Psychological Medicine*, 37:7 (2007), pp. 1027–36.

20. Jeffrey P. Dew, 'Two sides of the same coin? The differing roles of assets and consumer debt in marriage', *Journal of Family and Economic Issues*, 28:1 (2007), pp. 89–104.

21. Jeffrey P. Dew, 'Debt change and marital satisfaction change in recently married couples', *Family Relations*, 57:1 (2008), pp. 60–71.

22. The data used was the National Survey of Children and Households between 1987 and 1992–94. See Jeffrey Dew and John Dakin, 'Financial disagreements and marital conflict tactics', *Journal of Financial Therapy*, 2:1 (2011), pp. 22–43, at: http://jftonline.org/journals/jft/article/view/1414/1184

23. Jacob S. Hacker, Philipp Rehm and Mark Schlesinger, 'The insecure American: Economic experiences, financial worries, and policy attitudes', *Perspectives on Politics*, 11:1 (2013), pp. 23–49. See Table 3, in particular; quote from p. 32.

24. Alakeson and Cory, *Home Truths*, Figure 4.

25. Calculation assumes 5% of income is saved. See Resolution Foundation, *Squeezed Britain*, p. 13.

26. Lisa Kahn, 'The long-term labor market consequences of graduating from college in a bad economy', *Labour Economics*, 17:2 (2010), pp. 303–16.

27. Canadian data suggests similar scarring, though it fades over one decade rather than two. See Phil Oreopoulos, Till von Wachter and Andrew Heisz, 'The short- and long-term career effects of graduating in a recession: Hysteresis and heterogeneity in the market for college graduates', National Bureau of Economic Research Working Paper No. 12159, Cambridge, MA, 2006.

28. Kahn, 'Long-term labor market consequences', p. 303.

29. Komarovsky, *The Unemployed Man and His Family*, p. xvi.

30. Economic Policy Institute analysis of US Census Bureau data on real median family income. See Mishel and Shierholz, 'A lost decade, not a burst bubble', Figure 1.1.3.

31. Cribb et al., *Living Standards, Poverty and Inequality in the UK: 2013*, Figure 5.6 ('After Housing Cost' series).
32. Respondents were asked if they 'feel that your generation will have had a better or worse life than your parents' generation, or will it have been about the same?'. The column for 'same' includes a small proportion, 1% of the total, who say that they don't know. Data points are from Bobby Duffy, *Intergenerational Justice*, Ipsos MORI/Joseph Rowntree Reform Trust, 2013, at: www.jrrt.org.uk/sites/jrrt.org.uk/files/documents/Intergenerational_Justice_050613_IpsosMORI_JRRT.pdf
33. For the boomers, the proportion trusting the man/woman in the street actually improved over these years, from 53% to 70%; for Gen Y, by contrast, it stagnated at 45–46%. Ipsos MORI Generations data (2013). Supplied by Bobby Duffy.
34. YouGov (2013). Summary results and fieldwork details at: http://d25d2506sfb94s.cloudfront.net/cumulus_uploads/document/u7f0cyctl1/YGCam-Archive-results-040413-All-Countries.pdf
35. Borie-Holtz et al., *No End in Sight*, pp. 3–7.
36. Comparative data for the wider American workforce are drawn from another survey, conducted by the Heldrich Center in November 2009. See ibid., Table 2.
37. Valerie Walkerdine and Luis Jimenez, *Gender, Work and Community after De-Industrialisation: A psychosocial approach to affect*, Palgrave Macmillan, London, 2012, pp. 137–8.
38. The satisfaction scores of the continually employed group was essentially unchanged over these years – rounding to 5.3 in both years. This updated analysis was kindly provided by James Laurence and Chaeyoon Lim.
39. Between the 2002/03 and the 2008/09 waves, the satisfaction scores of those who have moved into unemployment drop by just over 0.5 (a fractionally larger fall than in the most recent data) while the 'newly re-employed' actually experience a marginal increase in happiness. As reported in Lim and Laurence, 'Economic hard times', Figure 4.
40. Strictly speaking, the 'newly re-employed' category covers workers employed in both waves with any experience of unemployment in between. Numbers quoted come from ibid., p. 13 and Figure 3.
41. In very rare years, such as 2009/10, rates have risen in real terms; but in others – including 2013 – they have been cut. All told, it is a fair summary to say that there has been no increase in British unemployment benefit rates in a third of a century.
42. An 'all-work' test has long been attached to Jobseeker's Allowance claims after a brief grace period, meaning that, in theory, job centres could require someone to take lower-paying (or very different) work than before. Historically, however, rates of sanctioning were low.
43. We vaguely state that we control for individual participation in 'youth' because the data has different information at different ages: the baseline for volunteering is age 23; for other measures listed it is instead participation at 33. For the full list of control variables, see James Laurence and Chaeyoon Lim, '"The scars of others should teach us caution": The long-term effects of job "displacement" on civic participation over the lifecourse: A cross-national comparative study between the GB and US', Institute for Social Change Working Paper 2013–2, Manchester, 2013, at: www.humanities.manchester.ac.uk/socialchange/publications/working/documents/JamesLaurenceHardshipandCivicParticipation.pdf
44. We are grateful to James Laurence and Chaeyoon Lim for converting the coefficients they report (in ibid., Table 1) into the odds ratios quoted here.
45. All the effects we cite are significant at the 5% level at least; ibid., Table 1.
46. In the *Bowling Alone* state-level data, Wisconsin is an above-average state on the majority of social capital indicators. See www.bowlingalone.org/data.htm
47. There is much overlap with the British controls, but some differences owing to data differences; for the full list see Laurence and Lim, '"The scars of others"', p. 11.

48. We are grateful to James Laurence and Chaeyoon Lim for converting the coefficients they report (in ibid., Table 1) into the odds ratios quoted here.

49. Emile Durkheim, *Division of Labor in Society*, Free Press, Glencoe, IL, 1933 [1893].

50. Because of differences in the available data, the potential mediators are somewhat differently adjusted for in the British and American data. See Laurence and Lim, '"The scars of others"', pp. 11–12.

51. Proportional reductions cited calculated by comparing Table 1 and Table 5 in ibid.

52. For one contemporary set of estimates of wages over the age range, see Gueorgui Kambourov and Iourii Manovskii, 'Accounting for the changing life-cycle profile of earnings', Mimeo, 2009, Figure 2, at: http://economics.sas.upenn.edu/~manovski/papers/accounting_for_profiles.pdf

53. H. Wilensky, 'Life cycle, work situation and participation in formal associations', in R.W. Kleemeier (ed.), *Aging and Leisure: A research perspective into the meaningful use of time*, Oxford University Press, New York, p. 214.

54. See, for example, Curtis, Grabb and Baer, 'Voluntary association membership', p. 147.

55. One American survey showed that volunteering rates rose in steps from 38% for those aged 18–24 up to 55% for those aged 35–54, before tailing off to 48% for those aged 55–64 and 45% for the age group 65–74. See V.A. Hodgkinson and M.S. Weitzman, *Giving and Volunteering in the United States: Findings from a national survey*, Independent Sector, Washington, DC, 1996. For the UK, James Laurence and Chaeyoon Lim's own analysis of the Citizenship Survey reveals the same pattern, with the volunteering rate rising from 35% or so among those in their early 30s up to around 45% by the mid-40s. For similar results for group membership, see J. Hendricks and S.J. Cutler, 'Volunteerism and socioemotional selectivity in later life', *Journals of Gerontology Series B: Social Sciences*, 59:5 (2004), pp. S251–S257.

56. The claims here are based on comparing the age-specific coefficients in Laurence and Lim, '"The scars of others"', Table 6 and Table 1. In the British data the cut-off point for 'middle aged' is 42.

57. This chart reproduces Figure 1 in ibid. The controls for personal characteristics have been applied to the 'predicted' membership rates shown.

58. This chart reproduces Figure 1 in ibid. The controls for personal and demographic variables detailed earlier in the chapter have been applied to the 'predicted' membership rates shown in this chart.

59. ibid., pp. 13–17.

60. ibid., Table 1.

61. John H. Goldthorpe and Colin Mills, 'Trends in intergenerational class mobility in modern Britain: Evidence from national surveys, 1972–2005', *National Institute Economic Review*, 205 (July 2008), pp. 1–18.

62. Steve Machin, Paul Gregg and Jo Blanden, *Intergenerational Mobility in Europe and North America*, Sutton Trust, 2005.

63. Using social-class measures, relative mobility rates have remained 'much the same'. See John H. Goldthorpe, 'Understanding – and misunderstanding – social mobility in Britain: The entry of the economists, the confusion of politicians and the limits of educational policy', *Journal of Social Policy*, 42:3 (2013), pp. 431–50.

64. Alan B. Krueger, 'The rise and consequences of inequality in the United States', speech at the Center for American Progress, 12 January 2012, prepared remarks at: www.whitehouse.gov/blog/2012/01/12/chairman-alan-krueger-discusses-rise-and-consequences-inequality-center-american-pro

65. See, for example, Nick Clegg's 'Hugo Young lecture' – delivered in London in November 2010, weeks after the spending review that set out the Coalition's first big cuts to benefits for the poor. Clegg dismissed 'a static, income-based definition of fairness' in favour of 'an approach focused on mobility and life chances'. Full text at: www.guardian.co.uk/politics/2010/nov/23/nick-clegg-hugo-young-text

66. The White House Great Gatsby Curve interactive is at: www.whitehouse.gov/blog/2013/06/11/what-great-gatsby-curve

67. For the elasticity estimates, see Miles Corak, 'Inequality from generation to generation: The United States in Comparison', in Robert Rycroft (ed.), *The Economics of Poverty, Inequality and Discrimination in the 21st Century*, ABC-CLIO, Santa Barbara, CA, 2013, pp. 107–25, Table 2. For the Gini coefficients, see OECD, 'An overview of growing income inequalities in OECD countries: Main findings', in OECD, *Divided We Stand: Why inequality keeps rising*, OECD, Paris, 2011, pp. 21–45, at: www.oecd.org/els/soc/49499779.pdf The underlying data is at: http://dx.doi.org/10.1787/888932535185

68. 'MP Jesse Norman defends Eton school's dominance in government', *Guardian*, 27 April 2013, at: www.guardian.co.uk/education/2013/apr/27/jesse-norman-eton-school-uk-government

69. To focus on prolonged (rather than transitory) worklessness, we characterise the families as having been 'workless' only if the head of household was found to be without work in successive waves of tracking data. For details, see Paul Gregg and Lindsey Macmillan, 'The intergenerational transmission of worklessness in the US and the UK', Institute for Social Change, Draft Working Paper 2013–1, 2013, at: www.humanities.manchester.ac.uk/socialchange/publications/working/documents/LindseyMacmillanpaper.pdf

70. The UK National Child Development Survey data covers people born in 1958; the US National Longitudinal Survey of Youth sample features people born between 1962 and 1965. Lindsey Macmillan kindly calculated and supplied the proportions of young adulthood shown, an alternative way of describing the results in ibid., Table 3: Panel A.

71. Lindsey Macmillan kindly calculated and supplied the proportions of young adulthood shown, an alternative way of describing the results in ibid., Table 3: Panel B.

72. All 24 reported coefficients linking worklessness of parents and their children are significant at the 99% level; ibid., Table 3: Panels A and B.

73. This additional analysis of the British Cohort Survey is included in the results tables throughout ibid.

74. '"Welfare Queen" becomes issue in Reagan campaign', *New York Times*, 15 February 1976.

75. A speech in which Iain Duncan Smith made the claim about three generations where no one had worked was removed from his department's website, but his words were quoted in 'Workless families: A convenient untruth', *Guardian*, 2 February 2012, at: www.guardian.co.uk/commentisfree/2012/feb/02/workless-families-convenient-truth-editorial For analysis demonstrating that families where two (never mind three) generations have never worked are a virtual myth, see Lindsey Macmillan, 'Measuring the intergenerational coefficient of worklessness', Centre for Market and Public Organisation Working Paper, 2011, at: www.bristol.ac.uk/cmpo/publications/papers/2011/wp278.pdf

76. Analysis of the NCDS data presented by Lindsey Macmillan at the SCHMI seminar in Sarasota, Florida, March 2012.

77. Analysis of the NLSY data presented by Lindsey Macmillan at the SCHMI seminar in Sarasota, Florida, March 2012.

78. Such differences in the heritability of worklessness across local labour markets can be seen in: Gregg and Macmillan, 'Intergenerational transmissions', Figures 1 and 2.

79. US rules have only been 'partially' mimicked in Britain, because lone parents with very young children are still exempt from work-search requirements, whereas even American mothers of babies face such obligations. Furthermore, the American requirements, which can be traced back to 1967, are strict. States administering Temporary Assistance for Needy Families must require lone parents of even children under six to spend at least 20 hours a week on work experience, job search and so on. A waiver can be granted for childcare only if it can be demonstrated that no friend or

relative was available to mind the child. See Gene Falk, *The Temporary Assistance for Needy Families (TANF) Block Grant: A primer on TANF financing and federal requirements*, Congressional Support Services, Washington, DC, 2011, at: http://greenbook.waysandmeans.house.gov/sites/greenbook.waysandmeans.house.gov/files/2011/images/RL32748%20v2_gb.pdf

80. Comparing the American sample with British baby boomers in the NCDS suggests that the inheritance of worklessness is more marked for sons in the US; there is no meaningful difference between British and American daughters in the boomer generation. Comparing the same American sample with the British Gen Xers in the British Cohort Survey suggests no meaningful difference in relation to worklessness. But with unemployment more narrowly defined, the inheritance effect for this later cohort appears somewhat more powerful in Britain. See Gregg and Macmillan, 'Intergenerational transmission', Table 3: Panels A and B.

81. For the relevant quotes from Peter Lilley's 1992 conference speech, see 'Daily Politics: Your favourite conference clips', BBC Two website, 3 October 2007, at: http://news.bbc.co.uk/1/hi/programmes/the_daily_politics/6967366.stm

82. See Chapter 3, note 42 for relevant citations.

83. Gregg and Macmillan, 'Intergenerational transmission', Table 4.

84. L. Loury, 'Some contacts are more equal than others: Informal networks, job tenure, and wages', *Journal of Labor Economics*, 24:2 (2006), pp. 299–318.

85. American children are more likely to get a job at the same plant as their parents; furthermore, this effect is particularly strong in high unemployment areas. See F. Kramarz and O. Skans, 'Nepotism at work? Family networks and youth labor market entry', unpublished manuscript, Symposium of Labor Economics (ESSLE), 2006.

86. Paul Gregg and Lindsey Macmillan, 'Intergenerational mobility and education in the next generation', Mimeo, 2008, cited in Cabinet Office Strategy Unit, *Getting On, Getting Ahead: A discussion paper: Analysing the trends and drivers of social mobility*, 2008, at: http://webarchive.nationalarchives.gov.uk/20081203181929/http://cabinetoffice.gov.uk/media/cabinetoffice/strategy/assets/socialmobility/gettingon.pdf

87. Danny Dorling, 'One of Labour's great successes', *Guardian* Mortarboard blog, 28 January 2010, at: www.theguardian.com/education/mortarboard/2010/jan/28/labours-great-successes-university-access-danny-dorling

88. 'The value of student maintenance support', House of Commons Library, Briefing Paper SN/SG/916, 2013, at: www.parliament.uk/briefing-papers/SN00916

89. See, for example, 'How the $1.2 trillion college debt crisis is crippling students, parents and the economy', *Forbes*, 7 August 2013, at: www.forbes.com/sites/specialfeatures/2013/08/07/how-the-college-debt-is-crippling-students-parents-and-the-economy/

90. Unpublished 2011 research report prepared for SCHMI, and supplied to the authors by Professor Ed Fieldhouse.

Chapter 8: A tale of two tragedies

1. 1979 personal election address to the voters of Ebbw Vale. Quoted in Mervyn Jones, *Michael Foot*, Victor Gollancz, London, p. 431.

2. Address to the New York State legislature, 28 August 1931. Quoted in Smith, *FDR*, p. 250.

3. Important qualifications in the UK would include the growing expenditure on the National Health Service, and – after the change of administration in 1997 – the minimum wage and the expansion of family tax credits. Qualifications in the US would include the Clinton administration's moves on minimum pay, tax credits and childcare. For a broader (if polemical) summary of the New Right's hegemony, see Tony Judt, *Ill Fares the Land: A treatise on our present discontents*, Penguin, London, 2010, Chapter 3.

4. The White Paper was presented by Minister for Reconstruction Lord Wooton. *Hansard*, 5 July 1944, vol. 132, cc649–700, at: http://hansard.millbanksystems.com/lords/1944/jul/05/employment-policy

5. Compared with the 1930s, mainstream policymakers now place less emphasis on the annual budget than on balancing budgets over the medium term, often explicitly targeting cyclically adjusted measures. Even UK Chancellor George Osborne acknowledges the importance of the so-called 'automatic stabilisers', the tendency for tax revenues to fall and for benefit spending to rise in a slump, and has said it would be wrong to offset this. When growth disappointed in 2011–12, he did not move towards immediate further retrenchment (which 1930s orthodoxies would have required), but instead proposed persisting with austerity for longer.

6. James Rowley and Roxana Tiron, 'Republicans see Obama second-term agenda as dead in water', Bloomberg, 14 February 2013, at: www.bloomberg.com/news/2013–02–13/obama-s-minimum-wage-increase-dismissed-by-boehner.html

7. Although with 1.7 million Americans paid precisely the federal minimum wage, the numbers directly affected are not insignificant. See Bureau of Labor Statistics, 'Labor force statistics from the Current Population Survey: Characteristics of minimum wage workers: 2011', at: www.bls.gov/cps/minwage2011.htm

8. The US Department of Labor's series on historic rates of the minimum wage is available at: www.dol.gov./whd/minwage/chart.htm Consumer price deflator from Lawrence H. Officer and Samuel H. Williamson, 'The Annual Consumer Price Index for the United States, 1774–2012', MeasuringWorth, at: www.measuringworth.com/uscpi/ We have deflated using the long-running CPI-U index, as used in official American poverty statistics. The alternative, CPI-U-RS, is a superior measure in certain technical respects, but is unavailable for earlier years, and can be applied to them using arbitrary assumptions. If this approach is taken, the minimum wage looks somewhat higher today relative to the distant past, but is still appreciably lower than it was in 1967. See Employment Policy Institute, 'The state of working America', at: http://stateofworkingamerica.org/chart/swa-wages-table-4-39-minimum-wage-1960-2011/

9. Edelman, *So Rich, So Poor*, p. 14.

10. ibid., p. 88.

11. For an appraisal of this legislation and a Clinton administration insider who resigned in protest at it, see ibid., pp. 81–100.

12. There is a transatlantic echo here of the 'Jobseeker's Allowance' reform of the 1990s. In subsequent bad years for the labour market, the count of unemployed claimants was reduced thanks to harsher benefit rules, but other measures of unemployment were not comparably reduced. See Gregg and Wadsworth, 'Unemployment and inactivity', p. 46.

13. Dan Finn and Rosie Gloster, *Lone Parent Obligations: A review of recent evidence on the work-related requirements within the benefit systems of different countries*, Department for Work and Pensions Research Report No. 632, London, 2010, available at: www.cesi.org.uk/sites/default/files/publication_additional_downloads/rrep632.pdf

14. Labour market participation (i.e. working or actively seeking work) among unmarried women with children was 74.6% in 1997, rose to 79.2% in 2002, but then fell to 74.9% in 2010 and 2011. Figures supplied on request by the Bureau of Labor Statistics.

15. 'Cuts and consequences: Key facts about CalWORK's program in the aftermath of the Great Recession', California Budget Project, Briefing 2012, at: www.cbp.org/documents/120224_CalWORKs_KeyFacts.pdf

16. Finn and Gloster, *Lone Parent Obligations*, p. 40.

17. In the Census Bureau's survey of programme dynamics, among low-wage women in service occupations who had received welfare, 6.5% were servants/cleaners in private homes, and 10.4% were janitors/cleaners – both numbers that had tripled since 1997. See John J. Hisnanick and Katherine G. Walker, 'Assessing employment outcomes

from the survey of program dynamics second longitudinal file: What type of jobs do welfare leavers get?', US Census Bureau, Washington, DC, draft paper presented at the Joint Statistical Meetings, American Statistical Association, San Francisco, CA, 2003, Table 7, at: www.census.gov/spd/workpaper/Assessing_Employ_Outcomes. pdf

18. OECD calculations at: www.oecd.org/els/benefitsandwagesstatistics.htm Select table 'Long term unemployed, 2001–2011'. Net replacement rate values for 2011, for single-earner couple with two children, on assumption family does not qualify for housing or other social assistance.

19. Finn and Gloster, *Lone Parent Obligations*, p. 41.

20. Sheila Zedlewski, Sandi Nelson, Kathryn Edin, Heather Koball, Kate Pomper and Tracy Roberts, *Families Coping Without Earnings or Government Cash Assistance*, Urban Institute, Washington, DC, 2003, pp. 24–5, 27, 29, at: www.urban.org/uploaded PDF/410634_OP64.pdf

21. Kristin Seefeldt's paper – 'When ends don't meet: Debt and its role in low-income women's economic coping strategies' – is forthcoming and under review. Quotes and précis are thus taken from her presentation to the 2012 County Welfare Directors Association of California, 3 October 2012, at: www.cwda.org/downloads/meetings/ conference2012/When-Ends-Dont-Meet-Seefeldt.pdf and from citation in Edelman, *So Rich, So Poor*, pp. 90–1.

22. Fitch Ratings, *Gauging the Benefits, Costs and Sustainability of the US Stimulus*, Fitch Inc., New York, 2012, p. 1.

23. On the politicking that compromised the stimulus, see Ryan Lizza, 'The Obama memos', *New Yorker*, 30 January 2012, section 2, at: www.newyorker.com/ reporting/2012/01/30/120130fa_fact_lizza?printable=true&currentPage=all For the resulting technical design flaws of the package, see Joseph E. Stiglitz, *Freefall: America, free markets, and the sinking of the world economy*, Norton, New York, 2010.

24. Table 1 of the Congressional Budget Office's revised and final 'Estimates for the insurance coverage provisions of the Affordable Care Act [Obamacare] updated for the recent Supreme Court decision', at: www.cbo.gov/sites/default/files/cbofiles/ attachments/43472–07–24–2012-CoverageEstimates.pdf

25. Ryan Lizza, 'The second term', *New Yorker*, 18 June 2012, at: www.newyorker.com/ reporting/2012/06/18/120618fa_fact_lizza?printable=true

26. Jack Grovum, 'States make "disturbing cuts" to unemployment benefits', *USA Today*, 11 July 2013, at: www.usatoday.com/story/news/nation/2013/07/11/stateline-unemployment-benefits/2508115/

27. For long-term unemployment figures, see Bureau of Labor Statistics, 'Economic news release', Table A–12, at: www.bls.gov/news.release/empsit.t12.htm On the North Carolina story, see Jordan Friedman, 'NC unemployment fight being watched across the US', *USA Today*, 28 July 2013, at: www.usatoday.com/story/news/ nation/2013/07/21/north-carolina-unemployment/2571889/ On the trend for the states to cut compensation, see 'The untimely death of unemployment insurance', Bloomberg, 28 August 2013, at: www.bloomberg.com/news/2013–08–28/the-untimely-death-of-unemployment-insurance.html

28. Stacy Dean and Dorothy Rosenbaum, 'SNAP benefits will be cut for all participants in November 2013', Center on Budget Policy and Priorities, Washington, DC, 2013, at: www.cbpp.org/files/2–8–13fa.pdf

29. Ron Nixon, 'House Republicans pass deep cuts in food stamps', *New York Times*, 19 September 2013, at: www.nytimes.com/2013/09/20/us/politics/house-passes-bill-cutting-40-billion-from-food-stamps.html?_r=0

30. Department for Work and Pensions and Office/National Statistics, *Households Below Average Incomes: An analysis of the income distribution 1994/95–2011/12*, 2013, Table 3.3tr, at: www.gov.uk/government/uploads/system/uploads/attachment_data/ file/206778/full_hbai13.pdf

31. Using a '50% of median income' poverty measure, the OECD reports rising hardship in many countries. By contrast, there was a fall in Britain that was substantially exceeded only in Estonia and Portugal, and in the former case only because plunging average incomes dragged down the poverty line. See OECD, 'Crisis squeezes incomes and puts pressure on inequality and poverty: New results from the OECD Income Distribution Database', 2013, Figure 6, at: www.oecd.org/els/soc/OECD2013-Inequality-and-Poverty–8p.pdf

32. Certain benefits were frozen in cash terms during the 1980s, but most were pegged to price inflation – or frozen in real terms. Taking the 1980s and 1990s as a whole, outright cuts to benefits made very little difference to inequality, whereas the failure to increase benefits in line with rising average real incomes had a huge effect – contributing almost half the total rise in overall income inequality over these years. See T. Clark and A. Leicester, 'Inequality and two decades of British tax reforms', *Fiscal Studies*, 25:2 (2004), pp. 129–58.

33. The ambition was first committed to in Tony Blair's Beveridge lecture at Toynbee Hall, East London, on 18 March 1999.

34. See Mike Brewer, 'Comparing in-work benefits and the reward to work for families with children in the US and the UK', *Fiscal Studies*, 22:1 (2001), pp. 41–77, especially Figure 7.

35. For a single-earner couple with two children on the median wage, for 2009 the OECD calculates that in Britain (assuming take-up of in-kind assistance), 71% of net income would initially be maintained in the event of unemployment, compared to 53% in the US. Strict time limits in the American system would likely widen these differences over time. Figures from OECD, Directorate for Employment, Labour and Social Affairs, spreadsheet for net replacement rates, 'During the initial phase of unemployment', at: www.oecd.org/els/benefitsandwagesstatistics.htm (last updated March 2013).

36. Gretchen Livingston and D'Vera Cohn, 'US birth rate falls to a record low; decline is greatest among immigrants', Pew Research Centre, at: www.pewsocialtrends.org/files/2012/11/Birth_Rate_Final.pdf

37. There was a decline of 2,500 live births in England and Wales in 2009, a small change compared with an average absolute change of 12,000 in the typical year since 1980. In 2011, there were 724,000 live births, compared with 595,000 born a decade earlier. See ONS, *Births and Deaths in England and Wales, 2011 (Final)*.

38. George Osborne, speech to Conservative party conference, 29 September 2008, at: www.guardian.co.uk/politics/2008/sep/29/toryconference.georgeosborne

39. Net public investment fell from about 3.5% of national income in 2009/10 to 1.5% in 2012/13. Institute for Fiscal Studies analysis, presented by Carl Emmerson at the Institute for Government, London, 7 June 2013, at: www.ifs.org.uk/docs/pre_spendinground_ce2013.pdf

40. Total expenditure on working-age benefits and tax credits is expected to be £91.2 billion; see Carl Emmerson, Paul Johnson and Helen Miller (eds), *The IFS Green Budget 2013*, Institute for Fiscal Studies, London, 2013, Table 8.2. The total of £23 billion cuts is made up of the £18 billion of eventual annual cuts which the chancellor claimed to have already set in train at the time of the 2012 autumn statement, plus the roughly £5 billion in eventual additional annual savings to which he committed in the same statement; speech and official analysis available at: www.gov.uk/government/topical-events/autumn-statement–2012

41. Various underlying drivers of total working-age welfare expenditure – including population growth, rising rents and stagnant wages – offset the cuts. Thus overall working-age welfare expenditure is set to fall by only about £5 billion in real terms, and even this is an overstatement owing to changes in the way that local tax rebates are scored. See official expenditure forecasts at: www.gov.uk/government/publications/benefit-expenditure-and-caseload-tables–2013 Select spreadsheet 'Medium-term forecast for all DWP benefits', then tab 'GB benefits and tax credits'.

42. HM Treasury, *Impact on Households: Distributional analysis to accompany Budget 2013*, London, 2013, Fig 2.F, at: www.gov.uk/government/uploads/system/uploads/attachment_data/file/221894/budget2013_distributional_analysis.pdf This figure excludes all the major benefit changes coming after 2013, but even so shows big losses for the poor, and a regressive pattern across most of the distribution – with the exception of heavy losses at the top end. The latter are very likely explained by the inclusion in the analysis (acknowledged in the document) of 'changes that were announced before June Budget 2010 that have been implemented by the Government'. These changes include the previous Labour government's reforms to National Insurance and income tax, which raised significant money from the high-paid.

43. Mike Brewer, James Browne, Andrew Hood, Robert Joyce and Luke Sibieta, 'The short- and medium-term impacts of the recession on the UK income distribution', *Fiscal Studies*, 34:2 (2013), pp. 179–201; projected poverty rates from Table 3; quotes from p. 192.

44. In remarks after Budget 2013, the Institute for Fiscal Studies director, Paul Johnson, put the total cost of change to the personal tax allowance, fuel duty and corporation tax at 'a pretty remarkable £24 billion a year . . . by 2016–17', at: www.ifs.org.uk/budgets/budget2013/intro.pdf

45. The theoretical advantages of merging several payments arises because of the opportunity to rationalise (though not to eliminate) certain perverse incentives. See Mike Brewer, James Browne and Wenchao Jin, *Universal Credit: A preliminary analysis*, Institute for Fiscal Studies, London, 2011, available at: www.ifs.org.uk/bns/bn116.pdf Potential practical problems include: IT disruptions, the difficulty of claimants in budgeting for high rents, and redistribution from men to women within the home. See Nigel Keohane and Ryan Shorthouse, *Sink or Swim? The impact of universal credit*, Social Market Foundation, London, 2012, available at: www.smf.co.uk/files/1913/4779/2202/20120916_Sink_or_Swim_web_ready2.pdf

46. The National Audit Office denounced 'weak management, ineffective control and poor governance'; see NAO, *Universal Credit: Early progress*, 2013, at: www.nao.org.uk/wp-content/uploads/2013/09/10132–001-Universal-credit.pdf

47. Historic UK retail price index series retrieved September 2013 from: Lawrence H. Officer, 'What were the UK earnings and prices then?', MeasuringWorth, 2012, at: www.measuringworth.com/index.php

48. The IFS's TAXBEN model calculates that: a workless couple with three children (of various ages) renting privately, and facing typical losses from the restriction of housing benefit to the 30th rather than the 50th percentile of local rents, will see real disposable (After Housing Cost) income drop from £287 to £256 between New Year 2010 and April 2015, a loss of about £31 or about 11%. This is an underestimate because TAXBEN cannot factor in locally varying reductions in council tax benefit. Dividing the assumed saving from these among the total number of potentially affected claimants implies an average loss of an additional £4 a week, which would push the total loss up to 12.5%. Since the move to temporarily over-index benefits in April 2010 pushed up living standards between New Year 2010 and the arrival of the Coalition in May, the actual decline in living standards since the change of administration will be sharper still. The IFS calculation assumes (in line with the government's assumption) that private rents grow at 4% a year.

49. Quote from George Osborne's Budget statement to the House of Commons, 20 March 2013: www.gov.uk/government/speeches/budget–2013-chancellors-statement

50. Between April and December 2012 alone, 140,195 appeals were heard regarding entitlement to Employment and Support Allowance. Of these, 59,493 – or 42% – found in favour of the appellant. Parliamentary answer by Justice Minister Helen Grant, *Hansard*, 15 May 2013, cc215W–216W.

51. 'Sickness benefit: "They try their damnedest to avoid paying"', *Guardian*, 20 March 2012, at: www.theguardian.com/society/2012/mar/19/sickness-benefit-try-avoid-paying For details on one man who died of lung disease while arguing with Atos over whether he was well enough to work, see 'Atos case study: Larry Newman', *Guardian*, 25 July 2011, at: www.theguardian.com/society/2011/jul/24/atos-case-study-larry-newman

52. 'Disability welfare changes delayed by assessment process', BBC News, 26 October 2013, at: www.bbc.co.uk/news/uk-politics–24680366

53. Social Security Advisory Committee, 'Sanctions in the benefit system: Evidence review of JSA, IS and IB sanctions', SSAC Occasional Paper No. 1, 2006, at: http://ssac.independent.gov.uk/pdf/occasional/Sanctions_Occasional_Paper_1.pdf

54. October 2011–October 2012 figures, given in: Parliamentary answer by Employment Minister Mark Hoban, *Hansard*, 11 March 2013, c104w.

55. Comparison of the six-monthly tables that YouGov kindly produced for us from its regular commercial work for January–June 2011 (based on 130,855 interviews) and January–June 2013 (217,478 interviews) reveals that the proportion of respondents feeling positive about: 'your relationship with friends' was down 4%; 'relationship with family' was down 2%; 'your health' is down 4%; 'the way things are going in your neighbourhood' is down 1%. There was, by contrast, stability in optimism about 'your financial situation'. The figures have been weighted and are representative of all GB adults (aged 18+).

56. Tim Leunig, 'Housing benefit cap: Can you live on 62p a day?', *Guardian*, 23 January 2012, at: www.theguardian.com/commentisfree/2012/jan/22/housing-benefit-cap-62p-a-day

57. On the suicide note story, see Keir Mudie and Nigel Nelson, 'Bedroom Tax victim commits suicide: Grandmother Stephanie Bottrill blames government in tragic note', *Daily Mirror*, 12 May 2013, at: www.mirror.co.uk/news/uk-news/suicide-bedroom-tax-victim-stephanie–1883600#ixzz2efG7r8A0 On the UN representative's intervention, see Amelia Gentleman, '"Shocking" bedroom tax should be axed, says UN investigator', *Guardian*, 11 September 2013, at: www.theguardian.com/society/2013/sep/11/bedroom-tax-should-be-axed-says-un-investigator

58. The exact number is 1.85 million. Department for Communities/Office for National Statistics, 'Local authority housing statistics: 2011–12', 2012, at: www.gov.uk/government/uploads/system/uploads/attachment_data/file/39457/Local_authority_housing_statistics_2011_12_v4.pdf

59. Zedlewski et al., *Families Coping Without Earnings*, pp. viii, 8–13.

Chapter 9: The veil of complacency

1. Jahoda et al., *Marienthal*, pp. 19, 43–4.

2. Orwell, *The Road to Wigan Pier*, p. 70.

3. John Rawls, *A Theory of Justice*, Harvard University Press, Cambridge, MA, 1971.

4. Franklin Roosevelt, Second Inaugural Address, 20 January 1937.

5. In very crude terms, creditors lose from expansionary 'cheap money' policies, while debtors gain. For sweeping historical analysis of how the tensions between them have affected monetary policy see Philip Coggan, *Paper Promises: Money, debt, and the new world order*, Allen Lane/Penguin, London, 2012. For political analysis of how the deflationary constituency prevailed in interwar Britain, see Ross McKibbin, *The Ideologies of Class: Social relations in Britain 1880–1950*, Oxford University Press, Oxford, 1994 [1990], Chapter 9; esp. pp. 264–70.

6. The Bank of England's own analysis states that by inflating asset prices, quantitative easing has boosted households' non-pension financial wealth, but that such 'holdings are heavily skewed with the top 5% of households holding 40% of these assets'. See

Bank of England, 'The distributional effects of asset purchases', 2012, p. 1, at: www.bankofengland.co.uk/publications/Documents/news/2012/nr073.pdf

7. Smith, *FDR*, p. x, and pp. 51–98 on his ideology-free early political career.

8. Beveridge reacted to the publication of Keynes' General Theory with scepticism; see Ben Pimlott, *Harold Wilson*, HarperCollins, London, 1992, p. 63. On his interest in sunspots, see José Harris, *William Beveridge: A biography*, Clarendon Press, Oxford, 1997 [1977], p. 351.

9. Francis Beckett, *Clem Attlee*, Politico's Publishing, London, 2000.

10. 'How a very different America responded to the Great Depression', Pew Center, 2010, at:www.pewresearch.org/2010/12/14/how-a-different-america-responded-to-the-great-depression/

11. Benjamin M. Friedman, *The Moral Consequences of Economic Growth*, Vintage/Random House, New York, 2006 [2005], p. 178.

12. ibid., pp. 158–79.

13. Paul Addison, *The Road to 1945*, Random House, London, 2011 [1975], Chapter 10.

14. While it is often claimed that rising spending during wars persists into peacetime (the so-called 'ratchet effect'), the persistence of high wartime taxes after the end of conflicts in Britain has in practice been more marked; the resulting increase in revenues is the underlying facilitator of any ratchet up in public spending. See Tom Clark and Andrew Dilnot, 'British fiscal policy since 1939', in Floud and Johnson (eds), *Cambridge Economic History of Modern Britain*, vol. 3: *Structural Change and Growth, 1939–2000*, Cambridge University Press, Cambridge, 2004.

15. Hacker et al., 'The insecure American', pp. 39–40.

16. Carole Walker, 'Analysis: George Osborne's Philpott gamble', BBC News, 5 April 2013, at: www.bbc.co.uk/news/uk-politics–22042399

17. Overall, 56% said the cuts were affecting them; of these, opinion ran 49% to 43% against Osborne. Among the 34% of the total who said they were not affected by the cuts, the balance was 58% to 35% in Osborne's favour. YouGov UK polling, 2013; fieldwork details and results at: http://cdn.yougov.com/cumulus_uploads/document/sk7o6dimmg/YoG-Archive-Cam-Guardian-results–120413.pdf

18. Republican National Convention, *We Believe in America: Republican Platform 2012*, at: www.gop.com/wp-content/uploads/2012/08/2012GOPPlatform.pdf

19. Greg Sargent, 'Romney: I'll never convince Obama voters to take responsibility for their own lives', *Washington Post*, 17 September 2012, at: www.washingtonpost.com/blogs/plum-line/post/romney-ill-never-convince-obama-voters-to-take-responsibility-for-their-lives/2012/09/17/0c1f0bcc–0104–11e2-b260–32f4a8db9b7e_blog.html

20. GSS variable 'natfare'; precise question: 'We are faced with many problems in this country, none of which can be solved easily or inexpensively . . . Can you tell me whether we're spending too much, too little or the right amount on welfare'. The proportion saying 'too much' fell from 59% in 1980 to 38% in 1984.

21. Only 11% accepted the idea of cutting these benefits. Gallup polling numbers, in Richard C. Auxier, 'Reagan's recession', Pew Center, 14 December 2010, at: www.pewresearch.org/2010/12/14/reagans-recession/

22. The final two GSS variables referred to are 'natfarey' (question wording as for 'natfare' at note 20 above, but with 'assistance to the poor' substituting for 'welfare') and 'helppoor' (respondents asked to place themselves on a 1–5 scale between people who 'think the Government in Washington should do everything possible to improve the standard of living of all poor Americans', and others who 'think that it is not the Government's responsibility and that each person should take care of himself'. The shifts towards the political Right are around 10 percentage points on both measures between 1990 and 1994.

23. GSS variable 'natfare' (see note 20); the proportion saying there was 'too much' welfare spending rose from 38% in both 2006 and 2008 to 42% in 2010.

24. For one empirical study that identifies the power of elite language in this field, in a UK context, see J. Curtice, 'Thermostat or weather vane? How the public has reacted to

new labour government', in A. Park, J. Curtice, K. Thomson, M. Phillips, E. Clery and S. Butt (eds), *British Social Attitudes 26th Report*, Sage, London, 2010, pp. 19–38.

25. GSS variable 'eqwlth'; precise question asks people to place themselves on a 1–7 scale between people who 'think that the government in Washington ought to reduce the income differences between the rich and the poor, perhaps by raising the taxes of wealthy families or by giving income assistance to the poor', and others who 'think that the government should not concern itself with reducing this income difference'. We treat individuals with response scores of 1–3 as supporting redistribution, and those responding 5–7 as opposed.

26. Data is drawn from a YouGov/Polimetrix national tracking sample of 3,000 respondents, interviewed four times between 2007 and 2011, and reported in Yotam Margalit, 'Explaining social policy preferences: Evidence from the Great Recession', *American Political Science Review*, 107:1 (2013), pp. 80–103; figures are quoted on p. 88 and include only respondents who were successively re-interviewed. Margalit reports that this exclusion has little effect.

27. ibid., Figure 4 and Table 4.

28. Hacker et al., 'The insecure American', pp. 39–40 (Table 6).

29. ibid., pp. 41–2 (Table 7).

30. ibid., p. 40.

31. Lindsay A. Owens and David S. Pedulla, 'Material welfare and changing political preferences: The case of support for redistributive social policies', *Social Forces* (forthcoming); final paper electronically pre-released at: http://sf.oxfordjournals.org/content/early/2013/10/14/sf.sot101.full?keytype=ref&ijkey=lpFDgu1y7FeFShp Quote taken from abstract; Figure 1a for changing policy preferences of respondents consistently in full-time employment. The big change in views among individuals moving into unemployment took place earlier – a 0.60 average increase in preferences for redistribution on a seven-point 'Likert' scale between 2006 and 2008 (and stability thereafter); among the continually employed, there was stability until 2008, and then a 0.55 drop in support for redistribution on the same seven-point scale between 2008 and 2010.

32. The crucial point here is less variation in wealth inequality (which bobs up and down, as the relative value of stocks held by the rich and more widely owned housing swings about) than the total amount of wealth relative to income. Since wealth is *always* far more unequal than income, rapid growth in wealth tends to increase dispersion in living standards. And growth has been very rapid indeed. Taking the UK as an example, private wealth (including private pensions) rose from about 300% of GDP in 1980 to 500% in 2005. See Hills et al., *Wealth in the UK*, Figure 2.4.

33. The Genetic Information Nondiscrimination Act of 2008; details at: www.genome.gov/10002328

34. Lars Osberg and Timothy Smeeding, '"Fair" inequality? Attitudes toward pay differentials: The United States in comparative perspective', *American Sociological Review*, 71:3 (2006), p. 471.

35. R. Andersen and M. Yaish, *Public Opinion on Income Inequality in 20 Democracies: The enduring impact of social class and economic inequality*, GINI Discussion Paper 48, Amsterdam Institute for Advanced Labour Studies, 2012, p. 33, at: http://gini-research.org/system/uploads/377/original/DP_48_-_Andersen_Yaish.pdf?1345039244

36. The precise BSA indicator is the proportion agreeing that 'Many people who get social security don't really deserve any help'. It declined from 28% in 1989 to 24% in 1993. We use a 1989 baseline, as the question was not asked in 1990.

37. More precisely, this BSA indicator is the proportion agreeing that: 'if benefits were less generous, people would stand on own feet'. It declined from 30% in 1989 to 25% in 1993. We use a 1989 baseline, as the question was not asked in 1990.

38. The precise BSA question asked what the government should do when forced 'to choose between the three options': 'Reduce taxes and spend less on health, education

and social benefits'; 'Keep taxes and spending on these services at the same level as now'; 'Increase taxes and spend more on health, education and social benefits'. The proportions preferring the last option rose from 54% to 63% between 1990 and 1994.

39. See statistics collated by the Institute for Fiscal Studies at: www.ifs.org.uk/fiscalFacts/ povertyStats Using an 'After Housing Costs' income definition, *all* summary measures of inequality – Gini coefficient, mean log deviation, coefficient of variation, and the 90/10, 50/10 and 90/50 percentile ratios – increased between the start of the 1990 downturn and 2008/09; the same is true if the peak of unemployment in 1993 is compared with that in 2011/12.

40. The exact BSA question asked is: 'Opinions differ about the level of benefits for unemployed people. Which of these two statements comes closest to your own view?': 'Benefits for unemployed people are too low and cause hardship' OR 'Benefits for unemployed people are too high and discourage them from finding jobs'.

41. Among those affected by the cuts, 45% believe them to be necessary, while 43% thought they were not; among those not personally affected the respective figures were 75% and 17%. YouGov UK polling, 2013; fieldwork details and results at: http:// cdn.yougov.com/cumulus_uploads/document/sk7o6dimmg/YoG-Archive-Cam-Guardian-results–120413.pdf

42. YouGov (2013). Summary results and fieldwork details at: http://d25d2506sfb94s. cloudfront.net/cumulus_uploads/document.net/u7f0cyctl1/YGCam-Archive-results– 040413-All-Countries.pdf

43. In more economically equal France, for example, there is only a 3 percentage point gap between the slump-hit and the slump-proof in support for redistribution, compared to an 11 point gap in Britain. (See note 42 for the relevant YouGov link.)

44. David Cameron's speech to the Conservative Party conference in Manchester, 8 October 2009, at: www.theguardian.com/politics/2009/oct/08/david-cameron-speech-in-full

45. Lane Kenworthy and Lindsay A. Owens, 'The surprisingly weak effect of recessions on public opinion', in David B. Grusky, Bruce Western and Christopher Wimer, *The Great Recession*, Russell Sage Foundation, New York, 2011, pp. 196–219.

46. John Curtice, Stephen D. Fisher and Rob Ford, 'The results analysed', in Dennis Kavanagh and Phillip Cowley, *The British Election of 2010*, Palgrave Macmillan, Basingstoke, 2010, pp. 385–426.

47. For analysis of decades of attitudinal data, see Tom Clark, Robert D. Putnam and Edward Fieldhouse, *The Age of Obama*, Manchester University Press, Manchester, 2010, pp. 112–38.

48. Respondents were asked how many benefit claimants were 'scroungers' in the sense that they 'lie about their circumstances in order to obtain higher welfare benefits (for example by pretending to be unemployed or ill or disabled) or deliberately refuse to take work where suitable jobs are available'. The proportion we quote is the total who answer either 'a significant minority', 'around half' or 'a majority'. YouGov's results were reported in Peter Kellner, 'A quiet revolution', *Prospect*, 22 February 2012, at: www.prospectmagazine.co.uk/magazine/a-quiet-revolution-britain-turns-against-welfare/#.Un9XcKVtf-Y

49. For a persuasive development of this point, see Runciman, 'Stiffed'.

50. George Osborne, speech to the Conservative Party conference in Birmingham, 8 October 2012, at: www.newstatesman.com/blogs/politics/2012/10/george-osbornes-speech-conservative-conference-full-text

51. By August 2012, less than six months after he announced a tax cut for incomes above £150,000, opinion polls showed the chancellor's popularity had dived. See John Burn-Murdoch, 'Half of voters believe Osborne should go in the cabinet reshuffle, poll reveals', *Guardian*, 28 August 2012, at: www.guardian.co.uk/news/datablog/2012/aug/28/poll-voters-say-george-osborne-lose-job-reshuffle

52. In the 2012 British Social Attitudes survey (published in 2013), the proportion saying that 'unemployment benefits were too high and discourage [the unemployed] from finding jobs' dipped from 62% to 51%. Data and results at: www.bsa–30.natcen.ac.uk

53. UK Polling Report blog, 15 September 2013, at: http://ukpollingreport.co.uk/blog/archives/8104

Chapter 10: Shelter from the storm

1. See, for example, Nouriel Roubini, 'The instability of inequality', Project Syndicate website, 13 October 2011, at: www.project-syndicate.org/commentary/the-instability-of-inequality

2. Off-the-record discussion between a Westminster City councillor and the *Guardian*.

3. Hacker et al., 'The insecure American', p. 44.

4. Komarovsky, *The Unemployed Man and His Family*, p. 124.

5. Kei Kawashima-Ginsberg, Chaeyoon Lim and Peter Levine, *Civic Health and Unemployment, II: The case builds*, National Conference on Citizenship, Washington DC, 2012.

6. For an informal summary, see Della Bradshaw, 'The pursuit of happiness in the workplace', *Financial Times*, 20 May 2013, at: www.ft.com/cms/s/2/6b1fd178–81cf–11e2-ae78–00144feabdc0.html

7. Between 2007/08 and 2008/09, the Charities Aid Foundation reports that individual donations in the UK fell away by 11%. In the United States, the foundation reports, there was a smaller fall-off, of about 6%, between 2007 and 2008. See National Council for Voluntary Organisations/Charities Aid Foundation, 'The impact of the recession on charitable giving in the UK', 2009, at: www.cafonline.org/pdf/UKGivingReport2009.pdf

8. Shiv Malik, 'Unemployed bussed in to steward river pageant', *Guardian*, 5 June 2012, at: www.theguardian.com/uk/2012/jun/04/jubilee-pageant-unemployed

9. For a sceptical review of the empirical foundations of the conventional wisdom, which concludes that – counter to that orthodoxy – regulation is relatively unimportant, see Howard Reed, *Flexible with the Truth? Exploring the relationship between labour market flexibility and labour market performance*, 2010, at: www.tuc.org.uk/extras/flexiblewiththetruth.pdf

10. After months of outrage about zero-hours contracts, and in the face of Conservative resistance, the Liberal Democrat business secretary, Vince Cable, finally produced a consultation document in December 2013, which canvassed opinions on outlawing 'exclusivity clauses'. But the paper also floated purely advisory alternatives, and one do-nothing option: 'rely on existing common law'. See Department for Business, Innovation and Skills, 'Consultation: Zero-Hours employment contracts', 2013, at: https://www.gov.uk/government/uploads/system/uploads/attachment_data/file/267634/bis-13-1275-zero-hours-employment-contracts-FINAL.pdf

11. Elke J. Jahn, Regina T. Riphahn and Claus Schnabel, 'Feature: Flexible forms of employment: Boon and bane', *Economic Journal*, 122:562 (2012), p. F120.

12. There are different ways to calculate replacement rates, but British benefits for the unemployed during the post-war decades consistently emerge as more generous than those of today. Comparing the headline rate of benefit for a single adult with earnings data, the proportion of average earnings replaced crept up over the 1950s, from 23% in 1948 to 27% in 1961, but has fallen substantially since the 1970s to reach just 14% by April 2010. (See HM Treasury, *Tax and Benefit Reference Manual 2009–10*, Table 7.4, at: http://data.parliament.uk/DepositedPapers/files/DEP2009–1987/DEP2009–1987.pdf; Gregory Clark, 'What were the British earnings and prices then?' (new series), MeasuringWorth, 2013, at: www.measuringworth.com/ukearncpi/) The OECD's 'gross replacement rates' factor in various family circumstances and a wider range of

benefit rates. On these calculations, the replacement ratio rose from 24% in 1961 to 27% in 1969, before oscillating during the 1970s, and finally sliding remorselessly to reach 16% in 2005. Data at: www.oecd.org/els/benefitsandwagesstatistics.htm Select spreadsheet 'Gross replacement rates, uneven years from 1961 to 2011'.

13. In common parlance, 'welfare' refers to Temporary Assistance for Needy Families and food stamps. Combined spending on the two is roughly £100 billion, which is 2–3% of the federal budget and a fraction of a percent of GDP. A broader definition might add in rental assistance and unemployment compensation, but even then the proportion of national income spent on working-age benefits would remain very low by European standards. See Tim Noah, 'Everyone's a queen: The Republicans' rapidly expanding definition of welfare', *New Republic*, 1 April 2013, at: www.newrepublic.com/article/112741/republicans-new-welfare-queens

14. Total expenditure on working-age 'welfare' (i.e. benefits and tax credits) is expected to be £91.2 billion in 2013/14. This figure represents around 13% of total managed expenditure. See Emmerson et al., *IFS Green Budget 2013*, Table 8.2.

15. See Shogo Takegawa, 'Workfare in Japan', in Chak Kawn Chan and Kinglum Ngok (eds), *Welfare Reform in East Asia: Towards workfare*, Routledge, Oxford, 2011, pp. 100–14.

16. Stanley White, 'Japan sales tax hike masks bigger problem of welfare spending', Reuters, 24 September 2013, at: www.reuters.com/article/2013/09/24/us-japan-economy-welfare-idUSBRE98N17A20130924

17. For a detailed and carefully costed menu of practical proposals to boost employment rates among parents and older workers, see Resolution Foundation, *Gaining From Growth*, pp. 192–3.

18. Tami Luhby, 'Romney-Ryan would aim to overhaul Medicaid', CNNMoney, 13 August 2012, at: http://money.cnn.com/2012/08/13/news/economy/ryan-medicaid/

19. Catalina Camia, 'Romney criticizes Obama's changes to welfare law', *USA Today*, 7 August 2012, at: http://content.usatoday.com/communities/onpolitics/post/2012/08/mitt-romney-welfare-reform-ad-barack-obama-/1#.UkbK-xbvz-Y

20. '0.7%, or £1.2bn, of total benefit expenditure is overpaid due to fraud', Department for Work and Pensions/ONS, 'Fraud and error in the benefit system: Preliminary 2012/13 estimates (Great Britain)', 2013, p. 1, at: www.gov.uk/government/uploads/system/uploads/attachment_data/file/203097/nsfr-final–090513.pdf

21. 'Benefit fraud could lead to 10-year jail terms, says DPP', BBC News, 16 September 2013, at: www.bbc.co.uk/news/uk–24104743 By way of comparison, the official figures for average punishments for some other crimes are reported on by Alan Travis, 'Rape sentences now average eight years, Ministry of Justice figures show', *Guardian*, 27 May 2011, at: www.theguardian.com/society/2011/may/26/rape-sentence-average-eight-years-justice-figures

22. Curtice, 'Thermostat or weather vane?'.

23. British polling by YouGov from spring 2013 suggests that a majority (52%) of poorer families (gross income below £20,000) anticipate a continuing fall in living standards, compared to less than one-third (31%) of households where income exceeds £70,000. Details reported in: Resolution Foundation, *2015: The living standards election*, 2013, at: www.resolutionfoundation.org/media/media/downloads/2015_-_The_living_standards_election.pdf

24. Tom Clark, 'Britons favour state responsibilities over individualism, finds survey', *Guardian*, 15 April 2013, at: www.theguardian.com/society/2013/apr/14/britons-sympathetic-unemployed-france-germany

25. Treasury Secretary Henry Morgenthau went in front of the House Ways and Means Committee and said that collecting payments from labourers, domestics and small firms would pose practical problems, with the result that these large chunks of the workforce were cut out of FDR's previously universalist proposal. See Smith, *FDR*, p. 353.

26. Arthur M. Schlesinger Jr, *The Coming of the New Deal*, Houghton Mifflin, Boston, MA, 2007, pp. 308–9.

27. Child Poverty Act 2010, at: www.legislation.gov.uk/ukpga/2010/9/contents

28. There are still many feasible options for raising more revenue from the wealthy, many of which would – by closing loopholes – also have the advantage of simplifying the tax system. In the British context, as well as increasing the higher rate of income tax and the additional rate of National Insurance, serious money could also accrue by abolishing 'entrepreneur's relief' in capital gains tax, and axing the exemption from capital gains tax on death. See Emmerson et al., *IFS Green Budget 2013*, pp. 245–80.

29. Claire Churchard, 'Government backs down over work experience scheme', Chartered Institute for Personnel Development blog, 1 March 2013, at: www.cipd.co.uk/pm/peoplemanagement/b/weblog/archive/2012/03/01/government-backs-down-over-work-experience-scheme–2012–03.aspx

30. Stiglitz, *Price of Inequality*, p. 84.

31. For a more precise development of these general arguments, see ibid., pp. 84–9; more specifically, on the way that inequality compromised the efficacy of the stimulus, see pp. 233–4.

32. Respondents thought it more important that benefits should 'penalise scroungers' than 'reduce poverty and inequality', but only by a narrow 49% to 44% margin; by contrast, 'making work pay' was seen as more important than poverty and inequality by an emphatic margin of 57% to 33%. Greenberg Quinlan Rosner, 'Winning on welfare', research presented by James Morris to a TUC conference at Congress House, London, 4 October 2013.

33. By 58% to 30%, respondents said they felt positively inclined towards 'National Insurance', a more favourable balance than for either 'benefits' or 'social security': ibid.

34. For some practical thoughts on how contributory social security might be revived in the UK, see Ian Mulheirn, 'Re-engineering contributory welfare', in Ian Mulheirn and Jeff Masters, *Beveridge Rebooted: Social security for a networked age*, Social Market Foundation, London, 2013, pp. 54–75.

Select bibliography

Comprehensive citations are provided in the endnotes. Here we detail only the more important books and papers, generally excluding the official and other primary sources of data which are indicated in the notes. Where particular chapters or papers within volumes are previously indicated, here we provide only the title of the book as a whole.

Addison, Paul. *The Road to 1945*, Random House, London, 2011 [1975].

Alakeson, Vidhya and Giselle Cory. *Home Truths: How affordable is housing for Britain's ordinary families?* Resolution Foundation, London, 2013, available at: www.resolution-foundation.org/media/media/downloads/Home_Truths_1.pdf

Almond, Gabriel A. and Sidney Verba. *The Civic Culture: Political attitudes and democracy in five nations*, Sage, Newbury Park, CA, 1989 [1963].

Andersen, R. and M. Yaish. *Public Opinion on Income Inequality in 20 Democracies: The enduring impact of social class and economic inequality*, GINI Discussion Paper 48, Amsterdam Institute for Advanced Labour Studies, 2012, available at: http://gini-research.org/system/uploads/377/original/DP_48_-_Andersen_Yaish.pdf?1345039244

Atkinson, A.B. and F. Bourguignon (eds). *Handbook of Income Distribution*, vol. 1, Elsevier, Amsterdam, 2000.

Atkinson, Anthony B. and Thomas Piketty (eds). *Top Incomes over the Twentieth Century: A contrast between continental European and English-speaking countries*, Oxford University Press, Oxford and New York, 2007.

Atkinson, Anthony B. and Thomas Piketty (eds). *Top Incomes over the Twentieth Century: A global perspective*, Oxford University Press, Oxford and New York, 2010.

Autor, David. *The Polarization of Job Opportunities in the US Labor Market*, Center for American Progress/Hamilton Project, Washington, DC, 2010, available at: www.brookings.edu/~/media/research/files/papers/2010/4/jobs%20autor/04_jobs_autor.pdf

Autor, David H. and Susan N. Houseman. 'Do temporary-help jobs improve labor market outcomes for low-skilled workers? Evidence from "Work First"', *American Economic Journal: Applied Economics*, 2:3 (2010), pp. 96–128.

Beckett, Francis. *Clem Attlee*, Politico's Publishing, London, 2000.

Bell, D.N.F and D.G. Blanchflower. 'UK unemployment in the Great Recession', *National Institute Economic Review*, 214 (2010), pp. R3–R25.

Bell, David N.F. and David G. Blanchflower. 'Underemployment in the UK revisited', *National Institute Economic Review*, 224 (2013), pp. F8–F22.

Blanchard, Olivier J. and Lawrence H. Summers. 'Hysteresis and the European un-employment problem', *NBER Macroeconomics Annual*, vol. 1, University of Chicago Press, Chicago, 1986, pp. 15–78, available at: www.nber.org/chapters/c4245.pdf

Blundell, Richard and Ian Preston. 'Consumption inequality and income uncertainty', *Quarterly Journal of Economics*, 113:2 (1998), pp. 603–40.

Blyth, Mark. *Austerity: The history of a dangerous idea*, Oxford University Press, New York, 2013.

Borie-Holtz, Debbie, Carl Van Horn and Cliff Zukin. *No End in Sight: The agony of prolonged unemployment*, Rutgers University, New Brunswick, NJ, 2010.

Boyle, David. *Broke: Who killed the middle classes?*, Fourth Estate/HarperCollins, London, 2013.

Brewer, Mike. 'Comparing in-work benefits and the reward to work for families with children in the US and the UK', *Fiscal Studies*, 22:1 (2001), pp. 41–77.

Brewer, Mike, James Browne and Wenchao Jin. *Universal Credit: A preliminary analysis*, Institute for Fiscal Studies, London, 2011, available at: www.ifs.org.uk/bns/bn116.pdf

Brewer, Mike, James Browne, Andrew Hood, Robert Joyce and Luke Sibetia. 'The short- and medium-term impacts of the recession on the UK income distribution', *Fiscal Studies*, 34:2 (2013), pp. 179–201.

Brinkley, Ian. *Flexibility or Insecurity? Exploring the rise in zero hours contracts*, Work Foundation, London, 2013, available at: www.theworkfoundation.com/Download Publication/Report/339_Flexibility%20or%20Insecurity%20-%20final.pdf

Brown, S., K. Taylor and S. Wheatley Price. 'Debt and distress: Evaluating the psycho-logical cost of credit', *Journal of Economic Psychology*, 26:5 (2005), pp. 642–63.

Clark, T. and A. Leicester. 'Inequality and two decades of British tax reforms', *Fiscal Studies*, 25:2 (2004), pp. 129–58.

Clark, Tom, Robert D. Putnam and Edward Fieldhouse. *The Age of Obama*, Manchester University Press, Manchester, 2010.

Coggan, Philip. *Paper Promises: Money, debt, and the new world order*, Allen Lane/Penguin, London, 2012.

Cohen, Philip N. 'Recession and divorce in the United States: Economic conditions and the odds of divorce, 2008–2010', Population Research Center, Baltimore, MD, 2012, available at: http://papers.ccpr.ucla.edu/papers/PWP-MPRC–2012–008/PWP-MPRC–2012–008.pdf

Congressional Budget Office. *Trends in the Distribution of Household Income between 1979 and 2007*, CBO, Washington, DC, 2011.

Cribb, Jonathan, Robert Joyce and David Phillips. *Living Standards, Poverty and Inequality in the UK: 2012*, Institute for Fiscal Studies, London, 2012.

Cribb, Jonathan, Andrew Hood, Robert Joyce and David Phillips. *Living Standards, Poverty and Inequality in the UK: 2013*, Institute for Fiscal Studies, London, 2013.

Crossley, Thomas F., Hamish Low and Cormac O'Dea. 'Household consumption through recent recessions', *Fiscal Studies*, 34:2 (2013), pp. 203–29.

Curtis, J.E., E.G. Grabb and D.E. Baer. 'Voluntary association membership in fifteen countries: A comparative analysis', *American Sociological Review*, 57 (April 1992), pp. 139–52.

D'Arcy, Conor and Alex Hurrell. *Minimum Stay: Understanding how long people stay on the minimum wage*, Resolution Foundation, London, 2013, available at: www.resolu-tionfoundation.org/media/media/downloads/Minimum_stay.pdf

DeParle, Jason and Robert M. Gebeloff. 'Living on nothing but food stamps', *New York Times*, 3 January 2010, available at: ww.nytimes.com/2010/01/03/us/03foodstamps.html?pagewanted=all&_r=0

Dew, Jeffrey P. 'Two sides of the same coin? The differing roles of assets and consumer debt in marriage', *Journal of Family and Economic Issues*, 28:1 (2007), pp. 89–104.

Dew, Jeffrey P. 'Debt change and marital satisfaction change in recently married couples', *Family Relations*, 57:1 (2008), pp. 60–71.

Dorling, D. 'Fairness and the changing fortunes of people in Britain', *Journal of the Royal Statistical Society A*, 176:1 (2013), pp. 97–128, available at: www.dannydorling.org/?page_id=3597

Duffy, Bobby. *Intergenerational Justice*, Ipsos MORI/Joseph Rowntree Reform Trust, London and York, 2013, available at: www.jrrt.org.uk/sites/jrrt.org.uk/files/documents/Intergenerational_Justice_050613_IpsosMORI_JRRT.pdf

Durkheim, Emile. *Division of Labor in Society*, Free Press, Glencoe, IL, 1933 [1893].

Edelman, Peter. *So Rich, So Poor*, The New Press, New York, 2012.

Elder, G.H. *Children of the Great Depression*, University of Chicago Press, Chicago and London, 1974.

Ellen, Ingrid Gould and Samuel Dastrup. *Housing and the Great Recession*, Stanford Center on Poverty and Inequality, Stanford, CA, 2012, available at: http://furmancenter.org/files/publications/HousingandtheGreatRecession.pdf

Falk, Gene. *The Temporary Assistance for Needy Families (TANF) Block Grant: A primer on TANF financing and federal requirements*, Congressional Support Services, Washington, DC, 2011), available at: http://greenbook.waysandmeans.house.gov/sites/greenbook.waysandmeans.house.gov/files/2011/images/RL32748%20v2_gb.pdf

Fenstein, Charles H., Peter Temin and Gianni Toniolo. *The European Economy Between the Wars*, Oxford University Press, Oxford, 1997.

Ferrie, J.E., M. Kivimäki, M.J. Shipley, G. Davey Smith and M. Virtanen. 'Job insecurity and incident coronary heart disease: The Whitehall II prospective cohort study', *Atherosclerosis*, 227:1 (2013), pp. 178–81.

Finn, Dan and Rosie Gloster. *Lone Parent Obligations: A review of recent evidence on the work-related requirements within the benefit systems of different countries*, Department for Work and Pensions Research Report No. 632, London, 2010, available at: www.cesi.org.uk/sites/default/files/publication_additional_downloads/rrep632.pdf

Floud, Roderick and Paul Johnson (eds). *The Cambridge Economic History of Modern Britain*, Vol. II, *Economic Maturity, 1860–1939*, Cambridge University Press, Cambridge, 2004.

Floud, Roderick and Paul Johnson (eds). *The Cambridge Economic History of Modern Britain*, Vol. III, *Structural Change and Growth, 1939–2000*, Cambridge University Press, Cambridge, 2004.

Friedman, Benjamin M. *The Moral Consequences of Economic Growth*, Vintage/Random House, New York, 2006 [2005].

Fry, Richard. *The Reversal of the Marriage Gap*, Pew Center, Washington, DC, 2010, available at: www.pewsocialtrends.org/files/2010/11/767-college-marriage-gap.pdf

Galbraith, J.K. *The Great Crash*, Penguin/Allen Lane, London, 2007 [1954].

Garside, W.R. *Japan's Great Stagnation: Forging ahead, falling behind*, Edward Elgar, Cheltenham, 2012.

Goldthorpe, John H. 'Understanding – and misunderstanding – social mobility in Britain: The entry of the economists, the confusion of politicians and the limits of educational policy', *Journal of Social Policy*, 42:3 (2013), pp. 431–50.

Goldthorpe, John H. and Colin Mills. 'Trends in intergenerational class mobility in modern Britain: Evidence from national surveys, 1972–2005', *National Institute Economic Review*, 205 (July 2008), pp. 1–18.

Goodman, Alissa and Steven Webb. 'The distribution of UK household expenditure, 1979–92', *Fiscal Studies*, 16:3 (1996), pp. 55–80, available at: www.ifs.org.uk/fs/articles/fsgoodman.pdf

Gordon, Robert J. and Timothy F. Bresnahan. *The Economics of New Goods*, University of Chicago Press for National Bureau of Economic Research, Chicago, 1997, available at: http://papers.nber.org/books/bres96–1/

Gregg, Paul and Stephen Machin. *What a Drag: The chilling impact of unemployment on real wages*, Resolution Foundation, London, 2012, available at: www.resolutionfoundation.org/media/media/downloads/What_a_drag_1.pdf

Gregg, P., S. Machin and M. Salgado. 'Real wages and unemployment in the big squeeze', Centre for Economic Performance, London School of Economics, Mimeo, 2013.

Gregg, Paul and Lindsey Macmillan. 'The intergenerational transmission of worklessness in the US and the UK', Institute for Social Change, Draft Working Paper 2013–1, 2013, available at: www.humanities.manchester.ac.uk/socialchange/publications/working/documents/LindseayMacmillanpaper.pdf

Gregg, Paul and Jonathan Wadsworth. 'Unemployment and inactivity in the 2008–2009 recession', *Economic and Labour Market Review*, 4:8 (2010).

Griffith, Rachel, Martin O'Connell and Kate Smith. 'Food expenditure and nutritional quality over the Great Recession', Institute for Fiscal Studies Briefing Note BN143, 2013, available at: www.ifs.org.uk/bns/bn143.pdf

Hacker, Jacob S., Philipp Rehm and Mark Schlesinger. 'The insecure American: Economic experiences, financial worries, and policy attitudes', *Perspectives on Politics*, 11:1 (2013), pp. 23–49.

Hall, Peter A. 'Social capital in Britain', *British Journal of Political Science*, 29:3 (1999), pp. 417–61, available at: www.abdn.ac.uk/sociology/notes06/Level4/SO4530/Assigned-Readings/Seminar%209.2.pdf

Hansard Society. *The Audit of Political Engagement 9: The 2012 Report*, Hansard Society, London, available at: www.hansardsociety.org.uk/blogs/parliament_and_government/archive/2012/04/27/audit-of-political-engagement–9-part-one.aspx

Harris, José. *William Beveridge: A biography*, Clarendon Press, Oxford, 1997 [1977].

Hendricks, J. and S.J. Cutler. 'Volunteerism and socioemotional selectivity in later life', *Journals of Gerontology Series B: Social Sciences*, 59:5 (2004), pp. S251–S257.

Hills, John, Francesca Bastagli, Frank Cowell, Howard Glennerster, Eleni Karagiannaki and Abigail McKnight. *Wealth in the UK: Distribution, accumulation and policy*, Oxford University Press, Oxford, 2013.

Jahn, Elke J., Regina T. Riphahn and Claus Schnabel. 'Feature: Flexible forms of employment: Boon and bane', *Economic Journal*, 122:562 (2012), pp. F115–F124.

Jahoda, Marie, Paul F. Lazarsfeld and Hans Zeisel. *Marienthal: The sociography of an unemployed community*, Transaction Publishers, New Brunswick, NJ, 2002 [1933].

Judt, Tony. *Ill Fares the Land: A treatise on our present discontents*, Penguin, London, 2010.

Kahn, Lisa. 'The long-term labor market consequences of graduating from college in a bad economy', *Labour Economics*, 17:2 (2010), pp. 303–16.

Kahneman, D. and A. Tversky. 'Prospect theory: An analysis of decision under risk', *Econometrica*, 47:2 (1979), pp. 263–91, available at: www.princeton.edu/~kahneman/docs/Publications/prospect_theory.pdf

Kaplan, George A. and Julian E. Keil. 'Socioeconomic factors and cardiovascular disease: A review of the literature', *Circulation: Journal of the American Heart Association*, 88:4 (1993), pp. 1973–98, available at: http://circ.ahajournals.org/content/88/4/1973.full.pdf

Kawashima-Ginsberg, Kei, Chaeyoon Lim and Peter Levine. *Civic Health and Unemployment, II: The Case Builds*, National Conference on Citizenship, Washington DC, 2012.

Keohane, Nigel and Ryan Shorthouse. *Sink or Swim? The impact of universal credit*, Social Market Foundation, London, 2012, available at: www.smf.co.uk/files/1913/4779/2202/20120916_Sink_or_Swim_web_ready2.pdf

Keynes, John Maynard. *Essays in Persuasion: The collected writings of John Maynard Keynes*, vol. 9, Cambridge University Press, Cambridge, 1978.

Kiernan, Kathleen, Sara McLanahan, John Holmes and Melanie Wright. 'Fragile families in the US and UK', Bendheim Thomas Center for Research on Child Well-Being Working Paper WP11–04-FF, Princeton, NJ, 2011, available at: http://crcw.princeton.edu/workingpapers/WP11–04-FF.pdf

Kingston, Jeff. *Japan's Quiet Transformation: Social change and civil society in the 21st century*, RoutledgeCurzon, Oxford, 2004.

Koeniger, W. and M. Leonardi. 'Capital deepening and wage differentials: Germany versus U.E.', *Economic Policy*, 22 (2007), pp. 71–116.

Komarovsky, Mirra. *The Unemployed Man and His Family: Status of the man in fifty-nine families*, AltaMira Press, Walnut Creek, CA, 2004 [1940].

Krueger, Alan B. 'The rise and consequences of inequality in the United States', speech at the Center for American Progress, 12 January 2012, prepared remarks available at: www.whitehouse.gov/blog/2012/01/12/chairman-alan-krueger-discusses-rise-and-consequences-inequality-center-american-pro

Laurence, James and Chaeyoon Lim. '"The scars of others should teach us caution": The long-term effects of job "displacement" on civic participation over the lifecourse: A cross-national comparative study between the GB and US', Institute for Social Change Working Paper 2013–2, Manchester, 2013, available at: www.humanities.manchester. ac.uk/socialchange/publications/working/documents/JamesLaurenceHardshipand CivicParticipation.pdf

Layard, Richard. *Happiness: Lessons from a new science*, Penguin/Allen Lane, London, 2005.

Leigh, Andrew. *Battlers and Billionaires: The story of inequality in Australia*, Redback, Collingwood, VIC, 2013.

Lewis, Michael. *Boomerang: The meltdown tour*, Penguin/Allen Lane, London, 2011.

Li, Yaojun. 'Hard times, worklessness and unemployment in Britain and the USA (1972–2011)', Institute for Social Change Working Paper 2013–4, Manchester, 2013, available at: www.humanities.manchester.ac.uk/socialchange/publications/working/documents/ EthnicunemploymentandworklessnessunderhardtimesinGBandUSA1972to2011.pdf

Lim, Chaeyoon and James Laurence. 'Economic hard times and life satisfaction in the UK and the US', Institute for Social Change Working Paper 2013–3, Manchester, 2013, available at: www.humanities.manchester.ac.uk/socialchange/publications/ working/documents/JamesLaurenceHardshipandWell-Being.pdf

Lim, Chaeyoon and James Laurence. 'Doing good when times are bad: Volunteering behaviour in economic hard times', *British Journal of Sociology* (forthcoming, 2014).

Long, Larry. *Migration and Residential Mobility in the United States*, Russell Sage Foundation, Chicago, IL, 1988.

Machin, Steve, Paul Gregg and Jo Blanden. *Intergenerational Mobility in Europe and North America*, Sutton Trust, London, 2005.

Margalit, Yotam. 'Explaining social policy preferences: Evidence from the Great Recession', *American Political Science Review*, 107:1 (2013), pp. 80–103.

McKibbin, Ross. *The Ideologies of Class: Social relations in Britain 1880–1950*, Oxford University Press, Oxford, 1994 [1990].

McKibbin, Ross. *Classes and Cultures: England 1918–1951*, Oxford University Press, Oxford, 2000 [1998].

Middleton, Roger. *Government versus the Market: The growth of the public sector, economic management and British economic performance, c. 1890–1979*, Edward Elgar, Cheltenham, 1996.

Mulheirn, Ian and Jeff Masters. *Beveridge Rebooted: Social security for a networked age*, Social Market Foundation, London, 2013.

National Conference on Citizenship. *Volunteering and Civic Life in America 2012*, National Conference on Citizenship, Washington, DC, 2012, available at: www. volunteeringinamerica.gov

Organisation for Economic Co-operation and Development. *Divided We Stand: Why inequality keeps rising*, OECD, Paris, 2011.

Organisation for Economic Co-operation and Development. *OECD Employment Outlook 2013*, OECD, Paris, 2013.

Orwell, George. *The Road to Wigan Pier*, Penguin Books, Harmondsworth, 1962 [1937].

Osberg, Lars and Timothy Smeeding. '"Fair" inequality? Attitudes toward pay differentials: The United States in comparative perspective', *American Sociological Review*, 71:3 (2006), pp. 450–73.

Owens, Lindsay A. and David S. Pedulla. 'Material welfare and changing political preferences: The case of support for redistributive social policies', *Social Forces* (forthcoming); final paper electronically pre-released at: http://sf.oxfordjournals.org/content/early/2013/10/14/sf.sot101.full?keytype=ref&ijkey=lpFDgu1y7FeFShp

Packer, George. *The Unwinding: An inner history of the new America*, Faber and Faber, London, 2013.

Park, A., J. Curtice, K. Thomson, M. Phillips, E. Clery and S. Butt (eds). *British Social Attitudes 26th Report*, Sage, London, 2010.

Peck, Don. *Pinched: How the Great Recession has narrowed our futures and what we can do about it*, Crown, New York, 2011.

Pember-Reeves, Maud. *Round About a Pound a Week*, C. Bell and Son, London, 1914, available at: http://archive.org/stream/roundaboutpoundw00reevrich#page/12/mode/2up

Pennycook, Matthew, Giselle Cory and Vidhya Alakeson. *A Matter of Time: The rise of zero-hour contracts*, Resolution Foundation, London, 2013, available at: www.resolutionfoundation.org/media/media/downloads/A_Matter_of_Time_-_The_rise_of_zero-hours_contracts_final_1.pdf

Perkins, Frances. *The Roosevelt I Knew*, Viking, New York, 1946.

Perri, Fabrizio and Joe Steinberg. 'Inequality and redistribution during the great recession', Federal Reserve Bank of Minneapolis Economic Policy Paper, Minneapolis, MN, 2012, available at: www.minneapolisfed.org/publications_papers/pub_display.cfm?id=4819

Pew Research Center. *A Balance Sheet at 30 Months: How the great recession has changed life in America*, Pew Center, Washington, DC, 2010, available at: www.pewsocialtrends.org/files/2010/11/759-recession.pdf

Piketty, Thomas and Emmanuel Saez. 'Income inequality in the United States, 1913–1998', *Quarterly Journal of Economics*, 118:1 (2003), pp. 1–39.

Plunkett, James and Alex Hurrell. *Fifteen Years Later: A discussion paper on the future of the UK national minimum wage and Low Pay Commission*, Resolution Foundation, London, 2013, available at: www.resolutionfoundation.org/media/media/downloads/FINAL_Future_of_the_minimum_wage_discussion_paper.pdf

Putnam, Robert D. *Bowling Alone*, Simon & Schuster, New York, 2000.

Putnam, Robert D. and David E. Campbell. *American Grace: How religion divides and unites us*, Simon & Schuster, New York, 2012.

Ransom, Roger L., Richard Sutch and Susan B. Carter. *Research in Economic History*, JAI Press, Greenwich, CT, 1992.

Rawls, John. *A Theory of Justice*, Harvard University Press, Cambridge, MA, 1971.

Rector, Robert. *How Poor are America's Poor? Examining the 'plague' of poverty in America*, Heritage Foundation, Washington, DC, 2007, available at: www.heritage.org/research/reports/2007/08/how-poor-are-americas-poor-examining-the-plague-of-poverty-in-america

Reinhart, Carmen M. and Kenneth S. Rogoff. 'The aftermath of financial crises', *American Economic Review*, 99:2 (2009), pp. 466–72, available at: www.ems.bbk.ac.uk/for_students/msc_econ/ETA2_EMEC025P/GZrhein.pdf

Resolution Foundation. *Gaining from Growth*, Resolution Foundation, London, 2012, available at: www.resolutionfoundation.org/media/media/downloads/Gaining_from_growth_-_The_final_report_of_the_Commission_on_Living_Standards.pdf

Rosenzweig, M. and O. Stark (eds). *Handbook of Population and Family Economics*, Elsevier, Amsterdam, 1997.

Runciman, David. 'Stiffed' (review of *The Occupy Handbook*), *London Review of Books*, 25 October 2012, available at: www.lrb.co.uk/v34/n20/david-runciman/stiffed

Shirakawa, Masaaki. 'Deleveraging and growth: Japan's long and winding road', lecture at the London School of Economics, 10 January 2012, available at: www.lse.ac.uk/asiaResearchCentre/_files/ShirakawaLectureTranscript.pdf

Skidelsky, Robert. *John Maynard Keynes*, vol. 2: *The Economist as Savior, 1920–37*, Penguin Viking, New York, 1995.

Smith, Adam. *An Inquiry into the Nature and Causes of the Wealth of Nations*, Electronic Classics Series Publications, Hazleton, PA, 2005 [1776], available at: www2.hn.psu.edu/faculty/jmanis/adam-smith/wealth-nations.pdf

Smith, Jean Edward. *FDR*, Random House paperback edition, New York, 2008 [2007].

Steinbeck, John. *The Grapes of Wrath*, Pan Books, London, 1975 [1939].

Stiglitz, Joseph. *The Price of Inequality*, Penguin/Allen Lane, London, 2012.

Stuckler, David and Sanjay Basu. *The Body Economic: Why austerity kills*, Penguin/Allen Lane, London, 2013.

Thomas, K. and D. Gunnell. 'Suicide in England and Wales 1861–2007: A time-trends analysis', *International Journal of Epidemiology*, 39:6 (2010), pp. 1464–75, available at: http://ije.oxfordjournals.org/content/39/6/1464.full

Tocqueville, Alexis de. *Democracy in America*, Fontana/HarperCollins, London, 1994 [1840].

Tversky, Amos and Daniel Kahneman. 'Judgment under uncertainty: Heuristics and biases source', *Science*, NS 185:4157 (1974), pp. 1124–31, available at: www.socsci.uci.edu/~bskyrms/bio/readings/tversky_k_heuristics_biases.pdf

Walkerdine, Valerie and Luis Jimenez. *Gender, Work and Community after De-Industrialisation: A psychosocial approach to affect*, Palgrave Macmillan, London, 2012.

Whittaker, Matthew. *On Borrowed Time? Dealing with household debt in an era of stagnant incomes*, Resolution Foundation, London, 2012.

Wilcox, W. Bradford (ed.). *The State of Our Unions, 2009*, National Marriage Project, University of Virginia and the Institute for American Values, Charlottesville, VA, 2009.

Willetts, David. *The Pinch: How the baby boomers took their children's future – and why they should give it back*, Atlantic Books, London, 2010.

Zedlewski, Sheila, Sandi Nelson, Kathryn Edin, Heather Koball, Kate Pomper and Tracy Roberts. *Families Coping Without Earnings or Government Cash Assistance*, Urban Institute, Washington, DC, 2003, available at: www.urban.org/uploadedPDF/410634_OP64.pdf

Acknowledgements

The research underpinning this volume was undertaken as part of a five-year collaboration between the University of Manchester and Harvard University, known as Social Change: A Harvard–Manchester Initiative (SCHMI). The collaboration was directed by Robert D. Putnam, the Malkin Professor of Public Policy at Harvard, and Ed Fieldhouse, Professor of Social and Political Science at Manchester. It was based at the Institute for Social Change at Manchester and ran from 2007 to 2012. This book draws especially heavily on work by the following individual scholars, whose work was funded through the programme and coordinated by Anthony Heath:

* Gabriella Elgenius (Oxford)
* Paul Hepburn (ISC)
* James Laurence (ISC)
* Yaojun Li (ISC)
* Chaeyoon Lim (Wisconsin)
* Siobhan McAndrew (ISC)
* Lindsey Macmillan (Institute of Education, London)

The correspondence between the research and the chapters that follow is not exact, but papers by Laurence and Lim particularly inform Chapters 5, 6 and parts of Chapter 7; the work of Li, Chapter 3; and the work of Macmillan, the final part of Chapter 7. McAndrew's work on suicide is used in Chapter 7, as is attitudinal data researched by Hepburn in Chapter 9, and they both helped with some of the historical trends documented throughout the book. Full details of the research papers are provided in the notes to each chapter. To say that we are grateful to these researchers is scarcely adequate – without them there would be no book. Particular thanks are due to Gabriella Elgenius, who joined the project late, and then worked tirelessly with modest resources to conduct the interviews with hard-hit families that run throughout the pages.

In addition, we would like to thank other SCHMI scholars – especially Robert Ford (ISC) and Maria Grasso (Sheffield) – who produced interesting papers on other aspects of the experience of hard times which ended up being less central to the book as it evolved. They also contributed valuable comments at SCHMI seminars in Manchester in 2011 and in Sarasota, Florida, in 2012.

At the same events and since, we benefited greatly from the advice and insight of Professor Putnam himself, who suggested many telling points and ringing phrases that have made their way into our text, including the tornado image, which twists its way through the book. Beyond his important direct input into the present work, we also need to thank Professor Putnam for his leadership over the five years of SCHMI, and Professor Fieldhouse for providing the day-to-day management with friendly dedication, as well as expert analytical support on quantitative aspects of the research. Professor Rachel Gibson has subsequently taken over as director of the Institute for Social Change, and we would like to extend thanks to her for efficiently tying up the managerial loose ends, as we would to Magdalen Faulds for helping with the final administration. The support of Jennifer Birchall, Tom Sander and Kyle Gibson is gratefully acknowledged in pulling off the major logistical task of bringing together scholars from both sides of the Atlantic. Tom Sander also played a major role in our intellectual debates and we are very grateful for his expert input throughout the project.

SCHMI would not have existed without generous funding from the University of Manchester, which we gratefully acknowledge. We would like to thank the then President, the late Alan Gilbert, and the Vice-President and Dean, Alistair Ulph, for their enthusiastic support in making SCHMI a reality.

Tom Clark would like to thank: Stephan Shakespeare, Joel Faulkner Rogers and Peter Kellner of YouGov for providing data and expert guidance on its interpretation, and likewise Bobby Duffy of Ipsos MORI and Martin Boon from ICM. Alison Park of NatCen Social Research was extremely helpful in providing BSA data. For providing additional numbers – and help in making sense of them – debts are owed to the Institute for Fiscal Studies (especially Robert Joyce and James Browne) and the Resolution Foundation (where James Plunkett, Gavin Kelly, Vidhya Alakeson, Warwick Smith and Matthew Whittaker were all invaluable). Simon Kirby from the National Institute has been another great help in providing data, as has Danny Blanchflower at Dartmouth College, Professor Steve Machin of UCL and Professor Paul Gregg and Mariña Fernández Salgado at Bath. John Goldthorpe kindly made time to talk over matters to do with social class and social mobility, as did Professor Janet Hunter of LSE on Japan.

For helping us assemble a rich range of case studies with great speed, we would like to thank the Resolution Foundation for a second time, as well as Citizens Advice, Save the Children and the London MPs Stella Creasy and Karen Buck.

Tom also owes a debt of thanks to Alan Rusbridger and Paul Johnson at the *Guardian* for allowing him time off, and to his leader-writing colleagues – David Hearst, Martin Kettle and Anne Perkins – for putting up with the consequences for their own workload. He also wishes to thank Aditya Chakrabortty from the paper, for reading a near-entire manuscript and providing insightful tips, as well as Simon Lancaster who cast an eye over the proposal at an earlier stage, and Yale's two anonymous readers for their expert suggestions. We are also greatly indebted to copy-editor Clive Liddiard, for turning his eagle eye to every last line of the text, and averting many mistakes in the process.

Tom would like to thank his family, particularly Helen, but also her parents and his own mother for providing out-of-hours childcare, without which the writing could never have got done.

As agent, Sarah Chalfant did a wonderful job in guiding us to flesh out what was initially a rather flimsy proposal into something substantial, and particularly in encouraging us to bring in the voices of the recession's victims directly. Together with Alba Ziegler-Bailey and colleagues at Wylie, she showed extraordinary patience in shepherding a project, which encountered more than its share of upsets, through to deal and publication.

Finally, we could not have been blessed with a more efficient or intelligent editor than Phoebe Clapham at Yale, who exceeded any reasonable expectation, at one point even pointing us to a valuable new data source. She, too, has been loyal to the book through many disruptions, and – faced with chaotic early drafts – she zoomed up and dived down across a messy landscape, and imposed some much-needed order on the map. The only thing she did wrong was to leave before publication, which could have been catastrophic, had not Rachael Lonsdale and Heather McCallum stepped forward and – with great energy – kept everything on track.

Index